THREE REVOLUTIONS

by the same author

1956, THE WORLD IN REVOLT
TEN DAYS IN HARLEM

SIMON HALL

THREE REVOLUTIONS

RUSSIA · CHINA · CUBA

AND THE EPIC JOURNEYS THAT CHANGED THE WORLD

faber

First published in 2025
by Faber & Faber Ltd
The Bindery, 51 Hatton Garden
London ECIN 8HN

Typeset by Faber & Faber Ltd

Printed and bound using 100 per cent renewable energy
by CPI Group (UK) Ltd, Croydon CRO 4YY

Parts of this book draw on material previously published in
1956, The World in Revolt and *Ten Days in Harlem*.

A CIP record for this book
is available from the British Library

ISBN 978–0–571–36715–3

MIX
Paper | Supporting
responsible forestry
FSC
www.fsc.org
FSC® C013604

Printed and bound in the UK on FSC® certified paper in line with our continuing
commitment to ethical business practices, sustainability and the environment.
For further information see faber.co.uk/environmental-policy

Our authorised representative in the EU for product safety is
Easy Access System Europe, Mustamäe tee 50, 10621 Tallinn, Estonia
gpsr.requests@easproject.com

2 4 6 8 10 9 7 5 3 1

For Brody

CONTENTS

Editorial Notes ix

Prologue 1

PART ONE: RUSSIA

Lenin

1. Zurich 9
2. Caged Lion 21
3. The Sealed Train 31
4. From the Finland Station 44

John Reed

5. Across the War World 57
6. Scandinavia in Wartime 71
7. Red Russia – Entrance 76
8. Red Petrograd 82
9. October 88
10. The Commissariat 102
11. Blocked 114
12. *Ten Days That Shook the World* 121
13. American Bolshevik 131
14. The Harvard Man in the Kremlin Wall 141
15. Afterlives 148

PART TWO: CHINA

Mao

16. Annihilation   159
17. Exodus   176
18. Zunyi   183
19. The Bridge of Chains   193

Edgar Snow

20. Red China Beckons   209
21. The Road to Red China   225
22. The Red Capital   237
23. *Red Star Over China*   250
24. Maoism   258

PART THREE: CUBA

Fidel

25. *Granma*   275
26. Shipwreck   287

Herbert Matthews

27. A Newspaperman's Newspaperman   301
28. A Chapter in a Fantastic Novel   313
29. Scoop!   324
30. Fidel's Secret Weapons   332
31. 'Comrade Matthews'   340
32. Venceremos!   355

Epilogue   368

Acknowledgements   377
Select Bibliography   380
Endnotes   385
Index   431

EDITORIAL NOTES

Russian dates

Until February 1918 Russia followed the Julian Calendar. At the time of the Bolshevik Revolution, this left the country thirteen days behind Western Europe, the United States of America and most of the rest of the world. This meant that, among other things, Lenin left Zurich on 9 April 1917 (Easter Monday) and arrived in Petrograd a week later on 3 April (which also happened to be Orthodox Easter Monday). Meanwhile, the February Revolution took place in March, and the October Revolution in November. To minimise confusion, and to respect the historicity of the events as experienced at the time, I have used the Julian dates, adding the odd clarificatory note where appropriate.

Russian transliteration

There are numerous systems in use when it comes to Russian transliteration. In an attempt at consistency, I have employed a simplified version of the British Standard system. I have also deferred to accepted, and widely used, English spellings (e.g. Alexander Kerensky, rather than Aleksandr).

Chinese names

At the time that Edgar Snow was working and writing in China, the Wade–Giles system was commonly used to romanise Mandarin Chinese: Mao Tse-tung; Peking; Pao An. In more recent decades, the Pinyin system – adopted officially by the PRC in 1958 – has predominated: Mao Zedong; Beijing; Bao'an. To further complicate matters,

EDITORIAL NOTES

many place names (including those of provinces) have changed over the years, so that Shensi province (where Mao's Red Army was based when Snow visited) is now officially known as Shaanxi, while Bao'an is part of present-day Zhidan county. I have endeavoured to use Pinyin romanisation throughout (including amending quotations from original sources) and modern place names. There are some exceptions, notably Chiang Kai-shek, which is well established in popular usage.

PROLOGUE

The journey that stirs you now is not far off.
– HOMER

Epic journeys – whether the heroic quest, the dramatic, against-the-odds escape or the triumphant return – have captivated mankind since the dawn of civilisation. The earliest surviving works of literature – the *Epic of Gilgamesh*, which was laid down on clay tablets in Mesopotamia some four thousand years ago, and Homer's *Odyssey*, written in Greece in the eighth century BC – are, tellingly, journey stories in which human endurance, resourcefulness, friendship and ingenuity are tested almost to destruction.[1]

This book uses journeys to tell the story of three defining events of the twentieth century: the creation of the first workers' state in Russia, in October 1917; the establishment of Communist rule in China, in 1949; and Cuba's transformation, under Fidel Castro, into a lodestar for a generation of sixties radicals. The six dramatic journeys that lie at the heart of this book proved fundamental not only to how the Russian, Chinese and Cuban revolutions ultimately played out, but also to the ways in which these revolutions came to be popularly understood. Three of the journeys that are told here centre on the leading revolutionary protagonists themselves. First, Lenin's return to Russia, from exile in Switzerland, at the height of the First World War, aboard the so-called 'sealed train'. This was a journey that took him through the heart of Kaiser Wilhelm's Germany, Russia's most hated enemy and a state that embodied everything – imperialism, rapacious capitalism and aristocratic power – that Lenin detested politically. Arriving triumphantly at Petrograd's Finland Station on 3 April 1917, Lenin proceeded, as perhaps only he could have done, to seize the political initiative: within months, his Bolshevik Party overthrew the Provisional Government of Alexander Kerensky, and set about establishing the world's first Soviet republic.

Second, the Long March of 1934–5, the epic military retreat that saw the Chinese Red Army, under the leadership of Mao Zedong, break the chokehold of its Nationalist opponents in the country's south-east, before finding sanctuary in Shaanxi, in the far north-west. The march, with its fierce battles, almost superhuman feats of endurance and six-thousand-mile trek across eleven of the country's twenty-eight provinces, would become a foundational myth for the Chinese Communists, and establish Mao's position as the movement's foremost leader.

Third, Fidel Castro's audacious return to Cuba, from exile in Mexico, in December 1956 aboard the *Granma* – a creaking, leaking leisure yacht – and subsequent escape into the vast fastness of the Sierra Maestra mountains, from where he launched an ultimately successful campaign of guerrilla warfare against the island's incumbent dictator, Fulgencio Batista.

While these three journeys proved to be key turning points in the trajectory of the Russian, Chinese and Cuban revolutions, this book also brings to life the decisive contribution made by three American journalists. Drawn by the exotic appeal of the foreign and unfamiliar, and eager to search out compelling, groundbreaking stories, these three men, at great personal risk, set out on remarkable quests. Their reward: extraordinary scoops that, for better or worse, framed how these revolutions were understood in the wider world.

John Reed, the poet, bohemian and writer, in the summer of 1917 travelled halfway across the world to investigate, first-hand, the unfolding revolution in Russia. Arriving in Petrograd that autumn, Reed was literally outside the gates when the Winter Palace fell to the Bolsheviks. An enthusiast for the cause, Reed worked for the People's Commissariat for Foreign Affairs, struck up friendships with Lenin, Trotsky and other leading Bolsheviks, and, at one point, even took up arms to defend the new government from counter-revolutionaries. His eyewitness account of the revolution, *Ten Days That Shook the World*, was published in 1919. Based on official documents, revolutionary newspapers, personal testimony and Reed's own colourful experiences, it was hailed not only as a classic of reporting but also as an account that, in the perceptive words of one contemporary analyst, would 'be remembered when all others are forgotten'.

Then there is Edgar Snow, a former advertising executive from Kansas City, Missouri, who, in the summer of 1936, crossed the front lines in China's bitter civil war and travelled hundreds of miles on mule and by foot to reach the city of Bao'an in North-West China – provisional capital of the Chinese Soviet Republic. Snow would spend some three months in 'Red territory', interviewing Mao and other key leaders, travelling with the Red Army, talking with rank-and-file soldiers and peasants, and all the while noting down his impressions of life under the Communists. Returning to Beijing that autumn, he immediately began work on *Red Star Over China*. At a time when the wider world – and indeed many millions of Chinese – knew virtually nothing about the Communists, the book's publication in 1937 was an international sensation, hailed for its gripping style and trail-blazing insights. Snow, declared one reviewer, deserved credit 'for what is perhaps the greatest single feat performed by a journalist in our century'. Whereas the Nationalist government of Chiang Kai-shek portrayed the Communists as 'Red bandits', little more than violent criminals, Snow stressed the idealism and discipline of Mao and his supporters. The Communists' commitment to land redistribution and social reform, and their insistence that China take the fight to the Japanese (who had invaded, and occupied, Manchuria in 1931), made them a powerful force. Indeed, Snow predicted that ultimately they would prevail.

Finally, Herbert L. Matthews, the *New York Times*'s veteran war correspondent who in February 1957 was smuggled by Havana-based supporters of Fidel Castro into the Sierra Maestra for a clandestine meeting with the man who had, just over two months earlier, launched an audacious bid to overthrow Batista's military dictatorship. Arriving at the rebel camp early on the morning of Sunday 17 February, Matthews chatted with Fidel's younger brother, Raúl, and Ernesto 'Che' Guevara over an improvised breakfast of dried crackers, ham and coffee. Then, as dawn broke, Fidel – wearing freshly pressed military fatigues and a khaki cap, and with a rifle slung over his shoulder – strode into the clearing. Over the next three hours, Fidel talked enthusiastically about both his hopes for the new Cuba and the strength of his forces, before signing Matthews's interview notes and posing for a photograph. Matthews's scoop, 'Cuban Rebel Is Visited in Hideout', hit the front page of the *New York Times* on Sunday 24 February. Blindsiding the Cuban government, which had been busily reassuring everybody that Castro was, in fact, dead, Matthews's heroic portrait of Fidel ('the very picture of idealism and moderation'), and his band of young followers, proved decisive in establishing the popular image of the Cuban firebrand as a Robin Hood of the Antilles and the world's first beatnik revolutionary.

These six epic journeys would prove central to the history of the twentieth century. To understand how and why this was the case, though, we must first travel to north-central Switzerland, in the spring of 1917.

PART ONE
RUSSIA

LENIN

Lenin, in his trademark worker's cap, at a military parade
in Red Square, May 1919.

1. ZURICH

Judging by the scanty information available in Switzerland,
the first stage of this first revolution, namely, of the *Russian*
revolution of 1 March 1917, has ended. This first stage of
our revolution will certainly not be the last.

– V. I. LENIN

Lenin first heard the extraordinary news just after lunch on Thursday
15 March 1917.* His wife, Nadezhda Krupskaya, was clearing away the
dishes, and the Bolshevik leader was putting on his coat in preparation
for the short walk back to Zurich's Central Library, when a breathless
Polish comrade, Mieczysław Broński, appeared at the door of their
apartment. 'Haven't you heard the news?' he cried out. 'There has
been a revolution in Russia!' It seemed barely believable, and Lenin
wondered at first whether the rumours were simply the work of German
propagandists. Eager to find out the truth, all three hurried down to
Bellevueplatz, on the shore of Lake Zurich, where the latest editions
of the newspapers were posted up. After reading, and rereading, the
reports, the news began to sink in: 'a revolution', Krupskaya explained,
'had really taken place in Russia.' Lenin, meanwhile, was in a highly
agitated state, as though hit by a sudden jolt of electricity. Writing to
Inessa Armand – a leading Bolshevik, close friend and former lover –
from a nearby café that same afternoon, he explained that 'Russia must
have been on the brink of revolution for days . . . I am so excited.'[1]

Russia at the dawn of the twentieth century was, in the words of
author and historian China Miéville, a 'great, sluggard, contradictory
power'. The vast empire stretched from the Arctic to the Black Sea,
and from the Pacific as far west as modern-day Poland. Its population

* Thursday 2 March in Russia.

9

of some 130 million was a great patchwork of Slavs, Turks, Georgians, Kyrgyz, Tatars, Armenians and countless other nationalities. While the country's cities boasted cutting-edge industries, which had been imported from Europe, some 80 per cent of the empire's population remained tied to the soil in a state of neo-feudalism. And while Russia was home to an exciting literary and artistic avant-garde, most ordinary Russians were unable to read. The empire was characterised by religious diversity: 10 per cent of the Tsar's subjects were Muslim (and a similar proportion Catholic); there were some five million Jews and almost half a million Buddhists. Yet at the very centre of the empire stood the Russian Orthodox Church – conservative, hidebound and intolerant of dissent.[2] And at the apex of it all, wielding (in theory) absolute power, was the Tsar, Nicholas II, the 'Emperor of All Russia'. Acceding to the throne in 1894, this dutiful, unimaginative and stubborn man was fully committed to the principle of autocracy, and averse to reform of any kind.[3]

Creaking, stiflingly oppressive and rife with discontent, dissent and political intrigue, the entire system was put under enormous strain by Russia's entry into the Great War. With its military underprepared for the realities of modern warfare, the casualties quickly mounted: the German offensive on the Eastern Front in the spring of 1915 cost Russia more than a million men and a vast amount of territory.[4] When Nicholas II took personal command of the army that August, it not only implicated him fully in the further battlefield humiliations that followed, but also left a power vacuum back in the capital, St Petersburg[*], where the Tsarina Alexandra – wildly unpopular due to the combination of her German background and her reliance on Rasputin, the self-styled 'Holy Man'[†] – exerted considerable influence.[5] Allies of the Tsar urged him, repeatedly, to change course; on 12 January 1917 the British ambassador, Sir George Buchanan,

---

* On 1 September 1914 the city was renamed Petrograd ('Peter's City'), in order to remove the German words 'Sankt' and 'Burg'.
† Rasputin was finally dispatched by court conspirators in December 1916.

even broke with diplomatic protocol to warn the emperor directly that he was headed for the abyss of 'revolution and disaster'.[6] The Tsar remained obdurate. Nicholas's cousin, Grand Duke Sergei, told Sir George soon afterwards that, had the ambassador been a Russian subject, he would have been banished to Siberia.[7] A month later, in an official dispatch to London, Sir George articulated his hopes that Russia would continue with the 'happy knack of muddling through', but warned that severe food shortages and labour unrest could 'at any moment fan the smouldering political discontent into a flame'.[8]

In the event, the real trouble started on 23 February, with a march to commemorate International Women's Day. Buoyed by thousands of striking female textile workers from the city's Vyborg district, the demonstration swelled to some fifty thousand. Even more turned out to support the unofficial strikes on 24 February, and the following day – the start of a three-day general strike – two hundred thousand people, including white-collar workers, teachers and students, took to the streets, singing revolutionary songs, carrying red banners and denouncing the 'corrupt' and 'criminal' government. When, on 26 February, Petrograd's military commander ordered his troops to fire on any demonstrators who failed to disperse, several young soldiers mutinied and joined the protests. It augured the chaos to come. Although the police stayed largely loyal (they would mow down hundreds of protesters over the coming days), members of the elite Pavlovsky Regiment mutinied that same afternoon. By 27 February a full-scale rebellion was underway, with as many as twenty-five thousand soldiers (more than 10 per cent of the total garrison) joining the revolutionaries, who promptly seized the city's armouries, attacked police stations, stormed the notorious Kresty Prison (freeing its political prisoners, as well as common criminals) and occupied key buildings.[9] General Alfred Knox, the British military attaché in Petrograd, witnessed the revolutionaries taking control of the city's artillery department. 'We first saw two soldiers – a sort of advanced guard – who strode along the middle of the street, pointing their rifles at loiterers to clear the road. One of them fired two shots at an unfortunate chauffeur.' Behind them, he continued, was 'a great disorderly mass of soldiery, stretching right across the wide street and both pavements. They were led by a diminutive but immensely dignified student. There were no officers. All were armed, and many had red flags tied to their bayonets.'[10] Those red flags, often little more than rags, or scraps of ribbon, were soon ubiquitous – pinned to hats and lapels, wrapped around rifles and bayonets, and hung on the public buildings that were being stripped of their hated Tsarist insignia.[11]

As Bolsheviks in working-class Vyborg fantasised about seizing power and establishing a revolutionary government, the real action moved to the Tauride Palace, home of the Duma, the Russian parliament, which Nicholas II had just prorogued. After much anguished discussion, some of its members formed the 'Provisional Committee of the State Duma for the restoration of order in the capital and the establishment of relations with public organisations and institutions'. At the same time, workers, socialists and revolutionaries who had begun to flood into the vast palace founded the Petrograd Soviet of Workers' and Soldiers' Deputies, electing an executive committee and setting to work on restoring essential services, creating a militia to keep the city safe, and solving – or at least easing – the food crisis.[12] With each hour that passed, Tsarist authority was visibly draining away: some ministers who had hidden in cupboards when the shooting had begun now gave themselves up, ashen-faced and broken; the seizure of key railway stations by the revolutionaries prevented Nicholas II from returning to his capital; and the units guarding the royal palace at Tsarskoye Selo abandoned their posts – and the imperial family. On 2 March, with the situation clearly irretrievable, the Tsar abdicated in favour of his brother.[13]

When, the following day, Grand Duke Michael – realising that he lacked the necessary political support – refused the throne, control over one of the world's largest empires now passed, at least in theory, to a new Provisional Government. Headed by the nobleman and statesman Prince Lvov, it was, from the start, forced to share power with the increasingly influential Petrograd Soviet.

The events of February had unfolded at a dizzying speed, unleashing a wave of jubilation on the streets of Petrograd. The French essayist and longtime resident of the city Amélie de Néry captured the mood brilliantly. 'You had to have lived here, you had to have seen the constraint impinging on all public life,' she explained, 'the strict supervision by the police, their lack of goodwill, the spying, the informing . . . in order to understand the joy which radiates in everyone's expression now.' 'At last,' she continued, 'this great people can breathe, they have cast off their chains,' and everyone, it seemed, was now smiling.[14] It was a similar tale in Moscow, where the British diplomat and spy R. H. Bruce Lockhart described a great throng of students and soldiers flooding into the city hall – 'the soldiers hot, greasy and officious; the students raucous and exultant'. He was also greatly moved by the sight of 'grey-bearded men, bent with years – men who had suffered exile, who had lived in mouse-holes, and who, with trembling knees and a strange light in their eyes, were now rejoicing over their hour of triumph'.[15]

After three hundred years, the seemingly all-powerful autocracy had collapsed in little more than a week. But while Russia succumbed to revolution, the country's most famous revolutionary was a thousand miles away, in exile in Switzerland.

Born Vladimir Ilyich Ulyanov on 10 April 1870 in Simbirsk, a city on the banks of the Volga, the boy who would become Lenin[*] enjoyed something of a charmed childhood. His father, Ilya, was a gifted bureaucrat who served as the regional inspector of schools; his mother, Maria, was the daughter of a wealthy doctor, landowner and nobleman; and the young Vladimir summered at the family's country estate at Kokushkino. Embracing (initially at least) the deep Orthodox faith of his mother, Vladimir was also a gifted student, with a fondness for

---

[*] Ulyanov adopted this alias in 1901, and the name was possibly based on the River Lena, in Siberia. He sometimes used the fuller pseudonym 'N. Lenin' (leading many, wrongly, to describe him as 'Nikolai Lenin').

classics and literature. Although he rebelled, becoming an atheist at the age of sixteen, there were no obvious signs that the young Vladimir was on the path to becoming one of the twentieth century's most notorious revolutionaries. This would change in the spring of 1887, however, when his beloved elder brother Alexander – who had fallen in with a group of extremists while studying science at St Petersburg University – was hanged for his involvement in a plot to assassinate the Tsar. (He had used his scientific expertise to prepare the bombs.)[16]

Enrolling that same year at Kazan University to study law, Vladimir was drawn to a group of clandestine radicals, inspired by the People's Will (a late-nineteenth-century organisation that advocated assassinations to overthrow the autocracy, and which had succeeded in killing Alexander II in 1881). In December 1887, during student demonstrations, Vladimir was among more than thirty members who were rounded up and expelled from the university. For the next three years, he retired to the family estate, and immersed himself in radical literature.[17]

According to the historian Orlando Figes, by far the biggest influence on Lenin was the novelist and socialist philosopher Nikolay Chernyshevsky. Figes argues that it was through reading him, not Marx, that Lenin became a revolutionary, injecting 'a distinctly Russian dose of conspiratorial politics into a Marxist dialectic that would otherwise have remained passive – content to wait for the revolution to mature through the development of objective conditions rather than eager to bring it about through political action'. It was, Figes declares, 'not Marxism that made Lenin a revolutionary, but Lenin who made Marxism revolutionary'.[18]

Moving to St Petersburg in the autumn of 1893, Lenin was initially rebuffed by the city's Marxists, many of whom dismissed him as a brusque and unsophisticated provincial. Soon, though, his dedication, fearsome intellect and natural leadership abilities were winning him admirers. Two years later, Lenin – along with fellow Marxist Yuli Martov – was among the leaders of a short-lived effort to organise the city's workers; arrested in December, and imprisoned, he was subsequently exiled to Siberia for three years. Allowed to live relatively comfortably, he was sustained by his books, a hunting rifle (though he was a notoriously bad shot) and his new wife and fellow revolutionary, Nadezhda Krupskaya, whom he had met shortly after arriving in St Petersburg.[19]

It was during this period that Lenin, appalled by the trend among some Marxists to advocate for a peaceful, electoral and reformist path to socialism, counter-attacked, denouncing those who would, as he put it, 'convert Social Democracy into a democratic party of reform' and 'introduce bourgeois ideas and bourgeois elements into socialism'. Fired by his own commitment to revolutionary socialism, on his release from exile Lenin, together with Martov, established a newspaper, *Iskra* ('The Spark'). Its aim: to transform the newly founded Russian Social Democratic Labour Party (RSDLP) into a centralised party capable of leading the country's workers' movement. (*Iskra* quickly became Russia's leading underground newspaper.[20]) Then, in 1903, at its Second Congress, the RSDLP voted, by a slender majority, in favour of Lenin's insistence that party membership be conditional on 'personal participation in one of the Party's organisations'. Martov, believing that this position was too authoritarian, had offered an amendment that initially won the day. But after several delegates walked out, following acrimonious votes on other matters, the balance of power swung back towards Lenin's faction. Following a second vote, Lenin prevailed; he immediately labelled his followers the 'Bolsheviks' (or the 'majority' faction) and those of Martov 'Mensheviks' (the 'minority'). It was a split that would define the coming political struggle, and hand the Bolsheviks a distinct psychological advantage.[21] Quite why the Mensheviks accepted their name remains something of a puzzle, but Lenin embraced the label 'Bolshevik' – as one of his comrades remarked, 'a name he knew was a programme, a distilled essence, more powerful in its impact upon the untutored mind than dozens of articles in learned journals'.[22]

Lenin would spend much of the next decade attempting to build up the Bolsheviks, and agitate for revolution, mostly from self-imposed exile in Europe.[23] During the revolution of 1905, safely ensconced in Geneva, Lenin called consistently (and recklessly) for the 'arming of the people', insisting that 'those who do not prepare for armed uprising must be ruthlessly cast out of the ranks of supporters of the Revolution.' At a time when there were barely a couple of hundred Bolsheviks in the Russian capital (half of them students), and virtually no chance at all that an armed uprising would succeed, Lenin was insistent. Victory, he argued, was beside the point: 'What do we care about victory? We should not harbour any illusions. We are realists . . . the point is not about winning, but about giving the regime a shake and attracting the masses to our movement. The uprising is what matters.'[24] In the end, what Lenin later termed the 'dress rehearsal' for the revolution of October 1917 was resolved when the Tsar, under enormous pressure, agreed to limited (and, as it turned out, short-lived) political reforms: the creation of a parliament, or Duma (with modest powers); the establishment of cabinet government; a partial extension of the franchise; and the granting of 'inviolable personal rights' to the population, including freedom of speech, conscience and assembly.[25] Lenin felt sufficiently emboldened to return to Russia in November 1905, but the level of police surveillance made political work all but impossible. As the Tsarist regime, now feeling more secure, began to crack down hard on unrest, Lenin was forced first underground, then to the relative safety of Finland (then an autonomous part of the Russian Empire), and eventually back to Switzerland.[26]

Lenin would continue to take what his opponents viewed as radical, uncompromising positions – notoriously, for instance, condoning the use of theft (or, as Lenin had it, 'expropriations') to help fund the party. Creating what was, in effect, a criminal operation – headed by Leonid Krasin and Joseph Stalin – the Bolsheviks used hired gangs to rob banks and attack post offices, railway stations and other targets. When Martov and his fellow Mensheviks recoiled from this criminal activity, insisting that they did not want to be 'regarded as thieves', Lenin was contemptuous, saying: 'You don't make revolution with kid gloves.'[27]

In the decade leading up to 1917, 'the Old Man' (as his close associates called him) lived an increasingly peripatetic lifestyle, basing himself in Geneva, Paris, London, Kraków and numerous other towns across Europe, as he sought to hone his arguments and advance the revolutionary cause. He was in Poronin, a little village at the foot of the Tatra Mountains, in Habsburg-ruled Galicia in modern-day Poland, when the Great War broke out. Its remote tranquillity had proved conducive to writing; its closeness to the Russian border allowed for a steady stream of visitors; and the clean air, magnificent scenery and opportunities for swimming and hiking had been fortifying. All this came to a sudden end with the guns of August 1914. Arrested and briefly imprisoned on suspicion of being a spy, Lenin – together with his wife – headed first to Bern, and then, in February 1916, Zurich.[28]

Lenin was a fan of Switzerland. He loved its lakes and mountains, and Zurich, which boasted a large émigré population, also had the added attraction of a newly opened public library. He spent as much time as he could there, seated at his favourite desk, surrounded by books, undertaking exhaustive research for a lengthy new essay. (*Imperialism: The Highest Stage of Capitalism* would eventually be published in mid-1917.)[29] Contemptuous of the world war – nothing more than 'a struggle for markets and for the freedom to loot foreign countries' – Lenin attacked Europe's leaders for seeking to 'deceive, disunite and slaughter the proletarians of all countries'. But he was particularly appalled by the reaction of Europe's social democrats, who had abandoned their collective opposition to war and cast aside the language of fraternity and peace in favour of patriotism and nationalism. When he learned that Germany's SPD (Social Democratic Party) had voted to grant war credits to the Kaiser's government, Lenin is supposed to have remarked: 'I am no longer a Social-Democrat; I am a Communist.'[30]

As the war itself began to drag on – and as its appalling costs in blood and treasure became increasingly evident – opposition to the conflict began to reassert itself on the Left. Lenin, though, was adamant: 'The propaganda of peace unaccompanied by revolutionary mass action', he declared in the spring of 1915, 'can only sow illusions and demoralise the proletariat, for it makes the proletariat believe that the bourgeoisie is humane.' 'In particular,' Lenin argued, 'the idea of a so-called democratic peace being possible without a series of revolutions is profoundly erroneous.'[31] It was a line that he continued to hold – most notably at the so-called Zimmerwald Conference, held on the outskirts of Bern in September 1915. Organised by Robert Grimm, a leading Swiss socialist, the meeting brought together thirty-eight delegates from across Europe, with the aim of relaunching the Socialist International on an anti-war platform.[32] At the four-day conference, a manifesto – reaffirming the 'international solidarity of the proletariat and of the class struggle', demanding a 'peace without annexations or war indemnities', and calling on 'Socialists of the belligerent countries' to take up the 'struggle against bloody barbarism with every effective means' – was adopted unanimously.[33] But Lenin also used the meeting to advocate for his wider goal: the destruction of the entire structure of imperialism. It was, he insisted, the 'duty of socialists' to 'develop the workers' revolutionary consciousness, rally them in the international revolutionary struggle, promote and encourage any revolutionary action, and do everything possible to turn the imperialist war between the peoples into a civil war of the oppressed classes against their oppressors'. The ultimate goal, he explained, was for the proletariat to seize political power and realise socialism.[34] This was the essence of Lenin's controversial doctrine of 'revolutionary defeatism': an extreme socialist position based on the idea that the working class would not benefit from a victory in a 'capitalist', 'imperialist' war. Instead, Lenin argued, the proletariat would gain from their nation's defeat if the war could be transformed into a civil war and then an international revolution.

In making his case, Lenin could count on the support of just a handful of other delegates – among them Germany's Fritz Platten, Grigory Zinoviev and Karl Radek. (Born in what is now Lviv, in Ukraine, Radek had been active in both the Polish and German socialist movements before the war.) But, according to the historian

Catherine Merridale, the Zimmerwald Conference had transformed Lenin into an international figure and the inspiration for a distinct, and growing, movement of radical European socialists, which would become known as the Zimmerwald Left.[35]

Although Lenin was securing greater prestige on the international stage, his influence in his homeland appeared to be on the wane. Under near-constant attack from the Tsarist secret police (the Okhrana), the Bolshevik Party itself appeared to be unravelling. Nadezhda Krupskaya's list of key organisers, for instance, had dwindled to just ten by 1917. The party's newspaper, *Pravda* – a key source of income as well as a critically important tool of propaganda – had been suppressed and many of the party's leading figures, including Lev Kamenev, had been rounded up and either imprisoned or sent into exile.[36] As for 'revolutionary defeatism', Lenin's message was, it seems, falling on stony ground. When, in December 1916, the French ambassador to Russia had asked one of his best informants whether Lenin's controversial idea was making any headway among the army, the response was brutal. 'No,' he was told: 'the only advocates of that doctrine here are a few lunatics who are supposed to be in the pay of Germany – or the Okhrana.' Even within Lenin's own party, it seemed, the defeatists were in a minority.[37]

Cut off from his homeland, and reliant on second-hand reports in the foreign-language press, Lenin now faced the very real prospect of watching from the sidelines as history marched on without him.

According to Nadezhda Krupskaya, as soon as he learned of the success of the February Revolution, Lenin's mind went into overdrive.[38] Within days he was issuing instructions to his Bolshevik comrades:

> Our tactics: no trust in and no support of the new government; Kerensky is especially suspect; arming of the proletariat is the only guarantee; immediate elections to the Petrograd City Council; no rapprochement with other parties.[39]

In an article written for the newly revived *Pravda*, which was published on 7 March,* Lenin declared that 'the first revolution engendered by the imperialist world war has broken out. The first revolution but certainly not the last.' He was openly contemptuous of the newly formed Provisional Government and its bourgeois ministers, dismissing the social democrat Alexander Kerensky, one of the revolution's leading lights, as a 'balalaika on which they play to deceive the workers and peasants'. Identifying the Petrograd Soviet as 'the embryo of a workers' government, the representative of the interests of the entire mass of the *poor* section of the population', Lenin argued that 'the only *guarantee* of freedom and of the complete destruction of tsarism lies in *arming the proletariat*, in strengthening, extending and developing the role, significance and power of the Soviet of Workers' Deputies.'[40] In private, Lenin went further, arguing that the proletariat would first need to 'smash' the '"ready-made" state machine' before merging the police, army and bureaucracy 'with *the entire armed people*'. The proletariat, Lenin explained, must 'take the organs of state power directly into their own hands, in order that *they themselves should constitute* these organs of state power'.[41]

These hard-line positions seemed extreme to many – including a good number of his own comrades – and certainly out of touch with the heady, optimistic mood on the streets of Petrograd, where the new government was busily enacting a series of liberal reforms that would have been unimaginable just weeks before.[42] What Lenin yearned for, more than anything else, was to be able to influence events directly. From the 'moment the news of the February Revolution was received', recalled Krupskaya, 'Ilyich was all eagerness to go back to Russia'.[43]

* 20 March in Switzerland.

2. CAGED LION

*You can imagine what torture it is for all of us to be stuck
here at a time like this. We have to go by some means,
even if it is through Hell.*

– V. I. LENIN

Lenin's old friend Grigory Zinoviev was in the Swiss capital, Bern, when news of the February Revolution broke. Like his fellow revolutionaries, he was elated by the news: 'The ice has broken,' he wrote, and 'what whole generations of Russian revolutionaries had dreamed of, had finally become a fact.' As he hurried home, still holding the news-sheet proclaiming the news, he discovered a telegram from Lenin already waiting for him. He was, he learned, to leave for Zurich 'immediately'.[1]

Born Hirsch Apfelbaum on 11 September 1883, on a dairy farm in what is now central Ukraine, Zinoviev joined the RSDLP in 1901 and sided with Lenin's faction when the party split. He was on the streets of St Petersburg, agitating among the workers, during the revolution of 1905, and became a member of the Bolshevik Central Committee two years later. In the decade or so that followed, Zinoviev – who lived in exile in France, Austria and then Switzerland – became Lenin's right-hand man. (When the Mensheviks described him as the Old Man's 'arms bearer', it was not meant as a compliment.) Described by one historian as 'stocky, clean-shaven, short-winded' and with a 'high-pitched voice', Zinoviev – a compelling and inspirational orator – was 'a supreme sycophant, famously cynical, who did a lot of Lenin's dirty work for him'. According to his fellow Bolshevik Angelika Balabanova (who later broke with the party), Zinoviev was 'simply the most despicable human being I ever met. Whenever there was an unfair factional manoeuvre to be made or a revolutionary reputation to be undermined,' she explained, 'Lenin would charge Zinoviev with the task.'[2]

As the two men walked the streets of Zurich that spring, one thought dominated all else: the urgent need to get back to Russia. Lenin, Zinoviev explained, was becoming increasingly frustrated, 'drawn to work, to fight, but in the Swiss "hole", there was nothing to do but sit around in the libraries. I remember with what "envy" . . . we looked at the Swiss Social Democrats, who in one way or another lived among their workers and were absorbed in the workers' movement of their country.' Lenin and his comrades, though, were 'cut off from Russia, as never before. We longed for Russian language, for Russian air. At that time, Vladimir Ilyich reminded us of a lion locked in a cage.'[3]

The problem, of course, was that Lenin's route home was blocked. The Allied powers, desperate to keep Russia in the war, were hardly going to provide safe passage to Europe's leading advocate of 'revolutionary defeatism'. Meanwhile, as a citizen of a hostile power, travel through Germany or Austria–Hungary was illegal.[4] In desperation, Lenin and his comrades conjured up a series of increasingly preposterous plans. Repeatedly Lenin sought to procure a false passport, so that he could travel in disguise ('I can wear a wig,' he explained), via France, England, the Netherlands, and then on to neutral Scandinavia. Then he toyed with the idea of returning to Russia by plane. But, as Zinoviev pointed out, they only lacked a few things: 'an aeroplane, the necessary means, the consent of the authorities, etc.' A false Swedish passport was easy to get hold of, but since Lenin neither spoke nor understood a word of the language, using the document presented a challenge. It was in seeming desperation, then, that he concocted a scheme to return to Russia using the passport of a deaf and mute Swede – and even went so far as to ask his comrade Yakov Ganetsky (Jakub Fürstenberg), then living in Stockholm, to 'find a Swede who looked like me'. It was left to Lenin's wife to point out the flaw: '"Imagine yourself falling asleep and dreaming of Mensheviks, which will start you off swearing juicily in Russian! Where will your disguise be then?" I said with a laugh.'[5]

For Lenin, however, being stuck in Switzerland while revolution played out in his homeland was no laughing matter. As he told

Ganetsky, 'You can imagine what torture it is for all of us to be stuck here at a time like this. We have to go by some means, even if it is through Hell.'[6]

Gradually, the comrades began to realise that they had no other choice. The only viable route home lay through Kaiser Wilhelm II's German Empire – Russia's deadly and most hated foe.

In the long, cruel months that had followed the outbreak of war in August 1914, German troops had killed or maimed hundreds of thousands of Russians, taken many more prisoner, and occupied vast tracts of Russian territory. Lenin himself had nothing but contempt for the imperialists, monarchists and bourgeois capitalists who, with the craven support of Germany's SPD, had sacrificed millions of their fellow citizens in order to 'enrich a few, open the road to Baghdad, [and] conquer the Balkans'.[7] To travel through Imperial Germany without permission risked almost certain arrest and imprisonment (not least because, as Karl Radek explained, the business of distinguishing between genuine traffickers and German spies proved impossible).[8] And yet to do a deal with the Kaiser's government smacked of treachery. The Austrian writer Stefan Zweig, who was in Zurich during the spring of 1917, later wrote that 'it is high treason, of course, to set foot on enemy land and cross it in the middle of a war and with the approval of the enemy general staff.' Lenin, moreover, would have been all too aware that, by enabling his opponents to level the charge that he was a paid agent of the German government, he risked compromising the Bolsheviks, and their cause – perhaps fatally.[9]

It is not clear who first suggested to Lenin the notion of returning to Russia via Germany. Writing several years later, Radek claimed that he had asked a journalist working for the *Frankfurter Zeitung* to sound out Gisbert von Romberg, the German ambassador in Bern, about whether Germany might allow Russian émigrés to travel through its territory.[10] In doing this, Radek may well have been influenced by his knowledge that Russians working in Copenhagen had recently received transit visas from Berlin.[11] At around the same time, though, Lenin's great rival Yuli Martov – addressing a meeting of Russian and Polish émigrés in the Swiss capital – floated the idea that the Provisional Government in Petrograd might release some German and Austrian civil internees in return for Germany allowing safe transit for the exiles. Zinoviev, who was at the meeting, reported back to Lenin, who deemed the idea 'excellent – we ought to get busy with it'.[12] As soon became clear, negotiations with the Provisional Government would likely be a long, drawn-out affair. (The hawkish foreign minister, Pavel Milyukov, was far from keen to assist anti-war 'defeatists'.) Lenin, who was kept awake at night by the fear that events in Russia might leave him behind, now moved to cut his own deal.

The complex, fraught and clandestine negotiations that unfolded in the early spring of 1917 involved a cast of individuals who were, by turns, unsavoury, disreputable and politically suspect. Lenin, understandably, insisted on leaving the heavy lifting to intermediaries.[13] Robert Grimm, the Swiss socialist leader, journalist and organiser of the Zimmerwald Conference, might have been, in Lenin's words, a 'detestable centrist', but he had useful contacts within the Swiss government, and so was recruited to try to broker a deal with Romberg.[14] At the same time, through his old ally Yakov Ganetsky, Lenin made contact with Alexander Helphand (who used the pseudonym 'Parvus'). Seventeen years earlier, Parvus had been a brilliant young Marxist who had helped churn out the early issues of *Iskra* from a printing press hidden in his Munich home. Now, though, he cut a very different figure: enormously fat, he had made a fortune in Constantinople (allegedly via dubious deals in wheat and arms) and then, with the outbreak of war, had offered his services to the German government, becoming a millionaire as an arms dealer, propagandist and exploiter of the black market in medicines, drugs, rubber and other goods. The once idealistic revolutionary had transformed, in middle age, into a caricature of a tycoon, with a penchant for luxury cars, champagne, cigars and glamorous young blondes. But, by convincing the German leadership that assisting Lenin and his comrades was in their interests, he changed the course of the twentieth century.[15]

By early 1917, the German government was under intense pressure. With the Royal Navy's economic blockade causing desperate hardship at home, the military command sought to use its formidable U-boat fleet to break the stranglehold and take the fight to the British. But, as the Germans well knew, the resumption of unrestricted submarine warfare was all but certain to bring the United States into the conflict. There would, however, be a crucial window, while the Americans were mobilising, in which Germany might win a decisive victory on the Western Front. That meant knocking out the Russians first – and, while advances on the battlefield had been encouraging, the collapse of the Tsarist regime offered the tantalising possibility that a separate peace might be made.[16] In a series of meetings with Ulrich von Brockdorff-Rantzau, the German minister in Copenhagen, Parvus (whose front company was based in the city) insisted that supporting the 'extremist' elements made sense. With Lenin back in Russia, he argued, the country would become destabilised, and those advocating for a separate peace would quickly gain the advantage.[17] Brockdorff-Rantzau agreed. In a cable sent to the foreign ministry on 2 April, the minister stated that it was 'essential that we now try to create the greatest possible degree of chaos in Russia', and 'deepen the differences between the moderate and extremist parties, for it is greatly in our interests that the latter should gain the upper hand'. In just three months, he predicted, the 'disintegration' should have reached the stage 'where we could break the power of the Russians by military action'.[18] As it turned out, he was knocking on an open door. The new foreign minister, Arthur Zimmermann – a covert-operations fan – readily agreed and immediately asked the German High Command whether they had any objections to allowing the 'transit of the revolutionaries' across German territory.

They did not.[19]

The first attempt by the Germans to secure Lenin's return to Russia ended in failure. Georg Sklarz, a business partner of Parvus, rocked up in Zurich offering to escort Lenin and Zinoviev through Germany and to pay their fare. The plan was dismissed out of hand: taking German money directly was simply far too incriminating.[20] Meanwhile, the negotiations that Grimm was undertaking with Romberg appeared to be going nowhere. On 3 April the German-Swiss socialist Willi Münzenberg attended a meeting at a Zurich restaurant, where he witnessed Lenin – 'excited and furious' – pacing up and down, venting his frustration to Zinoviev, Krupskaya and a handful of other comrades. Grimm, he claimed, had been deliberately blocking the return of the Bolshevik émigrés to Russia, and simply could not be trusted. It was eventually decided to appoint Fritz Platten, the secretary of the Swiss Socialist Party (and one of the few delegates to support Lenin at the Zimmerwald Conference two years earlier), to act as the go-between.[21] Platten, who visited Romberg at the embassy in Bern the following day, pressed for quick action. Romberg was persuaded and made an urgent recommendation to his superiors that permission for the journey be granted. He also encouraged his government to accept the various conditions that the exiles had drawn up.[22] As well as the famous clause that the carriage bearing the revolutionaries be granted 'extraterritorial rights' (a legal ruse which meant that – theoretically at least – the passengers would never enter German territory), the Bolshevik group also insisted that all communications with German organisations and officials would be undertaken, exclusively, by Platten. Permission to travel, moreover, would not be dependent on political beliefs or opinion and, to the extent that it was practicable, it was requested that the journey should be made without stops, and in a through train. In exchange, the exiles undertook to agitate for the release of a corresponding number of German and Austrian prisoners upon their return to Russia.[23]

On 5 April, word came back from Berlin: the deal was on.[24]

Lenin's secret agreement with the Germans did not remain secret for very long. Ernst Nobs, editor of Zurich's *Volksrecht* newspaper, had the scoop, and soon the story was the only topic of conversation among Zurich's writers, artists and journalists. At the Plauen Café, regular haunt of left-wing intellectuals, the news caused pandemonium. The leftist journalist J. Ley recalled how his fellow journalists and writers inveighed against the 'treachery' of working with the German imperialists, and roundly denounced Lenin. James Joyce quipped that Erich Ludendorff, first quartermaster general of the German High Command, 'must be pretty desperate'. Indeed, the idea of Ludendorff and Lenin – reactionary militarist and socialist revolutionary – working together, hand in glove, struck Joyce as absurd, an outlandish practical joke. But most of the writers, artists and radicals that Ley encountered did not see the funny side. Lenin's actions, they believed, would only strengthen Germany's military, prolong the terrible war and make a victory for the Kaiser more likely.[25]

Lenin was unrepentant. The night before his departure he addressed a meeting of Russian émigrés, workers and foreign correspondents, who had packed into a shabby, dimly lit hall, in the centre of Bern. The Bolshevik leader, pacing back and forth on the platform, gripping his lapels, had a defiant message. 'We have before us', he said, 'a struggle of exceptional gravity and harshness. Let us go into that battle fully conscious of the responsibility we are taking. We know what we want to do. The law of history imposes our leadership, because it is through us that the proletariat speaks.' The Spanish socialist and journalist Julio Álvarez del Vayo, who was in the audience that night, later wrote that he had 'never seen anybody more certain of winning a battle'.[26]

Early on the morning of 9 April – Easter Monday – Lenin, Krupskaya, Zinoviev, Radek and a number of other comrades (including Olga Ravich, Inessa Armand and Grigory Sokolnikov) gathered at the Volkshaus in Bern before catching the train back to Zurich.[27] After stopping off at their apartment to collect some belongings (a basket of clothes, two containing books and old newspapers, two boxes of party documents, and a portable kerosene stove for making tea), Lenin and Krupskaya repaired to the Zähringerhof hotel, on the square next to the city's railway station, for a farewell banquet.[28] At the end of lunch, Lenin stood up and, on behalf of the group, read aloud a 'farewell letter to the Swiss workers', conveying their 'fraternal greetings and expression of our profound comradely gratitude for your comradely treatment of the political émigrés'. Turning his attention to events in Russia, Lenin declared that 'to the Russian proletariat has fallen the great honour of *beginning* the series of revolutions which the imperialist war has made an objective inevitability.' The Old Man acknowledged that, 'single-handed, the Russian proletariat cannot bring the socialist revolution to a *victorious conclusion*.' 'But,' he continued, 'it can give the Russian revolution a mighty sweep that would create the most favourable conditions for a socialist revolution, and would, in a sense, *start* it. It can facilitate the rise of a situation in which its *chief*, its most trustworthy and most reliable collaborator, the *European* and American *socialist* proletariat, could join the decisive battles.' He signed off with the cry, 'Long live the proletarian revolution that is *beginning* in Europe!'[29]

At 2.30 p.m. – having put their signatures to a document in which they assumed responsibility for the journey and acknowledged that the Provisional Government had recently threatened 'to bring the Russian émigrés returning through Germany to trial for high treason' – they set off for the Hauptbahnhof.[30]

The Germans had agreed to transport a maximum of sixty émigrés but, in the end, just thirty-two (nineteen of whom were members of the Bolshevik Party) decided to risk it. The little band made for an incongruous sight: 'men and women and children in threadbare clothes, the men in black hats, the women in long skirts, ankle boots, their heads under varying types of covering ranging from scarves to Olga Ravich's big, broad-brimmed "chapeau"', carrying cushions, blankets and a handful of belongings.[31] Fritz Platten might have been smiling, but most members of the group approached the waiting train as if they were being forced to walk the plank.[32]

A crowd of about a hundred had turned out for the occasion. Some of those present were merely curious, while others had come to offer encouragement. Most, though, were hostile. Cries of 'Traitors!', 'Provocateurs!' and 'Spies!' rang out; others shouted taunts – 'The Kaiser is paying you for the journey!', 'They're going to hang you . . . like German Spies!' – or beat on the side of the carriage with sticks, jeering and hissing.[33] David Ryazanov, a friend of Leon Trotsky (who had been interned in Nova Scotia by the British while attempting to return to Russia), ran up to the train in a state of high agitation and pleaded desperately with Zinoviev: 'Vladimir Ilyich has let himself be carried away and has forgotten the dangers . . . Please understand that this is madness. Convince Vladimir Ilyich that he must abandon the plan to travel through Germany!'[34] Amid the chaos, the odd scuffle broke out – at one point Lenin seized the German socialist Oscar Blum by the collar and, mistaking him for a spy, threw him off the carriage and onto the track.[35]

Then, on the dot of 3.10 p.m., the train began to slowly inch its way out of the station. As it did so, a group of loyal Swiss socialists belted out the 'Internationale'. For the next couple of hours, the comrades relaxed as the train made its way through the valleys and hills north of Zurich. Then, after passing Neuhausen am Rheinfall – site of Europe's largest waterfall – they came to the border town of Schaffhausen, where the émigrés were promptly ushered off the train by Swiss customs officials. The revolutionaries could only watch, with dismay, as their luggage was searched and most of the provisions that they had carefully gathered for the long journey ahead, including cheese, sausages and chocolate, were confiscated. (The Swiss, it turned out, had strict rules about exporting food during wartime, and only a few bread rolls survived the cull.) Then, just down the line at Thayngen – and over the furious protests of Platten – a second posse of customs officials insisted on yet another examination.[36] Finally, the train reached Gottmadingen, in the German federal state of Baden-Württemberg, and the promise of the 'sealed train' to Sweden. As they pulled up at the station's only platform that evening, the émigrés were greeted by the sight of two German officers, in their grey uniforms and high black boots. Stiff and unsmiling, they ordered the passengers off the train and into a bare and deserted waiting room, where they were divided – the men on one side, and the women and children on the other. In the threatening silence that followed, most of the party – by now extremely jittery – began to wonder how they had been so naïve as to fall into a German trap. Anticipating disaster, they steeled themselves for imminent arrest.[37]

3. THE SEALED TRAIN

It was with a sense of awe that [the Germans] turned upon Russia
the most grisly of all weapons. They transported Lenin in a sealed
truck like a plague bacillus from Switzerland into Russia.
— WINSTON CHURCHILL

The two German officers, Captain Arwed Edler von der Planitz and
Lieutenant Ulrich von Bühring, had been selected specifically for the
job. Von Bühring, the younger of the two men, could speak fluent
Russian (although he was under strict orders to conceal this fact). Von
der Planitz – a lawyer who, after serving with an elite unit on the Western
Front, had been transferred to the domestic counter-intelligence branch
of the German General Staff – was described as 'politically tactful'. Just
days earlier, both men had received a top-secret briefing, in person,
from General Ludendorff. To the émigrés' enormous relief, it soon
became clear that Berlin had every intention of keeping to its side of the
bargain – the uncomfortable delay in the third-class waiting room was
merely to enable the Germans to make a final check of the numbers
travelling (and, perhaps, to make it clear to everyone exactly who was in
charge). After completing the formalities, and collecting the fares that
Lenin had insisted the group pay themselves, von der Planitz ushered
them towards the waiting train.[1]

The famous 'sealed train' consisted of a specially commandeered
military locomotive, a single green carriage that had been divided
into eight compartments – three of them second class and five of
them third – with a toilet at each end, and a baggage wagon. At the
comrades' insistence, Lenin and Krupskaya were given the second-
class compartment at the front of the train, so that the Old Man
could work in peace. (He put up only a token protest.) The other
two were assigned to women and families, while the single men had
to forgo the relative luxury of brown padded upholstery for the hard

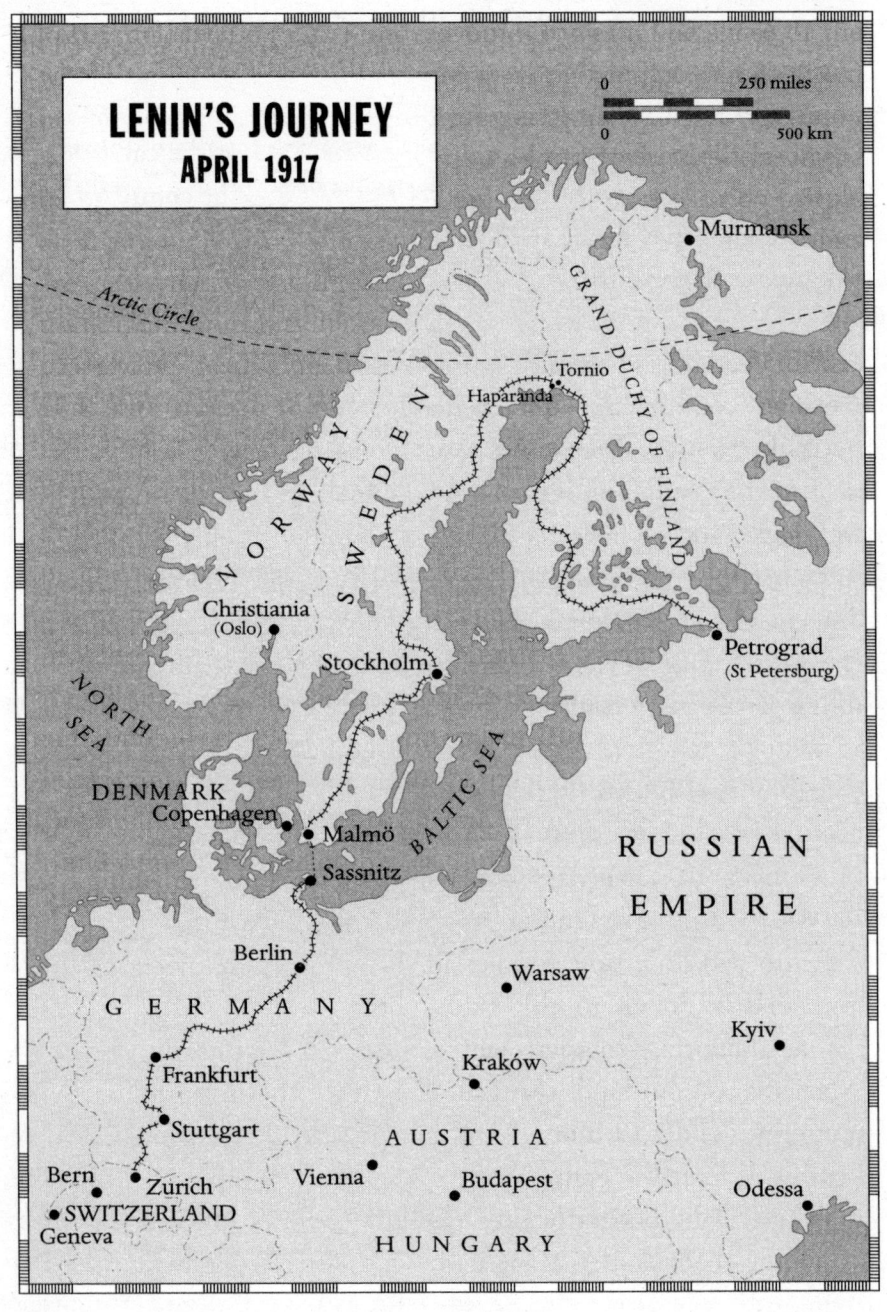

LENIN'S JOURNEY
APRIL 1917

0   250 miles
0   500 km

Murmansk

Arctic Circle

GRAND DUCHY OF FINLAND

N O R W A Y

S W E D E N

Tornio
Haparanda

Christiania
(Oslo)

Stockholm

Petrograd
(St Petersburg)

N O R T H
S E A

B A L T I C   S E A

DENMARK
Copenhagen

Malmö

Sassnitz

R U S S I A N

E M P I R E

Berlin

Warsaw

G E R M A N Y

Kyiv

Frankfurt

Kraków

Stuttgart

A U S T R I A

Bern   Zurich

Vienna

Budapest

Odessa

SWITZERLAND

Geneva

H U N G A R Y

wooden benches of third class. The two German officers occupied the compartment at the rear of the carriage. A chalk line, drawn on the floor by Platten, marked the border with 'German territory', and the three doors that opened at the 'Russian' end of the carriage were locked shut.[2] Now, with the shadows lengthening, the comrades began their long journey to the Baltic port of Sassnitz, more than a thousand kilometres to the north.

Lenin stood at the carriage window as the train rolled through the German countryside that evening, his thumbs characteristically hooked into his waistcoat. He would not have been able to see a great deal in the fast-fading light – just the firs and beech trees that lined the tracks, and perhaps a few early spring wildflowers. The train had, in fact, hardly got going when it came to a halt in a quiet siding in Singen, just a few kilometres north-east of Gottmadingen. Nestled at the foot of Hohentwiel, an extinct volcano, this little town was home to the giant Maggi plant, whose workforce of several hundred – many of them women – was dedicated to the production, and bottling, of the company's celebrated liquid condiment.[*3] As imposing as the tenth-century border fortress whose ruins topped the mountain, the factory, as the historian Catherine Merridale has explained, 'stood witness to the epic powers of the capitalist mode of production'.[4]

Lenin had little time to take all this in. His attention was almost immediately drawn to the raucous behaviour of the comrades in the neighbouring compartment – whose boisterous singing of the 'Marseillaise', and loud, shrieking laughter, proved too much. When muttering loudly to himself and banging on the wall proved futile, Lenin was forced to confront the troublemakers – who, it turned out, were fuelled by bottles of beer that the German officers had passed across the chalk border, along with a large pile of sandwiches for that

* According to Torsten Riotte, adjunct professor of modern and contemporary history at the Goethe University of Frankfurt – and a keen Anglophile – it tastes like a combination of Oxo and Marmite.

33

evening's supper.* Directing his focus away from the politics of world proletarian revolution, if only momentarily, Lenin began to draw up a list of in-train rules. Sleep, during designated hours, was now to be a matter of party discipline; when it came to smoking (a habit that Lenin detested), the solution was simple: it was confined to the toilet. Since that immediately caused a lengthy and uncomfortable queue for those who actually needed to use the facilities, Lenin cut up a sheet of paper and issued two types of ticket: 'second-class' passes for the smokers, and 'first-class' ones (which guaranteed priority entry) for everyone else.[5]

Early the following morning, Tuesday 10 April (28 March in Russia), the comrades were on the move again, as the train headed up the Neckar Valley, between the Black Forest and the Alps, bound for Frankfurt.†[6] As they contemplated the view from their carriage, the émigrés were struck by the desolate and disturbing scenes that greeted them.[7] Krupskaya explained that they all noticed 'the total absence of grown-up men. Only women, teenagers and children could be seen at the wayside stations, on the fields, and in the streets of the towns.'[8] And, as the train slowed down at little towns or crossings, the revolutionaries would see, up close, the pale, emaciated faces of a people worn down by three years of war, and brutal economic blockade.[9]

The monotony of the journey was broken later that afternoon when, with the train waiting at Stuttgart station, Fritz Platten was informed that the German trade unionist leader and Social Democrat Wilhelm Janson was requesting a meeting with Lenin.[10] Platten dutifully passed on the information, which sparked immediate concern for Karl Radek. As an Austrian citizen he was eligible to serve at the front, but he had

* They were also egged on by Karl Radek, who, for reasons that have never been explained, had managed to ensconce himself in a second-class compartment, despite travelling alone.
† The journey through Germany involved travel on 'four different state railways, and each time they crossed from one system to another, a new engine would take over'. Moreover, 'owing to military restrictions on lines to the front, they would at times move out of one state railway for a few miles and then return to it.' (Michael Pearson, *The Sealed Train*, 109–10.)

also enjoyed a fractious pre-war relationship with Germany's socialists, some of whom had accused him of embezzling party funds. Radek was promptly 'hidden in the luggage compartment and left with a supply of about fifty newspapers', so that he 'would keep quiet and not cause a scandal'.[11] The Old Man then carefully considered Janson's request: tell him, he said, to 'go to the devil's grandmother'; if he entered the Russian carriage, thereby violating their extraterritoriality, Lenin continued, then he would 'smash his nose' and throw him off the train.[12]

That same evening, now in Frankfurt, the émigrés' insistence that any communication with the German world that lay beyond their carriage be undertaken via Platten was violated in spectacular fashion. Before disappearing for the night (it was rumoured that he had a girlfriend in the city), their designated interlocuter had, it seemed, popped by the station buffet to order beer and sandwiches, and then tipped a group of soldiers to take them to the occupants of the carriage that had been discreetly parked in a quiet siding.[13] Radek explained what happened next. 'Suddenly the cordon was broken, as German soldiers came rushing up to us.' 'They had', he continued, 'heard that Russian revolutionaries, who were in favour of peace, were travelling through. Each of them held a jug of beer in both hands. Excitedly they asked us whether and when peace was coming.'[14]

The last thing the German authorities wanted was Russian revolutionaries spreading radical ideas or advocating for peace among the military rank and file, so when the train arrived in Berlin the following night, strict measures were put in place to avoid any repeat: there were military guards and barbed-wire barriers, and the formerly freewheeling Platten was informed that he could only leave the carriage if accompanied by a military escort.[15] Having missed the Wednesday-afternoon ferry to Sweden (whose government had finally, the previous afternoon, given authorisation for the revolutionaries to transit through the country), the Russians were held in the German capital for some twenty hours. The historical record is deafeningly silent on exactly what the émigrés got up to during this long layover. There is, though, no evidence at all to substantiate the rumours that Lenin met secretly with senior figures from the foreign ministry (whose headquarters was just a few minutes' walk from Potsdam station), or even perhaps the German chancellor, Theobald von Bethmann Hollweg.[16]

The following day, Thursday 12 April, the comrades endured a final five hours of confinement in the sealed train, as they trundled slowly through the countryside of Brandenburg and Western Pomerania, before reaching Stralsund, the beautiful old Hanseatic port. There, the carriage was loaded onto a ferry and taken across the Strela Sound to Rügen Island and on to the ferry port at Sassnitz.[17] Boarding the steamer the *Queen Victoria* for the voyage to Trelleborg, now just a few hours away, the émigrés were required to supply their names. Suspicious as ever, Lenin insisted that they use pseudonyms. The crossing itself was decidedly unpleasant: the Baltic Sea was choppy, and only five of the party – among them Lenin, Radek and Zinoviev – turned out to have decent sea legs. This little band stood, for a while at least, around the main mast, engaged in animated debate, while their comrades succumbed to seasickness or sought shelter from the cold in the downstairs saloon. There was one moment of tension when, over the ship's tannoy, the captain asked repeatedly if there was a 'Mr Ulyanov' on board. Lenin, who feared that he was about to be arrested – or worse – allowed himself a quiet chuckle on discovering that Yakov Ganetsky, who had waited in vain at the dockside in Trelleborg the previous night, had simply radioed the ferry to confirm their arrival.[18]

Ganetsky had organised an enthusiastic, if small, welcome at the quay: the mayor made a speech, a delegation of local socialists offered their fraternal greetings, and warm words were exchanged. What there was not, though, was a great deal of time: fifteen minutes after disembarking, the émigrés were on the train to Malmö, and a much grander reception at the city's Savoy Hotel.[19] It made for an incongruous sight: thirty or so of Europe's foremost revolutionaries, shabbily dressed and exhausted from days of travel, gathering amid the art deco splendour of Malmö's finest hotel, for a traditional Swedish smörgåsbord. Back in Switzerland, Radek explained, the émigrés had become 'accustomed to . . . no more than a herring for our dinner'. Now, confronted by huge tables weighed down with hors d'oeuvre – including salmon, smoked elk with berries, pickles, caviar, cream cheese and rye bread – the comrades swarmed like grasshoppers, demolishing the lot within minutes, as the appalled waiters looked on. Lenin – no gourmand, even at the best of times – was the only one not to indulge, preferring instead to grill Ganetsky about the latest news from Russia. The political discussions continued aboard the night train to Stockholm, joined by the Swedish socialist and journalist Otto Grimlund, and the lively conversation took in the current state of the Swedish Left as well as Lenin's own plans for Russia.[20]

Finally, as dawn broke on Friday 13 April, the train reached the Swedish capital.

As they climbed wearily down onto the platform that grey spring morning, the comrades were met by a melee of journalists, photographers and local dignitaries – including the city's mayor – before heading to the nearby Hotel Regina. Appalled by the slovenly appearance of Lenin's group, the staff initially refused to admit the new arrivals, only relenting after it was explained that the rooms had already been paid for. After freshening up, it was time to attend a breakfast that had been laid on by the local welcoming committee. As Radek quipped, 'Sweden is distinguished from all other countries by the fact that at every opportunity a breakfast is organised; when the social revolution comes in Sweden, the first thing they will do is give a breakfast in honour of the retiring bourgeoisie, and then a breakfast in honour of the new revolutionary regime.'[21]

With the next train to the sparsely populated Norrland (the 'northlands') not departing until the evening, most of the émigrés took the opportunity for some rest and relaxation. Lenin, in contrast, had a packed schedule: meetings with socialist leaders, some last-minute fundraising to further offset the cost of the trip home, and putting the final touches to plans to establish a Bolshevik Party foreign bureau in the city. Although Lenin refused a meeting with Parvus, who was – not coincidentally – in town, he deputed Radek to accept (in secret) the businessman's offer of massive financial help, much of it funnelled from the foreign ministry in Berlin, for the revolutionary struggle that lay ahead.[22] Lenin was eventually prevailed upon to take some time off and visit Stockholm's famous PUB department store. The goal, according to Radek, was to make him 'look something like a human being'. The Old Man had, for instance, travelled from Switzerland in hobnail boots. 'Even if he wanted to ruin the footpaths of the nauseating Swiss bourgeois cities with these boots,' Radek explained, 'we told him, his conscience must forbid him to take these tools of destruction to Petrograd, where perhaps there were no pavements left at all.' As well as some new shoes, they also persuaded him to purchase a pair of trousers, but he resisted all attempts to replace his ill-fitting woollen coat, asking whether, on returning to the Russian capital, he would be expected to 'open a ready-made clothing shop'.[23]

That evening, Lenin and the comrades (sans Radek who, as an Austrian citizen, was certain to be refused entry into Russia) made their way to the city's Central Station for the 18.37 sleeper service to Bräcke, five hundred kilometres to the north. A crowd of about a hundred had gathered, with the mayor and other socialists joined by dozens of well-wishers, many of them carrying bouquets of flowers. The scenes were witnessed by the Swedish socialist Hugo Sillén, who described how 'everybody was in a cheerful, elated mood, and Lenin was without doubt the centre of attention.' 'He had', Sillén explained, 'intelligent, sparkling eyes and made rapid, expressive gestures. The departing comrades were animatedly discussing something on the platform. Then we heard the "Internationale" and little red flags appeared from the carriage.' As the train began to move, the Swedish comrades 'set up a wild cheering for the coming revolution in the East and the cheers were enthusiastically echoed by all the departing Russians'.[24]

Pulling into Bräcke before dawn, the Russians changed trains for the journey to Boden, a little fortress town and key railway junction in Swedish Lapland. This was a journey through some of the country's most sparsely populated areas, whose snowy forests were home to deer, Arctic hares and the odd fox. Arriving around ten that night, the comrades loaded their bags onto yet another train: this one would convey them to the Swedish–Finnish frontier town of Haparanda, at the head of the Gulf of Bothnia, and the border with revolutionary Russia.[*][25]

During this final leg of the Swedish journey, Lenin addressed his comrades directly about the possibility that, on arrival in Russia, they might be arrested and charged with treason. He explained that a committee of five, to be led by him, would represent the entire group, emphasising their immigration rights as Russian citizens and attacking the Provisional Government for its failure to help them return home. No one else was to say, or to sign, anything. The stance was clear enough, and it drew on Lenin's legal training, but it is not clear how much comfort it offered to those who feared that, very soon, they might all be facing the hangman's noose.[26]

Originally a little fishing village, Haparanda's fortunes had been transformed by the Great War. As the only open land crossing, the town had become a strategic lifeline, offering one of the few ways to ship goods and other materials into the Russian Empire from Europe. In the absence of a railway bridge across the River Torne (which marked the border with the Grand Duchy of Finland), a vast overhead cable system had been erected, with goods loaded into giant buckets and transported across the border twenty-four hours a day. According to one estimate from 1917, in a single six-month period the customs post there processed some twenty-seven million mail items and packets, to say nothing of the bulkier goods that were stacked up as far as the eye could see.[27] Although it was now spring, the river was frozen solid (they were, after all, just fifty miles from the Arctic

* Finland, which had been incorporated into the Russian Empire in 1809 as an autonomous Grand Duchy, would gain its independence at the end of the year.

Circle), and the only way to reach the Finnish border post at Tornio was by sleigh. At around seven o'clock on the morning of Sunday 15 April, Lenin and the comrades trudged through the deep snow, down to the riverbank, where they were guided onto the waiting sleds. Drawn by ponies, these would carry the travellers across the mile and a half of thick ice.[28] Zinoviev recalled the 'long, narrow row of sleds', on each of which sat two passengers. As they slowly approached the Finnish customs post, with the red flag of revolution flying from its roof, tensions were running high. Lenin, though, remained 'outwardly calm'. According to Zinoviev, the Old Man was 'especially interested' in what was 'going on in faraway Petrograd. Over the frozen bay, covered with deep snow, he look[ed] eagerly into the distance, and his eyes seem[ed] to see a thousand and a half kilometres ahead of him the revolutionary country.'[29]

All that now stood between Lenin and his homeland were the British.

Back at the end of March, some influential voices within the German General Staff had offered only tepid support for the plan to transport Lenin and his fellow exiles back to Russia. Their reasoning was straightforward enough: given that the Finnish frontier posts had English officials attached to them,* it seemed doubtful that they would be minded to allow political activists who were publicly committed to knocking Russia out of the war to cross the border.[30] While the Germans ultimately gambled that the British would comply, the outcome was by no means certain. In early April, Alexander Kesküla, an Estonian political refugee living in Sweden, visited Sir Esmé Howard, Britain's ambassador in Stockholm, to deliver a blunt warning about the dangers of permitting Lenin to enter Russia. Kesküla, who had encountered the Bolshevik revolutionary in Switzerland, described him as a fanatic whose organisational abilities

* British officials were attached to the frontier post as part of an Allied wartime agreement.

might well enable him to build a large popular following. Keskülä's solution was ingenious: Lenin should be detained at the Swedish frontier on the grounds that he had just travelled through a country in the grip of a smallpox outbreak. This would, he believed, turn Lenin into a laughing stock. The ambassador was tempted but, in the end, informed London that he 'did not think it advisable to put it forward'.[31] In Moscow, meanwhile, Sir George Buchanan's concerns about permitting Lenin to return home were waved away. The very fact that the comrades had travelled home via Germany would, it was claimed, be enough to discredit them permanently.[32]

The Russian soldiers at the Finnish guard post that Sunday morning seemed friendly enough, talking with enthusiasm about the revolution and offering the returnees a loud cheer.[33] The British were a different matter. Once the party had filed into the little wooden hut, they were divided into two groups – male and female – and then subjected to what appeared to be a deliberately slow and humiliating interrogation.[34] Lenin, for instance, was strip-searched and pressed repeatedly on why he had left Russia, whether he planned to stay in Finland, and on his profession. Again and again Lenin explained that he was a political refugee returning home (he planned to stay at his sister's apartment in Petrograd), and that he was a journalist.[35] The Bolshevik leader did not know it, but just a few days earlier Boris Nikitin, a colonel working in counter-intelligence for the Provisional Government in Petrograd, had – at the behest of the British – attempted to secure ministerial support to prevent the 'traitors and sedition-mongers' from crossing the border.[36] His efforts had proved unsuccessful, and so it was in some desperation that Harold Gruner, the military intelligence officer on duty at Tornio, cabled the Provisional Government to ask whether some mistake might not have been made in allowing Lenin to return. With what was fast becoming his trademark haughtiness, the justice minister Alexander Kerensky replied that the 'new Russian government rested on a democratic foundation' and did not refuse entry to its own citizens.[37]

There was no choice but to let the party through.*

Lenin, of course, was delighted. Laughing, and embracing his comrades, the Bolshevik leader announced that, now that they were safely on native soil, 'our trials . . . have ended.' Raising a clenched fist into the air in triumph, the Old Man declared: 'We'll show them that we are worthy masters of the future.'[38] After making some brief remarks about Finnish freedom to the waiting crowds, and popping into the post office to telegram his sister, Mariya, in Petrograd, Lenin and his party boarded the Finnish State Railways train that would take them down the coast and then on to Riihimäki, just north of the capital, Helsingfors (Helsinki), where they would pick up the train to the Russian capital. The provision of a military escort caused some initial anxieties, but before long Lenin was chatting animatedly with the soldiers, arguing good-naturedly about the war and outlining his plans for the new Russia.[39] As the train passed by station platforms crowded with soldiers, one of the comrades 'leaned out and shouted, "Long live the world revolution!"'[40]

Lenin's high spirits, however, were soured by what he was reading in the latest edition of *Pravda*. For one thing, Lev Kamenev and Stalin were taking far too moderate a line when it came to the Provisional Government; other contributors appeared to be supporting an alliance with the hated Mensheviks; while yet another piece advocated 'revolutionary defencism' – continuing the war with Germany in order to defend the revolution at home. Perhaps the most bitter blow was the revelation that Roman Malinovsky, a prominent member of the party, had for years been working hand in glove with the Okhrana. The Old Man exploded: 'The swine,' he declared; 'shooting is too good for him.'[41]

A small delegation of Bolsheviks – including Kamenev and Fedor Raskolnikov, a young sailor and party propagandist – had travelled to

---

* Gruner would be haunted for years by this incident and was teased mercilessly by his colleagues for having let Lenin into Russia. One of his closest friends later wrote that 'were he a Japanese he would have committed hara-kiri.' See William Gerhardie, *Memoirs of a Polyglot* (London: Robin Clark, 1990), 130.

the little border town of Beloostrov that evening,* to formally welcome their leader back to Russian soil.[42] Raskolnikov described how, on hearing the bell that signalled the train's approach, they ventured out onto the platform. There, 'talking together excitedly beneath a broad red banner', was a crowd of workers from a nearby armaments factory, who had travelled ten miles on foot to meet the Bolshevik leader. Then, Raskolnikov recalled how 'the three blindingly bright lights of the locomotive rushed by us, and behind it the lighted windows of the carriages began to twinkle – more and more gently and slowly.' Disembarking from the train, Lenin was raised aloft by the workers, who carried him into the station hall. 'There,' explained Raskolnikov, 'all those who had come from Petrograd pushed their way through to him, one after the other, to congratulate him heartily on his return to Russia. All of us who were seeing Ilyich for the first time kissed him just as his old Party comrades did, as though we had known him for a long time. He was somehow serenely cheerful and the smile never left his face for a moment. It was clear that the return to his homeland, now embraced by the flame of revolution, gave him indescribable joy.'[43] Standing on a stool in the first-class waiting room, wearing his shabby woollen coat and a worker's cap, the Old Man made a few impromptu remarks. Then, as the bell for the service to the Russian capital rang out, the crowd cheered their farewells.[44]

Petrograd was now just twenty-five miles away.

---

* This was 3 April – Orthodox Easter Monday – in Russia (but 16 April by the Gregorian Calendar).

4. FROM THE FINLAND STATION

Comrades, soldiers, sailors, and workers! I am happy to greet
in your persons the victorious Russian revolution, and greet you
as the vanguard of the worldwide proletarian army . . . The Russian
revolution . . . has prepared the way and opened a new epoch.
Long live the worldwide Socialist revolution!

– V. I. LENIN

The Finnish State Railways locomotive, now adorned with red
flags and revolutionary bunting, pulled in to Petrograd just before
midnight on Monday 3 April. In comparison with the grand railway
terminuses that graced Paris, Budapest and other major European
cities, the Finland Station was decidedly modest. The American writer
Edmund Wilson described the single-storey stucco building – 'rubber-
gray and tarnished pink' – as being of 'a size and design which in
any more modern country of Europe would be considered appropriate
to a provincial town rather than to the splendors of a capital'.[1] But
what it lacked in architectural grandeur it more than made up for in
atmosphere that chilly April night. Despite having had less than a day
to prepare for their leader's arrival, the city's Bolsheviks had mustered
an impressive turnout – many of them attracted by the prospect of free
beer. Nikolai Sukhanov – the thirty-five-year-old writer, Menshevik
and founding member of the executive committee of the Petrograd
Soviet – was on hand to view the spectacle.[2] A great throng of
workers, sailors and soldiers blocked the square in front of the station,
'making movement almost impossible and scarcely letting the trams
through', orchestras were playing revolutionary hymns, and there
were countless red flags, dominated by a splendid, gold-embroidered
banner bearing the words 'The Central Committee of the RSDLP
(Bolsheviks)'. Amid the darkness, one could make out 'in two or three
places the awe-inspiring outlines of armoured cars thrust up from the

44

crowd'. Meanwhile, from one of the nearby side streets 'there moved out on to the square . . . a strange monster – a mounted searchlight, which abruptly projected onto the bottomless void of the darkness tremendous strips of the living city, the roofs, many-storeyed houses, columns, wires, tramways, and human figures.'[3] The atmosphere on the platform was even more impressive than on the square:

> Its whole length was lined with people, mostly soldiers ready to 'present A-a-a-r-m-s!' Banners hung across the platform at every step; triumphal arches had been set up, adorned with red and gold; one's eyes were dazzled by every possible welcoming inscription and revolutionary slogan, while at the end of the platform, where the carriage was expected to stop, there was a band, and a group of representatives of the central Bolshevik organizations stood holding flowers.[4]

Finally, an hour later than scheduled, Lenin's train pulled up. As it did so, a military band struck up the 'Marseillaise' (they had not yet had time to learn Lenin's preferred anthem, the 'Internationale'), and the crowd roared their welcome. As he stepped from the carriage – momentarily flustered by the unexpected reception (he had, up until the last, been fretting about arrest) – the Old Man was presented with a bouquet of flowers before being ushered along the platform towards the former Imperial Waiting Room. Within minutes Alexander Shlyapnikov, one of Petrograd's leading Bolsheviks and the self-appointed master of ceremonies that evening, 'appeared in the doorway, portentously hurrying, with the air of a faithful old police chief announcing the Governor's arrival'. Behind Shlyapnikov, at the head of a small delegation of Bolsheviks, was Lenin, who more or less sprinted into the room. Wearing his worker's cap, his face frozen and bouquet in hand, the revolutionary came to a sudden halt in front of Nikolai Chkheidze – the Menshevik lawyer and chairman of the Petrograd Soviet. It was, Sukhanov later wrote, as though Lenin had collided with 'a completely unexpected obstacle'. In a short speech (one that sounded more like a sermon), a glum-looking Chkheidze welcomed Lenin back to Russia on behalf of the Petrograd Soviet and issued an appeal for unity. Lenin, of course, had absolutely no intention of throwing his lot in with the Mensheviks, let alone offering support to the Provisional Government. Having stood expressionless, with the occasional glance up at the ceiling, during Chkheidze's remarks, Lenin now turned his back on his socialist rival to acknowledge the small crowd that had gathered in the waiting room.[5]

As the formal part of the welcome came to an end, Lenin made his way to the increasingly boisterous crowds in the square. As Shlyapnikov began to clear a path, the 'Marseillaise' rang out once more and, with the crowd roaring its approval, Lenin was raised aloft, before clambering onto the turret of an armoured car to speak. 'Preceded by the searchlight and accompanied by the band, flags, workers' detachments, army units, and an enormous crowd', the vehicle then made its way west across the Sampson Bridge, heading for the city

Lenin whips up the crowd from the back of a military vehicle in Petrograd, 1917.

centre. Sukhanov noted how, at virtually every intersection, Lenin would give a short speech – about peace, class struggle and worldwide revolution – to 'continually changing audiences'. 'The triumph', he wrote, 'had come off brilliantly.'[6]

Lenin's destination that night was a grand mansion on Kronverksky Prospect, close to the Peter and Paul Fortress, just a few doors down from the city's ornate new mosque. Built between 1904 and 1906 for the celebrated ballerina Matilda Kshesinskaya (a former mistress to three grand dukes, including the future Nicholas II), the house – with its two enfilades of reception rooms and splendid winter garden – had regularly hosted members of the city's cultural elite. The February Revolution had changed all that. Within days, Kshesinskaya and her teenage son had fled, and her beloved home had been commandeered by the Bolsheviks.* The beautiful art nouveau building was now bedecked with scarlet banners while, inside, almost all the furniture – aside from a grand piano – had been removed. The ballerina's silk-lined boudoir stank of onions and tobacco, and the marble Roman bath was full of cigarette butts, papers and used rags.[7]

In the upstairs dining room, tea and snacks had been laid out, and soon the comrades were tucking into the buffet. But Lenin, typically, was not there. Instead, he was out on the balcony, making yet another speech. The reaction of the crowd was largely positive, but towards the end the mood soured a little. When Lenin, by now rather hoarse, declared that 'the defence of the fatherland means the defence of one set of capitalists against another', a soldier shouted out, 'Ought to stick our bayonets into a fellow like that . . . If he came down here,' he continued, 'we'd have to show him!'[8] Rather than going out onto the street, Lenin retired to the downstairs reception room, where some two hundred activists, professional revolutionaries and Bolshevik Party leaders were waiting. The Old Man sat through a succession of

---

* Local rumour had it that Kshesinskaya had been targeted because she had been gifted a large store of boiler coal by one of her dukes.

rather dull and formulaic welcome speeches, smiling patiently. Then he rose to his feet, to deliver his extraordinary reply.

Sukhanov, who had been smuggled into the mansion by Lev Kamenev, later wrote:

> I shall never forget that thunder-like speech, which startled and amazed not only me, a heretic who had accidentally dropped in, but all the true believers. I am certain that no one had expected anything of the sort. It seemed as though all the elements had risen from their abodes, and the spirit of universal destruction, knowing neither barriers nor doubts, neither human difficulties nor human calculations, was hovering around Kshesinskaya's reception-room above the heads of the bewitched disciples.[9]

Standing in front of the grand marble fireplace, with its gilded supports, the Old Man harangued the comrades for two hours with such relentless ferocity that, as Sukhanov put it, 'I felt as though I had been beaten about the head that night with flails.'[10] Lenin again reiterated that the 'imperialist war' could only be resolved by a civil war and a worldwide socialist revolution, and he denounced the Petrograd Soviet for its support for 'revolutionary defencism'. This, he declared, was tantamount to a 'betrayal of socialism'. Lenin was dismissive of the Provisional Government, which was, he claimed, led by bourgeois imperialists, and also opposed coalition with other socialist parties, with the Mensheviks drawing particular ire for having supported the continuation of the war.[11] These positions made for uncomfortable listening for many of the comrades, who had only recently endorsed the policy of 'vigilant control' over the Provisional Government, opposed any 'disorganising activities' among troops at the front and agreed to hold unity talks with the Mensheviks that were due to start the next day.[12] But by far the biggest bombshell was Lenin's insistence that 'we don't need a parliamentary republic, we don't need bourgeois democracy, we don't need any Government except the Soviet of

Workers', Soldiers' and Farm-labourers' deputies!'[13] As Raskolnikov explained, 'The ultimate triumph of Soviet power, which many saw as something in the hazy distance of a more or less indefinite future, was brought down by Comrade Lenin to the plane of an urgently necessary conquest of the revolution, to be attained within a very short time.' It was this that made the speech 'in the fullest sense historic'.[14]

When he finished, Lenin was met with lengthy, rapturous applause. But, in a telling observation, Sukhanov noted that many of the comrades 'seemed to stare strangely in front of them; or else their eyes roved about unseeingly, showing complete confusion'.[15] It fell to Kamenev (on record as supporting a united front with other socialist parties) to make a formal reply. 'We may or may not agree with Comrade Lenin's views, we may differ from him in our evaluation of one proposition or another,' he said, but 'in any case, there has returned to Russia in the person of Comrade Lenin the brilliant and acknowledged leader of our Party and we shall go forward together with him, towards socialism.'[16] Despite the unifying words, the leader was – for now at least – politically isolated; even his wife, Nadezhda, told a friend, 'I am afraid it looks as if Lenin has gone crazy.'[17]

Over the next few days Lenin doubled down, reiterating his ideas before the Bolshevik Party's Central Committee, the Petrograd Soviet and in the pages of *Pravda*, which on 7 April published 'The April Theses'. Lenin had been working furiously on this famous (and uncharacteristically short) treatise throughout his long journey from Zurich, scribbling down his ideas and making continual edits from a makeshift desk in his compartment.[18] The final result, according to his biographer Robert Service, was a text whose significance is comparable to Constantine's Edict of Milan of AD 313 (which afforded Christianity legal status throughout the Roman Empire) or Martin Luther's Ninety-Five Theses of 1517 (which sparked the Protestant Reformation).[19] Having spent many hours on the train crafting what was the equivalent of a political hand grenade, Lenin was now ready to pull the pin.[20] Stating at the outset that the document was a summary of his 'personal' views, Lenin emphasised that the 'capitalist nature' of the Provisional Government meant that the current war 'unquestionably remains on Russia's part a predatory imperialist war'. No concessions to 'revolutionary defencism', therefore, were permissible. Acknowledging the 'undoubted honesty of those broad sections of the mass believers . . . who accept the war only as a necessity, and not as a means of conquest', Lenin held that it was the job of the party 'with particular thoroughness, persistence and patience to explain their error to them, to explain the inseparable connection existing between capital and the imperialist war, and to prove that without overthrowing capital *it is impossible* to end the war by a truly democratic peace, a peace not imposed by violence'. Lenin's second thesis held that the 'specific feature of the present situation in Russia is that the country is *passing* from the first stage of the revolution – which, owing to the insufficient class-consciousness and organisation of the proletariat, placed power in the hands of the bourgeoisie – to its *second stage*, which must place power in the hands of the proletariat and the poorest sections of the peasants'. This meant abandoning the system of 'dual power' (which saw the Provisional Government and the Petrograd Soviet vying for control and influence) and placing full authority in the hands of the soviets, or workers' councils, that had been formed in the wake of the February Revolution. Given this, Lenin was categoric in ruling out any support for the administration of Prince Lvov: 'The utter falsity of all its promises', he wrote, 'should be made clear.' The Old Man was, of course, no fool – he well understood that the Bolsheviks were currently in a minority (and a small minority at that) in most of the soviets that had sprung up across the country, including the most important one in the capital. The task, then, was to 'carry on the work of criticising and exposing errors' as well as preaching the 'necessity of transferring the entire state power to the Soviets'. 'The masses', wrote Lenin, 'must be made to see that the Soviets of Workers' Deputies are the *only possible* form of revolutionary government.' The rest of the document sketched out a rough schema for a future revolutionary government: the creation of 'a republic of Soviets of Workers', Agricultural Labourers' and Peasants' Deputies'; the abolition of the police and army; the confiscation of landed estates and the nationalisation of all land; and the 'union of all banks . . . into a single national bank'.[21]

In the immediate aftermath of the February Revolution most of the Bolshevik leadership in Russia had, in common with the other socialist parties, adopted the orthodox Marxist position. This, in the words of historian Marcel Liebman, held that, with Tsarism 'in ruins, economic, social and political power ought as a matter of course to pass to the bourgeoisie, whose reign would constitute the necessary prelude to socialism'.[22] The main task, as leaders like Kamenev and Stalin saw it, was to ensure that the gains of the February Revolution were consolidated and extended. Although a left faction took a more radical stance, the national Bolshevik Party conference, held at the end of March, had endorsed Stalin's view that they should give 'support to the Provisional Government in so far as it is consolidating the steps forward taken by the revolution, while regarding as inadmissible any support . . . in so far as it acts in a counter-revolutionary way'.[23] Virtually the entire leadership of the party, moreover, held that the second – socialist – stage of revolution would only be possible once capitalism in Russia (and the accompanying class consciousness of the proletariat) had developed to an advanced stage. As *Pravda* had put it on 7 March, 'There is no question among us of the downfall of capital, but only the downfall of the rule of autocracy and feudalism.'[24]

There is a lively debate among historians about just how new Lenin's ideas actually were.[25] The Bolshevik leader had a history of ideological experimentation, and had expressed doubts about the 'two-stage' theory of revolution before.[26] What does seem clear, though, is that in April 1917 Lenin's insistence that the first stage of the revolution had come to an end caused shock and consternation, unleashing a torrent of criticism from both friend and foe. Derision from his rival socialists was to be expected – one leading Menshevik, for instance, dismissed Lenin's views as 'claptrap', the 'ravings of a madman'.[27] Kerensky, meanwhile, thought that Lenin was 'living in a completely isolated atmosphere, he knows nothing and sees everything through the lens of his own fantasies'.[28] But more worryingly, even many in his own party remained unconvinced. Pavel Lebedev-Polianskii, a Bolshevik who hailed from Lenin's home region, told the Old Man to his face that, during his long years of exile, he had perhaps become detached from the realities of life in Russia.[29] Writing in the pages of *Pravda*, Kamenev explained that Lenin's 'general *schema* . . . seems to us unacceptable, in so far as it proceeds from the assumption that the bourgeois democratic revolution is finished and counts on the immediate conversion of that revolution into a socialist revolution'.[30]

Lenin's motivations for taking such an uncompromising stance in the spring of 1917 remain something of a mystery. (The Old Man remained frustratingly silent on the subject.) He had, clearly, been radicalised by the Great War, and had consistently opposed anyone who failed to take what he considered a sufficiently strong line against the 'imperialist' conflict.[31] He also seems to have sensed that the global conflagration had created the conditions for a wider collapse of the capitalist order and believed that a workers' revolution in Russia might spark a series of proletarian uprisings across Europe. In his magisterial biography, Robert Service raises the possibility that, like any good politician, Lenin was marking out 'an easily identifiable spot on the political spectrum; and, as an inveterate adherent of far-left socialist ideas, he felt himself at his most comfortable when criticising other socialist parties and groups for their insufficiency of radicalism'.[32]

Whatever the reason, over the coming weeks – helped by the force of his own conviction, the return of additional Bolshevik exiles (typically more radical than those who had remained in Russia) and the Provisional Government's declining popularity amid deepening economic and military crises – Lenin would gradually win over his internal critics and begin to build a wider base of support, particularly among younger factory workers, soldiers and sailors.[33] For now, though, he appeared to be something of a has-been. Writing to London on 9 April, the British ambassador, Sir George Buchanan, explained that Lenin's speeches had been 'exceedingly badly received' and, 'for the moment, this gentleman, whose arrival gave rise to the liveliest apprehensions in all moderate circles, seems to have lost all influence.'[34] Not everyone was quite so sanguine. Writing to his wife from Petrograd a few days later, the American cinematographer and celebrated war photographer Donald C. Thompson noted how Lenin was 'preaching to the soldiers daily not to fight any more and tells them that they are being sacrificed by the capitalists'. The Bolshevik leader was, he explained, 'a brilliant man' who constituted a genuine threat. By far the 'best thing for Russia to do', Thompson believed, would be 'to kill' Lenin. But, at the very least, they should 'arrest him and put him in prison'. If they failed to act, Thompson continued, 'I expect to write you a letter, some day, that this cur is in control of things here. Every day he is gaining strength and getting the support of the lowest element in Petrograd.'[35]

Thompson was spot on.[36]

JOHN REED

While living in New York's Greenwich Village, John Reed embraced
the neighbourhood's bohemian culture. 'Within a block of my house',
he explained, 'was all the adventure in the world.'

5. ACROSS THE WAR WORLD

Events grand and terrible are brewing in Europe, such as only the imagination of a revolutionary poet could have conceived.

– JOHN REED

When the news of the February Revolution first broke, the radical American journalist John Reed had instinctively dismissed the whole business as a bourgeois affair whose 'prime movers and dominating figures' were 'liberal-minded nobles, business men, professors, editors and army officers'. Neither a peasant uprising nor a revolt against militarism, the revolution's purpose, at least as Reed saw it, was to unify Russia behind the war effort, and to establish a Western European-style liberal, constitutional democracy.[1] But by the summer, as it became clearer that the Councils of Workers' and Soldiers' Deputies – or soviets – constituted a major, alternative source of power in the country, Reed's thinking began to shift.[2] In a piece co-written with his wife, Louise Bryant, for the left-wing magazine *The Masses*, published that July, the couple offered a bracing reinterpretation of the situation. The soviets, which represented 'the real revolutionary heart of the new Russia', were, they claimed, growing 'stronger hourly as the power of the awakened proletariat bursts up through the veneer of capitalism'. Offering their 'apologies to the Russian proletariat for speaking of . . . a "bourgeois revolution"', Reed and Bryant now acknowledged that the real story was the 'long-thwarted rise of the Russian masses'. The unfolding drama was captivating:

> The cumbersome medieval tyranny that ruled Russia has
> vanished like smoke before the wind. The bright framework of
> the complicated modern capitalistic tyranny that rules us all is
> crumbling from the face of Russia. And from the laden sea of
> dumb and driven conscripts, the rivers of workers bent with

hideous fatigue, the nations of mujiks [peasants] mud-colored and voiceless, something is taking shape – something grand, and simple, and human.

Little wonder that Reed was desperate to see what was happening with his own eyes.[3]

When Louise arrived back in New York in early August, following a two-month trip to France to report on the war for the *New York American*, her husband was waiting for her at the dockside in a state of high excitement. Dressed in a smart silk suit and wearing a panama hat, he rushed up to her. 'You got home just in time,' he declared; 'in four days we're going to Russia.'[4]

Born in Portland, Oregon, on 22 October 1887, John Silas Reed was raised in the mansion that had been built in the hills to the west of the city by his maternal grandfather, Henry Green – an industrial pioneer who had made his fortune in the fur trade and city utilities – and then in a substantial property in the exclusive West End neighbourhood.[5] Although Reed's father, Charles Jerome, was rather less successful – working for an agricultural implement company, and then as an insurance salesman – he moved in high social circles, and worked hard to ensure that his two sons, John ('Jack') and Harry, enjoyed the finest education that money could buy: Portland Academy, prep school in Morristown, New Jersey, and finally Harvard.[6]

Reed was, at best, an indifferent student. In fact, he failed the Harvard entrance exams the first time around before being permitted a second go.[7] From an early age, though, Reed had demonstrated literary flair. As a child, he regaled (and terrified) his friends with stories about 'Hormuz', a monster who 'lived in the woods behind the town and devoured little children'. He was enthralled by the tales of his uncle, Horatio 'Ray' Reed, a 'romantic figure who played at coffee-planting in Central America, mixed in revolutions, and sometimes blew in, tanned and bearded and speaking "spigotty" [broken English] like a *mestizo*'. Encouraged by his mother, Reed also developed a love of reading; aged nine, he determined to become a writer.[8]

Always something of an outsider at Harvard, Reed threw himself into sporting activities (he enjoyed some success in swimming and water polo) and sought, unsuccessfully, to secure coveted memberships in the more prestigious social clubs. He enjoyed far greater success when it came to writing. The *Lampoon*, a bimonthly humour magazine, was taking his doggerel and jokes within months of his arrival in Harvard Yard. At the end of his freshman year, Reed had two pieces published in the more highbrow *Harvard Monthly*. Soon he was an established part of Harvard's literary scene, mixing with a wider group of writers and editors.[9] But alongside his artistic pursuits, sporting achievements and love of a good time (beer halls, dances and weekend expeditions to Nantucket loomed large), Reed was increasingly drawn to the world of radical politics.[10]

For millions of ordinary Americans, capitalism – at least as it operated in the early twentieth century – seemed less a blessing than a curse. During the Gilded Age, the so-called 'robber barons' – notably Andrew Carnegie, J. P. Morgan and John D. Rockefeller – accumulated great wealth and political power by establishing monopolies in key industries (steel, railroads, oil, finance) and bearing down on any sign of organised discontent among their workers. At the same time, millions of Americans – many of them immigrants from Southern and Eastern Europe – were forced to live in unsanitary conditions in the nation's overcrowded, crime-ridden cities. Little wonder, then, that the decade or so before the Great War was the golden age of American socialism.[11]

Under its charismatic leader, Eugene V. Debs, the Socialist Party certainly appeared to be a rising force (Debs polled 6 per cent of the vote in the 1912 presidential election), while the Industrial Workers of the World (IWW, or 'Wobblies'), founded in Chicago in 1905, provided the cutting edge of a new labour militancy. The IWW was committed to industrial unionism (organising all the workers in a given industry, rather than those of a particular skill or rank) and was fiercely democratic (uniquely, they welcomed women, African Americans and Asian Americans as members). Organised around the principle of working-class solidarity, their ultimate goal was the overthrow of capitalism. In the meantime they sought to build 'the new society within the shell of the old'.[12]

Harvard – bastion of elitism and privilege – was not unaffected by these wider changes. Informal discussion groups quickly formed, in which students debated modern drama, anarchism and the writings of Marx; then, in the spring of 1908 – during Reed's junior year – new organisations with an avowedly political focus were founded. At the Cosmopolitan Club (Reed would later serve as its vice president) students held forth on such weighty topics as world peace, the merits of French syndicalism, and US foreign policy; Reed was also an irregular attendee at meetings of the Socialist Club.[13] Meanwhile, radicals sprang up 'all over the place . . . in music, painting, poetry, the theatre'. For Reed, like many of his contemporaries, the experience was electrifying: 'It made me, and many others, realize that there was something going on in the dull outside world more thrilling than college activities.'[14]

After graduating, Reed embarked on a tour of Europe – living it up in London, attending the cabaret in Paris and taking in a bullfight in San Sebastián – before, in the summer of 1911, setting up home in Greenwich Village, New York. Reed's run-down apartment on Washington Square South might have been a virtual slum, but he found the neighbourhood, with its 'delicatessens, bookshops, art studios and saloons, its long-haired men and short-haired women, artists, writers, radicals and Bohemians', enthralling. As he put it, 'within a block of my house was all the adventure in the world.'[15]

Thanks to the efforts of Lincoln Steffens – the famous muckraking journalist[*] and Reed family friend – Jack was hired by *The American*

---

[*] This term was used to describe the reform-minded journalists, prominent during the Progressive era, who exposed corporate and political corruption and raised awareness of poor, exploitative and unsafe living and working conditions.

Magazine as an editor and writer, supplementing his meagre $50-a-month income by writing short stories and non-fiction journalism for the likes of the *Saturday Evening Post* and *Metropolitan Magazine*.[16] Taking to heart Steffens's repeated injunction to go out, see the world and then write about it, Reed was increasingly drawn to the urgent social and political questions of the day. As he explained, 'in my rambles about the city I couldn't help but observe the ugliness of poverty and all its train of evil, the cruel inequality between rich people who had too many motor cars and poor people who didn't have enough to eat.' Although Reed had read plenty of radical literature and spent time among socialists, anarchists, labour leaders and others on the Left, his politics were really shaped by his own direct experiences. As he put it, 'it didn't come to me from books that the workers produced all the wealth of the world, which went to those who did not earn it.'[17]

In early 1913, Reed was elected to the board of *The Masses*, a magazine that, under its editor Max Eastman, was 'experimental, daring, clever, and openly disdainful of Victorian culture and the cant of middle-class values'.[18] Reed found the job supremely rewarding; it also placed him at the heart of New York's avant-garde cultural and political scene.[19] That spring, following a meeting with the legendary IWW leader William Dudley 'Big Bill' Haywood, Reed headed to Paterson, New Jersey, to report on the silk workers' strike that had begun in February, after labourers in the city's mills had walked out in protest against low wages, long hours and poor conditions. Arrested following an altercation with a police officer just hours after arriving in town, Reed spent four days in prison, forging friendships with – and a deep sense of affinity towards – the strikers who had filled the local jail.[20]

'War in Paterson', published in *The Masses* that June, was a brilliant, impassioned account of the strike, in which Reed's sympathies were in full view. On one side, Reed explained, were the mill owners, whose 'servants, the Police, club unresisting men and women and ride down law-abiding crowds on horseback. Their paid mercenaries, the armed Detectives, shoot and kill innocent people. Their newspapers . . .

publish incendiary and crime-inducing appeals to mob violence against the strike leaders.' On the other side were some twenty-five thousand strikers, led by Haywood, whose 'massive, rugged face, seamed and scarred like a mountain, and as calm, radiated strength'. These strikers – many of Italian, Lithuanian and Jewish heritage – were, Reed declared, 'gentle, alert, brave men, ennobled by something greater than themselves . . . They can not lose!'[21]

Reed's radical sympathies and journalistic flair were on show again at the end of the year when, at the invitation of *Metropolitan Magazine*, he headed to Mexico to cover the revolution. Two years earlier, the corrupt and tyrannical government of Porfirio Díaz had been overthrown and, in the chaotic aftermath, various factions were battling for control. Reed arrived in the country shortly before Christmas, and over the next few months he interviewed many of the major protagonists, conversed with ordinary soldiers and local peasants, witnessed the fighting up close, and finally embedded himself with Pancho Villa's rebel army as it advanced on the northern city of Torreón.[22] In his reports for *Metropolitan* and *The Masses*, Reed challenged Americans to take the revolution – too often portrayed as a kind of comic opera – seriously. To discover the truth about what was going on, they would need to follow his example: travel the country and talk to the people. If they did so, Reed remarked, they would discover that the revolution represented 'a slowly growing accumulation of grievances of the peons – the lowest class – that has finally burst definitely into expression. There is not one peon out of twenty who cannot tell you exactly what they are all fighting for: Land.'[23] Embodying the spirit of the revolution, as far as Reed was concerned, was Pancho Villa, the semi-literate military leader, passionate social reformer and popular folk hero who, Reed declared, 'has the knack of absolutely expressing the strong feeling of the great mass of the people'.[24]

Reed's reporting from Mexico for the *New York World*, *The Masses* and *Metropolitan* earned him high praise (America's answer, some admirers said, to Britain's Rudyard Kipling) and a reputation as one of the nation's foremost war correspondents.[25] But rather than bask in the glory – or catch his breath – Reed immediately followed up with a searing investigative report into the aftermath of the Ludlow Massacre of April 1914, in which National Guardsmen, hired by John D. Rockefeller's Colorado Fuel and Iron Company, had murdered two dozen coal miners along with their wives and children in the bloody denouement to a protracted strike. Poking about the ruins of the miners' tent encampment, Reed described 'a great square of ghastly ruins. Stoves, pots and pans still half full of food that had been cooking that terrible morning, baby-carriages, piles of half-burned clothes, children's toys all riddled with bullets . . . This', he explained, 'was all that remained of the entire worldly possessions of 1,200 poor people.'[26]

Reed might well have continued to focus his reporting on US labour unrest had it not been for events overseas. Within weeks of 'The Colorado War' appearing in *Metropolitan*, the Great War broke out and Reed was dispatched to Europe. Over two separate trips (September 1914–January 1915; April–October 1915) he would report from England, France, Germany, Eastern Europe and Russia.[27] The devastation and death that he encountered horrified him, and he found most of the countries he visited across the Balkans and Eastern Europe to be thoroughly depressing.[28] The one exception was Russia. To be sure, there was the vast secret police network, the military authoritarianism, the deep-rooted anti-Semitism and the corruption, inefficiency and incompetence that characterised the Tsarist regime. And yet Reed, captivated by this 'amazing and most interesting land', and drawn towards stories about labour conflicts, peasant discontent and clandestine political movements, could not help but wonder whether there might be 'a powerful and destructive fire' raging in the 'bowels' of the country.[29]

Born on 5 December 1885 in San Francisco, and raised in Nevada, Louise Bryant had, like Reed, cut her teeth in journalism – writing for the student newspaper while at the University of Oregon, before securing a job at the *Spectator*, a cultural weekly based in Portland.

An aspiring artist, women's suffrage campaigner and political radical, Bryant had long admired *The Masses* and was a fan of Reed's work. On 15 December 1915, the two met for the first time while Jack was making a rare trip home to visit his mother. The encounter most probably took place at the IWW Hall on NW Davis Street, which served as the hub for Portland's radical and bohemian community. Later that evening, they attended a dinner party hosted by mutual friends.[30] Their connection was electric. As Jack put it, 'she's . . . wild and brave and straight, and graceful' and a 'lover of all adventure of spirit and mind . . . an artist, a rampant, joyous individualist, a poet and a revolutionary'.[31] Within days, Louise – who, six years earlier, had married Paul A. Trullinger, a wealthy dentist – was making plans to leave her husband and move to New York. While the elopement might have scandalised Portland society, Louise was set firm. Writing on 28 December, just hours after Reed had headed back east, she wrote to him:

> It is nice and warm in my room where I am writing. The sides
> of the little stove are all red. I think it is the only warm thing left
> in Portland. This evening when I came home the streets were all
> slippery with ice and now when the first light of day is coming
> through my window the world seems quite frozen – This is all as it
> should be – silly old town – it had your glowing presence here for
> weeks without appreciating it – now a capricious old winter has
> turned it to ice as soon as you are gone. Wonderful man – I know
> there isn't another soul so free and so exquisite and strong.[32]

On New Year's Eve, Bryant departed from Union Station. Five days later she was in New York.

Sharing Reed's apartment at Washington Square South, Bryant was soon moving in the same circles – contributing pieces to *The Masses*, attending anarchist meetings and dancing at the Liberal Club.[33] Then, in the autumn of 1916, the couple followed the example of several friends by relocating to Croton, a small town in Westchester

County, which offered a quieter and more contemplative environment than the hectic pace and myriad distractions of Greenwich Village. Even more surprising – for a couple who forswore middle-class convention and embraced the doctrine of free love – on the morning of Thursday 9 November 1916 they married. The reasoning, though, was reassuringly prosaic: with Jack facing surgery to remove a kidney, they formalised things so that, if the worst happened, Louise would be his legal heir.[34]

On 3 February 1917, three days after Germany announced the resumption of unrestricted submarine warfare, President Woodrow Wilson – recently re-elected on a promise to keep America out of the war – broke off diplomatic relations with Berlin. Two months later the country was at war with Germany. Back in August 1914, Reed had denounced the war as a 'falling out among commercial rivals' – but had held out hope that 'out of this horror of bloodshed and dire destruction will come far-reaching social changes – and a long step forward towards our goal of Peace among Men.'[35] But on arriving in Europe that autumn, he had quickly become depressed by the surging nationalism that, in country after country, had seen radicals, artists, socialists, trades union leaders and the ordinary working man embrace the war.[36] For Reed, America's entry onto the battlefield was a profoundly gloomy development.

Writing in *The Masses* in April 1917, Reed told his readers that 'I know what war means. I have been with the armies of all the belligerents except one, and I have seen men die, and go mad, and lie in hospitals suffering hell; but there is a worse thing than that. War means an ugly-mob madness, crucifying the truth-tellers, choking the artists, sidetracking reforms, revolutions, and the working of social forces.' 'Whose war is this?' Reed asked. 'Not mine.'[37]

In 'Almost Thirty', a highly personal and introspective essay that he wrote that same spring, Reed lamented how the outbreak of world war had seen all 'but the engines of hate and destruction' come to a halt. The entire conflict, he wrote, 'is to me just a stoppage of the life and ferment of human evolution'. Reed, though, remained optimistic that a new chapter of his life was about to begin. 'The world', he explained, 'is so full of swift change and color and meaning that I can hardly keep from imagining the splendid and terrible possibilities of the time to come.'[38] These were prophetic words: within weeks of his arrival in Petrograd, in September 1917, the Bolshevik Revolution would change the course of world history, provide Reed with the defining cause of his life and make him one of the most famous writers of the twentieth century.

By the summer of 1917 Reed might have been set on travelling to Russia. But before he could go he faced the problem of compulsory military service. Under the provisions of the new Selective Service Act, passed on 17 May, the US government was empowered to use conscription to bolster the armed forces for the fight against Germany. On 14 August, the Croton draft board cleared the way when it exempted Reed from military service on health grounds. (His missing kidney now proved a blessing.) Then, after reassuring nervous government officials that he had no intention of attending a planned peace conference in Stockholm as a representative of the American Socialist Party (of which he was, in any case, not a member), the State Department issued his passport. With *The Masses* and the *New York Call* offering reporting credentials, and a $2,000 bequest from a sympathetic New York socialite to cover expenses, Reed was now ready to leave.[39]

On the eve of his departure, Reed penned one final article. Co-written with Louise, and based in part on her recent observations, it recounted the growing dissatisfaction with the war among workers and soldiers in Britain, France and Germany. Connecting this popular dissent with the dramatic changes already underway in Russia, the couple made a bold prediction. 'Out of the dull twilight that has hung over the world these three years like a winter mist in Flanders,' they declared, 'tremendous flames begin to leap, like bursting shells.

Events grand and terrible are brewing in Europe, such as only the imagination of a revolutionary poet could have conceived. The great bust-up is coming.'[40]

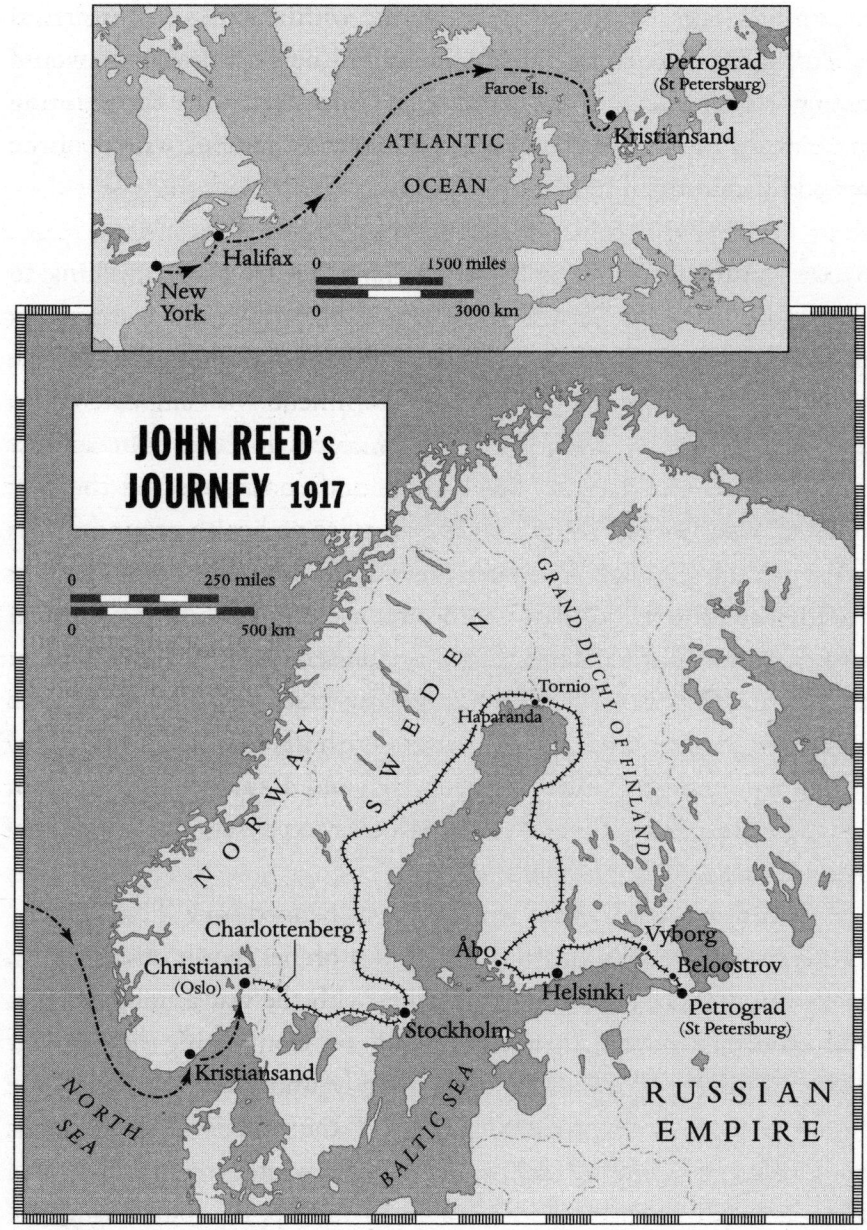

On Friday 17 August, as the *United States* slipped its moorings, 'lights going, band playing', Reed and Bryant took in their surroundings.[41] Launched on the River Clyde on 30 March 1903, and operated by the Scandinavian America Line, the ten-thousand-ton steamer boasted accommodation for almost 1,700 passengers. While those in first class could count on generously sized state rooms, a splendid, wood-panelled dining room, and a promenade deck, smoking room, music room and library, even third-class passengers enjoyed spacious cabins, meals served by uniformed staff, and ample deck space.[42] Travelling first class, Reed described the regular dances and black-tie dinners, and was struck by the lavishness of the food, with the ship's pastry cook rumoured to earn more than the Danish prime minister.[43] But it was politics, not pastry, that was at the forefront of his thoughts. In conversation with his fellow passengers, Reed encountered opposition to US conscription, deep-seated hostility towards Britain (which was using the Royal Navy to bully the neutral nations) and widespread war fatigue.[44]

Reed was, unsurprisingly, drawn to the seventy or more Russian exiles on board, mostly Jews from New York's East Side. These were, he noted, 'precisely the kind of people one sees in the Garment-workers' strikes, in Socialist local meetings – excitable, voluble, given to oratory and debate. In the middle of the cargo-deck they hold meetings, upon every conceivable subject, with chairman and all the paraphernalia of parliamentarianism.' Every evening they would gather on deck and 'sing the great slow Russian songs, which rise into the night like surf against rocks'. It was, Reed observed, 'strange how these people feel about Russia. In any other land, if life had been such a bitter thing as it was to these Jews in Russia, they would have never wished again to see the place of their suffering. But all these who have ever lived in Russia seem to love it inextinguishably, and only desire to return.'[45] Many of these political exiles, moreover, appeared to have been lifted from the pages of an extraordinary novel. One, a boy in his twenties, had 'killed the Chief of Police of Dvinsk, had been sentenced, with five others to die, and had seen his comrades hanged – and escaped!'[46]

And alongside a veteran of the *Potemkin*, whose crew had famously mutinied in 1905, was a Finn who claimed to have 'outwitted the police of three nations, with the aid of five dollars and a false birth certificate from a priest'.[47]

After docking in Halifax, Nova Scotia, the ship was held up for a week while the British authorities went over her 'inch by inch – and over the passengers as well – looking for contraband, spies, or any person or thing which for any reason should not be allowed to go to Scandinavia now'.[48] Concerned that he might be somehow prevented from reaching Russia, Reed hid a cache of letters from American radicals under the carpet. When a party of marines began to search his cabin, Reed distracted them with the offer of whiskey.[49] But the British were more interested in the Russian émigrés, who were frequently re-examined.[50] During these tense days, the whole ship seemed to crackle with suspicion, as rumours circulated about the presence on board of German spies and would-be assassins. But, Reed recalled, 'once out to sea . . . the tension slackened and people began to talk more freely; and then we all discovered, with a few violent exceptions, that our ideas about the war were pretty well agreed – the world was sick and tired of it, and extremely cynical about the rival claims and ideals.'[51]

As the ship sailed out beyond the Newfoundland Grand Banks, she left the steamer lanes and headed north, climbing towards the Arctic Circle, sweeping north-east, until 'one flashing blue morning the dazzling flank of an Iceland glacier lightly rested on the horizon, forty miles away.' Next came the Faroe Islands, emerging 'abruptly from the wine-dark sea, towering and jagged cliffs whose heads were veiled in mist, and about whose feet played slowly bursts of heavy surf', which reminded Reed of heavy artillery guns. Germany's resumption of unrestricted submarine warfare, and the presence of British minefields, meant that danger was never too far away, and the *United States* now headed north of the islands before bearing east towards the coast of Norway. For the ship's passengers, the grim realities of world war were forgotten, if only momentarily: 'That night,' Reed explained, 'we dined on deck, in costume – a <u>bal masqué</u> if you please – and all night long the revellers were shouting in the corridors.'[52]

The next day, eating fresh mackerel for lunch, one of the passengers remarked that the fish were 'extraordinarily fat'. Looking up from his plate, Reed noticed that 'everyone, a little smiling, a little pale, is thinking of what those fat fish have been eating, out there in the North Sea and along the coast of Flanders.'[53]

6. SCANDINAVIA IN WARTIME

[It was in Stockholm] that I first really knew that the Russian
revolution was not and could not be a failure.

– JOHN REED

Arriving in Christiania,* the Norwegian capital, in the first week
of September, Reed encountered a nation in crisis. Although the
Scandinavian countries had declared their neutrality following the
outbreak of hostilities in August 1914, they could not escape the wider
social, political and economic turmoil that the war unleashed. The
legitimacy of the existing political order was called into question as
discontent over the limitations on popular political participation boiled
over, and leftists, intellectuals and labour organisations pressed for
meaningful reform. In addition, the British government's determination
to use the power of the Royal Navy to enforce the Allied blockade
of Germany created significant economic challenges for Denmark,
Sweden and Norway, all of whom were heavily dependent on trade
with both Britain and Germany.[1]

By the autumn of 1917, the privations of war were clear to see. 'The
gardens of the King's palace', Reed observed, 'are given over almost
entirely to the raising of potatoes, and Christiania's glory as the
cheapest place to live in Europe has departed. Although the 'well-to-
do and the traveler can still get white bread, there is not much of it; as
for the peasants, fishermen and workers, they never had much to eat
but raw fish and black bread anyway, and now they have less of that
than ever. As in all the little neutral nations, a few speculators and
ship-owners have grown fabulously wealthy, and the workers haven't
enough to eat or to wear.' With the terrible northern weather on its

* The city changed its name to Oslo in 1925.

71

way, the railroads and factories crippled and the country running desperately short of grain, Reed despaired: 'What a black winter this will be for Norway.'[2]

In pre-war times, it would have been straightforward enough to catch one of the regular 'fast trains' to Stockholm – a journey that took six hours. But severe coal shortages now dictated a departure at four thirty in the afternoon, in cramped carriages, followed by a midnight change to an even smaller Swedish train that did not arrive in the capital until ten o'clock in the morning. At the little frontier town of Charlottenberg, Reed and Bryant endured a miserable hour as passports were checked, lengthy documents filled out, hand baggage searched, suitcases thrown onto the platform and rifled through, and bread rationing cards procured from the local police. Finally, they were permitted to board the smaller train for the journey on to Stockholm. Reed described how they and some forty other passengers – including many of the Russian exiles he had met aboard the *United States* – now crowded into a single second-class compartment:

> In that car-aisle, upon impossible mountains of baggage, we dozed and smoked and fought with orderly conductors all night . . . And in the morning looked out upon chill fields lying blanketed with white mist, through which spiked up the wisps of barley hung upon poles above the emerald grass.[3]

At one stop, an old woman boarded carrying a huge basket full of bread, and thermos bottles of hot coffee. 'With her scissors,' Reed explained, 'she snipped off bits of our bread-cards, and gave us each a few small slices of brown barley-bread, and a brittle biscuit made of potato-flour – and coffee brewed from roasted grain of some kind.'[4] And then, finally, they arrived in Stockholm.

Writing from his hotel room on Friday 7 September, Reed described a city fizzing with drama and intrigue. The Swedish capital was, he claimed, the 'last great spy-city, the last go-between of the belligerents'. Of the fifty thousand foreigners in the city, he estimated that three-quarters were 'spies and agents of various sorts'. All over the city, meetings, conferences and congresses were taking place, 'some openly, others with a good deal of privacy', involving Poles, Ukrainians, Finns, Czechs and anti-war socialists representing innumerable leftist factions. More formal political discussions were also taking place. 'Almost every month,' Reed noted, 'there are private meetings between diplomats . . . which generally take place in some little country town nearby.'[5]

Arriving at the start of the autumn season, Reed discovered the operas, theatres and cinemas 'going full blast', the hotels and restaurants packed and the city at its 'smart and sparkling' best:

Cloudless day follows cloudless day, and in the parks and public gardens the flowers are glorious, banked richly in the thick lawns around playing fountains. Everywhere are open-air restaurants and sidewalk cafés; in the evening the bands play under the lindens, in the glare of yellow arcs, and all the world, brightly uniformed or civilian, of twenty different nationalities, sips its coffee or schnapps or beer on the terraces, or strolls around under the trees.[6]

But while Stockholm was, on the surface at least, having a good war, Reed was alive to the difficulties faced by many of its ordinary citizens.[7] The workers, he explained, had seen little benefit from Sweden's war prosperity, and food rationing was in place: 'sixteen slices of brown bread and potato-cake per person per day, and two pounds of sugar per month'. Coffee, meanwhile, was virtually unobtainable. While those rich enough to be able to take their meals in restaurants could circumvent the hardships, those at the bottom had, of course, been hit hardest of all.[8]

Wandering around the city's streets and taking in the sights while waiting for the Russian consulate to issue his visa, Reed and Bryant encountered all manner of people – exiled aristocrats, foreign diplomats, South American socialists and Bolshevik agitators.[*][9] One morning, while he was exploring the warren of streets behind the Royal Palace, a 'crowd of workmen shouldered past – great husky blond fellows, tattooed on their arms, with their shirts open at the throat'.[10] As they passed by, one shouted out, and they all stopped. One of the party came back, touched Reed on the arm and, pointing to his own throat, began to signal his thirst. Startled and intrigued, Reed responded by handing over a crown. Noticing that he was wearing a red tie, one of the men pointed and asked, 'Sozialista?' When Reed nodded, a babble of enthusiastic cries erupted – 'Ik Sozial Demokrat! Ik!' After producing – and sharing – a bottle of yellow schnapps, the men ushered him towards a nearby bar:

> We turned into a door and through a black dark hallway, and up
> four flights of stairs to a small room in which there were three or
> four tables and some stools upon a reeking floor, and a wooden
> bar behind which stood a stout big blonde maiden . . . We sat
> down and she brought beer. We drank, and then, looking carefully
> around, the Social Democrats began softly to sing – something
> about 'bomba' and 'dynamita'. We drank some more. They sang
> other songs, each more blood-thirsty and violent than the last . . .
> pounded their chests, every once in a while, and affirmed that they
> were 'Ung-Socialisten' – or Young Socialists, the radical branch of
> the Social Democrats.[11]

Aside from drinking and sightseeing, Reed – ever the journalist – also used his time in Stockholm to take the wider political temperature. At the headquarters of the International Socialist Bureau, Reed met with Camille Huysmans, the organisation's secretary general, who, since the outbreak of war, had been working tirelessly (if fruitlessly) to establish socialist unity and bring about an end to hostilities.[12] From

---

* According to one wild rumour, Lenin was said to be in hiding somewhere in the city. (He was, in fact, holed up in Finland.)

Antonin Panin (the nom de plume of M. S. Makadzyub), a Menshevik delegate from the Petrograd Soviet, Reed heard first-hand the 'story of the rise and fall and rise of the Soviet, or Council, more dramatic and infinitely more inspiring than the history of the Romanovs'. It was during his conversations with Panin and his fellow Menshevik Pavel Axelrod that Reed 'first really knew that the Russian revolution was not and could not be a failure'.[13]

Buoyed by the news that the Russian Revolution was – apparently – inexorably moving towards socialism, Reed declared that 'there as in our own country, the greatest days are to come. Tomorrow I leave for Russia to see with my own eyes.'[14]

7. RED RUSSIA — ENTRANCE

Built by the cruel wilfulness of an autocrat, over the bodies of
thousands of slaves . . . this huge artificial city, by a peculiar irony has
become the heart of world revolution; has become *Red Petrograd!*

– LOUISE BRYANT

As their train from Stockholm steamed northward on the afternoon of
Monday 10 September, Reed and Bryant passed through 'interminable
forests of dark green fir and pine-trees, range on range of wooded
hills, stretching away east and west as far as one could see'. It was a
landscape that reminded Reed of his own Pacific Northwest. In some
of the more remote areas, Reed caught sight of the 'wilderness huts
and kilns of the charcoal burners, fierce, ragged figures with black
faces, more like beasts than men'.[1] September was hunting season, and
during the first part of the journey the train was constantly dropping
off men, with guns and dogs, dressed in elaborate Teutonic attire. But
as the afternoon wore on, the passengers thinned out until all that
were left were 'a few Prussian-looking officers, some Jewish traders,
and several of those shabby-looking, mysterious individuals who have
business in the vicinity of frontiers these troubled times'. 'The rest of
the train', Reed explained, 'is for Russia.'[2]

Travelling ahead, in the third-class carriage, was a group of
assorted Russian exiles – pale, haggard and wearing shoddy clothes
– who would regularly break into song. Alongside Reed and Bryant
in second class was an elderly Russian general, in civilian clothes,
'tall, thin, silent, with a pale, tragic face – evidently brooding over the
Revolution'. Returning from England after two years with a technical
mission, he was accompanied by a young Russian artillery captain
who spoke broken English and a cavalry officer with an interest in
Byzantine mosaics. As well as half a dozen young Russians, who had
just completed their training at British aviation camps, there was a

ruddy-faced British general with three adjutants and a servant on hand to black their boots. Perhaps of more interest to Reed was the 'tall old man with a grey beard, frock coat, wide-brimmed black hat, fat wife and child, his arms full of teddy bears and bundles of food, very emotional as he nears Russia; he is an anarchist, of the old-fashioned sort, who has spent a busy exile of thirty-eight years founding libraries of radical literature in Paris and London.'[3]

Following much the same route as Lenin had five months earlier, the train eventually arrived in Haparanda, the remote town at the head of the Gulf of Bothnia, just fifty or so miles from the Arctic Circle. Back in April, Lenin had been forced to traverse the frozen Torne river by sled. Thanks to the summer thaw, Reed and Bryant – together with their fellow passengers – were able to make the trip via boat.[4] And so, amid the morning drizzle, the little ferry boat, packed with travellers and piled high with baggage, pushed off from Sweden, bound for the Finnish frontier town of Tornio.[5] Reed described how, to the north,

> we catch a glimpse between great warehouses of a flat, treeless plain, stretching north – forever – to frozen swamps, and the grey arctic sea. The flat, sluggish water over which we go swells slowly in from the cold Baltic. Above us the sky is dull grey. A few hundred yards below steel piers stand up out of the water, carrying an endless chain of great buckets, which run night and day, weeks and months without halting, full of freight from Sweden to Russia; and yet without altering the look of those tarpaulin-covered mountains of goods which lie in the mud all along the Swedish shore.

Just over the water – a little more than a half a mile away – lay Finland: 'ugly great wooden and iron sheds, a couple of muddy tracks wandering down to the shore, and beyond, the roofs and Protestant church-steeples, all very drab and ordinary'.[6]

The scenes that met them on arrival, though, were very far from ordinary. Bryant explained how, stepping off the boat, she caught her 'first glimpse of the Russian army; great giants of men, mostly workers, in old, dirt-coloured uniforms from which every emblem of Tsardom had been removed. Brass buttons with the Imperial insignia, gold and silver epaulettes, decorations, all were replaced by a simple arm-band or a bit of red cloth.'[7] Reed also noted the 'complete absence of gendarmes – those yellow-bloused, booted giants with the red revolver-cords across their chests, who were so brutally omnipresent in the old Russia I knew'.[8] Instead, the revolutionary soldiers who were in charge of the border crossing were smoking and chatting away as they worked. When the Russian artillery captain suggested that his general be processed first, he was firmly put in his place. Generals were, he was told by one soldier, now no better than anyone else. (Indeed, his tone implied, they might be a little worse.[9])

Almost immediately, Reed and Bryant found themselves caught up in the ongoing drama of the revolution. Drawn towards an agitated, animated group that had crowded around a notice at one end of the hall, they heard astonishing news. Two days earlier, Alexander Kerensky, who had replaced Prince Lvov as head of the Provisional Government back in July, had placed Petrograd under martial law following reports that General Lavr Kornilov, commander-in-chief of the army, was marching on the capital. His aim: to destroy the Petrograd Soviet. This was, it seemed, nothing less than a full-throated counter-revolution; at stake, according to Kerensky, was the very survival of 'the country, of liberty, of democratic government . . . [and] the rights won by our citizens in the Revolution'. This news, though, was two days old, and in the absence of hard fact about what had happened since, rumours of all kinds took hold.[10] Advised by British officials against travelling to Petrograd, Reed and Bryant decided to press on regardless of what dangers might lie ahead.

Travelling south, Jack was struck by the strangeness of the Finns, with their 'flat, slant-eyed faces, round caps like the Mongols wear, and boots turned up at the toes'. Russian soldiers seemed to be everywhere, and the walls of every station en route were plastered with revolutionary proclamations and notices of political meetings, while the slogan 'Suomen Demokratialle!' – 'For Finnish Democracy!' – was ubiquitous. At each stop, meanwhile, extraordinary new claims were heard:

> Kerensky was assassinated. The Bolsheviks had risen again in Petrograd. Kornilov was capturing the city. The wild sailors from Kronstadt had brought the Baltic fleet up the Neva, and were shelling the Winter Palace. And then again it was that the army had turned against Kornilov – murdered him; that Petrograd had risen en masse, and there was hideous street-fighting. And in every mind was present a sinister or hopeful possibility, depending upon his sympathy or antipathy to the coup d'etat.[11]

Reed noted how the mood of their carriage varied according to the latest rumour. Their fellow passengers – Russian and British officers, a Greek princess, a Swedish drummer – all drawn from the upper echelons of society, struggled to conceal their conservative leanings.[12] On hearing news that Kornilov was supposedly on the brink of victory, for instance, some began to speculate on precisely how the revolutionary leaders would be brought to justice.[13] There was also a good deal of talk about the need for a 'strong man', capable of restoring law and order to the country. 'Both here and later,' Reed wrote, 'we began dimly to perceive that the Russian revolution had become a class-struggle, the class-struggle.' The bourgeoisie, who had helped to overthrow the Tsar, had, Reed explained, now turned against the revolution.[14]

As their train roared on through the night, belching out great showers of wood-fire sparks, Reed and Bryant tried to relax. It was hard, though, to avoid the overpowering sense of drama. At every stop, crowds of officers and soldiers with new morsels of information would pour into the corridors of the train.[15] At the major stopping points, the carriages would be locked while the military checked over the passengers carefully, on the lookout for potential counter-revolutionaries as well as for German spies.[16] As the journey progressed, the mood of the soldiers changed noticeably. Now, when the train pulled in at a station, the carriages were soon surrounded by irregular bands of soldiers, who peered through the windows, muttering 'Bourgeoisie! Bourgeoisie!' Reed felt, he said, like 'some English traveller from Boulogne by coach to Paris, in 1793, stopping to change horses at a little post-house, while the fierce, hairy faces of the local Jacobin militia were thrust in at the window'. Little surprise, then, that all talk of Kornilov suddenly disappeared; 'everyone', Reed noted wryly, was now 'engaged in keeping his mouth shut'. [17] And still the rumours flew. That final afternoon, as the train approached the Russian frontier, 'the reports came more quickly, more sensational, more contradictory. From all that we could gather, Petrograd swam in a sea of flames; but whether Kornilov or the government was winner, not two agreed.'[18]

Pulling in at Vyborg, about eighty miles from Petrograd, on the evening of Wednesday 12 September,* the atmosphere was ominous. The station was 'thronged with hundreds of soldiers, gathered in dense, silent groups about some speaker, or milling restlessly to and fro', and Reed and Bryant were 'suddenly afraid to enquire the news of the crowds on the platform'. The scraps of conversation that they did hear – 'All the generals must be killed', 'We must rid ourselves of the bourgeoisie' – did little to calm their nerves. It fell to a pale young man, sitting anxiously next to them, to blurt out the news. The day before, he explained, officers sympathetic to Kornilov had refused to act on orders to send troops to defend the capital. When the increasingly suspicious rank and file uncovered this deception, they had stormed into the officers' quarters and exacted a brutal revenge. Dragging a general and twenty-odd members of his staff out of the building, they had stamped on their faces with their heavy boots before pulling the men through the mud and dumping them in the canal, where they had drowned.[19] Faced with significant opposition

* This was 30 August in Russia.

from the rank and file, and the determined resistance of the Petrograd Soviet, the Kornilov revolt had fizzled out before it had begun.

Just after midnight, the train pulled up at Beloostrov, twenty-five miles from the Russian capital – the border town where, just a few months earlier, a delegation of Bolshevik leaders had formally welcomed Lenin back onto Russian soil. When troops suddenly boarded and ordered everyone off, Reed and Bryant feared, once more, that they would never reach their destination. It was with considerable relief, then, that they learned that this was just one final round of inspection and examination. Standing next to Bryant in the line was the indignant princess who objected vociferously as officials proceeded to confiscate her rouge, perfumes, French powder and hair dye. Her increasingly desperate pleas fell on deaf ears, and Bryant noted that only one person, an old monarchist, dared to show any concern. But even he took care to express his sympathies in English – a language that few of his countrymen could understand.[20]

At 3 a.m., their train finally pulled into the Finland Station. As Reed and Bryant stood, confused and disoriented, in the dark stillness of the pre-dawn, two young soldiers offered the couple a ride. In moments, they were hurtling through the empty streets in a big grey staff car, passing sentry posts, and hearing first-hand about the glorious early days of the February Revolution.[21] After the best part of a month, and a journey of more than four thousand miles, Reed and Bryant had finally made it to the Russian capital. Founded in the early eighteenth century by Peter the Great, who had ordered his new city, and Window on the West, to be built on reclaimed land from the Neva river delta, the vast construction project had cost the lives of thousands of conscripts, prisoners and forced labourers.[22] Now, two hundred years later, this city of two million souls had, as Bryant noted, become 'the heart of world revolution; has become *Red Petrograd!*'[23]

8. RED PETROGRAD

We are in the middle of things, and believe me it's thrilling.
– JOHN REED

Fumbling with his keys, the bleary-eyed porter finally managed to open the doors and, after bidding the soldier-chauffeurs goodbye, Reed and Bryant were ushered up the stairs and along the corridor into their suite at the Hotel Angleterre. It was, Bryant explained, an 'unfriendly room': all 'gold and mahogany with old blue draperies', an enormous granite bathtub and a 'musty, unused smell'. The hotel might have been lacking in home comforts but, situated on St Isaac's Square (the Reeds could see the splendid dome of the cathedral from their window) and close to the Winter Palace, Hermitage and Nevsky Prospect, it offered an ideal base from which to discover the city.[1] Exhausted, the couple quickly fell into a deep sleep.[2]

As they began to explore the city during early September, Reed and Bryant were struck by the harshness of everyday life. The shops were sparsely stocked and basic foodstuffs, including bread, milk and sugar, were in short supply; women, often with babies in their arms, would begin to queue in the cold, long before dawn, in the hope of securing some dull black bread. Other items, while available, were prohibitively expensive: at a time when the average wage was approximately thirty-five roubles a month, a five-cent chocolate bar or a half-kilo of candy cost between seven and ten roubles, while shoes would set you back more than a hundred.[3]

In stark contrast to the everyday hardship faced by the city's working classes, a semblance of bourgeois respectability continued to thrive. The theatres remained open. Tamara Karsavina – star of the Imperial Russian Ballet – performed to a packed house at the Mariinsky. Lectures on art and philosophy were held at the

Hermitage. The beautiful young officers, with their 'gold-trimmed crimson bashliki'* and elaborate swords, could be found in the lobbies of the city's upmarket hotels. And, as Reed observed acerbically, 'the ladies of the minor bureaucratic set took tea with each other in the afternoon, carrying each her little gold or silver or jewelled sugar-box, and half a loaf of bread in her muff, and wished that the Tsar was back.'[4]

These outward signs of normality could not, however, disguise the wider revolutionary milieu. All over the city one could see tangible signs of the revolution: Red Guards (the workers' militia) defended the factories; there were scars on the grand public buildings, where the imperial insignia had been torn down; and red banners flew everywhere. Even the statue of Catherine the Great, which stood in the square outside the Alexandrinsky Theatre, was not immune – a red flag fluttered, defiantly, from her raised sceptre.[5] Reed was also struck by popular enthusiasm for radical politics. It was there in the appetite for the working-class newspapers that had flourished since the fall of the Tsar; in the thousands of radical pamphlets that were, it seemed, pouring into every city, town and village in the country; in the explosion of political meetings and organisations; and in the enormous popularity of workers' councils and unions, which had mushroomed over the previous six months. The revolution had, Reed claimed, also seen a pent-up thirst for education and debate 'burst . . . into a frenzy of expression', as Russians 'absorbed reading matter like hot sand drinks water, insatiable. And it was not fables, falsified history, diluted religion, and the cheap fiction that corrupts – but social and economic theories, philosophy, the works of Tolstoy, Gogol, and Gorky.' Reed was particularly taken with the sight of the forty thousand employees of the Putilov metalworking plant lapping up the words of 'Social Democrats, Socialist Revolutionaries, Anarchists, anybody, whatever they had to say, as long as they would talk!'[6]

* A type of hood.

For Reed, these first days in Petrograd were exhilarating. Writing to his friend Boardman 'Mike' Robinson on 4 September (as the Russian calendar had it), he reported that 'the old town has changed! Joy where there was gloom, and gloom where there was joy. We are in the middle of things, and believe me it's thrilling. There is so much dramatic to write that I don't know where to begin – but I'll have a tale to unfold if ever . . . For color and terror and grandeur this makes Mexico look pale.'[7]

As for the chaotic political situation, discussions with radical émigrés and fellow journalists confirmed Reed's suspicions that the revolution had 'settled down to the class-struggle pure and simple'. Amid the 'tempest of events . . . which is beating upon Russia', Reed was sure of one thing: the Bolshevik star, he declared, 'steadily rises'.[8]

Reed would later date the start of what he called the 'true revolution' to 5 October, when the Bolsheviks withdrew from the newly created Provisional Council of the Russian Republic – a 'representative-consultative' body that had been created as a sort of pre-parliament. The Bolshevik refusal to support what they characterised as 'a Government of Treason to the People' was, he believed, 'a sign of the withdrawal of confidence from the Government by the whole mass of the Russian people'.[9]

In truth, pressure had been building for months. When Nicholas II had abdicated back at the start of March, power had passed – at least theoretically – to the new Provisional Government, headed by the nobleman and moderate politician Prince Lvov. Almost immediately, it had enacted a flurry of liberal reforms that would have been unthinkable just weeks earlier: the hated Okhrana was disbanded; Finland was granted limited self-rule and (German-occupied) Poland granted symbolic independence; the death penalty was abolished; discrimination based on religion or nationality was outlawed; and a bill guaranteeing universal women's suffrage was published (and became law that July).[10] But, from the start, the theoretically limitless powers of the unelected Provisional Government came up against the very real power of the soviets – and particularly the Petrograd Soviet (later the All-Russian Soviet of Workers' and Soldiers' Deputies) – with their thousands of elected deputies. Often characterised as a system of 'Dual Power' ('dvoevlastie'), the reality of the system was somewhat different.[11] As Alexander Guchkov, the newly appointed minister of war, noted in private, the Provisional Government did not wield any real power, and its policies could only be carried out with the support of the Petrograd Soviet – which controlled, among other things, the railways, postal service and telegraph. 'One can flatly say', he declared, 'that the Provisional Government exists only so long as it is permitted by the Soviet.'[12]

By the time that Reed and Bryant arrived in Petrograd, it was clear to almost everyone that power was fast draining away from the Provisional Government, which seemed chronically unable to deal with the problems of high prices, food shortages, crime, labour unrest and demands for land reform. Added to this already volatile mix was the increasingly unpopular war – which by now had cost more than two million lives. When the foreign minister, Pavel Milyukov, had issued a diplomatic note in April stating that the government 'will, in every way, observe the obligations assumed towards our Allies' and continue to fight for as long as was necessary, it had provoked mass street protests that had forced his resignation, and that of Guchkov. Then, in June, a military offensive against Austrian forces in Galicia had collapsed as exhausted, demoralised and poorly equipped Russian troops had simply refused to fight.

It was against this wider background of economic, social and military breakdown that, on 8 July, the minister for war and moderate socialist Alexander Kerensky had replaced Prince Lvov as chairman of the Provisional Government.[13] The thirty-six-year-old lawyer, with a penchant for drama and high fashion, had earned the nickname 'Speedy' during his time as a pre-war revolutionary, for his habit of evading the police by jumping on and off trams, and he certainly brought a certain vim and brio to proceedings.[14] But while he might have enjoyed some initial popularity – and apparent success in bearing down on the Bolsheviks in the aftermath of the so-called July Days* – his reorganised, liberal-socialist administration proved no more stable or effective than its predecessor. Pulled to the left by growing pressure from the soviets, and to the right by those who were alarmed by the apparent collapse of order, Kerensky was rapidly running out of road. Whatever popularity or credibility he enjoyed on 'the street', moreover, was destroyed by suspicions (not entirely unfounded) that he had privately encouraged the attempted coup by Lavr Kornilov.[15] In fact, in mobilising tens of thousands of armed workers to defend the city – diverting troop trains, sabotaging the publication of pro-Kornilov newspapers, organising armed militia, erecting barricades and appealing directly to the troops – the Petrograd Soviet had shown who was really in charge.[16]

All the while, the Bolsheviks were in the ascendant. As Reed saw it, the reason was simple. The entire Bolshevik programme, he declared, represented the desires of the masses. In calling for a general and immediate peace, the party won over much of the army, which was sick of the war. In calling for the redistribution of land, they won over much of the peasantry, while the proposal that workers should henceforth control industry appealed to much of the industrial working class. The Bolshevik cry 'All power to the Soviets!' was, Reed wrote, 'the voice of the Russian masses; and in the face of the increasing impotence and indecision of the ever-changing Provisional Government, it grew louder day by day'.[17]

---

* In July, amid growing discontent over Russia's war effort, workers and soldiers had taken to the streets, carrying rifles, red flags and knives. Egged on by the Bolsheviks, they denounced the Provisional Government and called for the soviets to take control of the country. In the street fighting that ensued, some seven hundred demonstrators were killed and the reorganised administration, headed by Kerensky, proceeded to bear down on the Bolsheviks: closing down their newspapers, arresting their most prominent activists (Lenin escaped jail by fleeing to Finland), and embarking on a vigorous propaganda campaign that framed the party's leaders as German agents. See Merridale, *Lenin on the Train*, 246–7.

At the end of August, the Bolsheviks secured a majority on the Petrograd Soviet and a few days later followed suit in Moscow. By the autumn, amid talk on the streets about a possible Bolshevik coup, the mood in Petrograd grew ever more fevered. In the factories, rifles and other weapons were stockpiled, and the Red Guard undertook public drills. In military barracks, soldiers engaged in animated debate while, on the streets, vast crowds would gather in the gloomy evenings to read the proclamations posted on the city's main streets or grab the latest editions of the newspapers.[18]

And 'in the rain, the bitter chill', Reed wrote, 'the great throbbing city under gray skies' was 'rushing faster and faster toward – what?'[19]

9. OCTOBER

For the first time in history the working-class has seized the power
of the state, for its own purposes – and means to keep it.

– JOHN REED

In the early hours of Thursday 26 October, Jack Reed, Louise Bryant
and three other Americans piled into the back of a huge motor-
truck which was waiting, engine roaring, at the steps of Petrograd's
Smolny Institute – headquarters of both the Petrograd Soviet and
the Bolshevik Party. As a group of sailors shuffled across to make
room, they issued a frank warning that they were sure to be shot
at. Undeterred, the intrepid little band took their seats alongside
guns, ammunition and bundles of leaflets. The truck 'jerked forward'
before turning onto Suvorovsky Prospect for the two-mile journey
downtown. Swaying and jolting as they picked up speed, one of the
revolutionaries 'tore the wrapping from a bundle and began to hurl
handfuls of paper into the air'. Reed and Bryant promptly followed
suit, and the car plunged 'down the dark street with a trail of white
papers floating and eddying out behind'. Although the streets of the
capital appeared empty, the showers of leaflets brought forth men
and women from their doorways or courtyards, who grabbed them
eagerly.[1] Intrigued, Reed picked one up and, aided by a 'fleeting
streetlight', read its extraordinary message:

TO THE CITIZENS OF RUSSIA!

The Provisional Government is deposed. The State Power has passed
into the hands of the organ of the Petrograd Soviet of Workers' and
Soldiers' Deputies, the Military Revolutionary Committee, which
stands at the head of the Petrograd proletariat and garrison.

The cause for which the people were fighting: immediate
proposal of a democratic peace, abolition of landlord property-

rights over the land, labour control over production, creation of a Soviet Government – that cause is securely achieved.

LONG LIVE THE REVOLUTION OF WORKMEN, SOLDIERS, AND PEASANTS![2]

Military Revolutionary Committee
Petrograd Soviet of Workers' and Soldiers' Deputies

When it came, the Bolshevik seizure of power was remarkably quick and bloodless. Back on 10 October, buoyed by growing support in many of the major cities, Lenin (recently returned from hiding in Finland) had finally persuaded his comrades to support plans for an armed insurrection. Meeting that evening in the dining room of Galina Flakserman, a journalist and Bolshevik stalwart, some of the party's biggest beasts – Trotsky, Stalin, Kamenev, Zinoviev and Lenin – thrashed out the issue. Kamenev and Zinoviev, concerned that the lower middle class were not yet ready to lend their critical support, argued that the Bolsheviks should wait and continue to build up their strength. But, after several hours of debate, Lenin prevailed.[3] By a vote of 10–2, they adopted a resolution – written, Trotsky recalled, 'hastily . . . with the gnawed end of a pencil on a sheet of paper from a child's notebook ruled in squares'.[4] Declaring that 'an armed uprising is inevitable' and 'the time for it fully ripe', the Central Committee instructed 'all Party organisations to be guided accordingly, and to discuss and decide all practical questions . . . from this point of view'.[5] With the matter, if not the timing, decided, the comrades finally relaxed over plates of cheese, sausage and bread.[6] A few days later, Lenin made the position public. Writing in the party newspaper on 18 October, he was clear: 'Either we must abandon our slogan, "All Power to the Soviets",' he explained, 'or else we must make insurrection. There is no middle course.'[7]

Aware of the growing threat, the Provisional Government exuded confidence: 'If the Bolsheviks act,' declared one minister, 'we will carry out a surgical operation and the abscess will be extracted once and for all.'[8] Kerensky even boasted that he would 'be prepared to offer prayers to produce this uprising' in order that it could be 'utterly crushed'.[9] But when it announced plans to evacuate the Petrograd garrison – sixty thousand strong, radical, many of them Bolsheviks – to the front, and replace them with more dependable troops, the Provisional Government played right into its opponents' hands. Fearful of a possible counter-revolution, the Petrograd Soviet now authorised the creation of a Military Revolutionary Committee that would oversee the defence of the city, and with it the revolution. With many of the city's regiments now proclaiming their loyalty to the Petrograd Soviet, and the General Staff refusing to recognise the MRC, the revolutionaries doubled down: in the early hours of 22 October they issued a directive that military orders to the Petrograd garrison that were not signed by the MRC should be considered invalid.[10] The following day, in a major boost to the Bolsheviks, soldiers at the formidable Peter and Paul Fortress – which contained most of the city's arsenal, and whose cannon looked out on the Winter Palace – came over to the MRC.[11]

Kerensky now prepared his response. Reed noted how some of the most loyal regiments were ordered to Petrograd; artillery, operated by the so-called junkers (or officer-cadets), was moved into the Winter Palace; and Cossacks were seen patrolling the streets for the first time since July.[12] Reed captured a city on the edge:

Up the Nevsky in the sour twilight crowds were battling for the latest papers, and knots of people were trying to make out the multitudes of appeal and proclamations pasted in every flat place . . .

An armoured automobile went slowly up and down, siren screaming. On every street corner, in every open space, thick groups were clustered; arguing soldiers and students. Night came swiftly down, the wide-spaced street-lights flickered on, the tides of people flowed endlessly . . . It is always like that in Petrograd just before trouble.[13]

On Tuesday 24 October – the eve of the opening of the Second All-Russian Congress of Soviets of Workers' and Soldiers' Deputies – the Provisional Government struck. Early that morning, a company of junkers and cadets forced their way into the headquarters of the Trud press, where the Bolshevik newspaper was printed, smashing equipment, destroying several thousand copies of the paper and posting a guard outside. With rumours soon circulating that the government had ordered the arrest of the leaders of the Petrograd Soviet, the MRC counter-attacked. 'Directive Number One' stated that the Petrograd Soviet itself was now in imminent danger and ordered that revolutionary regiments be brought to battle readiness. Any 'procrastination or interference in executing this order' would, it was stated, 'be considered a betrayal of the revolution'.[14] Kerensky, meanwhile, was on his way to the Mariinsky Palace to address the Provisional Council of the Russian Republic. Reed arrived towards the end of his 'passionate and almost incoherent speech . . . full of self-justification and bitter denunciation of his enemies'. Lenin and the other organisers of the rebellion were, Kerensky claimed, criminals, in league with the Germans, whose actions would expose the Russian front to 'the iron fists of Wilhelm and his friends'. Defending the Provisional Government, he called for the liquidation of those who 'have dared to lift their hands against the free will of the Russian people' and expressed his hope that 'perhaps at the last moment good sense, conscience, and honour will triumph.'[15]

Kerensky's hopes were soon dashed. That afternoon, sporadic clashes erupted across the city after the army General Staff ordered that the city's bridges be raised, to cut off working-class districts from the centre. Angry crowds, workers' militia and soldiers from the Petrograd garrison battled to ensure that, by evening, two of the city's four major bridges remained lowered. That night, under orders from the MRC, armed units occupied the city's telegraph office, electricity station, post office and the State Bank. Then, in the early hours of 25 October, the armoured cruiser *Aurora* and her crew of Bolshevik sailors came to anchor by the Nikolaevsky Bridge. Panicking in the glare of her powerful searchlights, the detachment of cadets guarding the bridge – now the last in government hands – promptly fled.[16]

The following day, Reed sought to get his bearings. Walking down Nevsky Prospect, he bought a copy of the Bolshevik newspaper, whose huge headline read 'ALL POWER – TO THE SOVIETS OF WORKERS, SOLDIERS AND PEASANTS! PEACE! BREAD! LAND!' The leader – penned by Zinoviev – declared that 'every soldier, every worker, every real Socialist, every honest democrat realises that there are only two alternatives to the present situation. Either', Zinoviev wrote, 'power will remain in the hands of the bourgeois-landlord crew' or 'power will be transferred to the hands of the revolutionary workers, soldiers, and peasants.'[17] Visiting the Military Hotel on St Isaac's Square, Reed noted that the building was 'picketed by armed sailors'. 'Suddenly', he recounted, 'came the sharp crack of a rifle outside, followed by a scattered burst of firing' from the direction of the Mariinsky Palace – home to the Provisional Council of the Russian Republic. Racing over, Reed was confronted with a dramatic scene. A large armoured car, red flag flying, with the slogan 'SRSD' (Soviet of Workers' and Soldiers' Deputies) daubed in red paint, was parked at the western corner of the building while revolutionary soldiers busied themselves erecting barricades.[18] Heading towards the large crowd of soldiers and sailors that had gathered at the main door to the palace, Reed overheard a sailor explaining how 'we walked in there and filled all the doors with comrades. I went up to the counter-revolutionist . . . who sat in the president's chair. "No more Council," I says. "Run along home now!"'[19]

Having failed to gain entry to the building, Reed – together with Louise Bryant and fellow American journalist Rhys Williams – headed for the Winter Palace, headquarters of the Provisional Government. Bluffing their way past the guards by waving their American passports and shouting that they were on official business, they made straight for Kerensky's office. Upon asking the nervous young aide, pacing around the anteroom, for an interview with the prime minister, they heard the astonishing news that he was not there.[20] Earlier that morning, Kerensky had fled for the front in a desperate bid to rally military support.[21] The palace itself made for a study in contrasts: at the end of one corridor, Reed noted, 'was a large, ornate room with gilded cornices and enormous crystal lustres, and beyond it several smaller ones, wainscoted with dark wood'. And yet, on either side of the 'parqueted floor lay rows of dirty mattresses and blankets upon which occasional soldiers were stretched out; everywhere was a litter of cigarette butts, bits of bread, cloth, and empty bottles with expensive French labels.' 'The place was', Reed explained, 'all a huge barrack, and evidently had been for weeks . . . Machine guns were mounted on window-sills, rifles stacked between mattresses', and soldiers 'moved about in a stale atmosphere of tobacco-smoke and unwashed humanity'. Reed stood for a while at the window, looking down at the large square in front of the palace, where 'three companies of long-coated junkers were drawn up under arms, being harangued by a tall, energetic-looking officer I recognized as [the] chief Military Commissar of the Provisional Government'.[22]

Leaving the palace late that evening, Reed's small group headed to the Hotel France for dinner, where 'right in the middle of soup the waiter, very pale in the face', insisted that they move to the dining room at the rear of the building, for fear that shooting might erupt at any moment. Despite having tickets to the ballet, they decided to skip the performance in favour of the drama that was unfolding on the streets.[23] As they walked along Nevsky Prospect, Reed described how:

the whole city seemed to be out promenading. On every corner immense crowds were massed around a core of hot discussion. Pickets of a dozen soldiers with fixed bayonets lounged at street crossings, red-faced old men in rich fur coats shook their fists at them, smartly dressed women screamed epithets; the soldiers argued feebly with embarrassed grins . . . Armoured cars went up and down the street . . . daubed with huge red letters, 'R.S.D.L.P.' [Russian Social-Democratic Labour Party].²⁴

Eager not to miss the much-anticipated opening of the Second All-Russian Congress of Soviets of Workers' and Soldiers' Deputies, the Americans now headed by car to the Smolny Institute, on the banks of the Neva river.

Reed had first travelled to Smolny earlier that autumn, aboard a packed, spectacularly slow streetcar. On reaching the end of the line, he had been struck by the 'graceful smoke-blue cupolas of Smolny Convent outlined in dull gold, beautiful, and beside it the great barracks-like façade of Smolny Institute, two hundred yards long and three storeys high, the Imperial arms carved hugely in stone still insolent over the entrance'. Founded as a convent school for the daughters of Russian aristocrats, the building's hundred or so rooms had been commandeered by various revolutionary organisations (including the Bolshevik Party), and its 'long, vaulted corridors, lit by rare electric lights, were thronged with hurrying shapes of soldiers and workmen, some bent under the weight of huge bundles of newspapers, proclamations, printed propaganda of all sorts', and 'the sounds of their heavy boots made a deep and incessant thunder on the wooden floor.'²⁵

Approaching the Smolny on the night of 25 October, Rhys Williams described how 'out of the dark we saw pencils of searchlights brush across its pale yellow surface, losing themselves in the lights streaming from its windows, then picking out the crenelated decoration beneath its roofs.'²⁶ A hive of activity, the building was now heavily armed and tightly secured: 'canvas covers had been taken off the four rapid-fire guns on each side of the doorway, and the ammunition belts hung snake-like from their breeches' while a 'dun herd of armoured cars stood under the trees in the courtyard, engines going'. Inside the building, the 'long, bare, dimly illuminated halls roared with the thunder of feet, calling, shouting'. There was, Reed claimed, 'an atmosphere of recklessness'.[27]

The Americans arrived just after the conclusion of a stormy meeting of the Petrograd Soviet. It had opened with Trotsky declaring, on behalf of the Military Revolutionary Committee, that the Provisional Government no longer existed. Then Lenin – making his first public appearance for months – had addressed the delegates. Hailing the beginning of a 'new era in the history of Russia', he called for the 'construction of a proletarian Socialist State', before ending with the familiar exhortation, 'Long live the worldwide Socialist revolution!'[28] Although these remarks were greeted with thunderous applause, not everyone was happy; some delegates baulked at what they viewed as a pre-emptory move, accusing Lenin of 'anticipating the will of the All-Russian Congress of Soviets'. When Trotsky replied coldly that the will of the Congress 'has been anticipated by the rising of the Petrograd workers and soldiers', a number of moderates withdrew in protest.[29]

Reed, Bryant and Williams now entered the great meeting hall for the formal opening of the Second All-Russian Congress. They were greeted by extraordinary scenes:

> In the rows of seats under the white chandeliers, packed immovably in the aisles and on the sides, perched on every window-sill, and even the edge of the platform, the representatives of the workers and soldiers of all Russia waited in anxious silence or wild exultation the ringing of the chairman's bell. There was no heat in the hall but the stifling heat of unwashed human bodies. A foul blue cloud of cigarette smoke rose from the mass and hung in the thick air.[30]

The session began with the election of the presidium, in which the Bolsheviks secured fourteen of the twenty-five places. They had barely had time to take their seats when, Reed recalled, 'a new sound made itself heard, deeper than the tumult of the crowd, persistent, disquieting – the dull shock of guns.' The cannon of the mighty Peter and Paul

Fortress had opened fire on the Winter Palace, last redoubt of the Provisional Government. 'With the crash of artillery, in the dark, with hatred, and fear, and reckless daring,' Reed exclaimed, a 'new Russia was being born'.[31] In the assembly hall, delegates initially rallied around a stirring call by Yuli Martov, leader of the Menshevik-Internationalist faction, for the creation of a cross-party socialist government. But as the debate wore on, old divisions began to re-emerge; some denounced the Bolsheviks' 'criminal political venture', while others called for negotiations with the Provisional Government. The latter demand drew a furious response from the hall, prompting a group of some fifty or so Mensheviks, Socialist Revolutionaries and representatives of the Bund (Jewish Social Democrats) to walk out – headed, they said, to the Winter Palace to stand with the government, even if it cost them their lives.[32] Trotsky's withering response has gone down in history. Standing up, with a 'pale, cruel face, letting out his rich voice in cool contempt', he declared: 'All these so-called Socialist compromisers, these frightened Mensheviki, Socialist Revolutionaries, *Bund* – let them go! They are just so much refuse which will be swept away into the garbage-heap of history.'[33]

With the assault on the Winter Palace now underway, Reed, Bryant, Williams, Bessie Beatty (of the *San Francisco Bulletin*) and Alex Gumberg (a Ukrainian émigré) were desperate to be where the action was. Reed described how they 'hurried from the place, stopping for a moment at the room where the Military Revolutionary Committee worked at furious speed, engulfing and spitting out panting couriers, dispatching Commissars armed with power of life and death to all the corners of the city, amid the buzz of the telephonographs'. Then the door opened, and as 'a blast of stale air and cigarette smoke rushed out, we caught a glimpse of dishevelled men bending over a map under the glare of a shaded electric-light'. One comrade, 'a smiling youth with a mop of pale yellow hair, made out passes for us'.[34]

And then out into the sharp, cold night, and the wild ride downtown.

*

Clambering out of a military truck just outside the City Duma, Reed and his compatriots were met by an extraordinary scene. 'Just at the corner of the Ekaterina Canal, under an arc light,' Reed later recalled, 'a cordon of armed sailors was drawn across the Nevsky, blocking the way to a crowd of people in columns of fours.' There were, he said, 'about three or four hundred of them, men in frock coats, well-dressed women, officers – all sorts and conditions of people', carrying sausages and singing the 'Marseillaise'. As they drew closer, the Americans realised that among the crowd were many of those who had recently stormed out of the All-Russian Congress, as well as the mayor of Petrograd, Grigory Shreider, and Sergei Prokopovich, minister of supplies in the Provisional Government. A journalist for the *Russian Daily News*, on spotting Reed, shouted cheerfully that he was off to 'die in the Winter Palace'.[35] At the barricade, an astonishing political performance began to unfold.[36] Reed captured the moment brilliantly:

Shreider and Prokopovich were bellowing at the big sailor who seemed in command.

'We demand to pass!' they cried. 'See, these comrades come from the Congress of Soviets! Look at their tickets! We are going to the Winter Palace!'

The sailor was plainly puzzled. He scratched his head with an enormous hand, frowning. 'I have orders from the Committee not to let anybody go to the Winter Palace,' he grumbled. 'But I will send a comrade to telephone to Smolny . . .'

'We insist upon passing! We are unarmed! We will march on whether you permit us or not!' cried old Shreider, very much excited.

'I have orders—' repeated the sailor sullenly.

'Shoot us if you want to! We will pass! Forward!' came from all sides. 'We are ready to die, if you have the heart to fire on Russians and comrades! We bare our breasts to your guns!'

'No,' said the sailor, looking stubborn, 'I can't allow you to pass.'

'What will you do if we go forward? Will you shoot?'

'No, I'm not going to shoot people who haven't any guns. We won't shoot unarmed Russian people . . .'

'We will go forward! What can you do?'

'We will do something,' replied the sailor, evidently at a loss. 'We can't let you pass. We will do something.'

'What will you do? What will you do?'

Another sailor came up, very much irritated. 'We will spank you!' he cried, energetically. 'And if necessary we will shoot you too. Go home now, and leave us in peace!'[37]

Amid a great wave of indignation, Prokopovich, now standing on a box and waving his umbrella, told his comrades that 'we cannot have our innocent blood upon the hands of these ignorant men.' 'Let us return to the Duma', he declared, 'and discuss the best way of saving the country and the Revolution!' At that, in the words of China Miéville, 'the self-declared *morituri* for liberal democracy' turned on their heels, 'taking their sausages with them'.[38]

Showing their MRC passes to the sailors, Reed and the others pressed on towards the Winter Palace. As they drew near, a series of shots rang out, and Red Guards, as well as regular soldiers and sailors, began to run towards the palace. As Reed and his friends picked their way over cobblestones strewn with broken glass, they suddenly heard a sailor cry out the momentous news: 'It's all over! They have surrendered!'[39] With many of the palace's defenders having long abandoned their posts, the ministers had wisely decided to avoid bloodshed,* and accept their fate.[40]

Clambering over a barricade, Reed's party now sprinted towards the Winter Palace, which was streaming with light, joining hundreds of Red Guards and revolutionaries. 'Carried along' by this 'eager wave of men', Reed recalled, 'we were swept into the right hand entrance, opening into a great bare vaulted room, the cellar of the East wing,

---

* Rhys Williams noted that none of the defenders of the Winter Palace had been wounded, while the revolutionaries suffered six fatalities and many more wounded.

from which issued a maze of corridors and stair-cases. A number of huge packing cases stood about, and upon these the Red Guards and soldiers fell furiously, battering them open with the butts of their rifles, and pulling out carpets, curtains, linen, porcelain plates, glassware.' One man, Reed observed, 'went strutting around with a bronze clock perched on his shoulder; another found a plume of ostrich feathers, which he stuck in his hat'. Within minutes the shout went out: 'Comrades! Don't touch anything! Don't take anything! This is the property of the People!' 'Many hands', explained Reed, 'dragged the spoilers down. Damask and tapestry were snatched from the arms of those who had them; two men took away the bronze clock. Roughly and hastily the things were crammed back in their cases, and self-appointed sentinels stood guard.' 'It was', he declared, 'all utterly spontaneous. Through corridors and up stair-cases the cry could be heard growing fainter and fainter in the distance, "Revolutionary discipline! Property of the People."'[41]

The Americans arrived in the palace's west wing just in time to see the ministers of the Provisional Government – pale, sullen and silent – being marched away by armed soldiers. While the former cabinet members were led off to the Peter and Paul Fortress, Reed's party headed upstairs, where they wandered through the seemingly innumerable rooms. Reed noted how the 'paintings, statues, tapestries and rugs of the great state apartments were unharmed' but, in the offices, 'every desk and cabinet had been ransacked, the papers scattered over the floor, and in the living rooms beds had been stripped of their coverings and ward-robes wrenched open.' Clothes were the most highly prized loot, Reed observed, and in a furniture storeroom 'we came upon two soldiers ripping the elaborate Spanish leather upholstery from chairs.' It was, they explained, for making boots.[42]

Finally, Reed's party made their way into the chamber where the ministers had been in session. The room 'was just as they had left it . . . Before each empty seat was pen and ink and paper; the papers were scribbled over with beginnings of plans of action, rough drafts of proclamations and manifestos. Most of these were scratched out, as their futility became evident, and the rest of the sheet covered with absent-minded geometrical designs, as the writers sat despondently listening while Minister after Minister proposed chimerical schemes.' Curious, Reed picked up one of these scribbled documents; it read 'The Provisional Government appeals to all classes to support the Provisional Government.'[43]

Engrossed as they were by the death throes of the old regime, Reed, Bryant and the others had not noticed an ominous change in the attitude of the soldiers and armed revolutionaries around them. By the time they reached the picture gallery, the Americans were surrounded by some one hundred men, suspicious of the foreigners who had been roaming the corridors at will. Challenged by one giant, sullen soldier, the group were accused of being either looters or provocateurs. Catching sight of an officer, Reed beckoned desperately for help. The man, who turned out to be the commissar of the Military Revolutionary Committee, was able to verify their passes and defuse the situation but, as he led them down the stairs and out of the palace, he explained how dangerous the situation had been and muttered, 'You have narrowly escaped.'[44]

Standing outside in the 'cold, nervous night, murmurous with obscure armies on the move, electric with patrols', Reed discovered that the sidewalk was 'littered with broken stucco, from the cornice of the palace where two shells* from the battleship *Aurora* had struck'. 'That', he explained, 'was the only damage done by the bombardment.' Hailing a cab, and stumping up an extortionate thirty-rouble fare, the intrepid band now headed back to Smolny, whose windows were still blazing, its corridors 'full of hurrying men, hollow-eyed and dirty'. It was, by now, around five in the morning and some people were asleep on the floor, their guns next to them. They entered the main hall just in time

* The very first shell it had fired, just as the Second All-Russian Congress was meeting, had been a blank.

to hear Kamenev announce, to great shouts of joy and thunderous applause, that 'the leaders of the counterrevolution ensconced in the Winter Palace have been seized by the revolutionary garrison.' Next, the congress passed a resolution, drafted by Lenin, declaring that, 'based upon the triumphant uprising of the Petrograd workmen and soldiers, the Congress assumes power.' Proposing a 'democratic peace' and promising to redistribute land, establish 'workers' control over production' and 'secure to all nationalities living in Russia a real right to independent existence', the resolution also warned of the risk of counter-revolution, and called for active resistance to supporters of Kornilov and Kerensky. 'Soldiers, Workers, Clerical employees,' it concluded, 'the destiny of the Revolution . . . is in your hands!'[45]

Reed would later recall how, standing on the steps of the Smolny in that 'cold, iron-grey dawn', he contemplated the momentous issues still to be resolved: 'Now there was all great Russia to win – and then the world! Would Russia follow and rise? And the world – what of it? Would the peoples answer and rise, a red world-tide?' 'There was', Reed later wrote, 'a faint unearthly pallor stealing over the silent streets, dimming the watch-fires, the shadow of a terrible dawn grey-rising over Russia.'[46]

10. THE COMMISSARIAT

I made a few speeches . . . I was a member of the Bureau
of International Revolutionary Propaganda . . . I was a very
small cog in the machine.

– JOHN REED

The Bolshevik seizure of power in October 1917 was, of course, only the beginning of the story. Following a week of bloody street fighting, the party soon gained control of Moscow; established a new (all-Bolshevik) Council of People's Commissars, headed by Lenin, which assumed the functions of the central government; and saw off an armed attack by a thousand Cossacks that Kerensky had hoped would take back the capital. But elsewhere the Bolshevik consolidation of power was far from smooth, and from 1918 to 1921 the new regime was engaged in an existential fight with the so-called 'Whites', as counter-revolutionaries, backed by Britain, the United States and France, plunged Russia into a terrible civil war.[1]

That bloody struggle, however, lay in the future. In the immediate aftermath of the revolution, Jack Reed exulted in the Bolshevik triumph. Writing on Saturday 4 November, a few days after Kerensky's Cossacks had been routed in an 'ugly and bloody' fight by a 'ragtag army of workers, sailors and soldiers', he described how, the previous evening, 'two thousand Red Guards – the proletarian militia organized and armed by Trotsky just before the final clash – swung down the Zagorodny* in triumph.' At their head a military band was playing the 'Marseillaise', and 'blood-red flags drooped over the dark ranks of the marching workers.' The militia were off to welcome back to 'Red Petrograd' the 'saviors of the new proletarian revolution', the men 'who had just fought so desperately and so successfully against

* Zagorodny Prospect is one of the city's grandest avenues.

Kerensky and his Cossacks'. 'In the bitter dusk they tramped, singing, men and women, their tall bayonets swinging, through streets faintly lighted and slippery with mud. And as they marched they passed always between crowds that were hostile, contemptuous, fearful.'

Reed spent several months working for the Bolshevik government, at one point even taking up arms to defend the foreign ministry from counter-revolutionaries.

The 'proletarian revolution', Reed explained, 'has no friends except the proletariat. The bourgeoisie – business men, shop-keepers, students, land-owners, officers, political office holders and their fringe of clerks and servants and hangers-on, are solidly in opposition to the new order.' Meanwhile the 'moderate Socialist parties – though they may find themselves forced by circumstances to combine with the Bolsheviks – hate them bitterly'. 'But,' Reed noted, 'these elements are so far powerless. Their military strength is represented only by part of the Cossacks, and the Junkers – cadets of the Officers Schools.' Lining up behind the Bolsheviks, in contrast, were 'the whole rank and file of the workers and the poorer peasants; and the soldiers and sailors are with and of them'. For Reed, the situation seemed deceptively simple: 'on one side the workers, on the other side, everybody else.' As things currently stood, the former were, he proclaimed, 'in complete control'. And, while no one could know for sure what the future might bring, he held out the possibility that this new 'proletarian government' would last 'in history, a pillar of fire for mankind forever'.[2]

The religious imagery that Reed conjured up was telling: here was a cause that he believed in, and one to which he was prepared to commit.

The sign hanging on the door of No. 6 Dvortsovaya Ploshchad (Palace Square), directly opposite the Winter Palace, read simply:

> All employees and functionaries of the Ministry of Foreign Affairs are invited to return to work immediately. Those who refuse to obey will be dismissed and their pension forfeited.
>
> LEON TROTSKY,
> *People's Commissar of Foreign Affairs*
> Seal of the Central Executive Committee
> of the All-Russian Soviets of Workers'
> and Soldiers' Deputies

On first entering the foreign ministry, one could almost imagine that the revolution had never taken place. After all, as Reed noted, the shveitzars (doormen) remained on hand to 'take your coat, hat and rubbers . . . with the same obsequiousness as erstwhile to Princes, Grand Dukes and Ambassadors'. But it did not take long for the new reality to intrude. For one thing, the visitors now were 'for the most part common soldiers and workmen, who address the shveitzars as "*tovarishchi* – comrades", and seem quite at home'. Upstairs, meanwhile, the corridors were 'peopled with lounging red-collared couriers, whose duty it was – and is – to run errands for the heads of departments. The beaten path is now between Palace Square and

Smolny Institute, the seat of power; and couriers' business is with the proletariat which somehow must be obeyed.'

Everywhere, it seemed, the old world and the new were colliding. Slowly returning to work, for example, were the chinovniks, or ranking civil servants. Reed recalled how 'one meets them time to time – dapper youths wearing immaculate frock-coats and a dazed expression.' Upstairs, near to the Department of War Prisoners, and next door to the Bureau of the Press, headed by Karl Radek (who had entered Russia shortly after the Bolshevik seizure of power), was the office of the newly formed Bureau of International Revolutionary Propaganda. The operation was led by Boris Reinstein, an American citizen and, Reed noted, 'incorrigible mainstay of the [radical] Socialist Labor Party of the United States – an excessively mild-mannered little man who burns with a steady revolutionary ardor'. It was here that, for two months during the winter of 1917, Reed, along with Rhys Williams, laboured to promote the cause of Bolshevism and international revolution.[3]

The atmosphere in which they worked was certainly chaotic. Reed wrote that 'things were done, but why or how they are done is beyond me.' The War Prisoners, Press, and International Propaganda departments were, he explained, 'organized in the most slip-shod manner, overlapping in many places, more or less ignorant of each other's activities, hampered by the sabotagers of the old regime, and crippled by the inherent Russian-penchant for tea and discussion'. At countless desks sat hundreds of people 'writing laboriously hundreds of documents by hand', which were then 'carefully placed where nobody could possibly find them'. 'The ancient and respectable ghost of the Bureaucracy', Reed lamented, 'still haunts the Foreign Office.'[4]

And yet, important tasks were somehow – miraculously – completed. Reed described how, almost immediately, his section began to publish a series of propaganda newspapers, aiming to encourage German troops to rise up, overthrow the Kaiser and embrace the socialist cause. The first of these papers was *Die Fackel* ('The Torch'), of which the bureau produced some half a million copies a day. These were, Reed explained, 'sent by special train to the central Army Committees in Minsk, Kiev and other cities, which, in turn, by special automobiles, distributed them to different towns along the front, where a regularly organized system of couriers brought them to the front trenches for distribution'.[5] Williams and Reed also devised a weekly illustrated news-sheet, just four pages long, which was aimed at the less educated soldiers. Consisting of a dozen or so photographs of revolutionary events, *Die Russische Revolution in Bildern* ('The Russian Revolution in Pictures') sought to convey the meaning of the Russian Revolution in plain, straightforward terms. A scene of a worker who was tearing the imperial eagles down from the roof of a palace, for instance, was captioned:

> On the roof of a palace, a workingman is tearing down the hateful emblem of autocracy. At the foot of the building the crowd is burning the eagles. The soldier is explaining to the crowd that the overthrow of autocracy is only the first step in the march of social revolution.
>
> It is easy to overthrow autocracy. Autocracy rests on nothing but the blind obedience of soldiers.
>
> The Russian soldiers merely opened their eyes, and autocracy disappeared.

While underneath a photograph of soldiers meeting in a palace, the text read:

> Socialists have often said, 'Those who build the palaces should live in them!'
>
> Here in Russia for the first time you can see workmen-soldiers, whose sweat and labor built the palace, whose blood was shed defending it, enjoying a palace as their home.[6]

Reed later described himself as just a 'very small cog in the machine', but he was clearly proud of his efforts.[7] In fact he believed – with some justification – that the propaganda newspapers, leaflets, flyers and translations of Bolshevik government decrees, together with the other activities of the bureau (indoctrination of prisoners of war, agitation among deserters, and so on), had eroded morale and stirred up significant unrest among the troops, thereby contributing to the German decision to sue for peace in November 1918.[8]

Alongside his propaganda efforts, Reed – who was desperately short of cash – took on paid work for the American Red Cross Mission, headed by Colonel Raymond Robins. A native New Yorker who had made a fortune prospecting for gold in Alaska, Robins – described by one historian as 'a bulky, two-fisted outdoorsman, half preacher, half political reformer' – was a realist who urged US recognition of the new Bolshevik regime (a move that he hoped would help dissuade Russia from agreeing a unilateral peace deal with Germany).[9] The job on offer was a simple one: Reed was tasked with fleshing out a proposal for an official English-language daily that would encourage friendly relations between Russia and the United States, urge the Bolsheviks not to pursue a separate peace with Germany and, in the longer run, facilitate US investment in the country. Reed was embarrassed that Robins, aware of his reduced circumstances, might have offered the job as a handout; he also fretted that, by taking it on, he was violating the ethics of the revolution. As he told Robins in January 1918, 'I am not corrupted by anybody's money' and 'I wouldn't like to be put down by anybody as having served the interests of the United States or any other capitalist Government, for I haven't – if I could help it.' In the end, Reed completed the job but, as he told Rhys Williams, in the sample front page that he mocked up he had 'dummied in a line under the masthead: "This paper is devoted to promoting the interests of American capital"!'[10]

For some historians, Reed's involvement in this project is evidence that he was prepared to betray the revolution; some have even suggested that he might have been an American spy or perhaps a double agent.[11]

But his own commitment to the cause, at least in the winter of 1917–18, appears to have been steadfast. On at least one occasion, according to the US embassy, he slung a rifle over his shoulder and joined the Red Guards who were on patrol outside the foreign ministry to defend it from a rumoured counter-revolutionary attack.[12] More typical, though, was his defence of the revolution through the various articles and speeches he produced during that winter. In a piece published by the *New York Call* on 22 November, for instance, Reed had broken news of the successful Bolshevik revolt, describing the 'entire insurrection' as a 'stirring spectacle of proletarian mass organization, action, bravery and generosity'.[13] On 10 January 1918, during the opening session of the Third All-Russian Congress of Soviets, Reed took the stage to speak as a representative of the 'American comrades'. After a few introductory words in Russian, Reed informed his audience that he was preparing to return to the United States. He would do so fortified by knowing that the 'victory of the proletariat' in one of the most powerful countries on earth 'is not a dream but reality'. Hailing the 'whole power, strength and invincibility of the revolutionary movement', Reed declared that, on returning to his homeland, he would 'tell the American proletariat about everything that is done in Revolutionary Russia'. 'I am convinced', he said, 'that this will call forth an answer from the oppressed and exploited masses.' As he took his seat, to the sound of thunderous applause, Reed turned to Williams and quipped, 'We never got such a reception at home.'[14]

Reed had, for some months, been intending to return to New York, not least so that he could begin work on his planned book about the revolution. When word finally reached him that *The Masses* had been suppressed by the government, and its editors – including himself – indicted under the 1917 Espionage Act, he determined to go home and face trial.[15] In planning his return trip, one thought above all preoccupied him: the safety of the substantial archive that he had built up over the previous months, amounting to some four cases of notes, flyers, Bolshevik proclamations, posters and newspapers – including samples of the work that he had produced for the Bureau of International Revolutionary Propaganda.[16] Louise had left for New York on 7 January and, worried about her own papers (on a previous journey through Finland her luggage had been confiscated), had secured the status of a 'courier' for the new Soviet government from Trotsky's deputy, Ivan Zalkind.[17] When her husband approached Trotsky with a similar request, the people's commissar went one better. On the evening of Tuesday 16 January, the US embassy in Petrograd received the following communication:

> The Russian People's Commissariat for Foreign Affairs have pleasure in informing the American Embassy at Petrograd that . . . citizen John Reed has been appointed Consul of the Russian Republic in New York.[18]

Rhys Williams recalled that this 'was just the sort of thing that would appeal to both Trotsky and Reed, and if Trotsky hadn't been so humorless, I would have considered it nothing but a spoof from start to finish'.[19] Jack, it seems, did not take the appointment entirely seriously, joking to one friend that 'when I'm consul, I suppose I shall have to marry people. I hate the marriage ceremony. I shall simply say to them, "Proletarians of the world, unite!"'[20]

Over in the American embassy – a somewhat dilapidated, poorly furnished building on Furshtatskaya Ulitsa – Ambassador David R. Francis did not see the funny side.[21] Already predisposed to view Reed with suspicion, the ambassador – a blunt Missouri businessman with a penchant for bourbon and cigars – now moved to get the appointment revoked.[22] The precise details remain murky, but it seems that, at the urging of the embassy, Alex Gumberg (with whom Reed shared bad blood) approached Lenin and, showing him a copy of the prospectus that had been drawn up for Colonel Robins, explained that Reed was impulsive, untrustworthy and wholly unsuited to the post.[23] On the evening of 24 January, Francis crowed to Robert Lansing, the secretary of state, that Reed had earlier that morning 'left for Sweden heartbroken because Lenin revoked his appointment'.[24]

In order to prevent Reed from travelling as a courier (as his wife had done) and to ensure the revocation of the consulship, Francis had issued the following order:

> To Passport Control Officers and Censors: The bearer, John S. Reed, an American citizen and the holder of Passport No. 62337 is also the holder of Visa 33/501 on Passport, for entrance to America. This will be authority and request for all officials to whom it is addressed to permit said John S. Reed to pass through their respective jurisdictions without examining the documents which he may be carrying as he is an editor and author and has been gathering data in Russia preparatory to writing a history of the Russian Revolution. Mr. Reed's papers have not been censored by the American Embassy at Petrograd, but same will be censored at the American port of entry by proper officials there and in this request those officials are not included.[25]

If Reed had hoped for a smooth journey home, he was to be deeply disappointed.

While Jack Reed was making his way from Petrograd to Christiania, the American military attaché in London cabled a report to the head of military intelligence at the War College Division in Washington DC. Initially compiled by officials in the Russian capital, the report warned that Reed was 'an anarchist and a Bolshevik sympathiser' who was 'contemplating returning to New York to stand trial on three indictments under espionage act'. He was, the report claimed, being 'urged by persons in Russia anxious to cause trouble with the United States to travel as a Bolshevist courier in order that if he is arrested, an international incident will be created'. If the State Department 'desire to obviate the possibility of such an incident', it continued, 'there may be time to stop him by warning diplomatic and Consular officers in Sweden and Norway not to visa his passport'.[26] Arriving in the Norwegian capital on 19 February, intending to sail for New York three days later, Reed now learned to his horror that the State Department had ordered its local officials to block his departure. With the next ship for New York not leaving for several weeks, he found himself stuck.[27]

While marking time in Christiania, Reed occupied himself by beginning work on his book, writing poetry, taking long walks and haranguing American officials to let him return home. According to a report written by the American consul in Christiania, George N. Ifft, Reed was also 'in constant communication with the Bolshevik element here and the Scandinavian socialists in sympathy with them'. On 21 February the *Social-Demokraten* published a short interview with Reed, in which he asserted that there was virtually no opposition to the Bolsheviks in Russia; indeed, he claimed that their influence was spreading. Asked about his own homeland, he lamented how 'free speech is suppressed everywhere and every trace of democracy is disappearing.'[28] Unsurprisingly, Ifft soon came to the view that Reed would be 'less harmful at home where his activities could be controlled' rather 'than wandering about Scandinavia posing as a political exile'.[29] He also notified the State Department that the local authorities were becoming twitchy: the chief of police had been asking whether there would 'be any hindrance to the departure of John Reed by the next steamer', while making not-so-subtle noises about possible deportation.[30] Eventually, on 25 March, the State Department issued Ifft with new instructions: 'Verify Reed's passport immediate return United States and telegraph date and steamer departure.'[31]

Reed sailed from Christiania aboard the SS *Bergensfjord* on 11 April. The crossing was rough, and Reed also went down with a nasty bout of food poisoning, but on the morning of Sunday 28 April he was home at last.[32] Before he could disembark, however, there was one further ordeal in store. Approached by two customs agents and a US Army lieutenant, he was now submitted to a lengthy interrogation, and a strip search. During the questioning, Reed was asked about his relationship with *The Masses*, his sources of financial support and his activities in Russia – including his short-lived appointment as consul to New York (which he dismissed as 'a joke'). Asked about his plans, now that he had returned home, Reed explained that he would write for the newspapers and give lectures, 'the same as other war correspondents do'. Pressed on whether he intended to 'engage in any Bolshevik propaganda', Reed replied: 'I am a Socialist and I am going to engage in Socialistic work within the law. If I do anything against the law I will take the consequences.' However, he continued, 'I am in this country to write my book and I would rather do that than anything else in the world.'

Towards the end of the interview, Reed appealed to the officials for the return of his papers, which had been taken away:

> Gentlemen, all my papers have been seized and I would like to be sure that they will not be lost, as I have a collection that is worth a great deal and which nobody else in the world possesses. Among them are copies of all newspapers issued during the first forty days of the Bolshevik Insurrection.

Collected under very difficult and challenging circumstances, this archive was, Reed explained, 'necessary for writing my book'. The papers, Reed was informed, were to be submitted to the State Department to verify whether 'they contain anything contrary to the interests of the American government'. As one of the officials put it, 'I don't think there is a chance of you losing them. Your interests will be looked after.'[33]

Finally, at eight o'clock that evening, Reed was released. As he walked down the pier, he was interviewed briefly by a *New York Tribune* reporter, who described him as 'in the best of health' and showing 'a great deal of cheerfulness at reaching once more a land of plenty and comparative security'. Waiting for him dockside were

Louise and a small welcoming party that included the lawyer and family friend Dudley Field Malone; Morris Hillquit, the labour attorney and Socialist Party leader; and Mike Gold, the writer, *New York Call* reporter and Bolshevik sympathiser.[34] Gold recalled how Reed 'kissed his girl again and again as our old-fashioned open carriage rolled through the New York streets, and how hungrily he stared at the houses, the people on the sidewalk, the New York sky, with his large, honest eyes'. The party headed to the Brevoort Hotel, whose basement dining room had long been a favourite among Greenwich Village writers, artists and intellectuals. As they entered, Reed was met by a sea of familiar faces, who greeted him 'in the casual New York manner'. Gold was particularly struck by an encounter with a 'beautiful, red-haired girl, an actress with dreamy white face and moon-struck eyes', who hailed Reed as they walked by:

'Hello, Jack,' she drawled.

'Hello, Helen,' he said.

'It seems to me you've been away, Jack,' she said.

'Yes, I've been away.'

'Where?' she asked.

'Russia,' he said.

'Russia?' she repeated dreamily. 'Why Russia, Jack?'

'There was a revolution,' he answered.

'A revolution? Oh! Was it interesting?' she drawled.

His face flushed and, for a moment, he struggled to find the words. After what seemed like an age, Jack eventually responded: 'Interesting. You wouldn't know.'[35]

11. BLOCKED

As for me, I am doing-nothing . . . unable to write a word
of the greatest story of my life, and one of the greatest in
the world. I am blocked.

– JOHN REED

Jack's great desire might well have been to begin work on his book, but he soon discovered that there were more immediate calls on his time. The first *Masses* trial had, he learned, ended in a hung jury* the day before the *Bergensfjord* docked in New York. With the Justice Department determined to press on, Reed remained under indictment. And so, on his first morning back in New York, Jack – accompanied by the newspaper's legal representative – dropped by the Federal Building to post $2,000 bail.[1]

Chronically short of money, Reed also discovered that the repressive wartime environment was, to put it kindly, far from receptive to his work. He did manage to place one piece, 'The Case for the Bolsheviki', in the *Independent* – although it came with an editorial warning about the author's commitment to socialism. Otherwise, he was forced to rely on left-wing (and perennially hard-up) publications like the *New York Call* and *The Liberator* (successor to *The Masses*) to publish his articles.[2] Throughout the summer of 1918, he also took to the stage as often as he could, speaking in union halls and socialist clubs across New York, Philadelphia, Boston and the Midwest.[3] Reed's consistent defence of the Bolshevik Revolution, his vivid and idealistic account of the workers' committees and his impassioned pleas for the new government to be granted official recognition by Washington usually went down well among his audience (typically made up of working-class immigrants). But controversy – and conflict – were seldom far

---

* After nine days of testimony, and two days of deliberations, the jury had split 10–2 in favour of conviction.

away. In Philadelphia he was arrested and charged with incitement to riot after attempting to address a thousand-strong crowd on the streets. (The police had refused a permit for a meeting.)[4] Art Young, the socialist cartoonist and fellow *Masses* indictee, described an incident in Cleveland, Ohio, in which:

> [Reed's] suitcase was seized, taken to police headquarters, and
> searched for bombs, seditious literature and other odds and ends
> for overthrowing governments. He narrowly escaped arrest after
> the lecture (which was not 'patriotic') by a strategic move through a
> basement exit. Boylike, he seemed to enjoy outwitting government
> officials.[5]

Although not a natural orator, Reed fired up his audiences by dropping in a few words of Russian – 'tovarishchi' (comrades) was a particular favourite – and he exuded an energy and fighting spirit that many found inspiring. As one observer put it, Reed 'spoke simply, with conviction and emotion . . . his earnestness and fighting mood were truly impressive' and 'at times he fairly leaped off the platform as he spoke.' His words 'seemed to carry a genuine message from the land of revolution and a challenge to the whole capitalist world'. But what was 'most striking to me was the great impatience that was apparent in his talk. He spoke rapidly, as if in a very great hurry. It seemed that John Reed felt that the revolution was near in America and time must not be lost in preparing for it.'[6]

On the evening of Saturday 18 May, Reed addressed a meeting of socialists at Carnegie Hall in Midtown Manhattan.[7] Among the five thousand or so Bolshevik supporters who packed into the vast auditorium was L. S. Perkins, an agent with military intelligence. In his top-secret report, filed a couple of days later, he described how Reed 'spoke entertainingly of what he had seen and heard in Russia, and gave an exhaustive description of the present Soviet (council) government'. Towards the end of his speech, Perkins reported, Reed declared that:

The masses supporting Trotsky and Lenin will die before they submit to Kerensky.

The Soviet government of Russia will not fall if it is left alone. It has faced the malignant hatred of the whole world and withstood it all. What does the Soviet government expect of you? Do you know what Trotsky said in his first message to the peoples of the world? 'Let all the people bring pressure upon their respective governments to stop this campaign against the Soviet government of Russia!'

A resolution calling on the United States to recognise the new Soviet regime was quickly passed by acclamation. In his summary, Perkins wrote that 'not a word of praise or promise of support of the United States Government; and not a note of patriotic American music was heard at this great meeting which, for the sentiments uttered, might have been held in Bolshevik Russia.'

As the meeting broke up, Perkins identified himself and ushered the speakers to a side room for questioning. Reed, who defended his remarks, also mentioned, in passing, that 'all of his notes and other papers brought over with him from Russia had been taken possession of by the State Department at Washington.'[8]

Throughout the spring and summer of 1918, with the continuing saga of his Russian archive increasingly on his mind, Reed turned to some of his influential friends for help. Writing to fellow journalist Lincoln Steffens on 9 June, he explained that he had a contract with Macmillan to publish a book on the Russian Revolution, but that the State Department's refusal to return any of his papers after almost two months left him 'unable to write a word of the greatest story of my life, and one of the greatest in the world. I am blocked.'[9] Steffens's reply, a week later, did little to lift Jack's spirits. While promising to do what he could, Steffens held out little hope of 'accomplishing any result'. Moreover, he advised Jack to bide his time: 'Really, I think it is wrong to try to tell the truth now. We must wait. You must wait. I know it's hard, but . . . I think it is undemocratic to try to do much now. Write, but don't publish.'[10]

Jack also approached William Franklin Sands, a veteran US diplomat and troubleshooter whom Reed had become acquainted with in Petrograd.* On 4 June 1918, Reed wrote to Sands in a state of some anxiety, asking whether there was anything that he could do to help. 'As you know,' Reed explained, 'I make my living by writing. I have orders from magazines, newspapers, and a contract for a history with Macmillan & Co. All of these I cannot fill. I cannot do anything . . . each day carries me further away from the time I knew in Russia and makes my story less valuable.'[11] The following day, Sands wrote to Frank Polk, a senior official at the State Department, to ask whether the return of the papers could be expedited. Dismissing fears that Reed was a Bolshevik, or anarchist, Sands described him as a 'sensational journalist, without doubt, but that is all'. Given Reed's close connections with the Bolsheviks in Petrograd (including his friendship with Trotsky), Sands argued that, rather than turning him into an enemy, it would be more productive to use Reed 'for our own purposes' in seeking to develop a more constructive relationship with the new revolutionary regime in Russia.[12]

The papers remained in government hands.

Reed was not to know it, but his tribulations stemmed in part from the machinations of Edgar Sisson, a fellow journalist, who had edited *Cosmopolitan* before joining the Committee on Public Information – a wartime propaganda outfit – in the spring of 1917. Arriving in Petrograd shortly after the fall of the Winter Palace, Sisson – 'prim, furtive and staunchly anti-Bolshevik' – was cut from very different cloth to Reed, with whom he soon had a series of run-ins. After Jack had gone on patrol with the Red Guards, outside the foreign ministry, Sisson had rebuked his 'silly' and 'florid' behaviour and cautioned that the Bolsheviks were

* For the historian Richard B. Spence, the connection with Sands – whom he describes as a 'spy-diplomat-capitalist' – is further evidence that Reed might have been either an American spy, or a double agent.

simply 'using' him for propaganda purposes; when, a few days later, Reed took to the stage at the opening session of the Third Congress of Soviets, Sisson was aghast. Having played a role in getting Reed's appointment as consul in New York rescinded (it seems that Sisson – whom Jack referred to openly as 'the weasel' – was the one who had asked Alex Gumberg to approach Lenin directly on the matter), he now set about exacting further revenge.[13] In a cable to the State Department, written while Reed was sailing home on the *Bergensfjord*, Sisson recommended that he be 'placed under close and intelligent observation from moment of arrival in New York'. As for his archive:

> Plenty of time should be taken in looking over all documentary matter. [Reed] may have particularly letters from Russians. If that inspection is still in progress on my return, it might be profitable to let me run through the stuff for handwriting and signatures that would interest me but which might not mean anything to the official inspectors.[14]

With the fate of his papers continuing to prey on his mind, Jack also had to face up to the prospect of a decade or more in jail. On 31 September, the second *Masses* trial got underway at the Federal District Courthouse in the Old Post Office Building opposite City Hall. The political backdrop was far from propitious: Eugene V. Debs, the veteran socialist and labour leader, had just been sentenced to ten years in prison, having been found guilty of obstructing the military draft. Meanwhile, the leaders of Jack's beloved Wobblies had been hit with lengthy jail terms, and draconian fines amounting to some $2 million, after being convicted for sedition.[15] The mood music hardly improved during jury selection, when all the candidates appeared to be pro-war patriots, hostile to political radicalism.[16]

In addition to a charge of conspiracy, the journalists on trial each faced accusations based on a specific piece of work: Max Eastman, for instance, had penned an editorial praising conscientious objectors, while Art Young had drawn a cartoon featuring businessmen, politicians and press barons engaging in a war dance, accompanied by an orchestra that was conducted by the devil.[17] As for Reed, he had added the headline 'Knit a Strait-Jacket for Your Soldier Boy' to a short article, reprinted from the *New York Tribune*, which argued that 'the frequency of mental disease among soldiers', much of it linked to so-called 'shell shock', 'had been the unexpected and staggering factor of the present war'.[18]

Once the trial began, it proved straightforward enough to rebut the charge of conspiracy – all the witnesses testified to the somewhat chaotic working practices at the magazine. (For various reasons Jack had barely been in the office during the first half of 1917.)[19] When Reed eventually took the stand on 3 October, he gave a vivid and moving account of his experiences as a war correspondent. Travelling with the Russian army into Galicia, for instance, he had seen the violence meted out to the Jewish population, how 'the Cossacks had ridden in there, how among the ruins of those Jews' houses their bodies lay, with the arms and legs taken off, hacked off, and people who had been badly cut by the Cossacks had been left to die among the ruins of their houses; utter devastation for no reason at all that one could see'.[20] From the German lines on the Western Front, Reed explained, he had seen 'a heap of bodies [that was] all that was left of the last French charge, and those bodies were slowly sinking in the mud, had been left out there, wounded, to die'.[21] About a third of the way through his testimony, Judge Martin Manton intervened to clarify his views on the Great War:

Q: You were opposed to the war?
A: I was opposed to our going in the war.
Q: Were you opposed to the war after going into it?
A: Yes, sir.
Q: Therefore, of course, you are opposed to obtaining the necessary military forces to prosecute this war?[22]

Warned in pre-trial preparation by his defence lawyers that answering yes to this question would spell certain doom, Reed prevaricated, only for Manton to press the case:

> Q: After we declared war you recognized it was necessary to have military forces?
> A: Yes, sir.
> Q: And then you were opposed to our obtaining the military forces?
> A: No.[23]

Denying that he had ever sought to 'obstruct the recruiting and enlistment service of the United States', Reed was emphatic when it came to the *Tribune* reprint (and its provocative headline).[24] When it was suggested to him that the article was intended to serve as a 'caution against mothers sending their sons to the army', or that it might have caused mothers to 'alter their attitude toward their sons enlisting', he responded: 'Nothing like that crossed my mind.'[25]

In his own testimony, former *Masses* editor Max Eastman put the argument for the defence plainly. 'He said,' reported the *New York Times*, that 'the whole case was simply one of a group of Socialists, none of whom had any intent to interfere with the Government's participation in the war, getting out a magazine in which some of them expressed their disfavor of the war policy of the country, an expression, he said, that they had a perfect right to make.'[26] The jury, it seemed, agreed; or, at least, enough of them did. Following deliberations that lasted almost twelve hours, the jurors remained, in the words of their foreman, 'hopelessly divided', with eight in favour of acquittal and four against. Once again, a mistrial was declared, and this time there would be no repeat. The defendants were, finally, free.[27]

And then, a month later, after Steffens had made a direct appeal to Colonel Edward House, confidential adviser to President Wilson, Reed's papers were returned.

12. TEN DAYS THAT SHOOK THE WORLD

The Russian Revolution is one of the great events of human history . . . and
historians . . . will want to know what happened in Petrograd in November
1917, the spirit which animated the people, and how the leaders looked,
talked, and acted. It is with this in view that I have written this book.

— JOHN REED

In his 1942 book *Heroes I Have Known*, Max Eastman recalled a
chance encounter with Reed, in the middle of Sheridan Square, during
the winter of 1918–19. Reed – 'gaunt, unshaven, greasy-skinned, a
stark sleepless half-crazy look on his slightly potatolike face' – had
just come down from his room, above Paula Holladay's Greenwich
Village Inn, for a cup of coffee. 'Max,' he pleaded, 'don't tell anybody
where I am . . . I'm writing the Russian revolution in a book . . . and
I'm working all day and all night. I haven't shut my eyes for thirty-six
hours . . . Don't for God's sake tell anybody where I am!' Eastman was
struck by the 'unqualified, concentrated joy' in Reed's 'mad eyes that
morning'. 'He was', his old friend explained, 'doing what he was made
to do, writing a great book.'[1]

Having tried, and failed, to write at the apartment he shared
with Louise in Patchin Place – a row of ten-storey brick houses in
Greenwich Village – Reed had retreated to Croton in search of peace
and quiet. Evidently it was to no avail; local legend has it that Reed, in
desperation, built a treehouse in a neighbour's oak tree and withdrew
there with his notepad and pencil. Finally, he found a suitable sanctuary
in his Greenwich Village garret. In this little attic room, surrounded
by hundreds of pages of his notes, as well as handbills, flyers, copies
of speeches, proclamations, decrees and a trove of newspapers, Reed
worked furiously, emerging only occasionally to grab a sandwich or
a coffee. After just ten weeks, he was done: he completed the book's
preface on New Year's Day 1919.[2]

*Ten Days That Shook the World** was a very different book from the one that Reed had originally planned to write. His early drafts, sketched out during his unwanted layover in Christiania, were, in the words of one historian, 'analytic and polemical'. But, during the summer of 1918, he decided that a narrative history, based on his own eyewitness accounts and personal experiences, would lend a powerful immediacy to the story, drawing the reader in and enabling them to make sense of what he viewed as 'one of the most marvellous' adventures that 'mankind ever embarked upon'.[3]

After a brief chronology of events, beginning with the February Revolution and ending with the Bolshevik seizure of power, Reed provided a helpful glossary to guide readers through Russia's often bewildering and byzantine political landscape, followed by two chapters outlining the wider context and causes of the Bolshevik Revolution. Finally, some fifty pages in, we arrive at the start of Reed's great drama. 'On the Eve', the book's third chapter, focuses on the growing struggle for power between the Provisional Government and the Bolsheviks. Reed pits Kerensky's defiant speech to the Provisional Council of the Russian Republic – delivered at the Mariinsky Palace on 24 October – against the withering remarks Trotsky made before the Petrograd Soviet about the country's 'pitiful and helpless' ministers, before pledging that any attack by the government would be answered 'blow for blow, steel for iron!'[4] Chapter four, which begins on the afternoon of 25 October, has Reed departing Smolny in a military truck, heading downtown just in time to witness the fall of the Winter Palace. The following chapters then chart the existential struggle between the new, insecure Bolshevik government, and the counter-revolutionaries, headed by Kerensky, which boasted strong middle-class support. With the routing of Kerensky's Cossacks on 31 October at Tsarskoye Selo, on the outskirts of Petrograd, the revolutionaries seized a decisive initiative. After a bloody six-day battle

* The title was suggested by the civil liberties lawyer Arthur Garfield Hays; when he first heard it, Max Eastman thought it not very good!

against the junkers and White Guards, on 2 November – the last of Reed's 'ten days' – Moscow finally fell to the Reds, amid an artillery bombardment of the Kremlin and other key sites. The book finishes with two summary chapters, followed by a lengthy appendix – full of appeals, decrees, proclamations and declarations that, in the words of one leading scholar, resembles 'a steamer trunk stuffed with handbills tumbling out on Reed's printed page'.[5]

In telling the story of what he described as a 'pageant of the Rising of the Russian Masses', Reed's sympathies for the factory workers and rank-and-file soldiers, in their contest with the bourgeoisie, shine through.[6] In a vivid passage detailing his return to the capital from Tsarskoye Selo, following the defeat of Kerensky's forces, Reed describes how:

I went back . . . riding on the front seat of an auto-truck, driven by a workman and filled with Red Guards. We had no kerosene, so our lights were not burning. The road was crowded with the proletarian army going home, and new reserves pouring out to take their places. Immense trucks like ours, columns of artillery, wagons, loomed up in the night, without lights, as we were. We hurtled furiously on, wrenched right and left to avoid collisions that seemed inevitable, scraping wheels, followed by the epithets of pedestrians.

Across the horizon spread the glittering lights of the capital, immeasurably more splendid by night than by day, like a dike of jewels on the barren plain.

The old workman who drove held the wheel in one hand, while with the other he swept the far-gleaming capital in an exultant gesture.

'Mine!' he cried, his face all alight. 'All mine now! My Petrograd!'[7]

Reed viewed the Bolshevik Revolution in quasi-religious terms. Attending the mass funeral, in Moscow's Red Square, of some five hundred revolutionaries who had perished in the battle for the city, he recalled being struck by a sudden realisation that 'the devout Russian people no longer needed priests to pray them into heaven. On earth they were building a kingdom more bright than any heaven had to offer, and for which it was a glory to die.'[8]

Clearly no cold, disinterested chronicler, Reed was nevertheless keen to emphasise that his book was based only on 'those events which I myself observed and experienced' as well as 'those supported by reliable evidence'.[9] In addition to his own contemporaneous notes, he had drawn on several hundred Russian newspapers, the English-language *Russian Daily News* and, most useful of all, an almost complete run of the *Bulletin de la Presse*. Issued by the French Information Bureau in Petrograd, it contained a summary of the major contents of the Russian press. Reed's archive also included 'almost every proclamation, decree and announcement posted on the walls of Petrograd from the middle of September 1917 to the end of January 1918', as well as copies of official government decrees and important documents from the Russian foreign ministry.[10] 'In the struggle,' Reed confessed, 'my sympathies were not neutral.' 'But,' he continued, 'in telling the story of those great days I have tried to see events with the eye of a conscientious reporter, interested in setting down the truth.'[11]

As for whether he had succeeded in this task – well, that was now for others to judge.

One man who was particularly keen to see the product of Reed's frenzied labours was Horace Liveright, the thirty-four-year-old president of the New York publishing house Boni & Liveright.* Born in December 1884 to German-Jewish immigrants, Horace had worked first in the securities and bond market and then, from 1911, in toilet paper manufacturing. He had, though, long harboured artistic ambitions. In the autumn of 1916 Liveright met Albert Boni – erstwhile owner of the Washington Square Bookshop (a favoured haunt of Greenwich Village

---

* Pronounced 'Bone-eye' and, to sound like a command, 'Live-right!'

intellectuals), part-time publisher and committed socialist. Almost on a whim, Liveright proposed that they go into business together and offered $12,500 in capital that had been loaned to him by his wealthy father-in-law. On 16 February 1917, Boni & Liveright was incorporated in New York City; Liveright was president, and Boni treasurer.[*12]

The firm's first commercial venture was the launch of the Modern Library – a series of reprints of modern European writers, including Oscar Wilde, H. G. Wells and Henrik Ibsen, which cost just sixty cents each.[13] That summer, the company also decided to move into trade publishing; one of its first releases was a reissue of Theodore Dreiser's *Sister Carrie*, a controversial and obscure novel that had first been published, and then quickly suppressed, in 1900. Then, in the spring of 1918, the company scored its first bestseller with the controversial publication of Leon Trotsky's *The Bolsheviki and World Peace*, which sold twenty thousand copies in its first year.[14]

During its 1920s heyday, Boni & Liveright occupied a grand four-storey brownstone at 61 West 48th Street that boasted a suite of offices, an opulent reception room (which functioned as a de facto club) and even a home-made still.[15] But in 1919 the company operated out of three small, nondescript rooms at 105 West 40th Street.[16] And it was here, in mid-January, that John Reed handed over his manuscript. When, as he had feared, Macmillan had cancelled his book contract, Boni & Liveright offered a natural home. The company, after all, had begun to carve out a reputation for publishing 'risky' books and Liveright was a denizen of Greenwich Village, on friendly terms with many of the writers that he would later publish.[17] Keen to secure the book, Liveright provided a $500 stipend to enable Reed to work on it full-time. (The total advance eventually ran to almost $1,200, the equivalent of about $20,000 today.)[18] Published on 19 March, and priced at $2, the book's dust jacket made much of Reed's insider status:

* In the summer of 1918, amid editorial and financial arguments and growing personal animosity, the future of the company was decided on a coin-toss, with Liveright taking control.

What occurred during the ten days of the Bolshevik Revolution in
Petrograd?
John Reed was there.

What did Trotsky prophesy seven days before the insurrection?
John Reed knows.[19]

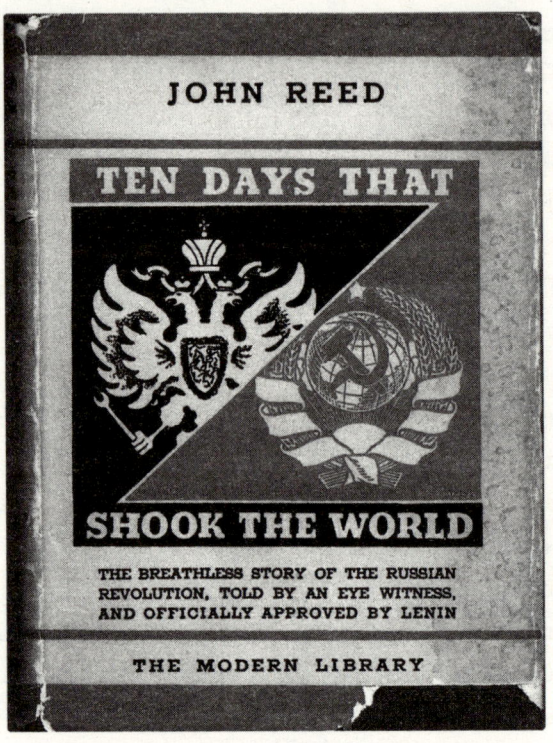

An early Boni & Liveright edition of John Reed's *Ten Days That Shook
the World*, widely acclaimed as one of the most influential non-fiction
books of the twentieth century.

'This is the book that will live after the passions of the moment have
died down,' wrote Eadmonn MacAlpine, associate editor of the
Revolutionary Age, that April. It was, he proclaimed, a 'history, written
not in the dry-as-dust language of the conventional historian, but in
the vigorous, picturesque style of an able journalist'.[20]

It would, of course, have been surprising if Reed had not received a glowing review from one of the most radical magazines in the United States, and one to which he was himself a contributor. And there was further praise from the pages of *The Liberator* – one of the few places that had been prepared to publish him during the previous year. In a review that appeared in the 1 May edition, the magazine's literary critic, Floyd Dell, declared that 'I find here exactly what I wanted – what we all want – the full story of what happened and how, in those ten never-to-be-forgotten days.' Emphasising the evidential, factual basis of Reed's book, Dell was also full of admiration for the quality of Reed's writing: 'the whole is lighted with those flashes of interpretation and description which make history when it is well done the most fascinating kind of imaginative literature.'[21]

Other reviewers were less than convinced. Writing in the *New York Times*, Charles E. Russell – the muckraking journalist and pro-war socialist – lauded Reed's brilliantly entertaining account. But, he complained, 'when less than one-sixth of a country's population undertakes with ruthless slaughter and horrible deeds to impose a program upon the unwilling remainder, persons not entranced with murder have some right to know what all this means. Assuredly their desires in this respect will not be supplied by anything in Mr. Reed's book.'[22] Perhaps the most scathing response was published in the conservative *Chicago Daily Tribune*, on 24 May. 'Mr. Reed states at the outset that he has tried to write as an unbiased observer,' intoned John Philip Morris, and 'he is as unbiased [an] observer as ever rode down a Petrograd street in a roaring camion at midnight, shrieking and throwing lurid literature to the canaille of the city.' *Ten Days* was, Morris declared, 'a book to read and shudder over. A book that makes you want total prohibition of immigration and universal military service and deportation of every I.W.W. in the country.' Morris ended his incendiary review by wishing for the speedy death of Lenin and Trotsky and expressing his fervent hope that the day would soon come when 'the sun will rise less red in Russia and a dawn not bathed in blood will give new hope to those who lie beneath the heel of the bolsheviki, whose ten days shook the earth but could neither affright God nor man.'[23]

One of the more thoughtful reviewers was Harold Stearns, the social critic and editor of *The Dial*, a fortnightly magazine of literature, philosophy and politics.[24] On Reed's own Bolshevik sympathies, Stearns praised how the author had declared his own interests from the outset. A 'prejudice admitted in advance is a prejudice robbed of nine-tenths of its power for evil', he declared. As a result, *Ten Days* offered 'a far more objective and impartial description of events' than those books written by 'men of integrity and rectitude – the avowed non-partisans'. 'Mr. Reed', Stearns explained:

> knew what he wanted to happen; the reader knows what the author wanted; the cards are on the table. It is not the things which are said in a historical volume that do harm; it is the things which are left unsaid – and it is a curious fact that Mr. Reed quotes more anti-Bolshevik statements and gives more generously the anti-Bolshevik point of view than do most of those industrious apologists so anxious to prove Bolshevism a menace to all civilization and decent living.

Stearns was also a fan of Reed's literary style. A story with 'emotional thrill', this was a narrative in which Reed's characters – the proletariat, the soldier, the worker and the peasant – were allowed to 'speak for themselves at just the correct dramatic moment'. More than a mere historical account, *Ten Days That Shook the World* was also 'a kind of handbook of reference for the future'. After all, Stearns explained, the 'Russian proletarian revolution is not likely to be the last', and Reed's microcosm of what had happened in Petrograd was 'also a microcosm of what, in varying forms, is certain to take place in many other countries, perhaps even here in safe America'.[25]

Jack was doubtless pleased with the positive notices, and by the promising early sales: the book, he told Louise, was 'going like hot-cakes'.

(It would ultimately sell a healthy six thousand copies that first year.)[26] But it was the book's impact on his fellow radicals that would have been particularly heartening. Sentenced to two years' imprisonment, following her conviction under the notorious Espionage Act of 1917, the anarchist and political activist Emma Goldman found comfort in Reed's great drama:

> John Reed's story, engrossingly thrilling, helped me to forget my surroundings. I ceased to be a captive in the Missouri penitentiary and I felt myself transferred to Russia, caught by her fierce storm, swept along by its momentum, and identified with the forces that had brought about the miraculous change. Reed's narrative was unlike anything else I had read about the October Revolution – ten glorious days, indeed, a social earthquake whose tremors were shaking the entire world.[27]

Meanwhile, at the newly built United States Penitentiary, Leavenworth, in Kansas, Big Bill Haywood and his fellow Wobblies passed around increasingly worn copies of the book, which they referred to, approvingly, as the 'Minutes of the Russian Revolution'.[28]

Reed himself was keen for the book to reach as many sympathetic hands as possible, and it was sold in union club rooms, lodges, meeting halls and miners' camps, as well as via advertisements placed in leading left-wing newspapers and magazines.[29] In May, concerned that, as he put it, 'the Capitalist Press is endeavoring to suppress the sale of the book by refusing to give it any mention whatever', he agreed a plan with Liveright to provide copies at a discounted rate of $1.20 by selling them directly through various labour organisations, who were able to take a small commission. Reed was at pains to stress that he was not looking to enrich himself: 'It really means very little to me personally, in a financial way, how many copies of the book are sold.' His motivation, rather, was the wider socialist cause: 'I think it extremely important for the Socialist Labor Movement of the United

States to know the truth about Russia, and to know the way in which the Social Revolution has been and is being made.'[30]

When, in speaking at radical meetings across the country, he discovered that his book was viewed as a kind of handbook of revolution, Jack was delighted.[31] As he explained in a letter (unpublished) to the *New York Times*, he 'heartily approved' of Bolshevism, and sincerely hoped that the principles of Bolshevism – 'workers' control of industry, socialization of the land, and the temporary dictatorship of the proletariat necessary to accomplish these things' – would 'be applied in every country on the face of the globe'. In seeking to accomplish this goal, *Ten Days That Shook the World* could, he thought, prove an effective weapon in the struggle. After all, as he put it, 'the great majority of persons who learn the truth about Russia become convinced Bolsheviki. Nothing else is needed.'[32]

It was a belief that, in the coming months, would be tested to destruction.

13. AMERICAN BOLSHEVIK

*I don't know just what it was that finally caught and took the joy out of
this poet and turned him into a poem . . . Anyhow . . . the revolutionary
spirit got him. He became a fighter; out for a cause; a revolutionist at home
here, and in Russia a communist. He didn't smile any more.*

– LINCOLN STEFFENS

'The main purpose of institutions, customs, laws, morals, etc., of
modern democratic countries,' wrote Reed in the spring of 1919, 'is
to create sentiments and conditions which operate to make people
support their own oppressors.' The working classes had, Reed argued,
been persuaded to act contrary to their own interests thanks to the
decisive influence that capitalists wielded via the education system, the
mass media and the wider culture. Inspired by what he had observed
first-hand in Russia, Reed's solution was the establishment of a
temporary dictatorship of the proletariat that would smash capitalist
power once and for all:

> This government – the Dictatorship of the Proletariat – will take
> all measures necessary to eliminate the capitalist class. It will take
> away their property and disenfranchise all who do not work. When
> this process is completed, the war between the capitalist class
> and the working class will be over, classes will have disappeared,
> and democracy follows, based on equality and the liberty of the
> individual.[1]

To some of his closest friends, this was a changed Reed – more
disciplined, less tolerant, and with a harder edge.[2] For Max Eastman,
Reed had 'lost much of his gaiety'. 'It seemed to me', wrote Eastman,
'that a person who had seen the victory of the working classes ought to
have joy in his eyes. Instead Jack came home in a state of tension that

was almost somber'.[3] According to his old mentor Lincoln Steffens, 'the revolutionary spirit got him. He became a fighter, out for a cause; a revolutionist at home here, and in Russia a communist. He didn't smile any more.'[4]

Reed spent much of 1919 immersed in the struggle to persuade the American Socialist Party – which he had joined shortly after his return from Russia – to endorse the Bolshevik view of class conflict and reject moderate or reformist versions of socialism. As one of the key leaders of the party's Left Wing (a sort of party within a party), Reed helped to draft the group's manifesto, published in the *Revolutionary Age* on 22 March. Denouncing 'bourgeois reforms' – such as old-age pensions, unemployment insurance and sick pay – it called for the overthrow of capitalism and the establishment of a proletarian dictatorship. In true left-wing style, Reed's own faction subsequently split, with the result that, at the end of August, America found itself blessed with two communist parties: the Communist Labor Party (with Reed as its international representative) and the Communist Party.[5]

Convinced that Moscow – and the newly formed Communist International (or Comintern) – would afford official recognition to only one of the American parties, Reed now readied himself to head back to Russia, to make the case for the CLP in person.

Reed's journey back to Russia reads like a passage from a Boy's Own adventure story. Travelling under an assumed name, 'Jim Gormley', and dressed in rough work-clothes, he left New York early in October aboard a Scandinavian freighter. At Bergen, during a period of shore leave, he disappeared into the welcoming arms of a band of radical socialists, who helped him to reach Christiania. A week later, he crossed the Swedish border on foot and, after a few days in Stockholm, was smuggled aboard a ship bound for the Finnish port of Åbo.[6] As the vessel approached its destination, Reed, as instructed, began to climb into a shaft that connected the engine room to the deck. There, for some four hours, in almost total darkness and amid the stifling heat, he clung desperately to a ladder, as Finnish police and customs officials searched the ship.[7]

After docking, a guide helped Reed onto the deck, where the harsh cold hit him hard. Hurrying past 'men in uniform, with gold-braided caps, and half a dozen grey-coated police, with revolvers strapped to their belts', Reed was virtually dragged to the gangway, and told 'Go!' Stumbling forward, he elbowed his way past the customs officials 'as if I were on business of importance'. Then, without daring to look around, he walked onto the dock. Told that he would be met by two sympathetic contacts, Reed began to follow a couple of loafers whom he spotted walking away from a warehouse.[8] When they responded blankly to the password, 'Woodrow Wilson', it transpired that they were the wrong men, and Reed had to make a perilous return to the dockside. There, he eventually located the comrades – by now frantic – who took him to a safe house. Then, after a couple of days' rest, he travelled to the Helsinki home of the writer and Bolshevik sympathiser Hella Wuolijoki. Finally, after two weeks in hiding, it was deemed safe to make the final journey to Petrograd – first by sleigh, then on foot and, once safely across the Russian border, by train.[9]

From Petrograd, Reed headed to Moscow – where, in the spring of 1918, the Bolsheviks had relocated their government. Renting a room in a working-class district of the city, he made his report to the executive committee of the Comintern (ECCI) and awaited its conclusions.[10] Reed jotted down his impressions of the Soviet leaders. Lenin was, he wrote, 'Genial . . . Hands in pockets. Chuckled while speaking sometimes. Joked. Gestures – more frequently than ever.' 'When you go to see him,' Reed explained, 'he hitches up his chair until his knees touch yours and looks *through* you with those terrible eyes . . . Gives one impression of being intensely interested.' His old friend Trotsky had 'filled out' and was 'surer of self, not impatient any more. Calmer.' He had, noted Reed, travelled to the front line during the defence of Petrograd and personally stopped the Red Army from retreating. Lev Kamenev, meanwhile, was 'plumper' and 'looks like a cocker spaniel'.[11] Reed particularly enjoyed his meetings with Lenin (to whom he gifted a copy of *Ten Days That Shook the World*) and was delighted to learn that the chairman of the Council of People's Commissars was a fan – later writing to Louise that she should 'tell Horace [Liveright] the big chief thinks my book the best'.*[12] But, ever the journalist, Reed was especially keen to take the measure of Soviet Russia by talking to ordinary people.

The country had changed considerably in the twenty or so months since his departure. Much to their shock, and despite (abortive) workers' uprisings in Germany, Hungary and elsewhere, the worldwide proletarian revolution predicted by the Bolsheviks had failed to transpire. They were thus faced with the unexpected problem of how to build socialism in one country. Under enormous pressure, both internally (from White counter-revolutionaries, opposition from segments of the peasantry, political defections and rising ethnic/ nationalist divisions) and externally, the Soviet government had created a two-million-strong Red Army to defend the borders. They had also established the Cheka, a secret police force headed by the ruthless 'Iron Felix' Dzerzhinsky, to bear down on domestic dissent, root out corruption and profiteering, and eliminate enemies both real and imagined. Moreover, the tumult that accompanied the effort to build the new socialist state was intensified by the particularly severe winter of 1919–20, one of the coldest on record, whose cruel hardships were exacerbated by the privations of civil war and the Western economic blockade.[13] It was a winter that, Reed explained, was 'horrible beyond imagination'. 'No one', he wrote, 'will ever know what Russia went through. Transport at times almost ceased, and the number of locomotives out of commission more and more exceeded those repaired.' Although there was plenty of grain in the provincial warehouses, it could not be transported. For weeks, Petrograd went without bread. It was a similarly grim story when it

* Lenin would later write a brief introduction to the book, in which he claimed to have read it 'with the greatest interest and never-slackening attention'.

came to fuel – with appalling results: 'In some houses there was no heat at all the whole winter. People froze to death in their rooms.' Even the country's leaders were forced to work in freezing offices, wrapped up in fur coats, hats and gloves. On several occasions, it was reported that passengers had starved or frozen to death when their trains broke down in the countryside.[14] In January, Reed travelled to the textile town of Serpukhov, a hundred kilometres south of Moscow, where the situation facing the town's thirty thousand mill workers was scarcely believable. An epidemic of typhus was raging, and in one mill a worker a day was succumbing to the disease. Chronically short of food, the workers would collapse from hunger while standing at their machines. And yet, Reed claimed, enthusiasm for the revolution seemed undimmed. In honour of the American's visit, the local party leadership had organised a regional meeting of Factory Shop Committee delegates. 'One dim kerosene lamp smoked on the speakers' desk,' Reed explained, 'and threw a faint light on the faces and ragged clothes of the assembly. They had come, some of them, from factories twenty versts* away in the country on foot through deep snow, with a little bread in their pockets. Their feet were bound with rags.' Reed was greeted by a rousing rendition of the 'Internationale', after which he gave a short speech, in which he offered comradely greetings from his fellow American revolutionists.[15] When he had finished, a pale youth jumped up and delivered an impassioned defence of the revolution:

From the workers of Serpukhov take this word to our brothers in America. For three years the Russian workers have been bleeding and dying for the Revolution, and not our own Revolution, but the World Revolution. Tell our American comrades that we listen day and night for the sound of their footsteps coming to our aid. But tell them, too, that no matter how long it may take them, we shall

* A verst is a Russian measure of length, equating to roughly 1.1km (0.66 miles).

hold firm. Never shall the Russian workers give up their Revolution. We die for Socialism, which perhaps we shall never see.[16]

Writing that July, Reed was optimistic about Russia's future. 'Just now,' he explained, 'it is a beautiful moment in Soviet Russia. Clear sunny day follows clear sunny day' and 'the fields are gorgeous with hundreds of varieties of wild-flowers.' The new Russia appeared as a 'rich, well-ordered land. Everywhere the green crops are going, occasionally a wood-burning factory sends up smoke, but more significant is the look of the people – none well-dressed but none in rags, none overfed, but none who look as if they were suffering.' Moreover, thanks to the free food, clothes, education and cultural entertainments that were provided by the new Bolshevik government, Reed explained, the streets of Russia were now full of happy children.[17] And everywhere, it seemed, were signs of renewal: the flowers blooming in Moscow's grand public gardens, the clean streets of Petrograd and the repairs to public buildings that were now underway.[18] Across the country, the People's Commissariat of Public Health had also been hard at work, ensuring that every township now boasted at least one new hospital.[19] And new Labour Armies had set about rebuilding damaged bridges and railway lines, cutting millions of feet of firewood for the cities and repairing locomotives.[20]

Reed painted a rosy picture, too, of the results of mass conscription into the Red Army, particularly the role of its political-cultural department, which not only provided 'political education' to the soldiers but also offered classes in literacy, technical education and vocational training, and provided ordinary soldiers with hitherto unimagined access to literature, drama and art. The results were remarkable. According to Reed, a previously illiterate peasant was, within six months, usually able to 'read and write, knows something of Russian drama, literature and art, understands the reasons for the war, and fights like a fury for the defense of the "Socialist fatherland", enters captured cities under red banners, singing – in short, has become a class-conscious revolutionist'.[21]

136

Although he never wrote about it publicly, Jack also appears to have taken a relaxed attitude when it came to the vexed question of the Cheka and its use of counter-terror. In his private notebooks he described the agency as a 'vast net-work of half-detective, half-revolutionary vengeance organizations all over Russia', and evidently believed that it had been necessary, and right, to act decisively against genuine counter-revolutionary plots and activists. It also seems he anticipated that, as the threat of counter-revolution abated, the power of the Cheka would wane, to be replaced by more conventional legal tribunals.[22] According to Emma Goldman, who arrived in Petrograd aboard the *Burford*· in January 1920, following her deportation from the United States, Reed was shockingly enthusiastic about the activities of the Cheka. He was, she recalled, particularly contemptuous of those Socialist Revolutionaries who had broken with the Bolsheviks and thrown their lot in with those calling for the return of the monarchy, and other reactionaries. 'I don't give a damn for their past,' Reed supposedly told her, 'I am concerned only in what the treacherous gang has been doing during the past three years. To the wall with them! I say. I have learned one mighty expressive Russian word, *"razstrellyat"*! (execute by shooting).'[23]

In February 1920, following the ECCI's decision to call for a merger between the Communist Labor Party and the Communist Party, Jack resolved to return to America – despite facing charges of criminal anarchy in Illinois, and the prospect of a five-year jail sentence: charges that had been levelled as part of a nationwide crackdown on left-wing radicals. Provided by the ECCI with $14,000 in small diamonds and $1,500 in cash to support the US communist movement, and sporting a dark moustache and slicked-back hair, with forged travel documents, Reed prepared to depart. His first attempt, which involved travelling through Latvia, failed when military clashes between Whites and

* Nicknamed the 'Red Ark', the ship transported more than two hundred anarchists, radicals and other 'undesirable aliens' from the United States to Russia.

Reds rendered the route to the coast impassable. The second attempt saw Reed cross into Finland and take refuge at the safe house near Helsinki. Then, on 13 March in Åbo, he was smuggled aboard a freighter bound for Sweden but was discovered, hiding in a coal bunker, by customs officials during a last-minute inspection. Interrogated and beaten by police, Jack was charged with smuggling and treason, and ultimately endured three months of imprisonment, locked in a tiny cell for nineteen hours a day and barely sustained by a meagre diet of bread and dry, salty fish. With the US State Department indifferent to his fate, and in an increasingly fragile mental state, he was eventually released after the Soviet leadership proposed a prisoner exchange. His limbs swollen, body covered in sores, and suffering from scurvy, an exhausted Reed finally left Finland for Petrograd on 7 June.[24]

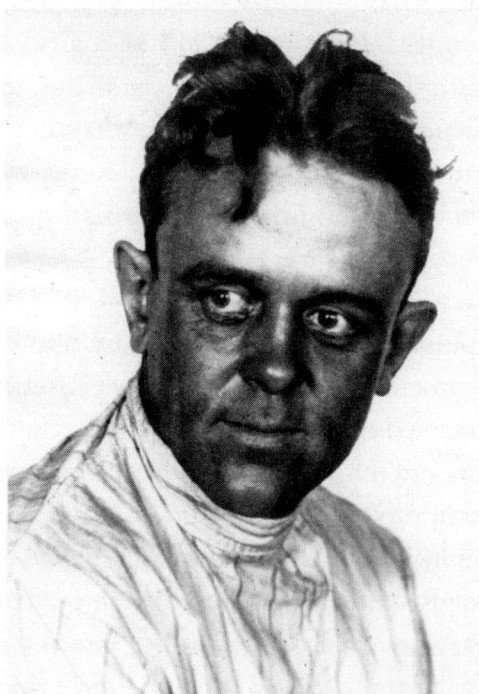

Reed, shortly after being discovered by Finnish customs officials hiding in the coal bunker of a freighter, during an abortive attempt to return to the United States, in March 1920.

Reed had barely had time to recover his strength before he was throwing himself into preparations for the second congress of the Comintern, scheduled to open on 19 July, and whose executive committee promised to act as a sort of 'General Staff of World Revolution', shaping policies for communist parties across the world. Holed up in the Delovoi Hotel, near the Kremlin, which was reserved for the delegates, Reed made a point of welcoming newcomers, showing them around the city and working hard to win over those who expressed scepticism of Bolshevism. The opening ceremony, held for symbolic reasons in Petrograd, saw the 169 delegates, representing almost forty countries, greeted by a raucous, seventy-thousand-strong crowd outside the Winter Palace. Jack was caught up in the spectacle, writing that the 'tremendous masses flowed like a clashing sea through the broad streets, almost overwhelming with their enthusiastic affection the delegates as they marched from the Tauride Palace to the Fields of Martyrs of the Revolution, protected on both sides by long lines of workers holding hands, forming a living chain'.[25]

But when the real business of the Comintern began in the Kremlin's grand Coronation Hall on 23 July, Reed's enthusiasm soon gave way to frustration. He was, for instance, appalled when foreign revolutionaries – many of them confident, intelligent individuals with impressive credentials – capitulated to Bolshevik leaders, even on issues about which they were much more knowledgeable.[26] For Reed, the real nub came with the so-called trades union question. The official position on trades unions, supported by Lenin and introduced by Karl Radek, the ruthless secretary of the ECCI, was that communists should infiltrate established unions with the aim of turning them into revolutionary organisations. For Reed, this policy made no sense when applied to the United States, where only one in five workers belonged to a union affiliated with the American Federation of Labor, whose conservative leader, Samuel Gompers, had prioritised organising skilled workers, belittled radical unions and adopted a 'no strike' policy during the Great War. Convinced that the AFL was a reactionary organisation, incapable of being used for revolutionary purposes, Reed and his allies instead advocated the policy of smashing the elitist craft unions, while concentrating on building up industrial unions (where all the workers in a particular industry, irrespective of their skill or trade, are organised into the same union – thereby securing greater bargaining power).[27] For Reed, who had long been inspired by the struggle of the IWW, this was deeply personal, and for a moment at least he seemed willing to take his criticisms to the very top.

After trying, and failing, to convince Radek to change his mind, Jack drafted a memo to Lenin, complaining about Radek's approach and explaining that the problem lay in the secretary's lack of knowledge. Realising that the new line on unions ultimately came from the 'big chief' himself, Reed eventually decided against sending the letter. He did, though, continue to mount a fierce rearguard action from the floor of the congress hall – despite the furious objections of Radek and Zinoviev, the Comintern chairman. The result was that, on 5 August, Radek's report was one of the few not accepted unanimously.[28] Reflecting on the congress a month later, Reed did not pull his punches, describing 'fundamental' differences, a 'long and bitter fight', and asserting that at the root of the problem was the fact that 'nobody in Russia' seemed to understand what industrial unionism, at least as practised in the United States, actually was. At the next congress, Reed predicted, the current position would have to be altered.[29]

Perhaps in revenge, Reed was almost immediately instructed by Zinoviev to attend the Congress of the Peoples of the East, in Baku – an oil-rich port city on the Caspian Sea. When he demurred – Louise was en route from Murmansk to Petrograd, and he had still not fully recovered from his ordeal in the Finnish jail – Zinoviev was clear: 'The Comintern has made a decision. Obey.' Unable to return home (the US government continued to refuse him a passport), and utterly reliant on his Bolshevik hosts, Reed had little choice but to agree.

It was a decision that very likely cost him his life.

14. THE HARVARD MAN IN THE KREMLIN WALL

Called by an urge he could not allay, nor put aside. John Reed . . .
gave his life to Revolutionary Russia. Dead in the flesh at 33!
Alive in the spirit for all time.
– *NEW YORK CALL*, 24 OCTOBER 1920

Jack returned to Moscow, and the much-anticipated union with Louise, on the morning of Wednesday 15 September, following an exhausting 4,500-kilometre round trip to the Caucasus. Although delighted to see him, she was shocked by his appearance. He seemed, she later said, 'older and sadder and grown strangely gentle and aesthetic'. His clothes were little more than rags, and the 'effects of the terrible experience in the Finnish gaol were all too apparent'. The following days were happy ones, though: Reed took her to meet new friends; they consorted with Bolshevik leaders, including Lenin, who granted her the rare privilege of an interview; visited galleries and museums; attended the ballet; and caught a performance of *Prince Igor* at the opera house. As they walked together 'in the park, under the white birch trees', their long separation 'seemed very far away'. There was, though, a new intensity about Jack, Louise recalled: 'he held me tightly by the hand . . . I could not leave him because he would shout for me.'[1]

Just ten days after his return from Baku, Jack fell ill with a fever. Initially diagnosed as influenza, as the symptoms worsened it soon became clear that he had contracted typhus; the probable cause, according to official reports, was 'eating unwashed fruit during a recent visit to Baku'.[2] Moved to the city's Mariinsky Hospital, where he was cared for by some of the country's leading physicians, Jack was provided with 'the best food, abundant linen, an electric stove, and all possible conveniences'. Ultimately a chronic shortage of medicines – exacerbated by the Allied blockade – sealed his fate. Near the end, 'old peasant nurses' resorted to slipping 'out to the Chapel [to] pray for him and burn a candle for his life'. Drifting in and out of delirium, paralysed down one side of his body and eventually unable to speak, Jack Reed finally succumbed in the early hours of Sunday 17 October. He was just shy of his thirty-third birthday.[3]

In death, John Reed was lauded as a hero of the revolution. His body, placed in an open silver coffin, 'banked with flowers and streaming banners', was taken to the Labour Temple, where it lay in state for seven days, guarded by fourteen Red Army soldiers. On Sunday 24 October, Reed's casket was taken in solemn procession to Red Square, accompanied by thousands of workers keen to pay their respects. Louise Bryant, who marched alone behind the hearse, recalled how the day was 'cold and the sky dark, snow fell as we began to march. I was conscious of how people cried and how the banners floated and how the wailing heart-breaking Revolutionary funeral hymn, played by a military band, went on forever and ever.' At the graveside, by the wall of the great Kremlin fortress, leading Bolsheviks – including Nikolai Bukharin (the editor of *Pravda*), Karl Radek, Boris Reinstein (Reed's old boss in the Bureau of International Revolutionary Propaganda) and Aleksandra Kollontai (the feminist who had served as the first people's commissar for social welfare) – gave eulogies.[4] While most of the speeches were rather formal, Kollontai praised Reed as a strong man and a 'generous soul', before offering a thinly veiled warning about the direction of the Communist Party:

> We call ourselves Communists, but are we really that? Do we not rather draw the life essence from those who come to us, and when they are no longer of use, we let them fall by the wayside, neglected and forgotten? Our Communism and our comradeship are dead letters if we do not give out of ourselves to those who need us. Let us beware of such Communism. It slays the best in our ranks. Jack Reed was among the best.[5]

For Bryant, who only recalled 'the broken notes of the speakers' voices', it was all too much. As the 'banners began to dip back and forth in salute', and 'the first shovel of earth' went rolling down, she fainted.[6]

In what turned out to be his last public address, delivered before two thousand Turks, Persians, Armenians and other representatives of Asiatic Russia in Baku, Reed had attacked the United States as one of the world's 'great imperialist powers'. From the Philippines to Cuba, Haiti to Mexico, Uncle Sam's record was one of oppression, exploitation and greed; he warned that American capitalists were eager to get their 'claws' into the mineral wealth of Armenia, Azerbaijan and other parts of the so-called Near East. Calling for 'solidarity between all the oppressed and toiling peoples', Reed proclaimed that there was 'only one road to freedom': 'Unite with the Russian workers and peasants who have overthrown their capitalists and whose Red Army has beaten the foreign imperialists! Follow the red star of the Communist International!'[7]

Even as Reed uttered these words, some have speculated that his own commitment to the cause was beginning to waver.

Writing in 1948, Benjamin Gitlow – a friend and ally of Jack's from their days in the Socialist Party's Left Wing – claimed that, while he was in prison in 1921 or 1922, Reed's widow had visited him, and recounted an extraordinary tale about the trip to Baku. The delegates travelling to the Congress of the Peoples of the East had, she said, been 'lavishly supplied with rich food and liquor, including rare wines and champagne'. Reed, who 'saw no excuse for flaunting such extravagance in the faces of the poverty-stricken masses', had complained, but 'Radek and Zinoviev laughed at him.' As their armoured train entered the Caucasus, 'Radek outdid himself in providing suitable entertainment for the delegates', as 'Old Mohammedan women boarded the train followed by beautiful Caucasian girls' who were 'disrobed before the delegates'. 'What followed', Bryant is alleged to have said, 'turned out to be an orgy of drunken lasciviousness . . . [that] thoroughly sickened and disgusted Jack.' Meanwhile, the congress itself was manipulated cynically by Radek and Zinoviev – who whipped up the delegates with demagogic appeals to anti-imperialism, but then produced heavily censored and sanitised reports of what was said for external consumption. Supposedly, by the time of the couple's emotional reunion in Moscow, Jack 'entertained grave doubts about the course he had taken', was concerned about 'how power and the lust for power' had 'affected the Bolshevik leaders' and was 'terribly afraid of having made a serious mistake in his interpretation of an historical event for which he would be held accountable before the judgment of history'.[8]

Gitlow's account should, however, be taken with a very large pinch of salt. He had become steadily more disillusioned with the politics of the radical left during the 1930s and, in 1939, made a dramatic and very public rejection of communism. Clearly, enlisting John Reed as a sort of proto-anti-communist served Gitlow's own political interests. Moreover, in his earlier memoir, published in 1940, he had made no reference whatsoever to the extraordinary revelations by Bryant.* And an account of the same journey from Moscow to Baku, written by Alfred Rosmer – a French communist and congress delegate who had himself broken with the Comintern – had the old peasant women offering fruit to the travellers, rather than nubile young girls.[9] At best, then, Gitlow's account would appear to have been somewhat embellished.

Other friends and associates of Reed's during his last months in Russia have, however, also furnished evidence of his supposed doubts. In her 1931 autobiography *Living My Life*, Emma Goldman recalled a conversation with Louise about Jack's final days. In his delirium, Louise said, Jack:

> kept on repeating all the time: 'Caught in a trap, caught in a trap.'
> Just that. 'Did Jack really use that term?' I cried in amazement.
> 'Why do you ask?' Louise demanded, gripping my hand. 'Because

* It is worth noting that Bryant, who died in January 1936, would not have been around to contradict him.

that is exactly how I have been feeling since I looked beneath the surface. Caught in a trap. Exactly that.'

'Had Jack also come to see that all was not well with his idol,' Goldman wondered, 'or had it only been the approach of death that had for a moment illumined his mind?'[10] Reed's friend and confidante Angelika Balabanova* seemed certain of the answer. Writing in 1938, she claimed that, during the spring and summer of 1920, Jack 'was becoming more and more depressed by the suffering, disorganization, and inefficiency to be found everywhere', and despaired about the 'indifference and cynicism of the bureaucracy of all gradations'.[11] When it came to Reed's battle at the second congress over the trades union question, Balabanova wrote that the 'tragedy lay not so much in his inability to defend himself effectively against [Radek and Zinoviev], as in the realization that he was struggling against a *system*, which had already begun to devour its own children'.[12] Balabanova saw Reed for the final time shortly after his return from Baku, when he and Louise paid a visit to her flat. 'Jack', she recalled, 'spoke bitterly of the demagogy and display which had characterized the Baku Congress' as well as 'the manner in which the native population and the Far Eastern delegates had been treated'.[13]

These accounts, all written many years after the events in question, and by people who had become fierce critics of the Soviet regime, need to be treated with caution. For one thing, it clearly suited anti-communists to be able to claim John Reed as one of their own. And that is what makes a top-secret memorandum, held in the files of US Military Intelligence, so intriguing. Dated 10 June 1921, and compiled by Colonel Mathew C. Smith, the document – which was sent to J. Edgar Hoover in the Justice Department shortly after it was written – was based on interviews with Bryant while she was in Riga, awaiting return to the United States. Bryant, Smith wrote, 'seems to

* Balabanova had served briefly as secretary of the Comintern, before being forced out by Zinoviev, who did not appreciate her strong independent streak.

be entirely in sympathy with the Russian Revolution, as she sees it as a means by which the people of Russia may obtain something better'. However, she stated – 'apparently sincerely' – that she was 'entirely out of sympathy with Communism, but . . . believes that Lenin will be able, helped by the great mass of the people . . . to lead Russia out of the present grip which the Communists and [the Cheka] have on the country'. As for her late husband, in highly confidential remarks she stated that Jack 'was carried away by Communism when he first went to Russia, but that she believes that, if she had been with him, he would never have gone to the extremes that he did'. 'She stated, however, that he was much disappointed with what he found in Russia and that she believes this is what brought on his illness.' 'He was', she said, 'so imbued with the idea of Communism, but when he got really in touch with the Russian situation, he found so few Communists and so many who used Communism as a means to get comfortable positions, extra food, homes, etc. that he was disappointed.'[14]

Amid all the competing and sometimes conflicting interpretations, a few things are clear: by the end of his life Reed had developed a deep personal animosity towards Zinoviev and Radek, and he remained willing to challenge the Comintern leadership, publicly, in a way that, as one leading historian writes, 'was unique even in 1920'.[15] There is also compelling evidence to suggest that Jack had become unsettled and disappointed by at least some of what he experienced and witnessed in Russia during 1920. But to ask whether these concerns and doubts might have developed into anything more substantial is to enter the realm of conjecture.

The news of Jack Reed's death prompted a wave of 'deep sorrow' among his friends and colleagues back in New York. In the restaurants, the cafés and the bookstores where he was well known, reported the *New York Call*, 'anecdotes of him formed the chief topic of conversation.' The tributes, too, came thick and fast:

Somehow one can't help feeling that he will fool them all again as he has so many times before and come back again triumphantly among us. With the same winning smile, the same good news of deeds in far corners of the earth. He will electrify us with inspiration to be up and doing for the revolution and bring the brave day of universal brotherhood and good will and plenty that lies ahead. He has always done so much to bring all these nearer.[16]

On the evening of Monday 25 October, an overflow crowd of thousands gathered in the city's Central Opera House for a highly charged and deeply moving memorial service. On the centre of the platform stood a large crayon drawing of Reed, the work of the talented Hungarian American illustrator and muralist Hugo Gellert. In his remarks to the mourners, the poet, socialist and leader of the famed 1912 Lawrence textile workers' strike Arturo Giovannitti declared that 'John Reed died as truly for the Russian revolution as did any of the brave soldiers of the Red Army . . . He gave his life for the revolution, even as if his heart had been shattered by shrapnel.'[17] In his own eulogy, Max Eastman made a similar point. Jack had, he said, 'sacrificed a life to the revolution', and 'if there is any special tribute I can add . . . it is a testimony to the splendor and gayety and wealth and magnificence of the life he sacrificed.' 'It was', Eastman explained, 'not only a great, laughing, lion-hearted fighter for truth and revolution, that lies buried among the first heroes under the wall of the Kremlin, but it is also a true genius who could have done almost anything else that he pleased.'[18]

In its 26 October editorial, the *New York Call* explained that the memorial service had demonstrated, powerfully and eloquently, that 'the spirit of John Reed' was 'alive and will continue to live as a compelling force' and as 'an inspiration'.[19]

It was a prescient observation.

15. AFTERLIVES

Art is a weapon in the class struggle.
– JOHN REED CLUBS

'The fact that John Reed wrote *Ten Days That Shook the World*, the fact that he devoted his writing to the portrayal of the class struggle in many parts of the world, and the fact that all his interests and desires were aligned with the proletarian revolution amply justify the use of the name for an organization of writers and artists,' wrote the Hollywood-based communist and labour journalist Mike Quin[*] in the summer of 1934. But 'what is less commonly known and too frequently submerged . . . is the enormous literary value of his writing.' 'When writers organize under the name of John Reed,' Quin explained, 'they are not only paying tribute to the proletarian consciousness of a man, but also recognizing some of the finest and most beautiful writing of the 20th century.'[1]

During the 1930s, a generation of young writers, artists and intellectuals – including John Dos Passos, Richard Wright, Langston Hughes and Josephine Herbst, as well as Quin – marched under the banner of the 'John Reed Clubs'. Like their hero, they sought to combine a commitment to the arts with the politics of class struggle. Affiliated with the Communist Party of the United States of America,[†] the John Reed Clubs also served for a time as a de facto propaganda arm of the wider radical left. The decision to name the clubs after Reed – made following an off-the-cuff remark by *New Masses* editor Walt Carmon, in October 1929 – proved inspired.[2] When he had returned from Russia, in 1918, Reed – eyewitness of the Russian Revolution,

---

[*] He was born Paul William Ryan.
[†] The CPUSA was born out of the merger between the Communist Labor Party and the Communist Party of America.

and on friendly terms with some of its most revered leaders – was in huge demand as a public speaker. As one historian has put it, 'with his native-born, educated accent and slouching, pants-hitching, boyish charm', he was able to reach people that no other left-wing speaker could. In fact, according to one leading scholar, *Ten Days That Shook the World* 'undoubtedly made more Soviet sympathizers than did all other left-wing propaganda combined'. Little wonder, then, that for a time he was viewed 'as if he were the No. 1 American Bolshevik'.[3] Reed's tragic and untimely death in Moscow only added to his allure in the years that followed.

Writing in the November 1927 edition of *The New Masses*,[*] Mike Gold sought to encapsulate Reed's appeal, a decade after the Bolshevik seizure of power. Reed had, he stated, 'lived the fullest and grandest life of any young man in our America'. Gold framed Reed as the example par excellence of the politically engaged left-wing artist; someone who had succeeded, spectacularly, in being both a 'revolutionist' and a 'revolutionary writer'. 'The revolution will grow in America,' Gold predicted, 'and there will be a new youth and Jack Reed will teach them how to live greatly again . . . There will be more Jack Reeds in America.'[4]

By 1934, there were more than 1,200 members spread across some thirty John Reed Clubs, in towns and cities throughout the nation. Their declared aim was to create a national organisation that would 'bring closer all creative workers' and 'maintain contact with the American revolutionary labor movement'. The JRC undertook a myriad of activities, including the publication of literary magazines (most famously *Partisan Review* in New York and *Left Front* in Chicago), organising discussion groups and lectures and hosting exhibitions of art and sculpture. In New York they even created a writers' school, with courses in Marxism and literature, poetry, fiction and prose. Alongside this artistic work the JRC also participated in a range of political

---

[*] A magazine associated with the American Communist Party that had been founded in 1926 by Mike Gold – the nom de plume of Itzok Isaac Granich, a Jewish American writer and lifelong Communist. The title was a nod to *The Masses*.

activity: protesting, for instance, against legislation proposed by the notorious anti-communist congressman Martin Dies that threatened to deport foreign-born communists; participating in annual May Day parades; supporting the struggle of organised labour; and engaging in anti-war protests.[5] Sometimes the group's activities attracted a violent counter-response. In Los Angeles, for instance, an exhibition of work by Black artists in support of the Scottsboro Boys – nine young African Americans who had been falsely accused, and subsequently convicted, of raping two white women – was attacked and broken up by the LAPD.[6] And, too often, these 'clubs of often famished and angry youth' (as the journalist Matthew Josephson described them) descended into factionalism and sectarianism. But, from their founding on the eve of the Great Depression, through to their formal dissolution in 1936, the John Reed Clubs operated at the cutting edge of efforts to build a new, radical, proletarian culture on the American Left, offering vital support to the coming generation of artists and helping to create a vibrant radical subculture in cities across the United States.[7]

If, during the 1920s and 1930s, Reed had served as a link with the revolutionary tradition of the early twentieth century and an inspirational model of the revolutionary writer, during the 1960s his status as a Greenwich Village bohemian, advocate of 'free love' and left-wing idealism, and his embrace of advocacy journalism, made him attractive to a new generation of radicals. This so-called 'New Left' – a loose coalition of organisations centred around Students for a Democratic Society and based largely on America's university campuses – championed the causes of civil rights and economic justice, and sought to build a new society within the shell of the old* and create a truly participatory democracy in the United States.[8]

Todd Gitlin was a prominent student activist and journalist who served as president of SDS in 1963–4, and who helped to organise the

---

* In a sign that the 'New' Left was not, perhaps, all that new, this idea had been central to John Reed's beloved Wobblies.

first national demonstration against the war in Vietnam, in Washington DC in April 1965. As a frequent contributor to the Liberation News Service, and the *San Francisco Express Times*, Gitlin was a key figure in the emergence of the 1960s underground press.* He described this effort to create an alternative, radical source of news, cultural commentary and political analysis as 'a romance' and 'marvellous adventure' for editors, photographers, writers and artists alike:

> With little money, less professional help or experience, we were improvising without blueprints, trying out unconventional forms of writing, learning design and layout and distribution as we went. On $40 a week – when it came – writers were staying up all night to do layout and set type. (Nobody did much bookkeeping.) Without a mainstream press to inspire us, we turned, cockily and half-consciously, to earlier generations of models, to the Orwell of *Homage to Catalonia*, the John Reed of *Ten Days That Shook the World*, to the pre-World War I *Masses* magazine of Max Eastman and Floyd Dell and Big Bill Haywood – if we turned to anyone.[9]

Ten Days, Reed's magnum opus, was also admired by sixties leftists of various stripes. In December 1967, for instance, *The Militant* (official publication of the Socialist Workers Party), hailed the International Publishers reprint, which was issued to commemorate the fiftieth anniversary of the Bolshevik Revolution. *Ten Days* was, declared columnist Dick Roberts, 'one of the best works of revolutionary journalism in American literature'.[10] In April 1974, *The Rag* – Austin's influential underground newspaper – carried a lengthy piece on *Ten Days*, praising Reed's 'genius for capturing the essence of the revolution through brief vignettes' and declaring that the book 'has become justifiably famous as the best account' of the Bolshevik seizure of

---

* At their height at the end of the 1960s, virtually every sizeable college town or city in the United States boasted at least one alternative newspaper, with an overall readership that stretched into the millions.

power.[11] Writing from his prison cell in the summer of 1970, Lawrence 'Pun' Plamondon – the minister of defence for the anti-racist, radical White Panther Party, who had spent the best part of two years on the run after being accused of bombing a CIA building – took heart from the pictures of contemporary revolutionaries that lined his wall (Huey P. Newton, Eldridge and Kathleen Cleaver, members of the Weather Underground), the music of B. B. King, and John Reed's *Ten Days That Shook the World*, which he deemed a 'most killer book about the Russian Revolution'.[12]

It was perhaps unsurprising, then, that Warren Beatty – supporter of Bobby Kennedy (1968) and George McGovern (1972), and high-profile opponent of the war in Vietnam – was driven to make a Hollywood movie about this rebel of an earlier age (and, apparently, a boyhood hero). Focusing on the love story between Jack and Louise, and foregrounding their embrace of bohemianism, feminism and the sexual revolution, *Reds* (1981) presents the couple, in the words of one historian, as 'well-intentioned', if at times confused, 'sixties-type idealists'.[13] Grossing $40 million in the US alone, the movie was nominated for twelve Academy Awards (picking up three, including for best director) and met with largely favourable reviews. Writing four decades later, in *Jacobin* magazine, Jim Poe hailed *Reds* as 'one of the best movies of its era', which 'stands up today as one of the greatest and most faithful depictions of revolutionary politics'. At the 'heart' of this 'beautiful film', Poe wrote, is the idea that 'our dreams and labors should be for the people and for revolution, not just ourselves.'[14]

Reed's masterpiece proved problematic during the Stalinist era – Uncle Joe was mentioned only in passing by Reed, whereas Trotsky (who was purged from the Communist Party, and subsequently expelled from the Soviet Union in February 1929) was one of the text's central heroes. The result was that the book was banned in Russia until Nikita Khrushchev's reforms of the mid-1950s.[15] But *Ten Days* has remained central to wider understandings of the Bolshevik Revolution, not least because director

Sergei Eisenstein based his 1928 epic, *October,* on Reed's text. More broadly, as biographer Robert A. Rosenstone has asserted, Reed's framing of the revolution as a ten-day drama came to enshrine 'the notion of what a twentieth century revolution should be'.[16]

In his lifetime, Reed's vivid, on-the-spot reportage helped to spread the message of the Bolshevik Revolution, and inspire left-wing revolutionaries, all around the world. In Tokyo in 1917 – then something of a haven for young Chinese radicals – Zhou Enlai, recently graduated from high school, was 'mesmerised' by the unfolding events in Petrograd. Noting down the latest developments in his diary and seeking out new sources of information, he eagerly read *Ten Days That Shook the World* as soon as it was published.[17] The events of that October, and Reed's immersive and idealistic reporting of them, helped to set Zhou on the path towards communism – and a critically important partnership with the man who would become a giant of twentieth-century revolution: Mao Zedong.

* The film was released internationally as *Ten Days That Shook the World*.

PART TWO
CHINA

MAO

Mao Zedong, aged forty-three. The photograph was taken by
Edgar Snow, and Mao – who back then liked to wear his hair long,
and rarely wore a hat – is wearing Snow's Red Army cap.

16. ANNIHILATION

They will be finished this year. They are surrounded on all sides.
The day of their collapse is not far away.
– *MINGUO RIBAO/REPUBLIC DAILY,*
10 OCTOBER 1934

The plan, it seemed, was working to perfection. For the best part of a year, beginning in September 1933, Chiang Kai-shek's Nationalist troops had been menacing Jiangxi – heartland of the self-proclaimed Chinese Soviet Republic – enforcing a brutal economic blockade on the Communist enclave's three million citizens. Working with German military advisers including Hans von Seeckt, one of Adolf Hitler's best generals, Chiang's forces had set about building new roads and a comprehensive network of concrete blockhouses, twenty feet thick ('turtle shells', the Communists called them), linked together with barbed-wire fences. Gradually, the cordon was tightened: trade in desperately needed salt, kerosene, cotton cloth and rice was stifled; virtually no one could travel in, or out; and, slowly but surely, the Nationalist troops began to advance. The intention, as one Red commander quipped, was clear enough: to dry the pond, and then get the fish.[1]

Taking personal command of the campaign, the Generalissimo (as he was often known) ultimately unleashed some half a million men, along with a modern air force of four hundred planes, to destroy the 'Red bandits' once and for all.[2] The Communists had survived Chiang's previous four encirclement campaigns by relying on partisan fighting and guerrilla warfare tactics. The blockhouse strategy, though, compelled the Communists to fight on Chiang's terms. Outnumbered by at least four to one, and heavily outgunned, their attempts to engage the Nationalist armies on the battlefield proved disastrous.[3] Red Army defeats in Lichuan and Xiaoshi in the autumn of 1933 augured the even greater disaster to come: in April 1934, Chiang's armies

159

completely overwhelmed the Communist forces at Guangchang – killing four thousand, and taking a further twenty thousand prisoners. With the back of the resistance broken, the road to Ruijin, the Red Capital, some seventy miles to the south, was now wide open. Beset by widespread desertion, an outflow of civilian refugees and severe economic hardship, and amid a savage campaign of political violence against counter-revolutionaries (real or imagined), the Jiangxi Soviet seemed on the brink of collapse.[4] Just weeks after the shattering defeat at Guangchang, it was decided that the Communists' proto-state, which had been assiduously built up, at great effort and expense, over several years, would have to be abandoned. Those responsible for this momentous decision were the Red Army's commander-in-chief, Zhu De, and its political commissar, Zhou Enlai, together with Otto Braun, a Comintern military adviser who had been dispatched by Stalin in September 1933, and Bo Gu, the twenty-seven-year-old Moscow-educated acting party leader. The rest of the Politburo was kept firmly in the dark, including the chairman of the Chinese Soviet Republic, and its titular head of state, Mao Zedong.[5]

Born on 26 December 1893 in Hunan, in South-Central China, Mao enjoyed a relatively comfortable childhood. His father, Rensheng, was a former soldier who had been able to save enough money to buy a couple of acres of rice paddy; his mother, Wen Qimei, was a devout Buddhist, warm and generous, who dutifully took her firstborn son to the local temple in Shaoshan and provided religious instruction at home. The growing family (two younger brothers, Zemin and Zetan, and an adopted sister, Zejian) lived in a 'large, rambling farmhouse, with a grey-tiled roof and upturned eaves, beside a cascade of terraced rice-fields tumbling down a narrow valley'. A pine tree wood was at the rear, and a lotus pond to the front. Mao and his brothers each had a bedroom of their own, which was an almost unheard-of luxury at the time. But life was far from easy. Four of Mao's siblings died at birth, and at the age of six he was put to work in the fields, keeping watch over the cattle and ducks, and carrying out other small tasks. Like his fellow peasants, the young Mao rarely bathed, and he cleaned his teeth by swilling a mouthful of tea. The family never went hungry, but the fare on offer was certainly not luxurious.[6] As Mao recalled, once a month his father 'made a concession to his laborers and gave them eggs with their rice, but never meat'. 'To me,' he continued, 'he gave neither eggs nor meat.'[7]

Mao's relationship with his father was difficult. Describing him as a 'hot-tempered man' and a 'severe taskmaster', Mao later claimed that he had 'learned to hate him'.[8] He would come to frame this relationship as an early education in the virtue of challenging authority: 'I learned', he explained, 'that when I defended my rights by open rebellion my father relented, but when I remained meek and submissive he only cursed and beat me more.'[9]

Mao's father might have been a bit of a tyrant but, if only for selfish reasons (to help with the farm accounts, and eventually take over the family business), he had stumped up five silver dollars a year* to send his eldest son to the village school. There, starting at the age of just eight, the 'family scholar' spent two years memorising, copying and reciting the contents of six textbooks that introduced Confucian ideas, emphasised the importance of studying and literary endeavours, and extolled the virtues of filial duties and responsibilities. Only when this onerous task had been completed were Mao and his fellow pupils permitted to explore the meaning of the texts they had memorised.[10] After graduation, Mao initially went along with his father's plan to have him apprenticed to a rice shop in the nearby town of Xiangtan. But shortly after his fifteenth birthday Mao declared his wish to enrol at Dongshan Upper Primary School, in the neighbouring county. Mao had heard about this new school, with its progressive teaching methods and modern curriculum, from a cousin who was a pupil there, but he initially found the elite surroundings, and the hostility and

---

* This was the equivalent of half a year's pay for an average labourer.

condescension of his fellow (and much richer) classmates, tough going. Academically, though, he thrived, excelling at classics and poetry, and he proved popular with many of his teachers. History was his favourite subject and, as well as immersing himself in the extraordinary story of China under its founding Qin and Han dynasties, Mao was also captivated by the feats of Peter the Great, Catherine the Great, Napoleon, Wellington, Washington and Lincoln.[11]

As he came of age in a China that, under the ruling Qing dynasty, was ossifying from within, mired in terrible poverty (in 1910 the vast majority of China's more than 350 million citizens were living in near-feudal conditions) and increasingly threatened and exploited by foreign powers (notably France, Britain, the United States and Japan), Mao's views about how to tackle the country's severe problems were shaped by his reading. He was particularly taken with *Words of Warning to an Affluent Age*, published by the entrepreneur and intellectual Zheng Guanying in 1893, which argued for the introduction of Western technology to help address China's chronic weakness. Three decades on, Mao could still recall the opening lines of one of the pamphlets he encountered as a young man – 'Alas, China will be subjugated!' – which warned of the looming dismemberment of the country.[12]

In the spring of 1910, amid a severe famine, the suicide of two peasants in the provincial capital, Changsha, seventy kilometres north-east of Mao's home village of Shaoshan, sparked a mass uprising: some thirty thousand people took to the streets, looting the offices of foreign steamship companies (which were accused of exacerbating the shortages by shipping rice downriver), attacking foreign missions and Western-style schools, and burning down the official residence of the local governor. The reaction of the Qing government was swift: the alleged leaders of the uprising were arrested, led through the streets in wicker cages and executed, their severed heads placed on poles as a visible warning to others. This incident made a deep impression on Mao. 'I never forgot it,' he later explained; 'I felt that there with the rebels were ordinary people like my own family and I deeply resented the injustice of the treatment given to them.' The uprising, and its bloody aftermath, Mao said, 'influenced my whole life'.[13]

Eighteen months later, Mao was in Changsha, studying at the city's secondary school, when the revolution that ultimately toppled the ailing and unpopular Qing dynasty broke out.[14] He was soon swept up in the excitement. Mao described how, just days after the initial uprising in Wuchang, three hundred kilometres away, one revolutionary visited his school and made a stirring speech before a spellbound audience. A few days later, Mao – together with a handful of his classmates – decided to join the revolutionary army.[15] His military career only lasted about six months, but he became popular with his platoon commander and fellow soldiers (most of whom were illiterate), who respected his 'great learning' and appreciated his willingness to write letters home on their behalf. It was during this time, too, that Mao first encountered socialist ideas, discussed in the pages of newspapers like *Xiangjiang Ribao* ('Xiang River Daily') and in pamphlets by Jiang Kanghu (a progressive who later founded the Chinese Socialist Party), who advocated: 'No government, no family, no religion: from each according to his ability, to each according to his need.' 'I wrote enthusiastically to several of my classmates on this subject,' Mao explained, 'but only one of them responded in agreement.'[16]

In the spring of 1912, following the abdication of the boy emperor Puyi and the establishment of a republic, Mao left the army and returned to his books.[17] For him, as for China, the following months were a period of great instability and uncertainty. The country first embraced new ideas and new freedoms – such as progressive education, greater equality for women, an independent judiciary and a free press – before slipping back into instability, political factionalism and violence as regional warlords vied for power, and the eighteen-year-old Mao struggled to find a purpose.[18] He considered a career as a policeman, a soap-maker, a jurist and an economist, and then spent several months, virtually penniless, holed up in the Hunan Provincial Library, where he devoured the Enlightenment works of Adam Smith, John Stuart Mill,

Herbert Spencer, Jean-Jacques Rousseau and Montesquieu.[19] Finally, in the spring of 1913, he decided to enrol at Hunan's Provincial First Normal School, where he trained to become a teacher. Mao, typically, chafed against many of the regulations: he particularly disliked the requirement to study natural sciences, in which he had no interest, and hated the compulsory class in still-life drawing. But his poor marks in these subjects were more than balanced out by strong performances in his favoured social sciences – history, literature, ethics and philosophy.[20] Mao was liked by his teachers, and soon fell under the influence of two charismatic professors. The first, Yuan Jiliu (known as 'Yuan the Big Beard'), helped him to improve his writing style. The second, Yang Changji, who had spent a decade abroad (in Aberdeen, Berlin and Tokyo), taught ethics and, as Mao recalled, 'tried to imbue his students with the desire to become just, moral, virtuous men, useful in society'.[21] During his time at the academy, Mao developed his ideas about the need for a strong, centralised state; the pre-eminent importance of individual will; and the complex, at times contradictory relationship between Western ideas and the Chinese intellectual tradition.[22] He also began to make forays into the wider world of politics and social reform. In April 1917, he had an article published in *New Youth*, the country's leading progressive magazine, in which he offered a practical solution to China's failings. The country was lacking in strength, he declared, because the martial spirit had been neglected, and the physical condition of the people had deteriorated. 'If our bodies are not strong,' Mao explained, 'we will tremble at the sight of [enemy] soldiers. How then can we attain our goals, or exercise far-reaching influence?' Railing against his fellow students, with their 'flowing garments', 'slow gait' and 'grave, calm gaze', he championed the cause of physical exertion. 'Exercise', he declared, 'should be savage and rude. To charge on horseback amidst the clash of arms and to be ever-victorious; to shake the mountains by one's cries and the colours of the sky by one's roars of anger.'*[23]

* Sadly, history has not recorded precisely how many of Mao's compatriots followed his suggestion that such exercise should be undertaken naked.

Mao also founded the New People's Study Society, a small, serious-minded group that discussed big questions about human society, the future of China, even the nature of the universe.[24] The half a dozen or so who initially joined also embraced Mao's enthusiasm for physical exertion. During the winter holidays, he explained, 'we tramped through the fields, up and down mountains, along city walls and across the streams and rivers.' When it rained, Mao noted, 'we took off our shirts and called it a rain bath. When the sun was hot we also doffed shirts and called it a sun bath,' and in the 'spring winds we shouted that this was a new sport called "wind bathing"'.[25]

In 1917 (aged twenty-three), Mao was named 'Student of the Year' and elected president of the Students' Society. Convinced as he now was that the 'superior men' – those who 'already possess lofty wisdom and morality' – were under a moral and practical obligation to help those less fortunate, he promptly revived plans for an evening school to provide practical knowledge, including literacy and basic accounting, to local workers; sixty were soon attending its classes. At a time when formal education was available only to a privileged minority, this kind of initiative was, Mao argued, vital to China's development.[26] It was a vision of an education system – open, anti-elitist and useful – that Mao would champion throughout his life.[27]

After graduating in the summer of 1918, Mao headed to Beijing, where his old mentor Professor Yang secured him a job as assistant librarian at the city's university. Beijing was expensive, and Mao's exceptionally modest salary of $8 a month meant that he was forced to rent a little room, with seven others, in the bustling Sanyanjing ('Three Eyes Well') neighbourhood, west of the Forbidden City.[28] 'When we were all packed fast on the *k'ang*,* Mao recalled, 'there was scarcely room enough for any of us to breathe. I used to have to warn people on each side of me when I wanted to turn over.' These rather dismal living conditions only made the beauty of China's ancient capital – with its parks, old palace

* A traditional brick platform, built across the end or side of a room, heated underneath, and used for sleeping on.

grounds and white plum blossom – even more striking.[29]

The wonders of the city also helped to compensate for Mao's dispiriting work at the university, where his lowly position rendered him virtually invisible to most of those visiting the library.[30] All the same, this was a particularly exciting time to be in Beijing: the New Culture Movement – which criticised traditional Confucian ideas and promoted modern, egalitarian values (including women's liberation, modern science, progressive education and an end to the patriarchal family) – was at its height. And, under its radical president Cai Yuanpei, Peking University* had become a centre of anarchist thought and activity.[31] Hardly surprising, then, that Mao was, in the words of one biographer, soon 'inhaling the literary, cultural, political, and scientific ideas sweeping Chinese intellectual circles'.[32] Chief among these ideas, at least as far as Mao was concerned, was anarchism. Indeed, he was just one of many young, progressive-minded Chinese citizens who were captivated by the ideology's rejection of authority and vision of a new society centred on peace, harmony and mutual friendship.[33]

In the end, though, it would be communism, not anarchism, that would define Mao's adult life.

As one of his biographers has explained, Mao 'did not become a revolutionary because he was a Communist; he became a Communist because he was a revolutionary'.[34] The Bolshevik seizure of power in 1917, following the October Revolution, had won admirers in China, particularly among leaders of the May Fourth Movement,† who

* Founded in 1898, it has continued to be known as Peking University despite the widespread adoption of the Pinyin system of romanisation.
† Named after the student-led protests that took place in Beijing, on 4 May 1919, following news of China's humiliation at Versailles (where her wartime allies handed Shandong province, which had been controlled by Germany, to Japan), the movement brought together a disparate group of reformers, radicals and thinkers, united in their desire to create a strong, reunified China, with the power to take on the country's warlords, reform the exploitative landlord system that left millions in penury, and stand up to foreign imperialism.

celebrated Russia's repudiation of its extraterritorial rights in China as a powerful blow against imperialism.[35] Encouraged by a handful of influential friends and colleagues, and with other options – including an attempt to establish village communes along anarchist lines – having run into the sand, Mao, tentatively at first, embraced Marxism.[36] Writing in December 1920, he expressed his sympathy with those who pushed for gradual reform. But with capitalists in control of everything – factories, banks, the instruments of state power, schools and the press – he had concluded that such an approach would not work. That left the option of a 'Russian-style revolution', which, in Mao's view, was 'a last resort when all other means have been exhausted'.[37] By the following summer, he was more effusive. Capitalism, he insisted, was 'strongly entrenched and hard to overcome. If it is not overthrown root and branch, no new construction will be possible.' To achieve what Mao characterised as the transformation of 'China and the world', a 'worker-peasant dictatorship' would be necessary. 'We should follow the Russian model,' Mao argued, 'for the Russian method represents a road newly discovered after all the other roads had turned out to be dead ends.'[38]

In July 1921, Mao, who had moved back to his native Hunan two years earlier, travelled to Shanghai for the founding Congress of the Chinese Communist Party (CCP), which immediately committed itself to the overthrow of capitalism and the abolition of class distinctions.[39] For the next decade or so, Mao was at the heart of the party's efforts to build up its support and agitate for the wider revolution. Back in Changsha, he established the Hunan Self-Study University, which functioned as a training school for future party activists, but most of his time was spent as a labour activist, seeking to organise textile workers, coal miners and railwaymen.[40] In 1923, at the Third Party Congress, Mao was one of those who argued in favour of forging a tactical alliance with the Guomindang – the Nationalist movement, headed by Dr Sun Yat-sen, that sought to eliminate warlordism, reunify the country and enact progressive reforms. His reasoning was entirely pragmatic: forced to operate underground, with a minuscule membership, and with the country's warlords cracking down hard on labour unrest, Mao argued that it was necessary for the Communists to unite, temporarily, with the Guomindang (which, in 1923, had begun to accept aid from the Soviet Union) against their common enemies.[41]

Mao – as both a member of the Communist Party's Central Committee and, now, an official of the Guomindang – worked hard to build a genuine alliance between the two organisations. He also began to refine his revolutionary ideas, focusing particularly on the role of the peasantry. In a famous article published in January 1926, he argued that peasants and farm labourers – 'the agricultural proletariat' – constituted a potential revolutionary force.[42] Even more controversially, he argued that, with sufficient leadership, vagrants – including thieves, beggars and prostitutes – could be mobilised too. In response to the rural movement that had been surging in his native Hunan, Mao predicted:

In a very short time, several hundred million peasants in China's central, southern, and northern provinces will rise like a fierce wind or tempest, a force so swift and violent that no power, however great, will be able to suppress it. They will break through all the trammels that bind them and rush forward along the road to liberation. They will, *in the end*, send all imperialists, warlords, corrupt officials, local bullies, and bad gentry to their graves. All revolutionary parties and all revolutionary comrades will stand before them to be tested, to be accepted or rejected as they decide. To march at their head and lead them? To stand behind them, gesticulating and criticizing them? Or to stand opposite and oppose them?[43]

Given the long history of exploitation and tyranny that the peasantry had been subjected to, Mao justified the use of revolutionary violence. Revolution was not, he famously wrote, 'like inviting people to dinner, or writing an essay, or painting a picture, or doing embroidery; it cannot be so refined, so leisurely and gentle'. Rather, it was an 'act of violence whereby one class overthrows the power of another'. The rural areas of China, Mao explained, 'must experience a great, fervent revolutionary upsurge, which alone can rouse the *peasant* masses in their thousands and tens of thousands to form this great force . . . To put it bluntly, it is necessary to bring about a brief reign of terror in every rural area; otherwise we could never suppress the activities of the counterrevolutionaries in the countryside or overthrow the authority of the gentry.'[44]

Mao's confidence in the revolutionary potential of the peasantry was strengthened by his experiences during the so-called Northern Expedition. Launched in July 1926, it saw the armies of the CCP–Guomindang United Front push forward from their base in Canton, with the aim of reunifying the country and finally breaking the power of China's warlords. The fall of Changsha in July, and Wuhan that autumn, signalled the wider victories to come. By the winter of 1926, the Nationalists controlled seven of twenty-eight provinces, and, by the time Beijing fell in the summer of 1928, the Guomindang had already established itself as the de facto government of the Republic of China.[45] In the early stages of the campaign, Mao had helped to pave the way for the Nationalists' success in his native Hunan by sending field operatives to organise the peasantry ahead of the military advance – and was honoured as a 'son of Hunan' for his efforts.[46] But Mao's emphasis on the peasantry put him at odds with most of his comrades on the Communist Party's Central Committee. For these activists – predominantly young, bourgeois intellectuals – the future lay with the modern, industrial working class (however small) rather than the peasantry who, with their superstitions and traditions, were inextricably linked with China's 'backwardness'.[47] But this ideological schism within the CCP would very soon be overshadowed by a much larger problem – one that posed a threat to the very survival of the Communist movement itself.

In the months that followed the death of the Guomindang's founder, Sun Yat-sen, in March 1925, Chiang Kai-shek, the commander of the

Nationalist garrison in Canton, eventually prevailed over his rivals. Appointed commander-in-chief of the National Revolutionary Army in June 1926, Chiang, whose sympathies lay with the movement's right wing, first used his Communist allies to help secure the success of the Northern Expedition before turning on them with astonishing brutality. In Shanghai, in the early hours of Tuesday 12 April 1927, Nationalist troops, aided and abetted by members of the 'Green Gang' – a notorious underworld organisation – unleashed a wave of terror against Communists that left hundreds dead, including many unarmed women and children. It signalled a new nationwide campaign of suppression and annihilation that killed hundreds of thousands of peasants and devastated the Communist Party.[48] In a report written in June 1927, Mao described in graphic detail the horrors that were inflicted by landlord militias with the support of the Nationalists. The 'brutal punishments', he explained, included 'gouging out eyes and ripping out tongues, disembowelment and decapitation, slashing with knives and grinding with sand, burning with kerosene, and branding with red-hot irons'. Not even women were spared the worst horrors: militia fighters would, Mao reported, 'run string through their breasts and parade them around naked in public, or simply hack them to pieces'. The entire province of Hubei was 'completely shrouded in white terror', and across Hunan, Jiangxi and Hubei, Mao estimated that more than ten thousand party activists, peasants and workers had been killed.[49]

In response to this unfolding disaster, the CCP leadership belatedly realised the need to establish its own armed force. That summer, the nascent Chinese Workers' and Peasants' Revolutionary Army (or Red Army) – a force of some twenty thousand men – took the fight to the Guomindang, with predictably dismal results.[*][50] Meanwhile, Mao was sent to Hunan, tasked with organising the 'Autumn Harvest Uprising' – an ambitious attempt to instigate a peasant revolt across

* Thirteen thousand men were lost in just two weeks, mostly to desertion.

the province. Mao's Red Army, made up of about a thousand regular troops who had defected from the Guomindang, along with a couple of thousand poorly armed peasants and unemployed coal miners, began their assault during the second week of September.[51] For Mao, in command of troops for the first time, it was almost all over before it began. Captured by Nationalist militia, he recalled how:

> I was ordered to be taken to the militia headquarters, where I was to be killed. Borrowing several tens of dollars from a comrade, however, I attempted to bribe the escort to free me. The ordinary soldiers were mercenaries, with no special interest in seeing me killed, and they agreed to release me, but the subaltern in charge refused to permit it.

Faced with certain death, Mao had no option but to attempt an escape. As the party approached the militia base, he 'broke loose and ran into the fields'. Reaching a 'high place, above a pond', surrounded by tall grass, he hid until sundown. Although on several occasions the soldiers came within touching distance, Mao somehow managed to evade capture. At dusk, and with the search temporarily abandoned, he set off across the mountains where, aided by friendly peasants, he was finally able to reunite with his forces.[52]

While Mao might have enjoyed good fortune, the same cannot be said for the soldiers under his command. Of the three thousand or so who started out on the campaign, almost half were lost, and the enterprise ended in total failure. Expelled from the Politburo following the disaster, Mao led the remnants of his army south, to the sanctuary of Jinggangshan, high in the Luoxiao Mountains.[53] 'Wreathed in cloud, with blade-sharp ridges, thickly forested with Chinese larch, pine and bamboo' and with waterfalls cascading 'down sheer gorges to lose themselves in thin, blue torrents, far below', it was, in the words of one historian, 'a poet's landscape, majestic but desperately poor'.[54] Establishing his forward operating base in the little town of Maoping,

Mao set about reorganising his forces. By the spring, he had drilled into them the essence of his military strategy (inspired by Sun Tzu's *The Art of War*), which was summed up in the pithy phrase:

> When the enemy advances, we withdraw,
> When the enemy rests, we harass,
> When the enemy tires, we attack,
> When the enemy withdraws, we pursue.

He also drew up guidelines for the treatment of civilians, insisting that his troops replace straw bedding when sleeping in the homes of peasants, return everything that they borrowed, pay for anything that they damaged, and generally behave in a courteous, respectful and humane manner. Politically, Mao and his allies established local soldiers', workers' and peasants' soviets, expropriated land for redistribution to the peasants and sought to win over (or at least refrain from alienating) market traders, shopkeepers and other members of the petty bourgeoisie.[55] After the multiple disasters of 1927, Mao's confidence was slowly returning and, at the end of August 1928, the Red Army – by now strengthened by several thousand troops commanded by Zhu De – successfully repelled a large Nationalist attack.[56]

That summer marked the high-water mark of the Jinggangshan base. At its peak, the territory controlled by the Reds extended across seven counties, covering a population of some half a million, all protected and defended by eight thousand regular Red Army soldiers.[57] But by the winter the mood had changed. In November, with the treasury running low, amid an acute shortage of food, cloth and medical supplies, and with Nationalist troops continuing to threaten, Mao drew up contingency plans for an evacuation. Then, in December, the Communists' meagre resources were stretched to breaking point by the arrival of Peng Dehuai's eight-hundred-strong Fifth Red Army. At virtually the same time, alarming reports began to filter in that up to twenty-five thousand Guomindang troops were gathering nearby, poised to launch a coordinated attack across five different fronts.[58]

As dawn broke on Monday 14 January 1929, Mao and Zhu led three thousand five hundred troops down the mountain, via a precarious and rarely used route. Making their way past pockets of snow, the force inched down to the valley – the men forced to crawl over large boulders in the face of an icy wind, hanging on to one another to avoid falling into the chasm below. As they headed first south and then east, the Communist forces endured harrowing conditions and suffered some bitter defeats before finally establishing a new base near Ruijin, in the Fujian–Jiangxi border area. Although they did not yet know it, the Jiangxi base would become the heart of the nascent Chinese Soviet Republic.[59]

Mao was thirty-seven years old when he founded the Jiangxi Soviet, and for the next four and a half years he dedicated his efforts to ensuring its success. By now, he had become convinced that the key to a successful Communist revolution lay in expanding the party's rural bases to encircle, and eventually capture, the cities.[60] As he put it, 'The development of the struggle in the countryside, the establishment of soviets in small areas, and the creation and expansion of the Red Army are prerequisites for aiding the struggle in the cities and hastening the revolutionary upsurge.'[61] Such a strategy relied on establishing strong economic, military and political foundations. Mao, as ever, began investigating local conditions and gathering detailed information – about class structure, trade, land ownership, taxes, education, even the price of chickens – to inform a programme of land reform that, while ambitious, treated the richer and middling peasants rather more leniently than many of his comrades would have preferred. Mao was clear: the priority was to build the maximum possible local support.[62] Not that he had suddenly become a cuddly liberal: between the autumn of 1930 and the spring of 1931, Mao's forces moved ruthlessly against alleged enemies, purging supposed Guomindang sympathisers from within the First Front Red Army (to give it its official name). Several thousand were killed, and the methods deployed by Mao's supporters were brutal – suspects were thrashed with ox-tailed sticks and hung up by their hands, burned with kerosene lamps, or had their hands nailed to a table while bamboo splints were inserted underneath the fingernails, to extract confessions.[63]

With Guomindang troops continuing to harass and threaten the base, Mao also refined the Red Army's use of guerrilla warfare – relying on local support and knowledge to lure the enemy in before striking. Mao's record was impressive – thirty thousand Communist soldiers managed to see off three 'encirclement and suppression' campaigns by Chiang's far larger forces. But Mao's refusal to adopt more conventional tactics and take the fight to the cities; his habit of ignoring, or reinterpreting, directives from the centre; and his deviance from orthodox positions on the class struggle made him a target. When the party's senior leadership relocated from Shanghai to Jiangxi in 1932, they quickly moved to clip his wings: stripped of his military responsibilities, Mao was instead tasked with administering the base area.[64] In his capacity as chairman of the recently proclaimed Chinese Soviet Republic, Mao had responsibility for a population of several million people. Characteristically, he threw himself into the challenge – reforming the tax system, relaxing the rules on divorce, seeking to improve literacy and education, and attempting to introduce a measure of democracy to local elections. Asked to head a Land Investigation Movement, Mao followed his own line. Rather than uncovering the supposedly hidden landlords and rich peasants who were ripe for appropriation, he instead sought to mobilise a mass movement that combined land reform and military recruitment with efforts to boost local economic production. This proved to be the final straw for Mao's superiors, who, in January 1934, removed him from all leadership positions; rumours even began to circulate that he had been placed under house arrest.[65] The Chairman, though, remained unrepentant. In a speech delivered before the Second Congress of the Chinese Soviet Republic that same month, he declared that 'the central task of the soviets is to mobilize the broad masses to take part in the revolutionary war, overthrow the imperialist Guomindang by means of such war, spread the revolution throughout the country, and drive imperialism out of the country.' The only path to victory, Mao insisted, lay in 'mobilizing the masses on a huge scale to participate and support the war'.[66]

Mao may have been defiant but, in truth, he appeared to have been comprehensively outmanoeuvred by his rivals. His speech, in the view of most of his comrades, was little more than a swansong.[67]

Personal salvation, it turned out, would lie in the almost complete destruction of everything he had been working for.

17. EXODUS

Adventure, exploration, discovery, human courage and cowardice,
ecstasy and triumph, suffering, sacrifice, and loyalty, and then through
it all, like a flame, an undimmed ardor and undying hope and amazing
revolutionary optimism of those thousands of youths who would not
admit defeat by man or nature or God or death – all this and more seemed
embodied in the history of an odyssey unequaled in modern times.

– EDGAR SNOW

On the evening of Tuesday 16 October 1934, Mao and some twenty
others left the little town of Yudu, seventy kilometres west of Ruijin,
where the Chairman had been recuperating following a bout of
malaria. His batman described how, after leaving via the North Gate,
the party turned 'to the left towards the river, which was all yellow,
roaring and foaming, as though calling on the armies to advance'.
'Soon,' the orderly explained, 'the sun set and the gusts of bitter wind
chilled us.' Mao, who was wearing a 'grey cloth uniform and an eight-
cornered military cap, with no overcoat', walked with 'enormous
strides along the riverbank'.[1]

The 'Long March' was finally underway.

Throughout the hot, wet summer of 1934, the Communists had
launched a mass recruitment campaign to swell the depleted ranks
of the First Front Red Army while simultaneously embarking on a
systematic programme of preparations for evacuating the base. Food
was requisitioned, winter clothing produced, rifles and other weapons
were repaired, everything from printing presses to the hospital's prized
X-ray machine was dismantled and packed up, and a propaganda
drive was launched to persuade peasant women to make straw sandals
for the soldiers – some two hundred thousand pairs were eventually
produced. Meanwhile the Red treasury – a vast trove of jewellery, gold,
silver ingots, more than one million silver dollars, and other valuables

– which had been hidden in the mountains near Ruijin, was dug up and brought back down to the capital, ready for distribution among the First Front Red Army.[2] At the end of September, news of the decision to abandon the base was made public. In an article ironically entitled 'All for the Defense of the Soviet', Zhang Wentian (one of the party's Moscow-educated leaders) emphasised the need for flexibility in taking the fight to the Guomindang. Tactics, he explained, would be shaped by circumstances, and it would be necessary to 'adopt different forms of struggle for attack, counterattack, defense, or even retreat'. All of these, he explained, would be 'used to carry out the party's general offensive line and achieve the complete victory of the soviet revolution'. Although the struggle would be long, and the path

CHINA

to victory far from smooth, Zhang ended with a rallying cry: 'Let us hold aloft the banner of the soviet,' he declared, and be 'tenacious in defense, firm in offense, fierce in pursuit and attack – and fight a bloody war in order to defend the soviet areas and smash the fifth "encirclement and suppression" by the enemy! We will win this bloody war; we can and must win at all costs!'[3]

On 15 October, a plane carrying Chiang Kai-shek took off from Nanchang, Jiangxi's provisional capital, for a trip north to rally support for the Guomindang. That morning's edition of the *Central Daily*, the movement's official newspaper, carried the headline 'Chiang Confident He Will Get Reds', and boasted of the Communists' imminent defeat. As the Generalissimo gazed from the window at the green hills and winding rivers below, it would have been understandable if he had allowed himself a moment of quiet satisfaction. And yet, at that very moment, his hated Communist foes were embarking on a daring escape from right under his nose.[4]

The Communists departed from Jiangxi amid scenes that could have been lifted from the pages of the Old Testament. Some ninety thousand Red Army soldiers, under the command of Otto Braun, Zhou Enlai, Bo Gu and Zhu De, were arranged into a 'long box' formation, consisting of two main columns. At the centre of the 'box' was the Military Commission – made up of four thousand communications and logistics personnel, engineers, hospital workers and the Red Army University* – and the remnant of the Jiangxi Soviet's civilian government, with several thousand reservists and porters carrying filing cabinets, sewing machines, the printing presses, the gold and silver reserves (packed into battered old kerosene cans), and even the contents of the Ruijin Library.[5]

There were just thirty women among those who evacuated the base: most of them the wives of senior Communist leaders or military commanders, as well as senior cadres in their own right.[6] Among

---

* Founded in 1931 as the Counter-Japanese Military and Political University, the Red Army University taught literacy and military tactics, and undertook political indoctrination.

MAO

them was He Zizhen, Mao's third wife,* who worked as his private secretary and party propagandist. Pregnant with her third child, she was compelled to leave their two-year-old son, Little Mao, behind.† In the chaos that followed the evacuation, the boy was lost; neither of his parents would ever set eyes on him again.[7] Little Mao was just one of many children who were left in what remained of the Jiangxi Soviet, along with some twenty thousand wounded soldiers, the elderly and almost all the women, protected by a rearguard force of six thousand. When the base was finally overrun, later that autumn, their fate was sealed. One report described how:

> The enemy used twenty full divisions to occupy the main Soviet cities and towns. They never succeeded in completely conquering the countryside where the people had arms, but they did succeed in slaughtering hundreds of thousands of people. Large numbers of women and girls were captured and sold at five dollars a head to [Guomindang] soldiers, officers, landlords, and brothel keepers.[8]

By the time this orgy of violence and retribution was unleashed, the Red Army was long gone.

Moving slowly – it managed only three kilometres that first day – the First Front Red Army inched its way south-west, into enemy territory, heading for the border with Guangdong.[9] Wang Quanyuan, who held senior posts in the Communist Youth League and in the Women's Department of the Central Committee, recalled how members of her unit were given some last-minute instructions on how to march silently:

---

* Mao was, technically, still married at the time of his third union in 1928; his second wife, Yang Kaihui, was executed by Nationalist forces in the summer of 1930. Mao's first union, with Luo Yixiu, was the result of an arranged marriage in 1908; while he participated in the ceremony, he thereafter refused to recognise the relationship.
† Their first child, a girl, had been abandoned to a peasant family in 1929 during the retreat from Jinggangshan to Jiangxi.

Everything we brought with us had to be wrapped up tightly so the enemy wouldn't hear us. We had to walk on tiptoe because if we put our heels down we'd make a *dong dong* noise which the enemy could hear.[10]

A combination of subterfuge, a catastrophic intelligence failure by the enemy (Chiang's forces were bombing Ruijin long after the Red Army had left), and a deal struck with a local warlord meant that the Communists made it past the first three lines of Guomindang defences without encountering any real trouble.[11] But the going was tough. Zhong Yuelin, who had joined the party as a teenager and was the youngest of the women with the First Front Red Army, recalled having to boil her underwear because there were so many lice, saying: 'If you didn't have lice, you're not a revolutionary!'[12] While exhausting, the night marches that the army undertook during this period were, in one senior officer's recollection, almost magical: 'When no enemy troops were near, whole companies would sing and others would answer. If it was a black night and the enemy far away, we made torches from pine branches or frayed bamboo, and then it was truly beautiful.'[13]

At the end of November, though, the Red Army's luck finally ran out. To begin with, the operation to cross the Xiang river, and break through the fourth and final blockhouse line, appeared to be going well. The advance forces made it to the north bank on 25 November, followed shortly thereafter by the battle-hardened troops of the First and Third Army groups.[14] As one soldier put it, 'It was as if we'd entered no-man's land . . . we had the river to ourselves.'[15] By 28 November, however, everything had changed. At the end of October, as Chiang came to terms with the scale and scope of the escape from Jiangxi, he had realised the Communists would need to cross the Xiang river to break the encirclement and link up with Communist forces in western Hunan. And so, in mid-November, he had hatched a plan to use fifteen Guomindang divisions, backed up by thousands more troops commanded by local warlords, to trap the Red Army by creating an 'iron triangle' in front of the river, bounded by the towns of Quanzhou, Xing'an and Guanyang. And now, as the slower-moving units of the Red Army, weighed down by heavy equipment, approached the Xiang, the first major battle of the Long March began.[16]

In the early hours of Saturday 1 December, Red Army military command issued the following order:

The battle of 1 December will affect our whole army. To be able
to move westward will open the path to future development. Any
delay will cause our army to be cut up by the enemy . . . Make all
soldiers and officers understand the significance of today's battle:
either we win or we lose.[17]

By now under near-constant attack from the air, and with its forces dangerously divided (half were still on the south side of the river), the situation facing the Communists was dire. It was, in the words of one local peasant, 'as if someone had overturned a beehive. You can't believe it. They put up pontoons over the river but there were so many people waiting to cross it. The horses were too frightened to walk on the pontoons, and men were pushing them, then they fell into the water themselves.'[18] Printing presses, lathes, sewing machines and other pieces of equipment were abandoned in the middle of the road, and one commissar was shocked to see, 'scattered in all directions', 'books and papers – military manuals, maps, books on strategy, the agrarian question, problems of the Chinese Revolution, works on political economy, on Marxism, Leninism'. To his horror, he learned that 'the library under which Red Army bearers had staggered all the way from Ruijin lay here, pages torn, books muddy, bindings crushed. All our ideological armory, all our military literature had been tossed aside.' As dazed and wounded soldiers struggled to find their bearings, and discipline began to break down, the casualties mounted.[19] One soldier described how 'the river was like a bath full of blood. There were so many bodies floating on the water, like dead locusts.' Dropping his rifle, he used his hands 'to push the bodies aside' and swim across.[20] By the time the battle was over, at least fifteen thousand Red soldiers lay dead, and tens of thousands more had been captured, wounded, or had simply fled.[21]

The encirclement, though, had been broken.

18. ZUNYI

It was obvious that Mao wanted revenge.
– OTTO BRAUN

Having crossed the Xiang, the Red Army – or what remained of it –
now sought refuge in Mount Lang, or Langshan ('Old Man'), in south-
west Hunan. Measuring 818 metres (2,684 feet) at its highest point,
the mountain posed a formidable physical challenge. The route up, one
soldier explained, was 'so steep I could see the sole of the man ahead of
me'. Some steps had been carved out of the face of the mountain, 'as
high as a man's waist', and, as the troops scrambled their way up, party
activists 'went up and down the columns' giving encouragement to
the 'struggling men and helping the sick and wounded'. But alarming
news soon travelled down the line that the 'advance columns were
facing a sheer cliff and that there was no way of getting the horses
up'; 'after a time came the order to sleep where we were and continue
climbing at daybreak.' Sleep, while easily ordered, was far from
straightforward: the path, the soldier noted, was no more than two
feet wide at any point, and even if one succeeded in lying down it
was not possible to turn over without rolling down the mountainside.
Moreover, there were 'great jutting boulders everywhere and even the
path was covered with sharp stones'. Awoken in the middle of the
night by the cold, the soldier 'lay and watched the twinkling stars in
the sky'. 'They looked like jade stones on a black curtain. The black
peaks towering around me were like menacing giants. We seemed
to be at the bottom of a well.' All along the narrow mountain path
were 'small fires lit by men also awakened by the cold. They were
sitting around and talking in low voices. Apart from their faint voices
the silence was so great that I could hear it. It was sometimes near,
sometimes far away, sometimes loud and sometimes faint, and at other

times like spring silkworms eating mulberry leaves. I listened intently and it sounded like a complaining mountain spring, then like the distant murmur of the ocean.'¹

The following morning, the soldiers reached Leigong Yai ('Thunder God Rock'), the cliff that had halted their progress the night before, and which jutted out into the sky at an angle of almost ninety degrees. They were now forced to make their way up some precarious carved steps, no more than a foot wide, without any ropes or handrails to aid them. Horses with broken legs lay at the foot of the ravine, and the wounded and sick were taken from their stretchers and pushed or dragged up the cliff face. Finally, after a march of almost twelve miles, the ordeal was over. Langshan was, the soldier explained, 'the most difficult mountain we had climbed so far'.²

On 12 December, just a few days after summiting Langshan, senior party leaders gathered in a farmhouse just outside of Tongdao, a little market town in the south-western corner of Hunan province, on the border with Guizhou. There, as a wedding took place in another part of the building, they took stock. Of the ninety thousand or so troops that had set off from Jiangxi in October, a combination of casualties and desertions meant that there were perhaps as few as thirty thousand remaining. The most pressing question now before them was whether to continue with their original plan to move north and meet up with the forces of fellow Communist He Long, who had established his own soviet base area. The latest intelligence reports indicated that they would have to take on between one hundred thousand and two hundred and fifty thousand Nationalist troops to reach the Communist base. It was at this critical moment that Mao, attending a meeting of the Military Commission for the first time in two years, seized the initiative. One senior general, Liu Bocheng, described how the Chairman 'came forward with a plan which saved the Red Army'. Rather than head north, Mao suggested that, for now at least, they should turn west, into the more lightly defended Guizhou province.

With the only alternative almost certain annihilation, and with some senior military commanders threatening to mutiny, it was perhaps not too surprising that Mao's proposal was accepted without opposition.[3]

Over the next few days, the Red Army would pass through some of China's most beautiful countryside: a land of 'great conical limestone mounds, thousands of feet high; mountains like camels' humps, like giant anthills'.[4] The pine and bamboo forests, crashing blue waterfalls, chain bridges and deep valleys certainly made for a spectacular sight. But it was the poverty of the region, and the oppressive conditions endured by its minority Miao and Dong people, that made the profoundest impact.[5] This was a land where infant mortality hit 50 per cent, illiteracy was near total and children were routinely sold to slave merchants (with five silver dollars considered a very good price). Opium, in the words of the renowned American journalist Harrison Salisbury, 'deadened, drugged, and immobilized the naked poor' and 'drenched the local armies'.[6] Late at night, after a hard day's marching, General Zhu De took to scribbling down his impressions of this strange, unfamiliar land:

> Corn, with bits of cabbage, chief food of people. Peasants too poor to eat rice; sell it to pay rent and interest. Rice seized by militarists as 'war rice tax' . . . Peasants call landlords 'rent gentry' and themselves 'dry men' – men sucked dry of everything . . .
>
> Poor hovels with black rotten thatch roofs everywhere. Small doors of cornstalks and bamboo . . . Have seen no quilt except in landlord houses in cities. One family of 10 persons here. Two board beds, one for husband, wife, baby; one a shelf for grandmother. Others sleep on earth floor around fire, without covering.

This was a land, he explained, where peasants could be found scrabbling in the ground under a landlord's old granary, digging out rotten rice – or, as the local Buddhist monks had it, 'holy rice': a gift, they said, 'from Heaven to the poor'.[7]

On Saturday 15 December, the Red Army arrived in the county seat of Liping, just over the Hunanese border in south-eastern Guizhou. The town, which was set in a valley flanked by low, terraced hills, was captured without much of a fight, and a military headquarters was quickly established in the home of a prosperous local merchant who, like the neighbouring Lutheran missionaries, had fled on hearing news of the Communists' advance. It was here, in this spacious, well-furnished home, which opened onto a 'narrow street of wood-fronted shops and houses with grey-tiled roofs and upturned bird's-wing eaves', that, on the evening of 18 December, the Politburo met in formal session for the first time since the Long March had begun. After several hours of tense discussions, Mao again won the day. Against the objections of party leader Bo Gu and the Comintern military adviser, Otto Braun – who remained committed to joining up with their fellow Communists in Hunan – the comrades agreed to change course: they would now move north-west, towards the city of Zunyi, and from there seek to establish a new base near the border with Sichuan.[8]

The two-hundred-mile trek to Zunyi, across mostly flat terrain, took the Red Army back into more prosperous country. Many of the county towns they passed through en route gave way without a fight. Marching at pace, the first troops reached the little trading post of Houchang ('Monkey Town') – some twenty-five miles south of the River Wu – on New Year's Eve. That evening, as the snow fell outside, the Politburo met once again. Although the details are murky, it seems that a fierce argument broke out after Braun urged the Red Army to make a stand and take on the three warlord divisions that, the leadership had just learned, were now closing in. His comrades were having none of it. They had, they reminded Braun, only recently decided to avoid risky set-piece battles. The priority now was to secure a new base. In a sign that Mao's ideas about guerrilla warfare were back in the ascendant, they also passed a resolution emphasising that 'no opportunity should be missed to use mobile warfare to break up and destroy the enemy.' Finally, the order of the day went out:

'Proceed to north Guizhou. Take Zunyi and Tongzi by surprise, and arouse the masses.'[9]

Advance troops reached the River Wu in the early hours of Tuesday 1 January. 'Slate-bottomed, carved through dark-gray basalt, few ferry points, fewer bridges, no fords, the water deep and boiling swift', the Wu was now the only remaining obstacle between the Reds and Zunyi, forty miles away. Initial reconnaissance was not promising: the river was 250 yards wide, the water apparently flowing at six feet a second, and the path down was steep, rocky and more than two miles long. In the event, the crossing was secured after forty-eight hours of fierce fighting – much of it at close range – and the use of bamboo rafts and a large pontoon bridge that had been constructed by army engineers.[10] The cost in lives was high: the Nationalists gleefully reported that 'those who fell into the water were countless', and somewhere between five hundred and two thousand Red Army soldiers were killed or taken prisoner.[11] But, by early on 4 January, the battle had been won. As the rest of the Red Army made its way across the Wu, the Sixth Regiment of the Second Division was ordered to press on and take Zunyi by storm.[12]

With the town guarded by a three-thousand-strong garrison, the success of the Red troops, who numbered only a third of that, was, on paper at least, far from guaranteed. Fortunately, though, at a village about ten miles outside Zunyi, the Communists deployed a classic pincer movement to capture an entire enemy battalion. (Crucially, no one escaped to warn the city's commanders of the impending advance.) Commissar Wang Jicheng explained how 'we lopped off the feelers of the enemy at Zunyi. Or rather, we turned them into our feelers. From among the prisoners we picked a company commander, a platoon leader and about a dozen soldiers who came of poor families, and asked them at length about the enemy's defenses.' A potent combination of party propaganda, the odd threat and a bribe of three silver dollars a man proved more than enough to turn the enemy. Soon they were divulging details of the city's fortifications, defensive lines and troop strength, and expressing surprise that the ruthless 'red-nosed' bandits they had been warned about were 'so nice'. With the key intelligence procured, Wang now hit upon the idea of entering the city via subterfuge: the men of Third Company, together with the thirty or so regimental buglers, would dress as enemy troops and, accompanied by the prisoners-of-war who had proved to be such cooperative interrogees, attempt to enter the city without firing a shot.[13]

It worked a treat.

Just before midnight, after a two-hour march through the pouring rain, the Communist troops and their new allies reached the outskirts of Zunyi. Approaching the city walls, they 'immediately started kicking up a din' and behaved as though they were 'running helter-skelter from some enemy in hot pursuit'. Commissar Wang described what happened next:

'Who goes there?' an angry voice challenged us from the gate-tower and we heard someone click his rifle-bolt.

'Friends. Your own men!' our captives calmly replied in the local dialect.

'What unit?'

This time our captive commander made his answer as we had arranged beforehand.

'The battalion stationed on the city outskirts,' he whined.

'Today the Communist bandits surrounded us. We lost the village – battalion commander killed. We're First Company. I'm in command – what's left of us. The bandits are after us. Open up. Let us in!'

After scanning the group with flashlights (all that could be made out were mud-covered figures in Guomindang caps), an officer – evidently grumpy at being awoken by all the commotion – ordered the gate open. The Reds, Wang explained, 'could hardly keep from laughing. Silently we fixed bayonets, held our rifles at the ready and waited anxiously for them to open the gate to welcome "their own men".'

Within moments, the bolts of the gate were being pulled back. 'Are the Communist bandits across the Wu?' asked a nervous guard. 'They are pretty fast, aren't they?' 'They are that,' declared one of the Red Army scouts, boldly, 'and now they've entered Zunyi. Listen, you! We are the Workers' and Peasants' Red Army of China!' Flooding through the gate, the Red soldiers immediately set about cutting the telegraph wires, disarming the guards and overpowering the town's surprised defenders. The Red forces 'streaked into the city like lightning', Wang recalled, and in moments the whole place was seething:

> The blare of the bugles mixed with the chattering of machine guns and rifles stirred the hearts of everyone who heard them. Everywhere we could hear the shouting of our brave soldiers as they pounced upon the enemy and the cries of the enemy trying to escape. We took the greater part of the garrison prisoner – many of them had just tumbled out of bed and hardly had time to put any clothes on. Only a few managed to escape through the north gate.[14]

By dawn on 7 January, the city had been captured; two days later, the Military Council and senior Communist Party leadership arrived. After halting outside the walls to brush the mud from their uniforms, they made a ceremonial entrance. As crowds lined the streets, and with red flags and propaganda banners hanging from the buildings, the Red Army soldiers struck up a favourite marching song – 'The Three Main Rules of Discipline and the Eight Points for Attention':

The rules:
Obey orders in all your actions.
Don't take a needle or a piece of thread from the people.
Turn in everything you capture.
The points of attention:
Speak politely.
Pay fairly for what you buy.

Return everything you borrow.
Pay for any damage.
Don't strike or swear at people.
Don't damage the crops.
Don't take liberties with women.
Don't mistreat captives.

While members of the women's work team set about collecting grain, recruiting soldiers, restructuring the local government and, as one of them put it, spreading 'propaganda among the masses', the Military Commission promptly established its headquarters in the 'liberated' home of Bai Huizhang, a merchant and local warlord. This imposing two-storey house, with its colonnaded veranda and wraparound balcony, was the finest in town. It made for an appropriately grand setting, then, for what one historian has described as 'the most important meeting' in the Politburo's history.[15]

Among the eighteen men who gathered after supper on the evening of 15 January were party leader Bo Gu, Zhou Enlai, Zhu De, Zhang Wentian, Wang Jiaxiang, Mao Zedong, Otto Braun and Red Army generals Lin Biao and Peng Dehuai.[16] The purpose of the meeting was to review recent events, establish what had gone wrong and agree on a way forward.[17] Writing about the so-called Zunyi Conference some three decades later, Braun claimed that 'it was obvious that Mao wanted revenge' for the earlier removal of his military and political power. Now, Braun explained, 'there emerged the possibility . . . that, by demagogic exploitation of isolated organizational and tactical mistakes, but especially through concocted claims and slanderous imputations, he could discredit the Party leadership . . . rehabilitate himself completely, [and] take the Army firmly into his grasp, thereby subordinating the Party itself to his will.'[18]

Bo Gu, who chaired the meeting, spoke first. Understandably, perhaps, he took a defensive position: stressing the difficulties the

Red Army had faced during the Fifth Encirclement Campaign, he emphasised the numerical advantages of the Nationalists, their superior firepower and the critical assistance (including financial support) that they had received from the 'imperialist' powers. The 'overall political and military line' that the leadership had adopted had, he asserted, been 'generally correct'.[19] Zhou Enlai, general political commissar of the Red Army, went next. Although he, too, argued that the basic strategy had been sound, he proved more willing to acknowledge errors – notably the tactic of 'fighting fortifications with fortifications' – and appeared prepared to accept a share of the blame.[20]

The next morning, Mao took the floor. In his memoirs, Braun described how the Chairman uncharacteristically 'made use of a painstakingly prepared manuscript' as he unleashed a volley of criticism against Bo and Braun for having 'waged positional warfare instead of a war of movement' in their attempt to 'check the enemy offensive' rather than, as Mao had advocated, adopting the flexible guerrilla tactics that had secured their earlier victories against the Nationalists. While Braun was singled out for his 'rude method of leadership' (his bullying, authoritarian style was widely resented), Bo was assigned most of the blame for the failure to 'exert adequate leadership' and correct the errors in military strategy. Sitting in his corner, chain-smoking furiously, Braun was seething. Although he later claimed to have remained silent throughout the meeting, other participants recall how, eventually, he defended himself as a mere 'adviser',* pointing out that the native Chinese leadership were ultimately responsible for their decisions.[21]

After Mao came Wang Jiaxiang. Everyone in the room knew that he was going to support the Chairman, who had been assiduously courting his support for weeks. Significantly, his tirade against Braun was followed up by further attacks on the leadership by Zhang and General Peng Dehuai, who, referencing the bitter loss of the Jiangxi base, derided Braun as 'a prodigal son, who has squandered his father's

---

* While true up to a point, this defence did not fully reflect the authority and influence that derived from being an official representative of the Comintern.

goods'. By the time Zhou Enlai took to the floor to make a second speech in which he engaged in lengthy self-criticism and accepted that the military strategy that had been adopted was 'fundamentally incorrect', it was clear that the game was up. The so-called 'troika' – the three-man military leadership of Bo, Zhou and Braun – was disbanded, and military command was placed in the hands of Zhou* and Zhu De; Mao was elected to the standing committee of the Politburo, and appointed Zhou's chief military adviser. Within weeks, Bo had been replaced as party leader by Mao's ally Zhang Wentian. And when, in March, a front headquarters was re-established, Zhu was appointed commander-in-chief, with Mao as political commissar.[22]

The Chairman was back.

* Although Zhou had been intimately connected with the military strategy adopted during the Fifth Encirclement Campaign, Mao – recognising the status and power that his chief rival still had – cleverly directed his criticisms against Bo and Braun, thereby offering Zhou a way to extricate himself and subtly switch his support. It was an offer that Zhou seized.

19. THE BRIDGE OF CHAINS

Victory was life, defeat was certain death.
– PENG DEHUAI

The Zunyi Conference might have confirmed that Mao's political fortunes were on the rise once more, but his plan to establish a new base in northern Guizhou was, it turned out, already dead in the water. On the very day that Mao and the other Communist leaders had entered Zunyi, crack Guomindang soldiers had occupied the provincial capital, Guiyang. Moreover, additional forces – perhaps as many as four hundred thousand – were being mobilised by Chiang in an effort to finish off the Red Army once and for all. It was also abundantly clear that, in economic terms, northern Guizhou was simply too poor to support a growing Red Army with some five thousand new recruits. Even the geography conspired against them: the Wu, Red and Yangtze rivers meant that to stay risked easy encirclement.[1]

Time, then, for yet another change of plan.

On the morning of Saturday 19 January 1935, with warlord armies now menacing from the south, the Red Army departed from Zunyi. Their eventual goal, it seems, was to unite with the Fourth Front Army of Zhang Guotao, a co-founder of the Chinese Communist Party who had established a successful soviet base in north-west Sichuan a couple of years earlier. Harried by enemy forces on all sides, the going was tough. At the end of January, an attempt to cross the upper reaches of the Yangtze almost turned into a rout: three thousand men were lost, and the army was forced to retreat.[2] It was during these chaotic days that He Zizhen gave birth to a baby girl. Knowing full well that it would be impossible to take the baby with her, it was a moment that she had been dreading. Qian Xijun, a political organiser and the wife of Mao's younger brother Mao Zemin, explained how, shortly after the birth, she carried the unnamed infant into the mountains to 'find someone to take care of her'. 'We looked and looked,' she explained, 'but there were very few around. Some had run away, some wouldn't open their doors.' Eventually, Qian found 'an old, blind lady, fifty or sixty years old'. Given ten silver dollars and told that she could raise the baby as her own, the old lady reluctantly agreed to take her.[3] Neither Mao nor He Zizhen would ever see the child again.

It was not until the end of February that the Communists' luck finally turned. By prevailing in the Battle of Loushan Pass they were able to retake Zunyi and, in the process, capture three thousand prisoners and destroy two crack Guomindang divisions. Mao – who must have been both exultant and enormously relieved – penned what one biographer has described as 'one of his loveliest poems'[4] in response to this triumph:

> Fierce the west wind,
> Wild geese cry under the frosty morning moon.
> Under the frosty morning moon
> Horses' hooves clattering,
> Bugles sobbing low.
>
> Idle boast the strong pass is a wall of iron,
> With firm strides we are crossing its summit.
> We are crossing its summit,
> The rolling hills sea-blue,
> The dying sun blood-red.[5]

That spring, Mao and the Red Army wove across Guizhou and Yunnan, crossing the Red River four times, before swinging south, passing within a few miles of Guiyang, where Chiang had established his provisional headquarters. From there they headed south-west, where they briefly menaced the key city of Kunming. Mao's forces then abruptly turned north, crossing the Golden Sands River in early May before setting up camp just outside the walled city of Huili* in Sichuan's far south. Mao might well have viewed the whole operation as the proudest achievement of his military career, but not everyone was convinced.[6] The feints and counter-feints were, after all, gruelling stuff. Otto Braun – admittedly no neutral observer – recalled that, such was the tiredness, not even the sound of bombs falling nearby could wake him up. On one occasion, he even fell asleep while marching and walked straight into a stream, only waking when immersed in the freezing water.[7] As deaths from disease and exhaustion began to mount, and morale began to waver, some even began to wonder out loud whether the troops were being exhausted to no good or obvious end.

It was against this backdrop that, as they caught their breath at Huili, one Red Army commander – the twenty-seven-year-old Lin Biao – now suggested that the Chairman be removed from operational command. Mao was incredulous: 'You're nothing but a baby!' he responded. 'What the hell do you know? Can't you see it was necessary for us to march along the curve of the bow?' With both Zhu De and Zhou Enlai firmly behind Mao, the challenge was quickly snuffed out. And, at yet another meeting of the Politburo, the comrades reaffirmed their support for marching due north, and a rendezvous with Zhang in northern Sichuan.[8]

Over the coming weeks, the Red Army would, in the words of one historian, 'perform feats of courage and endurance of which epics are made, weaving a dense myth of invisibility and heroism that their Nationalist opponents would try in vain to unravel'.[9] Their first major challenge, having made their way from Huili into 'broken, high plateau country, never lower than six thousand feet, where the hillsides were ablaze with Tibetan roses, pink and yellow oleander, azaleas, [and] rhododendrons', was to navigate the land of the Yi.[10] A fierce, aboriginal hill-people of Sino-Burmese origin, the Yi had a long-standing antipathy towards any Han encroacher. Determined to beat

* An attempt by the Red Army to take the city, which was defended by high, impregnable stone walls, failed.

Chiang's Nationalist troops to the strategically important Dadu river, Mao and the other Red Army leaders were now desperate to avoid getting bogged down in running battles with the Yi. They therefore resorted to bribery, emphasised their support for autonomy for all of China's minorities, and even pledged a blood oath, in an attempt to pass through the territory unmolested.[11] The oath, which was sworn by Liu Bocheng, the Red Army's chief of staff, and Xiao Yedan, a Yi tribal chief, took place next to a lake in the small mountain valley. There, the beak of a 'huge, majestic-looking cock' was broken, and the fresh blood sprinkled into bowls of clear, fresh water. Kneeling at the shore, Liu – the 'One-Eyed Dragon'* – now proclaimed that he was 'willing to become a sworn brother of Xiao Yedan'. 'If I ever violate this oath,' he continued, 'Heaven will kill me and the Earth destroy me!' Lifting the bowl to his lips, he drained it 'at one gulp'.[12] Although some stragglers were picked off – stripped of their clothes and their weapons and left to perish in the woods – most of Liu's troops made it through the area without incident. By the early hours of 24 May, the Red Army had reached the bluffs above the Dadu.[13]

Now all they had to do was make it across.

The Dadu, a powerful river whose source flows from high up in the Himalayas, was both spectacularly beautiful and – with its whirlpools, large rocks, steep banks and dangerous currents – fiendishly difficult to cross. The original plan was to cross at the little village of Anshunchang, where there was a ferry. This had to be abandoned when it was discovered that there were only three small boats available. Conscious that Nationalist troops were racing to secure the crossing points, Mao ordered the elite Fourth Regiment, commanded by Yang Dengwu, to race to a crossing point at Luding, a hundred miles upstream. Their route took them via a treacherous path that, Yang recalled, 'twisted like a sheep's gut around the mountains'. Battling

* He had lost the sight of one eye during battle.

the elements, Guomindang soldiers and the harsh physical terrain, the troops pushed on relentlessly. Dropping their heavy equipment and breaking into a jog, they covered the final seventy miles in just twenty-four hours.[14]

As dawn broke on Wednesday 29 May, Yang surveyed the scene. At the best of times the Luding Bridge – an iron-chain suspension structure, 120 yards long and built in 1701 – was a less than enticing prospect. As one American traveller described it, when visiting in 1908:

The thirteen chains provide side supports as well as those for the bridge floor, but when one notes the open spaces, the irregularly laid planking of the flooring, the infrequent palings connecting the side chains, and the general airiness of the whole construction hanging so jauntily over wild and swirling water, one cannot help but feel that the bridge is sketchily built.[15]

Now, Yang noted, the Nationalist troops had removed the planks on the western side, leaving the chains swinging free. At the eastern end, meanwhile, a machine-gun post had been mounted on the gatehouse, and the town was defended by as many as two hundred soldiers. In his 1935 account, based on the first-hand testimony of those who were there, the American journalist Edgar Snow explained how, just before four o'clock that afternoon, some two dozen volunteers stepped forward to lead the assault. With hand grenades and Mausers strapped to their backs, they were soon:

swinging out above the boiling river, moving hand over hand, clinging to the iron chains. Red machine guns barked at the enemy redoubts and spattered the bridgehead with bullets. The enemy replied with machine-gunning of its own, and snipers shot at the Reds tossing high above the water, working slowly towards them. The first warrior was hit, and dropped into the current below; a second fell, and then a third. But, as others drew nearer the center, the bridge flooring somewhat protected these dare-to-dies, and most of the enemy bullets glanced off, or ended in the cliffs on the opposite bank.

The enemy soldiers, Snow speculated, had probably never before encountered 'fighters like these – men for whom soldiering was not just a rice bowl, and youths ready to commit suicide to win. Were they human beings or madmen or gods?' In desperation, the bridge's defenders tossed paraffin onto the remaining planks and set them alight. But it was too late: 'By then about twenty Reds were moving forward on their hands and knees, tossing grenade after grenade into the enemy machine-gun nest.' As the climactic battle unfolded, great shouts of joy began to ring out from the western bank of the river: 'Long Live the Red Army!'; 'Long Live the Revolution!'; 'Long Live the Heroes of Dadu Ho!' With the panicking enemy forces in full flight, Red Army soldiers began to swarm over the bridge; within the hour, the crossing had been secured. In the skies overhead, Chiang's planes roared 'angrily and impotently', and the Reds 'cried out in delirious challenge to them'.[*][16]

From Luding, the Red Army continued north, marching through the Great Snow Mountains to avoid being ambushed by Chiang's armies.[17] Mao's bodyguard, Chen Chang-Feng, described how the peak of Jiajin Mountain 'pierced the sky like a sword point glittering in the sunlight. Its whole mass sparkled as if decorated with myriad glittering mirrors'

* That, at least, is the story as handed down by the Chinese Communist Party over the decades. In recent years, historians have cast doubt on at least some aspects of the narrative. Although few would agree with Jung Chang and Jon Halliday, who claimed in their controversial 2005 book *Mao: The Unknown Story* that 'there was no battle at the Dadu Bridge', there is a growing consensus that the bridge was relatively lightly defended – by poorly motivated and poorly armed warlord troops, most of whom fled in the face of the Red Army – and that claims that the battle was the most important of the entire Long March were overblown. See, for example, Sun Shuyun, *The Long March: The True History of Communist China's Founding Myth* (New York: Anchor Books, 2008), 140–8, and Ed Jocelyn and Andrew McEwen, *The Long March: The True Story Behind the Legendary Journey That Made Mao's China* (London: Constable, 2006), 247–55.

Zhou Enlai, Mao Zedong and Zhu De during the Long March. The gruelling year-long ordeal had, Mao declared, 'proclaimed to the world that the Red Army' was an army of 'heroes'.

and 'its brightness dazzled your eyes.' With snow clouds occasionally forming around the peak, it made for 'an unearthly, fairyland sight'.[18] But the series of fourteen-thousand-foot passes posed one of the hardest, and cruellest, ordeals of the Long March. The soldiers, wearing straw sandals and shirts, desperately short of food and with only ginger and chilli to ward off the cold, were woefully underprepared. Mao's ally Dong Biwu described how:

> We started out at early dawn. There was no path at all, but peasants said that tribesman come over the mountains on raids, and we could cross if they could. So we started straight up the mountain, heading for a pass near the summit. Heavy fogs swirled around us, there was a high wind, and halfway up it began to rain. As we climbed higher and higher we were caught in a terrible hailstorm

and the air became so thin that we could hardly breathe at all. Speech was completely impossible and the cold so dreadful that our hands and lips turned blue. Men and animals staggered and fell into chasms and disappeared forever. Those who sat down to rest or to relieve themselves froze to death on the spot.[19]

Exhausted, and now down to just ten thousand men, Mao's forward forces finally met up with soldiers from Zhang Guotao's Fourth Army near the little village of Dawei, just twenty-five miles from the foot of Jiajin Mountain, in Sichuan province. It was Wednesday 12 June. On uniting with their comrades, one soldier recalled, 'We embraced, we sang and wept.' For the Chairman, though, this was a moment of great peril. Zhang commanded a much larger force, perhaps as many as seventy thousand strong, and his troops were well provisioned, familiar with the local terrain and nicely rested. Zhang, moreover, was one of the few party leaders able to go toe-to-toe with Mao on matters of both political and military strategy. In short, he was now the single greatest threat to the Chairman's political pre-eminence. At a banquet held to celebrate the union of the two armies in the village of Lianghekou, on the evening of 25 June, one comrade reported how Mao, 'a Hunanese, who was fond of chili, made chili-eating the topic of merry conversation, discoursing at length on the theme that chili-eaters were revolutionaries . . . Such talk was fun and helped create an atmosphere of light-heartedness.' The atmosphere of relaxed bonhomie, however, was not to last. Soon enough, the two men's personal rivalry – and the question of how to balance out military power, where Zhang had the upper hand, and political power, where Mao enjoyed the support of the central leadership and the Politburo – spilled over into debates about the ultimate destination of the march. Mao was by now committed to establishing a new soviet base in Gansu–Shaanxi (not least because it would add credence to his propaganda claim that the Communists were preparing to take the fight to the hated Japanese, who had occupied Manchuria in 1931). Zhang, in contrast, favoured heading west, towards Xinjiang, where contact with the USSR would be easier, or establishing a permanent base in the Sichuan–Xikang border area, where his forces had already secured a foothold. From 26–29 June, the Politburo met in Lianghekou's old monastery – its walls 'black with the smoke of Yak's butter' from the monks' lamps – to thrash things out. When it was over, Mao seemed to have prevailed: Zhang, appointed vice chairman of the Military Commission, had agreed, albeit reluctantly, with the plan to march north.

Almost immediately, the compromise began to unravel. In July, Zhang appears to have deliberately sabotaged an effort to take the garrison town of Songpan, a hundred miles north, which controlled the main pass to Gansu. Then, in August, Mao's First Front Red Army made its way through the treacherous grasslands of Sichuan, close to the Tibetan border, alone. Floods, Zhang claimed, prevented his army from advancing any further north. Despite several entreaties from his comrades to change course and join them, he refused, and instead headed south, to set up a base in western Sichuan.[*][20]

The grasslands – a 'vast and trackless swamp' that stretched across five thousand square miles along China's border with Tibet – provided the Long Marchers with a last major hazard.[21] In *The Great Road*, her magisterial biography of Zhu De, the American journalist Agnes Smedley drew on prodigious research and interviews with key participants in the Long March to paint a vivid picture of the terrain. She described how:

As far as the eye can reach, day after day, the Red Army saw nothing but an endless ocean of high wild grass growing in an icy swamp of black muck and water many feet deep. Huge clumps of grass grew on dead clumps beneath them, and so it had been for no man knows how many centuries. No tree or shrub grew here, no bird ventured near, no insect sounded. There was not even a stone. There

* This proved to be a fatal mistake. Zhang's Fourth Front Army was virtually wiped out by Nationalist troops; the shattered remnants eventually reunited with Mao, in Shaanxi, in 1936, by which time Zhang's challenge to the Chairman had long since evaporated.

was nothing, nothing but endless stretches of wild grass swept by torrential rains in summer and fierce winds and snows in winter. Heavy black and gray clouds drifted forever above, turning the earth into a dull, somber netherworld.[22]

It was into this desolate landscape that the Red Army troops now advanced. It must have made for an incongruous sight as the soldiers, dressed in an array of mismatched uniforms with blankets flung around their shoulders, linked hands, and inched their way forward in long lines.[23] It was a route fraught with hazard. Otto Braun explained how:

> A deceptive green cover hid a black viscous swamp, which sucked in anyone who broke through the thin crust or strayed from the narrow path. I myself witnessed the wretched death of a mule in this fashion. We drove native cattle or horses before us which instinctively found the least dangerous way. Grey clouds almost always hung just over the ground. Cold rain fell several times a day, at night it turned to wet snow or sleet. There was not a dwelling, tree, or shrub as far as the eye could see. We slept in squatting positions on the small hills which rose over the moor. Thin blankets and large straw hats, oil-paper umbrellas or, in some cases, stolen capes, were our only protection. Some did not awaken in the morning, victims of cold and exhaustion. And this was the middle of August! Our sole nourishment came from the grain kernels we had hoarded or, as a rare and special treat, a morsel of stone-hard dried meat. The swamp water was not fit to drink. Still it was drunk, for there was no wood to purify it by boiling. Outbreaks of bloody dysentery and typhus . . . again won the upper hand.

The only consolation, Braun noted, was that 'the enemy could attack us neither from the air nor on land.'[24]

The First Front Red Army lost about as many men in the grasslands as they had in crossing the Great Snow Mountains. Yet, remarkably, they were able to win one final battle – the last, as it turned out, of the Long March – when a twenty-man commando unit successfully stormed the heavily defended Lazikou Pass. It was a victory that opened up the road east, to Shaanxi, in China's far north-west.[25]

The final six hundred miles took the marchers, by now just a few thousand in number, across a barren, lunarlike landscape, marked by towering conical hills of fine, light-brown soil carved into high terraces like wedding cakes, and vast ravines that plunged hundreds of feet down into the wide, flat-bottomed canyons below.[26] Although they were harassed by local cavalry units, the threat was minimal. As Mao quipped to his bodyguard, Chen, 'They wouldn't dare to fight when they know it's the Chinese Workers' and Peasants' Red Army. They are only "expert" in running away!' Standing atop the ridge that marked the border between Gansu and Shaanxi on 20 October, Mao was in high spirits: 'We have crossed ten provinces already,' he said. 'When we go down this mountain, we'll be in the eleventh – Shaanxi. That's our base area – our home!'

Two days later, they reached the little town of Wuqizhen, just 150 kilometres or so west of Yan'an. While the troops enjoyed a well-deserved rest, Mao headed on to Xiasiwan, where the headquarters of the provincial soviet was based. According to Chen, 'large snowflakes were falling when we set out' but 'nobody felt the cold as we trudged over the rough mountain paths.' Arriving at dusk, they 'heard the beating of gongs and drums and the noise of a crowd of people' who, on catching sight of the Chairman, cheered wildly. Then, amid 'a tremendous din of gongs and drums, the crowd rushed up, waving small red and green banners bearing the words: *Welcome Chairman Mao! Welcome the Central Red Army!*' Standing tall and wearing the battered overcoat he had brought with him from Jiangxi, Mao nodded his head and waved repeatedly at the crowd as cheers of 'Welcome Chairman Mao!' and 'We've won through! We've won through!' rang out.

Finally, the Long March was over.[27]

*

By almost every measure, the Long March was epic. Over the course of a year, some six thousand miles were covered, at an average rate of seventeen miles per day. The route, which took in eleven provinces, involved the crossing of twenty-four major rivers and eighteen mountain ranges. Some sixty towns and cities were taken or occupied by the First Front Red Army, and more than a dozen major battles were fought. As well as an almost unimaginable triumph of human perseverance, determination, endurance and courage, the Long March was also a staggeringly catastrophic military defeat: not only had the vital Jiangxi base been lost but, of the ninety thousand Red Army soldiers who had set out in October 1934, barely five thousand made it to Shaanxi. The Reds, it seemed, were finished.[28]

Mao, who was soon busy rebuilding the Red Army and establishing the new soviet base in Shaanxi, had other ideas, of course. Writing that December, he declared the Long March to have been 'unprecedented in the annals of history'. 'Since the time when Pan Gu* divided the heavens from the earth,' he asked, 'has history ever witnessed such a Long March as ours?' After all, Mao continued, 'for a period of twelve months we were subject to daily reconnaissance and bombing from the skies by scores of planes, and on the ground to encirclement and pursuit, obstruction and interception, by a huge force of hundreds of thousands.' The Long March, he asserted, was a manifesto that had 'proclaimed to the world that the Red Army is made up of brave heroes, whereas the imperialists and their running dogs, Chiang Kai-shek and his ilk, are utterly useless. The Long March proclaimed the total failure of imperialism . . . in encircling, pursuing, obstructing, and intercepting us.' The Long March was, moreover, 'a propaganda team. It has announced to some 200 million people in eleven provinces that the road of the Red Army is their only road to liberation. If it were not for this undertaking, how would the broad popular masses have learned so quickly about the existence of the great truth embodied by

* In Chinese mythology, Stuart R. Schram has explained, Pan Gu was the 'earliest being brought into existence, who set the universe in order and constructed the world'.

the Red Army?' Finally, Mao argued, the Long March had 'sown many seeds that will sprout, leaf, blossom, and bear fruit, and eventually will yield a harvest . . . the Long March has ended with victory for us and defeat for the enemy.'[29]

In the end it was the heroic version of the Long March – a story for the ages that emphasised survival, against-the-odds triumph and derring-do – that would prevail.[30] Mao might well have been correct to claim, in the winter of 1935, that the march 'would have been inconceivable' without the Communist Party, whose 'leading organs, its cadres, and its members fear no difficulties or hardships'.[31] But, as it turned out, the creation of the Long March of legend owed much to a talented former advertising executive from the American Midwest: Edgar Parks Snow.

EDGAR SNOW

Edgar Snow, in Shaanxi, wearing the Red Army cap that
was gifted to him on arrival in Red territory.

20. RED CHINA BECKONS

Intensely excited by the prospect that lay ahead, I was aware,
as I took the express for Xi'an, that I was crossing a Rubicon.
For once I was absolutely right.
– EDGAR SNOW

On Monday 1 June 1936, Edgar Snow wrote from Beijing to L. M. McBride, his editor at London's *Daily Herald* newspaper, informing him that he was planning a trip to China's north-west to 'visit the scene of warfare between the Chinese Reds and the government troops'. In truth, an informal truce – agreed to forge a united front against the Japanese – meant there had been little in the way of warfare for several months. But Snow had a much bigger prize in sight. He had, he explained, 'been assured, by men in whose word I place confidence, that it might be possible for me even to enter into the Red districts of Shaanxi and Gansu, and interview important Communists, including Mao Zedong, the Lenin of China'.

'I do not know', he continued, 'whether you fully realize how extraordinary the material from such a trip might prove to be.' For the past decade, the Red Army had been engaged in a near-constant battle with the military forces of the national government in Nanjing. And yet, Snow explained, 'in all the years that the Reds have been in action no foreign newspaperman has penetrated a Red-controlled region.' There were 'no first-hand accounts of conditions in the Soviet areas' and 'no interviews with any of the famous Red leaders . . . have been published.' 'If I succeed,' Snow declared, 'it will be a world scoop on a situation about which millions of words have been written, based only on hearsay and highly colored government reports.'[1]

A couple of days later, 'Ed packed up his sleeping bag, his Camel cigarettes, his Gillette razor blades, and a can of Maxwell House coffee – his indispensable artifacts of Western civilization,' recalled his wife,

Helen Foster. Still feverish following a last-minute flurry of inoculations, and with his cameras slung casually around his neck, he bade farewell to his dogs and the servants who lined up at the gate, before departing for the railway station at midnight. 'Overhead were the immense desert stars and a crescent moon,' Helen wrote, and 'we were silent, except for the slow pad-pad of the jogging rickshamen.' Arriving at the railway station with little time to spare, Snow clambered aboard the express train for Xi'an, two days away. Standing on the steps, 'grinning as if he were Caesar at one of his triumphs', he offered a final mock-salute to his wife, before the hissing, wheezing locomotive inched off into the night.[2] They would not see each other again for five months.

Edgar Parks Snow was born in the Midwestern rail hub of Kansas City, Missouri, on 19 July 1905, the youngest of three children to James Edgar Snow and Anna Catherine Edelman. His father had used savings accumulated while working for a livestock company to purchase a small printing business, and had a fierce work ethic and a strong independent streak. The paternal line on the family tree was rooted deeply in the American past – a great-great-great-grandfather had fought in the Revolutionary War. Ed's mother, though, was a second-generation immigrant of Irish and German stock, and – controversially, given the Snow family's staunchly Protestant lineage – a devout Catholic.[3]

Although he had other interests – the Eagle Scouts, jazz (he played the drums and the saxophone) and the novels of Mark Twain – Ed displayed an early enthusiasm for the world of journalism. When dropping off packages for his father at the imposing red-brick offices of the *Kansas City Star*, he would chat animatedly to the journalists in the newsroom; at high school he founded a newspaper, *The Delt* (named for his Delta Omicron Omicron fraternity); and, during a year at junior college, he worked on the school paper.[4] Snow also had a strong sense of wanderlust, and was keen to explore the world beyond the American Midwest. In the summer of 1922, he and two other boys took a road trip out west, as far as Los Angeles. When their Model T touring car eventually gave out, he jumped the rails back home. It was a formative experience: 'If I had not seen the Pacific that summer,' he later recalled, 'I might never have fixed so firmly in my mind the ambition to sail across it.' He also learned a powerful lesson in social justice. Arriving in Kansas, asleep on a flatbed truck, he was awoken by armed 'harvest bandits'. They stole just fifty cents from him (he had $5 hidden in a shoe), but 'looted more than a hundred migratory workers on the train of their entire summer's earnings'. 'To me,' Snow explained, 'they were the meanest kind of thieves, robbing the poor,' and 'I realized that under these circumstances I would shoot a man if I could.'[5]

In the autumn of 1925 – after a few months living with his older brother, Howard, in New York – Ed enrolled at the University of Missouri to study journalism (working for a time as campus correspondent for the *Star*). But, after just a year, he was back on the East Coast. Renting an apartment with his brother on West 55th Street, he took a low-level job at Scovil Brothers & Company, a New York advertising firm. After winning an international letter-writing competition, he considered a career as an author or independent writer. But when, towards the end of 1927, a modest investment on Wall Street yielded him the princely sum of $800 (the equivalent of about $13,500 today), his mind was set: he would quit his job and spend a year travelling the world.[6]

In a letter written to his parents in February 1928, shortly before he left New York, Ed outlined his motivations. He had, he explained, 'been somewhat depressed by the monotony of existence and the thought that I labored, a cog in a gargantuan machine, while youth, life, was slipping by'. He noted his strong desire for 'Adventure! Experience! I wanted to overcome difficulties – physical hardships – and enjoy the tokens of my triumph! I wished to know peril and danger!'[7] Snow's plan was to 'return to New York after the year, make a fortune before I was thirty, and devote the rest of my life to leisurely study and writing'.[8]

CHINA

The SS *Radnor* departed from Brooklyn Pier on Friday 24 February. Aboard the merchant ship were two newly appointed deckhands: Snow and Alvin Joslin – an old friend and fraternity brother from Kansas; the jobs had been secured after a personal appeal to Kermit Roosevelt, son of the former Republican president and founder of the Roosevelt Steamship Line. Two days later, the *Radnor* slipped her moorings at Newport News, Virginia, bound for Shanghai, with stops in Panama, Hawaii and the Philippines. Snow stood on the chilly deck, eager to catch the sunrise. 'I had a sensation', he wrote in his diary, 'of thrilling poignancy. This was the dawn of another life for me.' Ed loved life onboard ship – sandpapering, painting and sweeping in the mornings, and taking his turn at lookout in the evening, from the prow of the vessel. The *Radnor* finally arrived in Honolulu on 29 March. Her boilers had sprung a leak on the way, and when it became clear that the repairs would take six weeks, Snow and Joslin took advantage, setting out to explore the 'Paradise of the Pacific'. As well as driving around Waikiki, selling pineapple juice at a makeshift stand, swimming and attending a traditional luau, Snow penned what would be his first published article. 'In Hula Land' – which *Harper's* carried that September – earned its proud author $300. It was, noted his editor, 'a splendid article . . . you have found your literary stride.'[9]

After more than two months in Hawaii, and with the *Radnor* now long departed, Snow looked for alternative means to continue his journey. When a plan to work his passage to Japan aboard the *Yomachichi* came to nothing, Ed prevailed upon a new American acquaintance, Dan Crabb, who was booked onto the *Shinyo Maru*. Crabb's lavish first-class cabin was, it turned out, easily big enough to accommodate two and so on 12 June, with one Edgar Parks Snow safely stowed away onboard, the liner began its nine-day voyage to Yokohama, the port city just south of Tokyo. Sleeping on the sofa and waking early before the cabin boy came in to clean, Snow survived on Crabb's ham-and-eggs breakfasts (which were served in the room) before filling up on sandwiches during cocktail hour. He also used his wits, as well as a couple of carefully placed bribes, to evade detection.[10]

Arriving in Japan on the morning of Friday 22 June, Snow faced one final hurdle: although he had a passport, he did not have the required landing pass to go ashore. Salvation arrived in the form of a posse of journalists who had come aboard to cover the arrival of Setsuko Matsudaira, daughter of the Japanese ambassador to the United States, who was returning home to marry the emperor's second son, Prince Chichibu. With the support of an English reporter, Snow was encouraged to pass himself off as one of the journalists. Waving a sheaf of official-looking papers that he had been given, and confidently shouting out '*Japan Times*', he marched nonchalantly down the gangplank and straight past the waiting officials. Later that day, Snow and Crabb, along with the journalists, celebrated the triumph in Tokyo's American Club.[11]

Offered a job with the *Japan Advertiser* by one of his new friends, Ed decided instead to continue with his travels – and his freelance adventure-writing. After making his way down the coast to Kobe, by way of Fuji, Nagoya and Kyoto, Snow – accompanied by Crabb – travelled third class across the Seto Inland Sea, 'awash with green inlets and oddly rigged sailing vessels'. Then, from Nagasaki, they set sail for China.[12]

On 6 July 1928, Snow arrived in Shanghai, a city that embodied the West's economic and political presence in – and ruthless exploitation of – China. Following the granting of concessions in the mid-nineteenth century, a separate Western city had mushroomed at the edge of the old walled town, located on the western bank of the Huangpu river. The result was that China's centre of banking, commerce, industry and foreign trade was divided into three distinct areas: the International Settlement (run by a council made up of British, American and Japanese members); a French Concession; and the much larger Chinese area. In addition to fifty thousand foreign nationals, and significant numbers of refugees from the Russian Empire, the city was home to some three million Chinese citizens (half of whom lived in the foreign-administered areas of the city), who were packed into overcrowded tenements, exploited by ruthless factory owners (both foreign and Chinese) and treated by most Europeans as second-class citizens in their own country.[13]

After the immense 'beauty' of Hawaii and the 'charm and order' of Japan, Snow initially thought that Shanghai 'looked anything but appetizing'. But, offered a position on the *China Weekly Review* by John Benjamin Powell (an alumnus of the University of Missouri), Snow decided with some reluctance to stay – at least for a few weeks.[14] The city, then Asia's largest, was, he explained, a 'vast, unkempt, exciting, primitive and sophisticated village', and he would later recall how the 'bizarre contrasts of very old and very new, the sublime ugliness of the place, its kind of polyglot glamor . . . and its frank money-is-all vulgarity held me in puzzled wonder'.[15]

Taking an apartment on Seymour Road, which he shared with future American diplomat John Allison, Snow soon found his bearings. His job, he quickly discovered, paid well: the monthly salary of 600 Chinese dollars, he told his mother, allowed him to 'become simply filthy with luxury out here on the fringes of the world'. Rent was negligible, transport cheap, while even the best meal at the American Club cost the equivalent of just thirty cents. Tailored suits were half as expensive as off-the-peg clothing back in America, and the Seymour Road apartment was soon being cleaned and catered for by two Chinese servants. It was, Snow recalled, all rather easy. Most of the hard graft in the office was undertaken by Chinese subordinates, and working hours were short. Lunch lasted for at least two hours and, after an hour back in the office, 'the average American or Englishman or Frenchman was ready to call it a day and go home or drop in at his club for a swim and a "peg" or two before his valet dressed him for dinner.'

It was the kind of life, Snow realised, that was not really for him.[16]

Gradually, towards the end of 1928, Snow began to broaden his horizons, visiting Nanjing in mid-October and, early the following year, travelling to Jinan – an important rail junction in the country's north-east that had been occupied by the Japanese under the pretext of protecting their foreign nationals.*[17] That April, he took a four-month railway journey across China, which the government had laid on to promote tourism. The eight-thousand-mile expedition saw Snow travel from the lower Yangtze Valley through central China, before heading north to Beijing, and onwards to Manchuria and Korea. In July, Ed insisted on taking the train as far as the southern edge of the Gobi Desert, an area of North-West China that was in the grip of a dreadful famine.[18] In a moving article, published in the *China Weekly Review* on 3 August, Snow recounted a visit to Saratsi, a city in Suiyuan† province that, in normal times, was home to four hundred and fifty thousand. Snow was profoundly shocked by what he encountered. Walking the city's desolate streets, he was met with near-apocalyptic scenes. 'For many blocks – seated in doorways, on curbstones where there were any, or on top of the wrecks of houses, or merely lying exhausted in the gutters . . . [were] men and women and children in the last reaches of starvation.' Having passed by three bodies, 'naked except for loin cloths, lying prone on the street', Snow then came across 'a picture that was surely the most heart-wrenching I have ever seen':

A little boy, scarcely six years old, sat beside an old man, either dead or in the last moment of earthly life. The child was thickly coated with dust and filth – and nothing else. He was pushing against his father's side . . . and with all the effort of his emaciated twisted young body, he was exhorting him to sit up, and to speak. I walked over to the spot, knelt down beside the child and put my hand on the old fellow's pulse. There was no response . . . Gently pulling the bewildered infant away from the body, we took him with us and I saw to it that at least one empty stomach was well fed that day.[19]

* Japan viewed Chinese unification as a threat to its own regional power, and its ongoing interests in Manchuria, and developed the so-called 'Strong China' policy in response.
† Suiyuan is today part of the Inner Mongolia Autonomous Region.

In the spring of 1930, Snow left the *Review* to take up the role of 'roving correspondent' for the Consolidated Press Association, a newly formed foreign service that would serve a dozen or so major American newspapers. Although the pay was nothing to write home about, the job promised freedom to study, and to travel.[20] When a planned trip to Turkestan, in the Soviet Union, fell through, Ed turned his attentions instead to the south, and an epic journey to India via Formosa (modern-day Taiwan), French Indochina (modern-day Vietnam), Yunnan, Tibet and Burma. Leaving Shanghai on Thursday 25 September, he reached Kunming, the capital of Yunnan province – known as 'the eaves of the foot of the world' – on 7 December. From there, Snow travelled through hundreds of miles of bandit country, by mule, before finally descending into Burma. After recovering from a bout of malaria, it was on to India, where he stayed for four months, before finally returning to Shanghai.[21] The trip, naturally, provided Snow with plenty of copy, but it also offered a political education. In Formosa he saw first-hand how the Japanese (who had occupied the island since 1895) were systematically eradicating the local culture. In Hanoi he learned something of the growing nationalist opposition to the French (a movement in which communists had a leading role).[22] And in Burma, where a peasant uprising was underway, he 'found the same discontent with alien rule and among youths the same rebellious spirit and yearning for national freedom that were rapidly infecting every Eastern colony'.[23] India, meanwhile, offered him the opportunity to meet, up close, two of the giants of the movement to cast off the British Raj. When it came to Gandhi's commitment to nonviolence, Snow was, for now at least, unconvinced, but he was taken with Nehru, who struck him as practical, realistic and above all dynamic.[24] As for China, Snow's experiences in Yunnan – where, it turned out, many government officials were on the make, even as the region's endemic poverty led thousands to sell their children into slavery – convinced him that a modern, progressive China was all but impossible under the Guomindang.[25]

*

Arriving back in Shanghai in August 1931, Snow barely had time to unpack before he was on the road yet again. In early September, he travelled up the Yangtze river, which, swollen by a series of extreme cyclones, had unleashed a catastrophic flood over an area of some sixty-nine thousand square miles. It was one of the great natural disasters of the twentieth century, affecting perhaps as many as fifty million people. Millions of homes were destroyed and vast areas of farmland submerged; some estimate that the floods claimed as many as four million lives.[26] Snow wrote movingly of the plight of the flood's victims, while also framing the disaster as the latest in a series of afflictions – corrupt tax officials, looting soldiers, roaming bandits and the warlords who, between them, had left the granaries and treasuries bare, and the peasants seething with resentment.[27]

By the time Snow's piece on the great flood appeared in the *New York Herald Tribune Sunday Magazine* in early December, China had been rocked by an even greater crisis. On 18 September 1931 – the day that Snow had arrived back in Shanghai from his trip up the Yangtze – the Japanese, using an explosion on the South Manchurian Railway as pretext, overwhelmed Chinese forces in Mukden (modern-day Shenyang), the ancient walled capital of Manchuria, and quickly seized control of the entire north-eastern province. In early November, Snow arrived in Manchuria as part of a small group of journalists. The fighting had now ended, but the signs of the recent battle were everywhere, not least in the frozen bodies of Chinese soldiers that littered the outskirts of the capital. Snow described the local resistance, in the face of overwhelming odds, as 'the most heroic thing I have seen in China'. In Mukden, he interviewed both the Japanese commander and the new puppet governor, who readily admitted to his impotence.[28] Privately, Snow suggested that 'such a phantasmagoria as existed in Manchuria under the name of government' had not deserved to survive. 'But,' he continued, 'the ethical problem still remains: has any nation the right to take over the land, property and government of another merely because the latter is hopelessly incompetent?'[29]

Ed would soon get to see the military clash between China and Japan up close.

By the start of 1932, Shanghai had become the centre of bitter anti-Japanese sentiment, with a widely observed boycott of Japanese goods and a series of unofficial strikes targeting Japanese-owned factories, and the city's bankers refusing to complete Japanese transactions. When, on 18 January, several Japanese monks were killed, the Japanese issued an ultimatum calling for an end to the boycott and the suppression of the anti-Japanese movement. Although the Chinese authorities eventually agreed – just hours before the deadline – it was pretty clear that Japan was spoiling for a fight. At midnight on Thursday 28 January, naval and marine forces attacked the city. Snow, who was travelling back from the railway station in the northern neighbourhood of Zhabei, later claimed to have seen the first Chinese soldier to fall in the battle. His scoop on the outbreak of hostilities made the front page of the *Chicago Daily News* and the *New York Sun*. Over the next month, Chinese forces put up fierce resistance, and, although they were eventually forced to retreat, the military defeat was, Snow claimed, 'an incredible spiritual victory'.[30] In his account of the war, *Far Eastern Front*, which was published by a small New York publishing house the following year, Ed declared that the Shanghai war 'stimulated in all classes, particularly in the youth both in and out of the army, a new manhood, self-reliance and self-respect, with an apparent determination to resist'.[31] This faith, that a China 'united in patriotic struggle' would, or could, be 'invincible', helped to create a political climate in which Chiang Kai-shek (who had moved his government away from the fighting) 'would finally have no choice but to compromise with his "first and worst enemy"' – the Communists – and 'join it against Japan'. 'It was that fact', Snow later wrote, 'which was to change the history of Asia in the most decisive way.'[32]

Amid the geopolitical turmoil, Snow was also building a domestic life: by the time his book was out, he had moved to Beijing, accompanied by his new wife, Helen Foster. The twenty-three-year-old aspiring journalist from Cedar City, Idaho – known to her friends as 'Peg' – had met Ed, whose work she admired, within days of arriving in Shanghai in the summer of 1931. Having hit it off over ice cream sodas at the Chocolate Shop, a favourite haunt of Americans in the city, they undertook a somewhat 'fitful courtship' (it was interrupted by, among other things, the Yangtze flood and the Japanese attack on Shanghai), before marrying on Christmas Day 1932, in the US embassy in Tokyo. In a private letter, written a few months after their first meeting, Helen confessed that she liked Ed 'better than anyone else I have ever known . . . and he really does seem to have a good deal of talent, and a wonderful adventuring spirit'. Ed, for his part, enthused that 'we believe or disbelieve in . . . the same things, have similar dreams, aspirations [and] hopes.' He also held her literary talent, as a poet as well as a journalist, in high regard.*

After a two-month honeymoon that took in Formosa, the East Indies, Singapore, Hong Kong and Macao, the newlyweds arrived in Beijing in early March 1933.[33] They lived in several places – including a villa on the outskirts of the city – before, in the summer of 1935, settling at 13 Kuijiachang, a large one-storey house on the corner of the old city walls, just down from the famous Fox Tower. The property featured a substantial conservatory, palatial rooms, a marble bathroom, stables and a tennis court. Rent came in at just $10 a month, and the Snows shared the staff of servants with the resident of the house's other wing, a Swedish geologist.[34] After the hustle and bustle of Shanghai, Beijing – which Snow described as 'the grandest and most interesting capital in Asia' – offered a slower and more relaxing pace of life. Like many foreigners (and indeed like Mao fifteen years earlier), the Snows were captivated by the city's great beauty. Its 'ancient temples and palaces with their rose-colored walls' conveyed 'a sense of classical antiquity', Ed wrote, while, from the top of the 'great Tartar Wall you could see vistas open through

* It was Ed who came up with her nom de plume, 'Nym Wales', which combined the Greek word for 'name' with a nod to her family's Welsh roots.

wide acacia-lined avenues around the Winter Palace, across the gold and purple roofs and parks, and the toy lakes mirroring constant azure skies'. The atmosphere struck Snow as 'friendly and intimate'. 'Everybody', he recalled, 'seemed to know everyone else.'[35]

In Beijing, Ed led a more scholarly kind of life. His friends included the young sinologists John and Wilma Fairbank and Owen and Eleanor Lattimore, the foreign correspondent F. McCracken Fisher and the iconoclastic French philosopher Pierre Teilhard de Chardin. Meanwhile the novelists John P. Marquand and Pearl S. Buck (whose 'rich and truly epic descriptions of peasant life in China' would, in 1938, win her the Nobel Prize in Literature) were regular visitors. Over the coming months, Snow began to learn Chinese and edited *Living China* – an English translation of contemporary Chinese short stories whose authors, often in hiding or in exile, shared a commitment to social justice and were critical of the Guomindang. Ed also worked intermittently on his long-planned, and much-delayed, Yunnan travel book, and taught journalism at Yenching, then one of the country's leading universities. It was a job that brought him and Helen into contact with a new generation of politically conscious students, fired by a recent influx of refugees from Manchuria. During visits to the Snows' home (which operated as a de facto safe house), the students borrowed banned books from Ed's growing library and helped with translation work. But inevitably talk would quickly turn to politics, notably the students' simmering frustrations over the Nationalists' repeated unwillingness to stand up to Japanese aggression. When, in late 1935, it seemed likely that Chiang would yet again capitulate – this time to demands to grant autonomy to an area just south of the Great Wall, which included Beijing – the students, with the active encouragement of both Ed and Helen, resolved to act.[36]

Just before dawn on Monday 9 December 1935, students began to gather at a dozen different gates and memorial arches across the city. From there, their columns moved towards the main streets, before uniting at the wide boulevard that led to the Winter Palace and the offices of the city's leading Guomindang official. Caught by surprise, the police initially made only half-hearted efforts to stop the protests, but when the 'political gendarmes, in black leather jackets . . . descended on the main column in motorcycles and sidecars with mounted machine-guns', things turned ugly. Pushing into the crowds, they 'indiscriminately clubbed boys and girls alike. Several dozen were arrested at random.' With a posse of foreign journalists on hand, cameras at the ready, offering a modicum of protection, the students pressed on – their spirits buoyed by the enthusiastic support of local shopkeepers, housewives and passers-by who stood on the streets applauding and shouting out 'Save China!' and 'Down with Japanese Imperialism!'[37] The demonstration made headlines around the world, achieved its immediate objective (spooked, the Nationalists called Japan's bluff) and sparked copycat actions in other major cities, including the capital, Nanjing.[38] Within months, a full-fledged student movement had emerged.[39] For Ed, the experience taught him that the 'total loss of confidence by educated youths in an existing regime' was an 'indispensable' precondition of revolution. The 'profound failure of the [Guomindang] to play any dynamic role of guidance or inspiration' during this critical period, he explained, 'made it a symbol of pessimism, stagnation and repression' and, in the fateful years that lay ahead, would drive 'hundreds of the ablest and most patriotic young men and women to the Red banners as China's last hope'.[40]

Snow had long been intrigued by the Chinese Communists and, during his lengthy travels around Asia, he had also seen first-hand the influence of local communist parties in the anticolonial struggles that were flaring across Burma, India and Indochina.[41] His political education had continued on his return to Shanghai in August 1931, when he grew close to Madame Sun Yat-sen (Soong Qingling), the widow of the Guomindang's legendary founder, Dr Sun. Supportive of the movement's left wing, which Chiang had set about obliterating, she lamented the corruption, incompetence and repression that increasingly characterised the Nationalist government. Her political sympathies, she explained, lay – as her late husband's had – with the poor. As for the Communist Party: it was, she told Snow, the sole authentically revolutionary force in the country. Through Madame Sun, Ed was also introduced to a wider coterie of left-wing sympathisers, writers and political activists, who encouraged him to further question the line, emanating from Nanjing, that the Communists were nothing more than 'Red bandits'.[42]

Alarmed by growing evidence of repression, including book-burnings, censorship and the political persecution of leftists, Snow became increasingly critical of Chiang. The Generalissimo was, he wrote in January 1934, no great statesman or military commander, but 'in some ways a mediocrity' whose 'traditional conservatism, strengthened by his acquisition of wealth and power, seems to have narrowed his social and political outlook'.[43] At the same time, Ed was willing to give the Communists a hearing. As he told his brother Howard in July 1935, 'the real revolution in China, just as anywhere else in the world, is tried only when every other means of resolving intolerable situations has been exhausted.' 'This revolution', he continued, 'is merely an expression of a historic need of the masses, too long suppressed, too long denied.'[44] Snow, who had seen something of their daily struggles up close, sympathised with China's rural poor: 'Peasants who call themselves Communists', he wrote to his father in early 1933, 'are in reality men who have been crushed, oppressed, robbed, bullied' and 'are at last in a revolt for freedom'.[45] A host of questions remained unanswered. Was China's Red Army a 'mass of conscious Marxist revolutionaries, disciplined by and adhering to a central program'? Who were the leaders? What did they believe in? How did the Chinese soviets operate? Who supported them and why? Did the great mass of those who rallied around the red banners amount to anything more than 'ignorant peasants blindly fighting for an existence'?[46] With one eye, as ever, on the next big story, Snow was itching to find out more.

The problem was that there was almost no reliable first-hand information available about the Communist movement. With the remote, Red-controlled areas either shut off or besieged by Chiang's forces, and the secret police bearing down on radicals in the cities, Western journalists were forced to piece together information taken from propaganda, second-hand accounts and snippets gleaned from activists from the urban underground.[47] As Snow explained, 'here was a story, growing in interest and importance every day; here was *the* story of China . . . Yet we were all woefully ignorant of it.' 'We all knew', he stated, 'that the only way to learn anything about Red China was to go there.' In late 1932, Snow had told his literary agent that he had almost succeeded in gaining the papers required to travel to a Red area, but at the last minute his contact had become suspicious and disappeared without trace. Then, in March 1934, a lull in the fighting seemed to offer the chance to travel to the Jiangxi Soviet – the largest and most important part of the Communist Party's incipient state. Snow received a $750 advance from his publisher for a book on 'Red China', to be completed by the end of the year. Within weeks of signing the contract, though, intense fighting had broken out again and, in the bloody aftermath of the Nationalists' Fifth Encirclement Campaign, the Long March was underway.[48] At the start of November, Snow wrote to his editor, lamenting that his plans for the book were 'fast dwindling'. He had spoken recently with Chiang and, if what the government claimed was true, it appeared that the Communists' Jiangxi base had been 'virtually wiped out'.[49] Snow's project seemed doomed.

Salvation eventually came in the spring of 1936, when he learned through an intermediary that Zhang Xueliang ('the Young Marshal'), commander of the Northeastern Army, had concluded a secret truce with the Communists with the intention of presenting a united front in the face of Japanese aggression. With the civil war in the region on hold, Snow realised that it might now be possible to pass through the Nationalist lines and into the Red-controlled areas of northern Shaanxi.[50] It was, he told America's ambassador in China, Nelson T.

Johnson, 'a powerful temptation – a world scoop on a nine-year-old story', and his instincts as a reporter were 'fully roused'.[51]

Ed turned to Madame Sun, and her formidable network of contacts, for assistance in getting to Shaanxi. Within days he was contacted by Hsu Ping, a local university professor (and secret party activist), who handed him a letter of introduction to Mao Zedong written in invisible ink, as well as instructions on how to contact the party underground in Xi'an, the capital of Shaanxi province that lay eight hundred miles south-west of Beijing. Liu Shaoqi, the new party secretary in North China (and a veteran of the Long March), had, it later transpired, authorised the trip.[52] From the Communists' perspective, Snow was the ideal person to tell their story to the outside world. As an American with extraterritorial legal protections, his articles did not have to be approved by the Chinese censors; he was incredibly well connected, not least with the mainstream press (his work appeared in the *New York Herald Tribune*, *Saturday Evening Post* and *Foreign Affairs*); and he was widely viewed as trustworthy and independent. Snow's reports, then, unlike those of a partisan* like Agnes Smedley (a fellow Missourian), would carry more weight.[53]

As he embarked on his odyssey, Ed was aware of the dangers involved. On the eve of his departure, Chiang had announced preparations for a 'final annihilation drive' against the Reds, while, if popular reporting were to be believed, the Communists themselves were little more than bandits, with a bloody record of atrocities against civilians. Despite the risks, Snow consoled himself with the knowledge that many lives had been sacrificed for the Red cause, and it was well worth trying to find out why. As he prepared to depart, he did so with a sense of genuine excitement. Boarding the express train that June night, Snow was 'aware that I was crossing a Rubicon. For once I was absolutely right.'[54]

---

* In 1937 Smedley attempted (unsuccessfully) to join the Chinese Communist Party. She also, almost certainly, undertook espionage on behalf of the Comintern and the Soviet Union.

21. THE ROAD TO RED CHINA

We passed the legendary burial mountain of Ch'in Shih Huang-to,
the greatest revolutionary builder in ancient Chinese history.
It struck me then as oddly appropriate that the Communists
should here work out a destiny for China with aims no less radical
than those . . . imposed 2,200 years ago.

– EDGAR SNOW

On arriving in Xi'an on the evening of 7 June, Snow made his way past the various gendarmes and police officers, who were insistent about checking his identity papers and inspecting his luggage, before heading straight to the Sian Guest House, where he had been told to 'await a visit from a gentleman who would call himself Wang, but about whom I knew nothing else'.[1]

While he waited for the mysterious Red emissary to materialise, Snow paid a call on General Yang Hucheng, commander of the Northwestern Army and pacification commissioner for Shaanxi province. This former bandit-cum-warlord who had allied himself with the Guomindang was, Snow discovered, living alone in his newly finished stone mansion, after each of his two wives, who detested one another, had refused to move in 'unless the other stayed behind'. Suffering from a bad headache, and distracted by his domestic troubles, the general was in no mood to talk politics, and politely dispatched one of his secretaries to show Snow around the city – including a visit to the famous Giant Wild Goose Pagoda.[2]

Xi'an was, Ed recorded in his diary, 'full of tobacco shops. Everybody smokes, young, old, women, children.' There were also 'many new provision shops and clothiers', a modern flour mill and a newly built cotton mill. Merchants, he observed, 'wander the streets . . . with their wares, carried on poles'. Snow also recorded how the modern pharmacies competed, side by side, with the numerous medicine shops with their 'great displays of snakes, turtles, deer horns, musk, frogs, etc.', and he described 'one lad with a syphilitic knee waiting to get some of the black viscous-looking tar made of the various ingredients described above. He was in great pain . . . and sat bargaining for the plaster, for which the apothecary, with a glum face, outrageously demanded 20 cents.'[3]

Ed also met with Shao Li-tzu, the charming and well-educated governor (whose reach, Snow noted, did not extend much beyond the grey walls of his capital). Shao, a former Communist who had gone on to serve as Chiang's personal secretary, granted Snow an audience 'in the garden of his spacious yamen,* cool and restful after the parching heat of [X]ian's dusty streets'. Asked about the fortunes of the Reds, he replied that there were not many left; those in northern Shaanxi were, he explained, mere 'remnants'. To Snow's evident relief, Shao – a 'little man with a wrinkled face like a walnut' – also confirmed that the fighting between the Guomindang and the Communists in the region had, temporarily at least, come to an end.[4]

Finally, a few days after Snow's arrival, Pastor Wang – a 'large, somewhat florid and rotund, but strongly built and dignified' man, dressed in a long, grey silk gown – strode into Ed's hotel room. 'In the week that followed,' Snow wrote, 'I discovered that Wang alone was worth the trip to Xi'an.' He would spend 'four or five hours a day listening to his yarns and reminiscences' as well as to his more serious take on the political situation. A former priest who was on friendly terms with both Chiang and the notorious Shanghai gangster Tu Yueh-sheng, Wang had served as a senior official in the Chinese Red Cross. Having been working for some time with the Reds, he had in early 1936 helped to facilitate the face-to-face talks between Zhou Enlai and Marshal Zhang of the Northeastern Army that had resulted in the ceasefire. Wang was, Snow noted, a 'wholly unexpected' figure.[5]

He was also one who liked to spring a surprise.

* A yamen was the name given to the administrative office or residence of a local bureaucrat or mandarin in imperial China.

One morning, Wang pulled up outside the hotel to take Snow to see the ruins of the ancient Han capital on the outskirts of the city. As Ed clambered into Wang's car, he noticed a man sitting in the back wearing sunglasses and the uniform of a Nationalist official. During the long and dusty drive to the Weiyang Palace, the man remained silent. But, as Snow gazed at the raised mound of earth from where the great Han emperor, Wu, had ruled, he wandered over and removed his dark glasses and white hat. Moving up close, and grasping Snow firmly by the arms, the man now grinned and, with a conspiratorial wink, whispered, 'Look at me! Look at me! Do you recognize me?' Ed did not know what to make of the man, who was bursting with excitement and whose uniform – he had come to realise – was a disguise. Lost for words, Ed could only shake his head and offer a rueful smile. 'I thought,' the man continued, that 'maybe you had seen my picture somewhere.' By now almost 'dancing with pleasure', he revealed his name: Teng Fa – the chief of the Red Army's security police, and a man with a $50,000 bounty on his head. Teng was apparently 'overjoyed' at meeting this American journalist who was so eager to travel into Red territory. Hugging Snow repeatedly, he offered him his horse (the 'finest in Red China!'), his pictures, his diary – whatever he needed. Providing some details about how Ed would travel into the Communist territories, and what he should expect on arrival, Teng also assured him that he was guaranteed the warmest of welcomes. On the drive back, he allayed Snow's concerns about his personal safety ('Aren't you afraid for your head?' he had asked) by explaining that he was currently living, secretly, in the house of Marshal Zhang. 'What a Chinese!' exclaimed Snow. 'What a Red bandit!'[6]

Snow would spend about a month in Xi'an, seeing the sights and talking with missionaries and various officials, as he waited for the arrangements for smuggling him over the front lines to be worked out. He also whiled away the time by playing cards with a fellow American, George Hatem – a young physician and political radical, who had responded to the Communists' desperate appeal for doctors and was similarly hoping to cross into Red territory.* Then, finally, word came through: it was time to depart.[7]

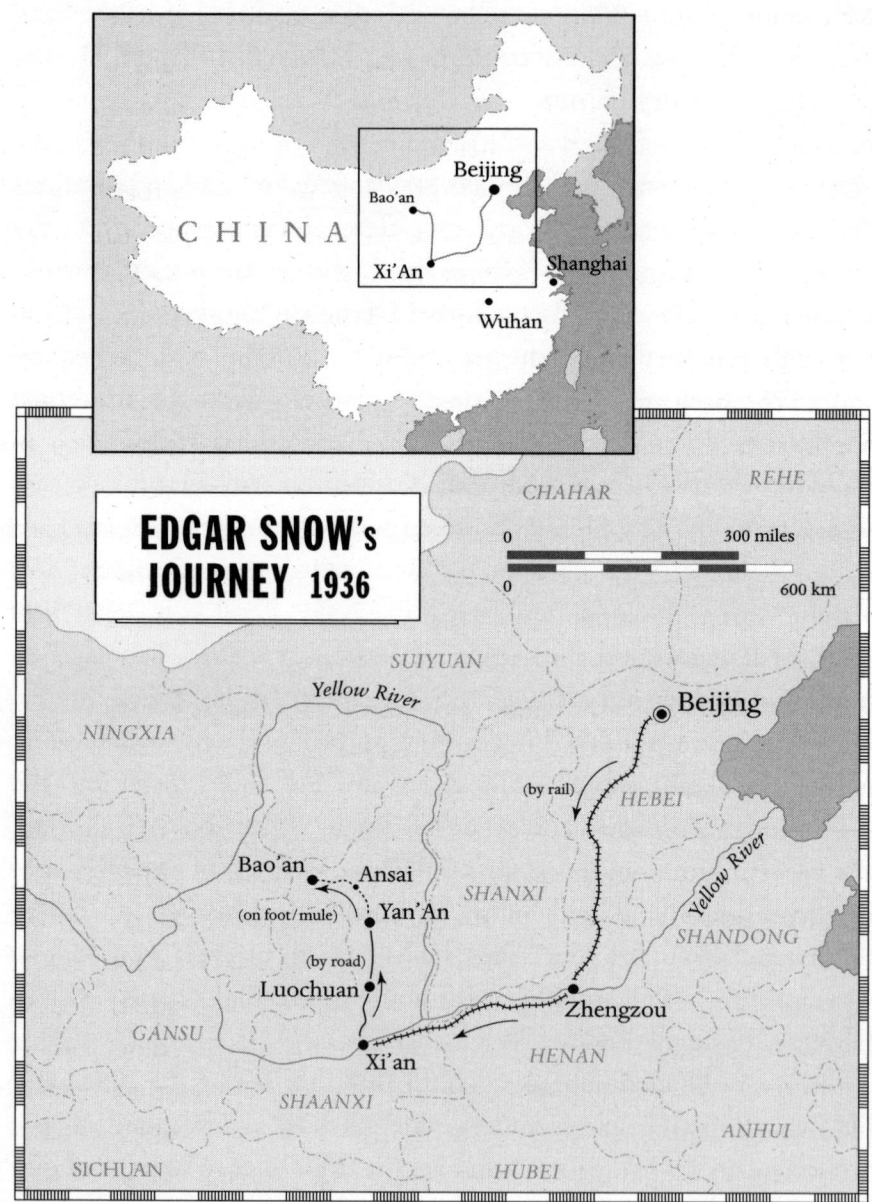

Snow and Hatem left Xi'an on the morning of Sunday 5 July, in a six-ton Dodge truck, after an earlier plan to fly into Red China aboard Marshal Zhang's private aeroplane was deemed far too risky.[8] They departed before sunrise, the city's high wooden gates swinging open as they showed their military pass. Great army trucks made their way past the nearby airfield from which daily reconnaissance and bombing expeditions over Red territory set off. Every mile of the road north, Snow explained, evoked in the Chinese traveller episodes from the country's rich history. An hour in, they were crossing the Wei river, whose fertile valley had been a cradle of early Chinese civilisation, and where the country's first emperor, Qin Shi Huang – the legendary unifier of China and builder of the Great Wall – lay buried. It seemed appropriate, Snow wrote, that this latest historical phenomenon in China, the Communist movement, should have chosen this place in which to 'work out a destiny'.[9]

The newly built road along which they travelled was, Snow noted, already scarred by washouts and ruts, and progress could be painfully slow. That evening they came to a stop in Luochuan, a hundred kilometres or so south of Yan'an, and Snow hunkered down in a dirty hut. The rats, along with the donkeys and pigs in the room next door, made sleep almost impossible.[10]

As they continued their journey northwards the following morning, the previously ubiquitous poppy fields gave way almost immediately to the magical landscape of the Loess Plateau. Loess – a silt-like sediment, thought to have been formed by dust blown down from Mongolia and on the great winds from Central Asia – made this area both richly fertile and extraordinarily beautiful. Snow described a landscape dominated by great castle-like hills, and others that looked like rows of woolly mammoth or perfectly rounded scones. Some, Snow continued, appeared 'like ranges torn by some giant hand, leaving behind the imprint of angry fingers'. This was an awesome, and sometimes frightening, place – 'a world configurated by a mad god – and sometimes a world also of strange surrealist beauty'.

The rich topsoil, some ten feet deep, meant that this area was intensely cultivated, but, Snow noticed, there were hardly any houses. The peasants, he discovered, lived in cave dwellings (yao-fang) that had been dug from the 'hard, fudge-colored cliffs'. These were not caves as Westerners typically understood them: even the wealthiest landlords called them home. Some of the dwellings, Snow explained, contained many rooms, with stone floors and high ceilings, that were lit via rice-paper windows and boasted strong, black-varnished doors. At one point, a young army officer gestured into the distance, pointing out just such a cave village a mile or so ahead, and warned that those living there were 'Reds'. A few weeks earlier, it transpired, a detachment from Zhang's Northeastern Army had sought to buy millet from the villagers, only to be rebuffed; when they had attempted to seize it by force, shots had been fired. The whole area, the soldier noted gravely, was 'Red-bandit territory'. Snow recalled how he 'gazed toward the spaces indicated with keener interest, for it was into that horizon of unknown hills that I intended, within a few hours, to make my way'.[11]

Early that afternoon, the party reached the outskirts of Yan'an. In January 1937, the Red Army would enter the city, and the Communists would make it their new capital that September. When Snow arrived, though, it was the Guomindang's last outpost in the region. Beyond the city, Snow noted, 'everything was Red territory – reaching a hundred miles or more northward to the Great Wall, and westward two hundred miles to the plains of Ningxia.'[12] Yan'an was, Snow observed, perfectly suited for defence. Nestled in a cradle of high, rocky hills, the city's ancient stone walls had been enhanced with new fortifications, including machine-gun posts that looked out towards Red territory. Although a siege had recently been lifted, its impact was, Snow noted, evident in the city's gaunt, hungry-looking inhabitants and the empty shelves in many of the shops. What little food was available was extortionately expensive.[13]

Early the next morning, Tuesday 7 July, Snow and Hatem, accompanied by a single army officer, were escorted past the last

Guomindang sentinel. After shaking hands with their escort, who offered a salute, the two Americans now made their way 'through the thin strip of territory that divided "Red" from "White"', accompanied only by the muleteer who had been hired to carry their belongings – Hatem's medical supplies and Ed's cameras, as well as bedrolls and a small amount of food.[14] For four hours, as they tracked a winding stream, the little band saw no sign of human life. There was, as Snow described it, 'no road at all, but only the bed of the stream that rushed swiftly between high walls of rock'. It was the 'perfect setting', he began to fear, 'for the blotting-out of a too inquisitive foreign devil', and his nerves were hardly calmed by the muleteer's oft-expressed admiration for his expensive leather shoes. Then, to the guide's shout of 'Tao-la!' ('We have arrived!'), the rock walls 'at last gave way and opened out into a narrow valley, green with young wheat'. In the distance Snow spotted a small village in the side of the hill, 'where blue smoke curled from the tall clay chimneys that stood like long fingers in the face of the cliff'. A few minutes later and they were being greeted by a young farmer, wearing a white turban and with a revolver strapped to his waist. Ed, as instructed by Pastor Wang, explained that he was an American journalist, and that he wanted to meet the local chief of the Poor People's League (a peasants' association affiliated with the Communist Party). Liu Lung-hue ('Liu the Dragon Fire') received him warily at first but, after Snow added that he planned to visit the county seat of Ansai and interview Mao Zedong – who was believed to be there – he seemed reassured. A cup of hot tea was soon followed by tobacco, wine and food. At around four o'clock that afternoon, and with the fearsome heat of the midday sun now dissipated, the Americans prepared to depart. Ansai was, Liu insisted, only 'a few steps away', and he provided a youthful guide and a new muleteer to help them on their way.[15]

By sunset, and with their destination still some way off, the Americans prepared to spend their first night in Red territory, bedding down in a village that was nestled in the curve of a river, with hills rising steeply on either side. Chalked onto the walls of the slate-roofed houses, Snow explained, were such slogans as:

Down with the landlords who eat our flesh!
Down with the militarists who drink our blood!
Down with the traitors who sell China to Japan!
Long live the Chinese Revolution!
Long live the Chinese Red Army!

The local Communist representative here was a young man, perhaps twenty years of age, who wore a blue cotton jacket and a pair of white trousers, which contrasted with his bare, leathery feet. The man was kind and welcoming, but Snow declined the offer of a room in the village meeting house (which seemed rather gloomy and uninviting) and instead slept out in the open, using blankets spread out on dismantled wooden doors. The following morning, Wednesday 8 July, Snow was awoken at sunrise by the local chief, who warned him that White bandits were rumoured to be in the area.[16] After a quick breakfast of coffee, crackers and jam, and some eggs provided by the locals, Snow and Hatem, with two donkeys, made their way along the bed of the stream, which they were informed would take them to Ansai. Now and then they would pass little cave villages where dogs would growl menacingly, and young child sentinels would emerge to inspect their road pass. Then, after an hour, the Americans reached a beautiful pool set in a natural basin hollowed from the rocks. It was there that Snow laid eyes on a Red warrior for the first time. The man, wearing a sky-blue coat and a white turban with a red star, had a pistol hanging at his hip with a red tassel dangling from its holster-stock. He was standing next to his white horse, which was wearing a striking blue saddle-blanket, emblazoned with a yellow star. On being questioned, Snow outlined their situation, and the man – Liu, a twenty-two-year-old who had already served six years in the Red Army, and who was on his way to visit district government officials – offered to accompany them.[17] At about eleven o'clock they arrived at Ansai. The town, with its well-preserved walls, looked impressive from a distance, but was in fact deserted: the streets were overgrown, and the once fine buildings lay in ruins. The settlement had, Liu explained, been destroyed in a flood a decade earlier, and its former residents now lived in the yao-fang that had been carved out of a nearby hillside. Rumours that Mao was based here were false, and the local Red leaders were themselves out of town, meeting a provincial official in the nearby village of Pai Chia P'ing. Liu offered to escort them there, and after snacking on crackers and chocolate they were off again.[18] After walking for several hours, and with dusk falling, the party finally rounded a small hill, and a modest village came into view. At that exact moment, Snow recalled, 'I heard a chorus of yells that seemed to come out of the porous yellow earth.'[19] Raising his head in the direction of the shouts, Snow saw – standing on a ledge above the road – a dozen or so peasants, wielding spears, pikes and a few rifles. 'The question of my fate as a blockade runner – whether I was to be given the firing squad as an imperialist, or to be welcomed as an honest inquirer – was', he wrote, 'about to be settled without further delay.'[20]

Snow need not have worried. Seeing the concern on his face, a laughing Liu explained that the village was home to a partisan school, and the peasants were simply practising their war cries. As Ed later noted in his diary, 'Every day this kind of thing goes on, to harden the lungs, build up the enthusiasm & spirit of the men. The war cry still plays an important part in Chinese partisan warfare.' Rather than being shot, Snow was received 'joyously' by the Communist leaders in Pai Chia P'ing, who informed him that he had only narrowly avoided an encounter with White bandits during the journey from Ansai. (A detachment of Red troops had been sent to see them off.) While he was still digesting the news of his lucky escape, a thin young officer appeared, wearing a thick black beard. He approached Snow and, speaking in a 'soft, cultured voice', asked whether he was looking for someone. The officer had, Snow realised, 'spoken in *English*!' and, in a moment, he learned that he was speaking with Zhou Enlai, senior Red Army commander and Mao's right-hand man. They talked for only a few minutes, but Zhou invited Snow to visit him the next day at his nearby headquarters. Then, with Zhou gone, Snow sat down for dinner with members of the communications department, teachers in the partisan school, a radio operator and several Red Army officers. Their hearty meal of chicken, cabbage, bread and millet was served by two youths – wearing oversize uniforms and caps that kept sliding down over their eyes – who, Snow learned, were members of the Young Vanguards: volunteer revolutionaries, destined to become the Red warriors of tomorrow.[21]

The following morning, accompanied by one of those 'Sons of Lenin', Snow set off for Zhou's headquarters, in a village just a mile and a half away. He found the vice chairman of the Chinese Soviet government – a man with an $80,000 price on his head – in a little mud cave, with a single sentry posted at the door. The room was clean, and sparsely furnished: a mosquito net hanging over the k'ang platform was the only concession to luxury. Zhou looked up from his wooden table – where he was reading the latest reports from the front – to welcome his American visitor. Addressing him directly, Zhou explained that he had been told that Snow was an honest journalist, sympathetic to the Chinese people, who could be relied on to tell the truth. The fact that he was not a Communist was, Zhou declared, irrelevant.[22] Snow recorded his initial impressions of the leading revolutionary in his diary:

> a slight figure, wiry, strong, wearing a thin beard, dark but with
> a reddish tinge. He wears a simple gray cotton uniform, without
> markings of any kind except the red bars on the collar – the uniform
> of all R[ed] A[rmy] soldiers . . . entirely without affectations of
> any kind, spoke at first in hesitant but correct English . . . Also
> speaks French, Russian and some German . . . showed a familiarity
> with world events & politics amazing in a man completely cut off

from outer world for four years . . . Good health. Does not smoke. Occasionally drinks alcohol . . . has a retentive memory.[23]

Snow interviewed Zhou over the course of the next two days – about the movement's leaders, strategy, history, strength and motives, and other topics. As well as lengthy and eloquent answers, he also received a draft itinerary – a hand-drawn map, complete with 'the names of people and institutions for me to see in each place' – that involved a journey of some ninety-two days.[24] Ed left enormously impressed with Zhou: when he spoke, he wrote, 'color flushed from his cheeks, his eyes sparkled and his enthusiasm mounted. After 10 years of struggle his faith in the certain triumph of the revolutionary forces he led, seemed absolutely unshaken.' Zhou was, he continued, 'every inch an intellectual' and so 'this great determination is all the more remarkable.'[25]

As Snow prepared to depart Pai Chia P'ing, he noted down in his diary some of his initial thoughts. He had interviewed two young soldiers ('Old Dog' and 'Local Cousin') and, while they relished, above all else, the chance to 'fight for their rights', they also recounted how the Red Army had afforded them the opportunity to learn to read, write and study. Despite being away from home for four years already, their enthusiasm for the cause remained undimmed. 'It is astonishing', wrote Snow, 'what men can endure when they know that their sufferings are equally shared . . . and that the rewards will [be] likewise.' This, he claimed, was 'the secret' of the Red Army's 'splendid morale'.[26] The Communists in general also struck Snow as rather cheerful. 'There is', he wrote, 'nothing grim about life here or about any of the people one meets. They go about remaking the world like college boys to [an American] football match. It seems strange to see two soldiers, fully armed, walking along a path hand in hand and singing, yet that is what you see here very often.' 'Every house rings with singing at night, laughter and good humor' and the peasants would, he noted, 'come out & join the Reds in singing'.[27]

These early, tantalising glimpses of Red China had more than whetted Snow's appetite. He was now more eager than ever to see what awaited him in Bao'an: provisional capital of the Chinese Soviet Republic.

22. THE RED CAPITAL

I was overcome with emotion at the warmth of the greeting [and] the
incredible experience of receiving it far in the interior in this little city
fortified by many ribbed ranges of mountains, and the strange thrill of
solemn military music in the stillness and vastness of those mountains.

– EDGAR SNOW

Snow set off for Bao'an on the morning of Saturday 11 July, accompanied by a military escort of some twenty men commanded by
Li Chiang-lin – 'an old Bolshevik' and veteran of the Nanchang
Uprising of 1927 – whose wife, Snow learned, had been killed by the
Nationalists. Riding a nag (the best horses, he was told, were sent
to the front), the experience was far from comfortable, and he was
particularly anxious as the party made its way along the narrow cliff
trails. 'Any sudden shift of my weight,' Snow feared, risked sending 'us
both hurtling to the rocky gorge below'.[1]

Northern Shaanxi was among the poorest areas of China that Snow
had seen during his seven years in the country. The fields, he explained,
were 'mostly patches laid on the serried landscape, between crevices and
small streams', and the steep gradients of the hills limited the quality
and quantity of the crops that could be grown.[2] On Sunday, the party
marched some twenty miles over dreadful roads, tracking 'the bed of
a stream running through high rock gorges, the road at times lifting
200 or 300 feet high . . . and dwindling to the narrowest foothold
on the flank of the cliff, with a perpendicular drop sheer to the river
on one side'. They passed few villages, and those that they did were
'mostly caves dug into walls of rock high above the river', accessible
only via ladders made of pegs that had been driven into the cliffs. They
spent the night in one such place, where, unable to stomach another
meal of boiled millet, Snow persuaded an old peasant woman to sell
him and George Hatem four eggs. Appealing to her sense of pride, he

stated that 'here are two foreigners come all the way from their own countries, hundreds of miles distant . . . do you want us to go away and say that the peasants do not have anything to eat, or that they have eggs but will not give them to a visitor?' When, soon after, Snow spotted the woman's clearly undernourished children, he felt a burning sense of shame; his attempts to return the eggs were to no avail. 'The old woman pressed them upon us', refusing any payment with a 'charming toothless smile'. The villagers were, Snow observed, 'mostly illiterate' and yet 'they talked glibly of Marx and Lenin and they knew that in Soviet Russia there were no exploiters, no capitalists, no landlords.'[3] Even some of the children that Snow encountered had a rudimentary understanding of the struggle. A capitalist, one told him, was 'a man who makes other people till his land & does no work himself'.[4]

On the final morning of their journey, Snow talked with some of the young Red Army soldiers. One, a handsome young man of twenty-one, formerly a cook in Hunan, had 'dropped his pots & pans' and rushed out into the road to join up, wearing only a pair of sandals and some trousers, when the Red Army arrived in his district. Another, a peasant boy from Sichuan whose 'parents were poor farmers, with only four mou* of land, not enough to feed him and his sisters', explained that the Red Army had been welcomed in his village. He had joined up with the enthusiastic approval of his family. Although one of the men stated that his primary motivation had been to take on the Japanese, the rest all said that they had joined up to 'fight the landlords'.[5] Snow was evidently impressed by the soldiers, describing how they 'sang nearly all day on the road' – spontaneously, whenever the spirit moved them. He also admired their self-imposed discipline, describing how, while they would happily fill their pockets when passing wild apricot trees, they would never touch the fruit in private orchards, and were diligent in ensuring that any grain or vegetables eaten in the villages were paid for, in full. As for the locals, as far as Snow could make out 'they bore no

* A Chinese unit of land measurement equivalent to approximately 0.165 acres.

resentment toward my Red companions. Some seemed on close terms of friendship, and very loyal – a fact probably not unconnected with a recent redivision of land and the abolition of taxes.' He also described how local peasant women would frequently 'laugh and joke with Red warriors, in a very emancipated way for Chinese women'.[6]

Just after noon on Monday 13 July, the party reached a knoll over-looking the former frontier stronghold of Bao'an ('Defended Peace'). It made for an impressive sight. Remains of the city's fortifications, 'flame-struck in that afternoon sun, could be seen flanking the narrow pass through which once emptied into this valley the conquering legions of the Mongols'. And there was also 'an inner city, still, where the garrisons were once quartered; and a high defensive masonry, lately improved by the Reds, embraced about a square mile in which the present town was located'.[7] As they began their descent, the sound of bugles rang out, and a great mass of people could be seen 'hurrying toward the South gate'. 'They seemed', Snow explained, 'to be assembling in some kind of formation.' As they neared the city, it was clear: a welcoming party was readying to receive them.[8] On entering Bao'an, they were met by banners – proclaiming 'Welcome to the American journalist to investigate Soviet China!' and 'Long live the Chinese revolution!' – held aloft by 'a curious crowd'. At the end of the street stood a reception committee, consisting of most of the government officials (although not Mao, who was still asleep).[9] Snow described how 'the cadets from the military academy were lined up, & the band blared a welcome as we marched between the lines of spectators. The band & troops fell in behind us and marched up the main street' as revolutionary shouts rang out. Snow was 'overcome with emotion at the warmth of the greeting [and] the incredible experience of receiving it far in the interior in this little city fortified by many ribbed ranges of mountains, and the strange thrill of solemn military music in the stillness and vastness of those mountains'.[10]

'In this dusty, poorly provisioned lair,' Snow explained, 'the Communists had set up the paraphernalia of a tiny state: ministries of foreign affairs, finance, agriculture, public health, defense, education, planning – the works.' A Red Army University, headed by Lin Biao, the future 'liberator of Manchuria', occupied a series of caves with room for around eight hundred students, while so-called 'publishing caves' brought forth a steady stream of textbooks, newspapers and party propaganda. Food, meanwhile, 'consisted mostly of millet, cabbage and squash grown along the river, with pork, lamb and chicken rare luxuries'.[11]

Snow and Hatem were taken to the Wai Chiao Pu (foreign ministry), 'a cluster of houses at the edge of town', where they were put up in a one-storey mud-brick hut, furnished with 'a newly made table & benches and curtained windows'. It may have been simple but, Snow noted, after three days of sleeping outdoors it seemed like the height of luxury. That evening, the Americans joined leading government officials for a banquet of eggs, mutton, beef, pork balls, shredded liver soup and vegetables, at which Mao, 'still looking somewhat sleepy, his mass of black hair uncombed', put in an appearance.[12] He struck Snow as a 'gaunt, rather Lincolnesque figure', relatively tall, with a mild stoop, piercing eyes and prominent cheekbones. He also, thought Snow, had an 'intellectual face of great shrewdness'.[13]

Snow would interview the chairman of the provisional Central Soviet Government extensively in the coming days, sitting down with Mao in his hillside cave (guarded by a single sentry) and chatting over hot-pepper bread, or sour-plum compote that had been prepared by his wife, He Zizhen.[14] During these sessions, Snow questioned Mao about his background and early life, his involvement with the Communist Party, his political ideals, the experience of the Long March and his vision for China's future – accumulating some twenty thousand words of notes in the process.* The two hit it off, and Snow would come to write admiringly

* In his 1960 memoir, *Journey to the Beginning*, Snow described himself as Mao's 'American Boswell' (p. 163) – a reference to Samuel Johnson's famous amanuensis, James Boswell, author of the landmark biography *The Life of Samuel Johnson*.

about this energetic man and brilliant strategist.[15] As one of Snow's biographers has put it, the Chairman was keen to emphasise a series of key messages that functioned as a leitmotif throughout Snow's visit: the 'fundamental issue before the Chinese people today is the struggle against Japanese imperialism'; that this must be 'realized simultaneously with the liberation of the oppressed peasantry'; 'the Communist Party of China was, is, and will ever be, faithful to Marxist–Leninism'; and finally, as Mao put it, 'we are certainly not fighting for an emancipated China in order to turn the country over to Moscow!'[16]

Edgar Snow and Mao Zedong. Snow described the Communist leader as 'a gaunt, rather Lincolnesque figure' who might 'become a very great man'.

In the coming weeks and months, Snow would interview other important Communist leaders, including Bo Gu, the former party leader who had been appointed chairman of the North-West Branch Soviet Government; Hsu Teh-li, the minister of education; and the senior Red Army commander Lin Biao. He would also travel extensively in northern Shaanxi, observing village life and meeting front-line troops as he built up a richly textured picture of life in Red China. From

Bo, Snow learned that, unlike in Jiangxi, land here was 'plentiful & landlords are not numerous' and, as a result, 'the main effort of the Red Movement here has been against high taxation rather than landlordism.' Usury had been abolished, the land tax repealed and opium was being eradicated. Regular trade was actively encouraged (and thus only lightly taxed) and, Snow was informed, 'there are no beggars . . . All men & women who want to work are readily absorbed in farming enterprise, the small industries that exist, and the government or army service.'[17] Bo also gave an insight into how the local soviets were formed. On occupying an area, he explained, the Red Army would immediately call a meeting of the local inhabitants to lay out the movement's aims. At this stage, some confiscated property would typically be redistributed to those present to build support – and encourage a larger turnout at subsequent meetings. Next, the people would be asked to elect a revolutionary committee to organise the village soviet. Sometimes a local 'elder', typically a landlord, would be elected to the revolutionary committee, because the peasants did not understand that the Red Army was deadly serious when it said that it would eliminate landlords, tax collectors and usurers. As they became emboldened, the villagers would then proceed to depose the elders and elect 'poor youths' in their place; sometimes they would even demand the death of a particularly oppressive landlord. In such cases, Bo emphasised, the Red Army would not interfere. In fact, 'to demonstrate its sincerity' it would sometimes take the initiative in the 'mass prosecution of some local villain about whom it has been informed by the peasants'.[18]

During his extensive sojourn in northern Shaanxi Snow saw 'little that could be called a "terror"' and doubted 'if any then existed'.[19] As he observed in his diary on 16 September, 'In general one does not get the impression here of a people at war (except at the very front) with an army in movement.' There was, he claimed, 'no violence practiced upon the peasantry; at any rate, I have not seen it. I have not seen even a fist fight between soldier and civilian, or between civilians or between soldiers.' Women, moreover, appeared to move about freely, without concern for their safety: 'I have seen comely young girls sit down beside the bellows and pump the ancient instrument cheerfully for an hour or more to cook the soldiers' dinner, talking and joking with them meanwhile.' In the two months that he had been in Red territory, Snow continued, 'I have never seen a child struck nor an old man abused.' Even examples of political prisoners had been hard to come by. He had encountered a landlord family, under arrest, who were being taken to Ho-lien-wan for 'investigation'. The father, 'a poorly dressed man', looked (understandably) glum, his two sons walked in silence, while his wife 'continually cursed the young soldiers who were guarding them'. But, Snow noted, none of the family were chained, and the soldiers, rather than being menacing, appeared to be in good humour. Besides this group, a Guomindang tax collector, and a half-dozen or so deserters who had been set to work digging ditches and latrines, he had seen only one other political prisoner:

> One morning in [Bao'an] I passed several soldiers leading a young
> man wearing soiled cotton garments, with a look of despair on his
> peasant face. I learned that he was a 'confessed spy,' who had been a
> member of the district soviet revolutionary committee. He had been
> caught sending out reports to the [Guomindang] (as I was told).
> Later on I saw him in the [Bao'an] jail, a stone cave in the hills.[20]

Based on his first-hand observations, Snow concluded that 'persuasion and gradualism' were the primary methods used by the Communists to win over the peasantry and build support for their social, economic and political reforms.[21]

Towards the end of July, Snow made a two-week journey to the western front to see the Red Army up close. It was, he later wrote:

> quite apart from any other military organization I had seen: the
> incorruptibility of its officers, the equality of pay and rations . . .
> the great emphasis placed on political training, and the army's role

in the organization of revolutionary committees among the poor in every village. In brief, the Reds sought to make every man, woman and child active in some organization.

Ed was particularly taken with the children – many of them orphans and runaway slaves – who accompanied the army, serving as mess boys, buglers and scouts, and who were referred to, with evident affection, as 'little devils'.[22] The Red Army's rank and file was, Snow learned, made up primarily of young men (the average age was just nineteen), drawn overwhelmingly from the peasantry and the agrarian and industrial working class, and over half were members of either the Communist Party or the Communist Youth League.[23] Attending a political class one afternoon, he took the opportunity to question the men about whether the Red Army was any better than China's Nationalist or warlord armies. His question prompted half a dozen men to leap to their feet, keen to emphasise how, as one put it, 'Here we are all equals; in the White Army the soldier masses are oppressed. Here we fight for ourselves and the masses.' When Snow asked how the men knew that they had the support of the peasants, it brought forth a torrent of first-hand testimony about peasants bringing them food and water, engaging in sabotage against the enemy and providing intelligence on Nationalist troop movements, and actively seeking to join the ranks. As one teenage recruit put it, 'Our Red Army *is* the people, and this is what I have to say!'[24]

Snow spent the last week of September and the early part of October back in Bao'an, collecting 'enough biographies to fill a *Who's Who in Red China* . . . every morning turned up a new commander or Soviet official to be interviewed.' He also lived something of a 'holiday life' – riding, swimming and playing fiercely competitive games of tennis with faculty from the Red Army University, and high-stakes poker* with Bo Gu and other senior Communist officials. All the while, though, he was becoming ever more anxious. Alarmed by reports

* Bo Gu apparently lost $120,000 in a single evening; fortunately, Snow wrote, 'it was all in matches anyway.'

that thousands of new troops, loyal to Chiang, were flooding into Shaanxi, strengthening the border in preparation for a fresh assault on the Communists, Snow feared that, if he did not leave soon, he might not get the chance.[25]

On Monday 12 October, after more than three months in Red territory, Snow set out for home. He knew that he had a terrific story. To tell it, he now just had to make it out alive.

Snow departed Bao'an just after nine o'clock that morning. As he walked down the main street for the final time, heading towards the city gates, people leaned out of offices to shout their farewells, and his poker club confederates turned out to bid him goodbye. Snow was followed by some of the city's children as far as the old city walls and there, at the river's edge, he saw that the 'whole Red [Army] University was seated out in the open, under a great tree, listening to a lecture'. As Snow passed by, they 'all stopped and rose and waved and shouted "Yi p'ing hao lu!" ["Have a smooth journey!"] and "Shih Lo T'ung-chih, Wan Sui!" ["Long Live Comrade Snow!"]' Just about the only person not to make an appearance that morning was Mao (who, characteristically, was still asleep). After crossing the stream, Snow turned – a lump rising in his throat – to give a final wave. Then he mounted his horse and rode off briskly, escorted by two Red soldiers and Fu Chin-kuei, a young Communist who had been deputed to accompany him during much of his stay in Red territory.[26]

The three months Snow had spent in Red China had been utterly exhilarating. The people he had encountered, in Bao'an and elsewhere, seemed, he said, 'the freest and happiest Chinese I had known'. 'I was never afterward', he recalled, 'to feel so strongly the impact of youthful hope, enthusiasm and human invincibility in men dedicated to what they conceived to be a wholly righteous cause.' Compared with the inefficiency and corruption he had witnessed among Nationalist officials over the years, 'the Reds were men of probity and selflessness', and he admired their willingness 'to die to affirm the worth of an ideal they cherished more than personal survival'. Snow's affinity with the Communists also owed much to 'their enthusiastic espousal of science, the practice of equality and fraternity among men and women, their insistence on racial equality' and 'their positive attitude toward the future', which contrasted with the fatalism he had encountered elsewhere in China. While he acknowledged that the reforms the Communists 'enforced or advocated were not the country-club ideals of political freedom by any means', they did, Snow felt, 'offer the essential satisfactions of food, shelter and some kind of democratic equalitarianism for all'. Meanwhile, their call to form a united front to take on the Japanese struck Snow as essentially 'right'. After all, he explained, the simple fact was that 'the Chinese could not defend the nation by killing one another.' But perhaps the Communists' strongest appeal for Snow 'as a Westerner' was what he termed 'their decisive rejection of mysticism and the gods that had failed the poor, in favor of the rationalist's faith in man's ability to solve the problems of mankind'.[27]

Little wonder that, as he left the Red capital that autumn day, Snow felt he 'was not going home, but leaving it'.[28]

Although Snow's horse had already been travelling for several days, and was fuelled by a meagre diet of cornstalks and grass, all day it trotted briskly at the head of the 'small cavalcade'. The party followed the Bao'an river until sunset, when they made their camp in a farmhouse at the foot of an imposing sandstone hill. Towering up from the stream to a height of some two hundred feet, the hill – with its hundreds of caves that had been carved out from the stone – resembled a giant beehive. There was, Snow recorded, not very much to eat, but their farmer-host was prevailed upon to sell them a chicken. This, together with the Chinese cabbage and millet rolls they had brought with them, resulted in a modest banquet. After supper, their host was encouraged to play his sanxian – a long, three-stringed lute – and the songs, Snow wrote, 'had a queer melancholy' that 'fitted into this weird country quite exactly'.[29]

The following day, the party stopped in a 'small village with a broken-down temple and many young and broken-footed women'. The house where they were quartered was home to four women – three daughters-in-law and 'one despotic mother-in-law'. That night, they feasted on fried cabbage, hash browns, fried chicken, steamed bread and turnips. Ed was struck by the festive atmosphere that surrounded the village, 'with the red and green peppers drying everywhere, and the green cabbages and golden pumpkins lying in the autumnal sun'.[30] By 15 October the party had reached Fu-ts'un. The hills, Snow recorded, 'were interminable and thickly wooded and the brown rust of autumn lay everywhere around us'. They saw many pheasants, wild deer and pigs, as well as 'two tigers streaking from one thicket to another, far out of range'. 'The whole day', as Snow described it, 'was one of sheer beauty, and immense comfort to the eyes after months and months of barren hills and deserted valleys.' As in the other villages, Snow's party was hosted by the local representative of the Poor People's League – this one a 'bright young farmer', who informed them that the main highway to Xi'an was now held by soldiers of the Guomindang's Northeastern Army, under the command of General Yang Hucheng. 'No one could travel without a pass,' he explained, and 'if you didn't have it the soldiers would take what they pleased from you: money, clothes, food or anything you might have.' Many peasants, suspected of being Communists, had in recent days been killed by Yang's men and now, the farmer continued, peasants avoided the main highway and travelled instead at night 'by the small mountain roads'.[31]

While the final arrangements were being made to escort Snow across the front, he spent four days 'loafing around' in An-chia-pan. Here, he noted, 'the peasants are amazed at the sight of a foreigner. The word has travelled fast and people come from miles distant to have a look at me. Many have invited me to visit their homes, to dine with them.' He asked one of his visitors, a young partisan girl, 'armed and smiling', whether there were many landlords left in the area. Not many, she said, 'they have fled', although elsewhere they had 'all returned and some land has been given back to them, in accordance with the new policy'.[32]

On Monday 19 October, Snow was escorted to the front lines by twenty Red soldiers. There, Pien Chang-wu, a Red officer whom Snow had met back in early July, was waiting for him. Pien, Snow recalled, then 'personally took me across no-man's land and led me up to a few Manchurian soldiers' who were commanded by 'an immaculate young officer wearing a gold sword and white gloves'. In his diary, Snow noted that 'we exchanged greetings; I shook hands with Pien and he turned and marched back across the plain.' The next morning, He Zhuguo, one of the more talented Nationalist generals (and one who was increasingly sympathetic to calls to form a united front), questioned Snow extensively about the Communists' morale, determination, equipment, policies and 'their patriotism and determination to fight Japan'. He 'seemed pleased with what I told him', and 'expressed his impatience with the delay in reaching an agreement to end the civil war'. Soon afterwards, Snow was 'put aboard' an army truck and smuggled into Xi'an, past its famous Drum Tower, and on to a safe house that had been provided by Marshal Zhang.[33]

On 27 October, the *Kansas City Times* carried unconfirmed wire reports, circulated by missionaries in Xi'an, that Snow had recently met his death 'at the hands of unidentified persons'. The claim was quicky retracted – Snow was very much alive. His return to Nationalist territory had, though, skirted disaster.[34]

As he jumped from the military truck on the evening of 20 October, Ed immediately asked one of the soldiers to toss him his bag, which contained a dozen notebooks (including interview transcripts, biographical sketches and diary entries), thirty rolls of film ('the first still and moving pictures ever taken of the Chinese Red Army') and a substantial collection of Red newspapers, magazines and documents. As the search for the bag dragged on, Snow grew increasingly anxious. After several minutes, his worst fears were confirmed: the bag was gone. The truck, Ed now learned to his horror, had been 'loaded with gunnysacks full of broken [Nationalist] rifles and guns being sent for repairs'. To avoid being discovered in case of a search, his own bag had been stuffed into one such sack. When they had reached Xianyang, twenty miles from Xi'an and on the opposite bank of the Wei river, the entire cargo – including Snow's notebooks – had been unceremoniously unloaded. Like John Reed some two decades earlier, Snow now faced the possibility that he would never see his precious archive again.

By now, it was already dusk, and the driver suggested returning the following morning to collect the bag. But Snow was insistent. After a prolonged discussion – watched, from a distance, by bemused traffic police – the soldiers finally agreed to set off straight away. After a sleepless night, dawn brought happy news: the bag, and its contents, had been recovered. As Snow recalled, he was in fact 'doubly lucky'. Shortly after his papers and film had been returned, 'all traffic was completely swept from the streets, and all roads leading into the city were lined with gendarmes and troops', in preparation for a surprise visit to Xi'an from Chiang Kai-shek. 'It would', Snow explained, 'have been impossible then for our truck to return over that road to the Wei River, for it skirted the heavily guarded airfield.'[35]

A couple of days later, Ed was safely back in Beijing. His wife, Helen, answered a knock at the side door to find her husband 'grinning foolishly behind a grizzled beard' and looking 'like the cat that had swallowed the canary'. On entering, he opened his bag and put his notebooks and papers on the floor, before taking out 'an old gray cap with a red star on its faded front'. Placing it on his head, and pulling it down over one eye, he 'capered around the room', the dogs 'leaping and dancing with him', before demanding scrambled eggs, Camel cigarettes, Maxwell House coffee and some American canned peaches. As well as simply being happy to be alive, Ed was, Helen recalled, 'exploding with pride at his achievement'.[36]

23. RED STAR OVER CHINA

I believe in my right as an American journalist to tell the truth as
I have found it . . . I believe it quite enough to describe what I
have seen and explain this phenomenon of the Red Army – a task
which I feel will supply some much-needed materials of history.
I am not the person best suited for this enterprise, but circumstances
have bestowed it upon me, and I intend to have a stab at it.

– EDGAR SNOW

Ed's delight was entirely justified. As he told the *Daily Herald*'s
L. M. McBride, nobody before had 'entered Red territory, visited
Red chieftains, investigated Soviet life, interviewed Red warriors and
commanders, Red peasants and workers' and 'brought back a story
for the world'. In breaking the nearly decade-long 'news-blockade
around all Soviet life in China', he had, he explained, secured an
unprecedented scoop: 'I do not know', he wrote, 'that anything of the
sort has occurred elsewhere in modern journalistic history, for the
situation is so unusual that it can scarcely have had a counterpart.'[1]

Now at home in Beijing, Snow wrote frantically, producing a series of
articles on Mao, the Red Army and life in Red China. *Life*, the weekly
photo magazine recently launched by the publisher Henry Luce, also
paid $1,000 to publish more than forty of Snow's photographs, which
appeared across the 25 January and 1 February 1937 editions of the
magazine.[2] When Nationalist ministers in Nanjing dismissed Snow's
stories as a hoax, he stated flatly that all he had done was to try to 'give
a more coherent and reasonable picture of the Northwest situation than
has in general been furnished'. 'This ambition', he continued, 'has been
based not on any fancies of my own, but on facts I have ascertained from
reliable persons or from my own observations.' Rejecting claims that he
was a propagandist, and in the face of veiled threats from government
officials, Snow insisted on his right to 'publish the truth as I find it'.[3]

During 1937, other reporters, inspired by Snow's singular achievement, began flocking to northern Shaanxi to see for themselves what conditions were like. (Agnes Smedley, Earl Leaf of the United Press, the *New York Herald Tribune*'s Victor Keene, and the New Zealander James Bertram, who wrote for *The Times* and the *New Statesman*, were among those who made the trip.) Anxious that he might have his thunder stolen at the last minute, Snow worked furiously on his book.[4] In preparing the manuscript, Helen Foster played a vital role – not only freeing up time by answering the flood of mail that now poured in, and by transcribing his copious, hand-written notes, but in insisting that he place Mao's life at the centre of the narrative. When Ed requested that she 'cut down Mao's story and digest it for [the] book', explaining that he was planning on rewriting great chunks of it in any case, Helen was horrified:

'But this is a classic. It's priceless,' I protested. It would be the heart of Ed's book, the backbone. It gave Mao's whole background in perfect form. I argued that Ed shouldn't touch it, but should use every word as Mao had told him. 'Why, this is like having George Washington at Valley Forge tell the story of the Revolution.'

They had, she recalled, numerous arguments over this issue. Indeed, she was so fearful that her husband might 'cut most of it out in my absence' that she even contemplated abandoning her own trip to Red territory – to interview Zhu De, He Long and other leading Communists whom Ed had been unable to meet – which she undertook in April 1937.[5]

In the end Helen's good judgement prevailed. Although Ed added a few paragraphs of explanation, and made a few minor cuts and edits elsewhere, Mao's autobiography 'was published authentically as told to him'.[6] He finished his manuscript in late July, just as the Japanese were preparing their assault on Beijing. (The city would fall on 8 August.) At more than four hundred pages long, it was organised into twelve sections.[7] Weaving together Snow's own extraordinary journey with compelling pen-portraits of Communist leaders, generals, soldiers and peasants, *Red Star Over China* presented an epic story of adventure and heroic, against-the-odds struggle. It made for a gripping read.[8]

The book's wider claims, too, were bracing. While Chiang had dismissed the 'Red bandits' as irrelevant, Snow stressed the idealism and discipline of the Red Army and its supporters, arguing that the Communists' commitment to sweeping domestic reform, and eagerness to take on the Japanese,* made them a force to be reckoned with. Like John Reed in *Ten Days*, Snow wrote with evident affection and conviction when describing the everyday transformations that had occurred in the lives of ordinary Chinese people as a result of Communist rule. In a sympathetic narrative, he pointed out that, in areas where the Reds had established themselves, 'land was redistributed and taxes were lightened'; unemployment, prostitution, opium and child slavery had been abolished; literacy rates, political consciousness and cultural horizons raised; and working and living conditions improved. As for Mao, this 'Lenin of China' was a man of the people, with an iron constitution and a fierce work ethic, who combined a keen intellect with 'the personal habits of a peasant' – at one point Snow described how the Chairman turned down the belt of his trousers to check for lice. Although there was no 'ritual hero worship built up around him' (not yet, at any rate), Mao's influence over the Communist movement was, Snow claimed, greater than any of his rivals', and the role of his personality was immense. 'One felt a certain force of destiny in Mao,' Snow wrote; 'it was nothing quick or flashy' but grew out of his uncanny ability to embody the demands of millions of his fellow citizens – above all the peasantry. If, as he

---

* During the Long March, Mao had, of course, insisted that the Red Army was heading north to take on the Japanese. This was, though, little more than propaganda (and an attempt to boost morale). The Red forces, both during the Long March and in the months after arriving in Shaanxi, were in no position to take the fight to the Japanese. See Lee Feigon, *Mao: A Reinterpretation* (Chicago: Ivan R. Dee, 2002), 62.

thought they might, the Communists proved capable of regenerating China, then, Snow argued, Mao might 'become a very great man'.[9]

RED STAR

OVER

CHINA

BY EDGAR SNOW

RANDOM HOUSE · NEW YORK

Title page of the Random House edition of Edgar Snow's *Red Star Over China*. 'Like a bright star shining in a dark sky', Snow's masterpiece 'guided thousands on the road of revolution'.

Snow might have predicted a great future for the Chinese Communists, but he was far less confident about the prospects for his own book. Writing to Helen shortly before it was finished, he conceded that there were parts that made for 'surprisingly good reading'. But when it came to the manuscript as a whole, he was far from content: 'I'm afraid', he said, 'I can't say much for it.'[10]

He need not have worried.

Red Star Over China was published in Great Britain by Victor Gollancz in October 1937. Selected for the widely influential Left Book Club,* it was reprinted three times in the first month, and rapidly clocked up sales of one hundred thousand.[11] Writing anonymously (as was then standard practice) in the *Times Literary Review*, the adventurer and travel writer Peter Fleming (older brother of Ian) offered a note of caution: the book was, he said, 'repetitive' and 'far too long', and Snow's evident enthusiasm for the Communists (which Fleming, needless to say, did not share) meant that he would be read not only with interest but also with 'a grain of salt'.[12] Overall, though, the reviews were laudatory. From the pages of the *Daily Herald* (which had of course helped fund Snow's trip to Bao'an), William Norman Ewer praised *Red Star Over China* as not only a 'historical document of the first order' but also as 'exciting and enthralling a tale of exploration as anyone can want to read'. This 'epic story, superbly told', was, he predicted, destined to become a classic.[13]

The book came out in the United States at the start of 1938. As his editor Bennett Cerf explained, the publication ended up being 'one of the biggest rush jobs we ever undertook'. Originally scheduled for release on 15 January, the date was brought forward at the last minute when Random House learned that a rival publisher was about to release a book on China. They were, he explained, 'darned if we were going to let *anything* dim the lustre of [Snow's] achievement'. With publication day now 3 January, the ink had scarcely had time to dry before the first copies were rushed to the bookstores.[14] Although US sales were much more modest (the Random House edition sold a total of 23,500), the

---

* Other selections that year included George Orwell, *The Road to Wigan Pier*, Stephen Spender, *Forward from Liberalism*, and Sidney and Beatrice Webb, *Soviet Communism: A New Civilisation*.

reception was, if anything, even more effusive.[15] In the *Atlantic*, foreign policy expert Walter H. Mallory judged the book to be 'the most superb piece of reporting' that he had ever read – and one that presented 'the authentic inside story of the Chinese Communists'.[16] From the pages of the *Saturday Review of Literature*, meanwhile, David H. Popper – staff member at the Foreign Policy Association and future diplomat – wrote that *Red Star Over China* 'deserves the accolades which will be bestowed upon it'. It would, he explained:

> be a significant book if it were simply the saga of the Chinese Communists' dramatic struggle to maintain their beleaguered government against five smashing [Guomindang] offensives. It would be a first-rate tale of heroic adventure if it did no more than chronicle that master military achievement of modern times – the incredible six-thousand-mile march across all China to the far Northwest. It would be an illuminating social document if it were only a biographical account of the Chinese Soviet leaders, a record of the evolution of Soviet policy, and a description of the Reds' achievements.

'In all these fields,' Popper declared, 'it blazes new trails for the historian.' Snow had, he concluded, 'accomplished a magnificent feat'.[17] It was a judgement shared by others. Malcolm Cowley of the *New Republic* declared that Snow deserved all credit for 'what is perhaps the greatest single feat performed by a journalist of our century', while *Time* claimed that 'as a piece of journalistic enterprise' *Red Star Over China* 'ranks with John Reed's *Ten Days That Shook the World*'.[18]

Snow, to be sure, had a tremendous story: as the *New Yorker* put it, the tale that he had brought out of 'the mysterious, insulated' provinces of North-West China was 'one of the most interesting of its kind since the days of Marco Polo'.[19] But there were other forces at work, too, that helped to explain the book's popularity. In particular, a series of dramatic events following Snow's return from Bao'an had helped to keep China on the front pages. First, on 12 December 1936, while on a visit to Xi'an to oversee the start of the latest offensive against the Communists, Chiang was kidnapped by Marshal Zhang and other rebellious commanders. Their aim: end the civil war, organise a coordinated national defence against the Japanese and secure meaningful political reforms (including the release of all political prisoners). Although this sensational development led to an initial outpouring of jubilation in the Red capital, the Communist leadership – under pressure from Moscow – soon struck a more conciliatory tone. (Stalin, it seems, wanted nothing to do with such 'banditry'.) Later that month, Zhou Enlai headed a delegation to Xi'an, where he pressed for both Chiang's release and the creation of a united front. The Generalissimo was eventually freed on Christmas Day, and while the details of any deal were deliberately obscured by the Nationalist government, it was clear that the planned assault on the Communists was now off the table, replaced by a spirit of national cooperation.

The desperate need for a united front, as well as the scale of Japanese ambitions towards China, was made painfully clear just a few months later. On 27 July 1937, following a military skirmish on the outskirts of Beijing, Japan launched bombing and artillery raids on the South Barracks (the ancient capital's last line of defence), killing two thousand troops with the loss of just fifty of their own. A week later, the Japanese entered the city. As the Communists and Guomindang finalised the details of their cooperation agreement, the enemy pressed on, brutally occupying Tianjin, Shanghai and finally Nanjing, which fell in mid-December.[20] As one of Snow's biographers has argued, there could hardly have been a better backdrop against which to publish *Red Star Over China*:

> Everyone, it seemed, was interested in China. Executive branch cabinet heads now paid day-to-day attention to the country, rather than leaving diplomacy to foreign-service officers. For the general

public the heroic Chinese peasant, personified in the 1937 movie version of Pearl Buck's *The Good Earth*, became, increasingly, an object of sympathy. Polls showed 2 percent of the public pro-Japanese, 74 percent pro-Chinese.[21]

Meanwhile, Snow's message – that the Chinese Red Army was made up of committed, well-organised, battle-hardened patriots, ready and willing to take on the Japanese menace – was one that resonated deeply with an American public, and political class, increasingly worried by the advance of fascism and militarism across Europe and the Far East.[22] After reading Snow's book, Harold Ickes, secretary of the interior and right-hand man to President Franklin D. Roosevelt, noted that 'any people that can do what the Red Army did during the Long March and after' were 'positively invincible'.[23]

Ickes, it turned out, was dead right.

24. MAOISM

Snow came when no one would. He made a study of our situation
and he helped make known to the world the facts about us . . .
We shall always remember this great deed he did for our country.
He was the first to open up the way to friendly relations.

– MAO ZEDONG

At the conclusion of *Red Star Over China*, Snow had predicted
that, although the revolutionary movement he had documented so
assiduously might suffer setbacks and defeats, might retreat temporarily
or languish for a while underground, in one form or another it would
'eventually win, simply because . . . the basic conditions which had
given it birth carried within themselves the dynamic necessity for its
triumph'.[1]

When, on 1 October 1949, Mao formally proclaimed the formation
of the People's Republic of China, following the Communists'
decisive military victory over the Guomindang,* Snow was proved
spectacularly right.

These were, though, difficult years for Ed. The so-called 'loss' of
China to communism, just a year or two into the Cold War, constituted
a major trauma for America and unleashed bitter recriminations about
who was to 'blame'. Republicans, locked out of the White House
since FDR's victory in 1932, seized on the opportunity to assail the
Truman administration, denouncing left-wing officials in the State
Department – and the 'China Hands'† who advised them – for the
catastrophe. Although President Truman had already established a

* The United Front collapsed at the end of the Second World War; fighting between
the Communists and the Guomindang resumed in the summer of 1946.
† The term refers to a group of American diplomats, journalists and soldiers, known
for their knowledge of China and supposed influence on American policy, before,
during and after the Second World War.

'loyalty program' within the federal government, designed to weed out communists and subversives and strengthen national security, the politics of anti-communism now became supercharged. In his notorious speech before the Ohio County Republican Women's Club on 9 February 1950, Wisconsin Senator Joseph R. McCarthy declared that 'the reason why we find ourselves in a position of impotency is not because our only powerful potential enemy has sent men to invade our shores, but rather because of the traitorous actions of those who have been treated so well by this nation.' The State Department was the focus of much of his scorn. Its 'bright young men' who had been born with 'silver spoons in their mouths' were, he claimed, among 'the worst'. Asserting that this, 'one of the most important government departments', was 'thoroughly infested with Communists', McCarthy claimed to have in his hand a list of '205 cases* of individuals who would appear to be either card carrying members or certainly loyal to the Communist Party, but who nevertheless are still helping to shape our foreign policy'. McCarthy – who would give his name to the anti-communist crusade that swept the country over the next few years – ended his speech with a call for 'the whole sorry mess of twisted, warped thinkers' to be 'swept from the national scene so that we may have a new birth of national honesty and decency in government'.[2]

Although Snow was never called to testify before either the House Committee on Un-American Activities or the Senate Internal Security Subcommittee – the bodies that spearheaded the congressional response to the so-called Second Red Scare[†] – his name came up repeatedly during hearings, with witnesses questioned about their own associations with Snow, or views of his work. The FBI, with the active encouragement of its director, J. Edgar Hoover, amassed

---

* He later downgraded the number to fifty-seven, but never produced any names, or evidence to back up his claims. In December 1954, the Senate voted by 67 to 22 to censure him.
† An earlier period of intense anti-communist and anti-subversive politics had followed the end of the First World War.

a substantial – if ultimately rather anodyne – file on him during an investigation that lasted for more than two decades.[3] Conservatives, meanwhile, repeatedly accused Snow of having duped his readers into believing that the Chinese Communists were little more than 'agrarian reformers'* and of generally peddling a pro-Communist line.[4] In a September 1947 article for the right-wing monthly *Plain Talk*, Freda Utley (a former party member who was, by now, a full-throated anti-communist) launched a ferocious attack on Snow, who had joined the solidly conservative *Saturday Evening Post* as foreign correspondent in 1942. 'Students of totalitarian propaganda', she wrote, 'have long recognized that the readers of the *Saturday Evening Post* have had the Communists' views regularly distilled for them by Edgar Snow for years past.' Eschewing Marxist jargon, Snow used 'language and arguments readily understood by American readers' and 'represents himself as standing aloof and merely "informing" his readers of "facts" they ought to know'. But really, she claimed, Snow was a 'conjurer' who used semantics and assertion to 'trick' the public into believing that the Chinese Communists were 'really nice liberal democrats' or that, once in power, they would not slavishly follow the Moscow line. Snow, she concluded, was, 'without doubt, one of the cleverest, smoothest, and most subtle advocates the Kremlin has ever had on its side'.[5] Robert Welch, president of the right-wing John Birch Society, offered a typically sensationalist spin: Snow's writings on China had, he claimed, 'helped mightily in the brainwashing of the American people which enabled the Communist influences in our midst to manipulate the sell-out of China to the agents of the Kremlin'.[6] Right-wing suspicions about Snow were, of course, hardly allayed by the unpopular positions he continued to take during the 1950s, supporting, as FBI agents duly noted, 'the necessity for peaceful

---

* This charge was unfair. As Snow explained in 1941, 'my personal feeling in the matter is that liberals who build up hopes that the Communists of China are "different" and "only reformers" and have abandoned revolutionary methods . . . are doomed to ultimate disillusionment.' (Edgar Snow, *Battle for Asia*, 290–1).

coexistence with the Soviet Union' and advocating for 'the recognition of Red China'.*⁷

Rumours that Snow was a communist had begun to circulate back in the 1930s: his public opposition to racial segregation as practised in Shanghai; his growing sympathy for the plight of the Chinese peasantry; and his determination to challenge the 'Red bandit' thesis and take the Communist movement seriously, were more than enough to draw suspicion. In a letter to his brother Howard in July 1935, Ed rebutted the charge. He was not, he explained, a member of any political organisation, nor did he 'attempt to interpret facts as I find them from any ready-made economic or political doctrine whatever, whether Marxist or Leninist or Mussolinian or Rooseveltian'. 'The worst handicaps I have', he continued, 'are a lingering belief in such things as the rights of men to equal opportunity, a belief in the fundamental soundness of such concepts as freedom of speech, freedom of press, freedom of assembly, and a somehow undying faith in the notion that the highest degree of individual freedom (in the largest social sense) is not necessarily incompatible with democratic political forms.' Finally, he explained, he believed it was possible 'that we Americans will be able to maintain a certain consistency with the original ideas of the founders of the great republic . . . and work out a decent civilized system of life and economics which will fairly soon put the control of the means of production in the hands of the people, and for the widest social benefit'. 'If this is treason,' he concluded, then 'tell the Liberty League, or whatever it is called, to prepare the noose.'⁸ Although during the Cold War he quickly grew sick of the Red-baiting, Snow remained dogged in his defence. 'It is a lie', he wrote in a letter published in the *New York Times* in December 1953, 'to state or infer in any way that I

* It was not until the early 1970s, under the presidency of Richard Nixon, that the United States began to work towards normalising relations with the People's Republic of China. Although formal diplomatic recognition did not come until 1 January 1979, the PRC had officially taken China's place in the United Nations (including its permanent seat on the Security Council) in the autumn of 1971, just weeks before Nixon's historic visit to China.

am or have ever been a Communist.'⁹ The year before, the same paper had carried Snow's emphatic response to testimony before the Senate Internal Security Subcommittee that, once again, had identified him as a suspected Communist sympathiser: 'There is', he said, 'no basis for any statement that I am a Communist or Pro-Communist. I am not and never have been.' 'If anyone makes that statement outside Congressional immunity,' he continued, 'I will consider it grounds for a libel or slander action and will act at once.'¹⁰

The damage, though, was done.

Snow, who had finally returned to the United States in January 1941, now found it increasingly difficult to earn a living as a journalist. Although he had served as its distinguished foreign correspondent during the 1940s, the *Saturday Evening Post* carried only three of the twenty-five articles he suggested for publication in 1950 (he resigned as associate editor the following year), and his books were banned in US government-sponsored libraries overseas. Reliant on his second wife, the actress Lois Wheeler (they married in May 1949, after Ed's protracted divorce from Helen), the generosity of friends and the small amounts of work he was able to obtain, Snow eventually decided to leave the United States in 1959, for Geneva, for a year of teaching and travel. It turned out to be a permanent exile.¹¹

In his 1963 book *How the Far East Was Lost*, Anthony Kubek – a historian and spokesperson for the China Lobby* – identified Snow as 'the one American who has done more than any other to portray and to explain the Chinese Communists, their principles, and objectives in a favorable light'. *Red Star Over China*, which supposedly offered an 'exultant account of life among the Chinese guerrillas', was, he continued, 'the opening gun in what subsequently became

* The China Lobby was a constellation of advocacy groups and activists who were fiercely pro-Nationalist and anti-Communist. After the founding of the People's Republic of China, they continued to support Chiang (who had fled to Taiwan) and opposed efforts to recognise the PRC at the United Nations.

a tremendous effort to impress the general public with the virtue, courage, bravery, and humanity of the Chinese Communists'.[12] Edgar Snow was no communist, and *Red Star Over China* no crass work of propaganda. But, as it turned out, Kubek was on to something. In her landmark 2019 book *Maoism: A Global History*, the historian Julia Lovell has shown how *Red Star Over China* served to bolster the Communists' appeal among many young, urban, liberal Chinese citizens, elevated the status and reputation of Mao Zedong as the party's driving force and pre-eminent leader, and ultimately helped to make 'Maoism' a genuinely global phenomenon. Indeed, she has even claimed that, without Snow, 'both a domestic and an international cult of Mao would be hard to imagine'.[13]

A complex, and at times bewildering and contradictory set of ideas, Maoism (or, as the Chinese Communist Party prefers, 'Mao Zedong Thought') represented an innovative and highly consequential attempt to adapt Soviet-style Marxism to China's predominantly rural peasant society. Described by Lovell as a 'potent mix of party-building discipline, anti-colonial rebellion, and "continuous revolution"', it would prove enormously influential throughout the second half of the twentieth century.[14] Given its inconsistencies, its mutability and the different guises that it has taken in different locales at different times, scholars have – understandably – struggled to define Maoism. As one historian has quipped, 'Maoism doesn't exist. It never has done. That, without doubt, explains its success.'[15]

Popularised by journalists and foreign visitors (including actors, musicians, writers and activists) and summarised in short, pithy quotations from Mao (most famously those collected in the *Little Red Book*), Maoism – with the personality of the Chairman at its centre – was rooted in a handful of core ideas: the primacy of political violence as an organising philosophy (summed up in Mao's famous phrase, 'Political power comes out of the barrel of a gun'); the revolutionary potential of the peasantry; the importance of guerrilla warfare; an emphasis on practice rather than theory; and a staunch anti-imperialism. In fact, as movements to throw off colonialism flared across Asia and Africa in the aftermath of the Second World War, Mao was quick to place the newly founded PRC at the centre of the global anti-imperialist movement. Characterising the 'imperialists' and 'reactionaries' as 'paper tigers', he declared that 'the countries of the Americas, Asia, and Africa will have to go on quarrelling with the United States till the very end, till the paper tiger is destroyed by the wind and the rain.'[16]

Although it only came into formal existence during the 1940s, Maoism drew on ideas and practices that Mao had been developing since co-founding the Communist Party in 1927, if not before. And, in popularising Maoism, both in China and around the world, Edgar Snow – or, more accurately, his brilliant book – played a starring role.[17]

On returning from Bao'an, Ed was keen for his story to be known in China as well as in the West. He passed on some of his early articles to academics and writers with the National Salvation Front (which had been formed by Manchurian exiles to pressure the Nationalists into taking on the Japanese) and they were published, secretly, in April 1937. A brief account of Snow's interview with Mao appeared in *Yanda zhoukan*, a magazine produced by students at Yenching University, in December 1936, while more substantial – and accessible – pieces on the Communist leader were carried in the Shanghai-based *Wenzhai* in August and September 1937. Then, in early 1938, the first Chinese edition of *Red Star Over China* was published. Translated by a small but dedicated team headed by the fearless and talented Hu Yuzhi (an intellectual, and underground party member), the book appeared under the relatively innocuous title *Xixing manji* ('Narrative of a Journey West') in a bid to evade the Guomindang censors.[18] With the war against Japan now raging, the book proved a huge hit. As Lovell has explained:

Student political groups were mesmerised by *Red Star* and its author; it circulated secretly across universities and high schools in

Shanghai, where 50,000 copies were printed; pirate versions spread over China and sinophone Asia. Readers were so avid that some copies were ripped into individual chapters, to enable Snow's words to travel more rapidly.[19]

Dong Leshan, who worked on a new translation of *Red Star* during the 1970s, recalled the 'delight and excitement' that he had felt on first encountering the text. Despite it being banned, countless young Chinese readers had, he noted, nevertheless gained their initial understanding of both the Communist Party and the Chinese Revolution via the book. 'Like a bright star shining in a dark sky,' he explained, *Red Star Over China* 'guided thousands on the road of revolution'.[20]

Many of those who had been inspired by Snow's book now flocked to Yan'an, the new Red capital, joined the party's urban underground or took up arms – either for the Red Army or as guerrilla fighters – in the war against the Japanese. Some were encouraged directly by Snow. In March 1937, Zhao Rongsheng was one of about twenty students who attended an informal afternoon seminar at the house of an American professor in Beijing. There, Ed passed around some two hundred photographs and several pages of typescript from his book, showed film footage that he had shot in Shaanxi and discussed his interviews with Mao and experiences with the Red Army. He also told the students that, if they wanted to find out more, 'you'd better go there and have a look for yourselves.' The experience was electrifying, and Zhao recalled how 'Snow's stories of what he had seen and heard and the photos he brought back created a lasting impression.' A few weeks later, Zhao and nine of his fellow students headed to Yan'an. 'We learnt a great deal,' he recalled. While one of the party remained in Yan'an to study, the rest returned to Beijing to organise the student movement there, under instructions from Mao to be 'models for the people'.[21]

The Chairman and his allies must have been delighted by *Red Star*'s impact. From the outset, the Communist leaders had taken great care to ensure that the image they presented to Snow was as positive and congenial as possible. In this, Snow turned out to be the first in a long line of foreign guests who were exploited by China's Communist leaders to present their (carefully curated) message to the outside world.[22] Although the archives relating to the planning of Snow's visit in 1936 remain closed, Mao's summary instructions are nonetheless highly revealing: 'Security, secrecy, warmth and red carpet.' Snow was, as we have seen, given a tremendous (and emotionally charged) welcome on his arrival at Bao'an. At a time of great scarcity and hardship, he was often provided with baked bread, meat, sugar, coffee and other relative luxuries, for which his offer of payment was almost always declined. When it came to the set-piece interviews with Mao, the final transcripts were checked carefully.[23] Although he spoke reasonable conversational Chinese, Snow was reliant on an interpreter, Wu Lianping, to translate Mao's answers into English. After diligently writing down what Wu reported, the transcript was translated back into Chinese and submitted to Mao for a final check, before being translated back into English again. In *Red Star*, Snow described this process of corroboration (or, as some critics unfairly have it, 'censorship'), explaining that Mao was 'noted for his insistence upon accuracy of detail'.[24] Back in Beijing, Snow also agreed to some (though by no means all) requests to excise or rewrite certain passages of his book – toning down criticisms of Chiang, for example, over concerns that they might damage efforts to establish a united front (a project that, it is worth emphasising, Snow fully supported). But when Mao suggested, through an intermediary, that he downplay the Communists' commitment to the class struggle, Ed simply ignored it.[25]

Given what we now know about the reality of life in Mao's China during the 1950s and 1960s – the terrible famines, the political violence and the millions of lives lost or ruined – it is very easy to be critical of Snow; to see him as naïve, a dupe, or worse. His own disillusionment with the Nationalist government, instinctive support for the underdog, sympathy for the plight of the long-suffering Chinese peasantry and left-of-centre political beliefs certainly predisposed him to view the Communists in a positive light. But, in the final analysis, *Red Star Over China* conveyed his honest impressions of Red China and the Communist movement – as he saw and experienced them personally – in Shaanxi in the autumn of 1936. Writing to the American ambassador in Nanjing, in February 1937, Snow readily conceded that he had been 'subjected to certain doses of propaganda'. While he did not claim 'any supernatural powers in this respect', he explained that 'certain experience has enabled me to distinguish fact from fiction, and wherever my personal sympathies may lie,' he explained, 'I continue to be from Missouri' – the Show-Me state.'[26]

In fact, Snow worked hard to check evidence, took detailed notes and left out material that he felt was unreliable.[27] As one scholar has noted, 'the quality of Snow's research and methodology gave *Red Star Over China* a ring of authenticity which could hardly go unnoticed even by those with only a casual knowledge of Chinese affairs.'[28] Still, the overall picture that he painted was, without doubt, a sympathetic one. He had found his time with the Red Army 'exhilarating' and, while in the Shaanxi Soviet, had developed both a good rapport with, and a high opinion of, the senior Communist leadership.[29] Both of these things were reflected in what he wrote and said. Responding to an article published in his hometown newspaper on 27 April 1938, criticising *Red Star* and accusing the Reds of being 'baby-killers', Snow retorted that the 'Chinese Communists, who are now leading China's war of independence, represent a very high type of political morality indeed'.[30]

At the apex of that struggle, of course, was Mao Zedong. In the autumn of 1936, Mao's pre-eminent position within the Communist

---

* The best-known legend attributes the state's unofficial motto to Congressman Willard Duncan Vandiver. In 1899, he gave a speech at a naval banquet in Philadelphia in which he declared, 'I come from a state that raises corn and cotton and cockleburs and Democrats, and frothy eloquence neither convinces nor satisfies me. I am from Missouri. You have got to show me.' See www.sos.mo.gov/archives/history/slogan.asp.

Party was, unbeknownst to Snow, far from assured; indeed, the following year he would face a stiff challenge from Wang Ming, Moscow's preferred candidate, for control of the movement. Moreover, the Chairman was, as Julia Lovell has put it, 'not even first among equals'. Seen as a 'practical man of military strategy', Mao was viewed as an unoriginal thinker who routinely deferred to his better-educated comrades (many of whom had spent time in Moscow). *Red Star Over China* – with Mao's biography as its centrepiece – helped to change all that.[31] Snow's Mao was earthy and relatable, a poet and a philosopher, a military innovator and an expert political organiser. He was, in the words of one Indian admirer of *Red Star Over China*, 'the most dazzling star of all mankind'.[32]

As that comment suggests, the influence of Snow's extraordinary book was by no means restricted to China. Revolutionaries and anticolonial nationalists in Burma, Malaya, India and elsewhere were inspired by *Red Star*'s discussions of guerrilla warfare, the revolutionary potential of the peasantry and the apparent charisma of the Chairman.[*][33] After being appointed to head the newly founded uMkhonto weSizwe ('The Spear of the Nation') in 1961, Nelson Mandela set about learning how to start a revolution. Among the numerous sources he consulted was 'Edgar Snow's brilliant *Red Star Over China* [in which] I saw that it was Mao's determination and non-traditional thinking that had led him to victory'.[34] Meanwhile, *Red Star* helped to introduce Mao, and Maoism, to a new generation of student radicals across Western

---

* Snow was also responsible for an early, and widely circulated, image of Mao. As one of his translators, the young Yenching student Huang Hua, explained, just before heading to the front to visit the Red Army, Snow asked to take a photograph of the Chairman. Huang recalled that, 'as we stepped out of the cave, Mao looked quite smart in the sun. His clothes were neat but his hair was somewhat ruffled. So Snow took off his own brand new army cap with the red star and suggested the Chairman wear it. This was a shot that Snow was most proud of and which had become well known to most Chinese people.' See www.chinadaily.com.cn/china/2006-10/22/content_713979_2.htm.

Europe (including in France, Germany and Italy) and – to the horror of conservatives – in Snow's own United States of America.

Barney Rosset, the legendary president of Grove Press, had read *Red Star* while stationed in China with the Army Signal Corps during the Second World War. (It had convinced him that the Communists would ultimately prevail.) In 1961, he published a new edition under the Black Cat imprint, for the mass market, which was advertised as a kind of handbook for revolution. Not only was it a 'satisfying and enlightening tale for the general reader' and an essential source for understanding the history of modern China, but – as the book's frontmatter pointed out – *Red Star Over China* had also served as a 'handbook of guerrilla warfare during World War II for anti-Nazi partisan fighters in Europe and anti-Japanese guerrillas in Southeast Asia'.[35]

During the 1960s, *Red Star Over China* was discussed, and publicised, in the pages of the vibrant underground press, and praised by a range of countercultural and radical groups. Those organising discussion evenings around the book, or encouraging activists to read it, included local chapters of Students for a Democratic Society; the University of Wisconsin Committee to End the War in Vietnam; the White Panther Party; and Control, Conflict and Change, an offshoot of the Motor City Labor League in Detroit, which sought to build support among the white working class for the black liberation movement, the anti-war movement and other radical causes.[36] More than a quarter of a century after its publication, it turned out that Snow's words were still capable of moving people to political action.

The young student radical Dennis O'Neil had first encountered Mao via the *Little Red Book*, but his admiration for the Chairman and his ideas was only strengthened after reading *Red Star Over China*.[37] In an intellectual and political odyssey that took in SDS, the anti-war movement and the revolutionary left, O'Neil was not alone. As he put it, 'I made the same evolution as hundreds of thousands of people in that age cohort . . . At first you're against the [Vietnam] war because war's horrible . . . And then you're against the war because it's a system: the system of imperialism . . . So we need to have a revolution . . .'³⁸ For radicals like O'Neil, Maoism – with its uncompromising commitment to revolution, searing anti-imperialism and support for liberation struggles across the globe* – seemed to offer an attractive template, one unencumbered by the well-documented excesses of the Soviet Union (not only Stalin's bloody purges, but also the crushing of the Hungarian Revolution in 1956 and the Prague Spring twelve years later).

Alex Hing became a revolutionary after reading *Red Star Over China* and *The Autobiography of Malcolm X* while a student at the City College of San Francisco, in early 1968. 'Both these books', he recalled, 'struck me as right on.'³⁹ Putting aside a life of petty crime, and rebelling against the oppressive atmosphere of his native Chinatown, Hing threw himself into radical causes: joining SDS, opposing the military draft and attending the Poor People's Campaign in Washington DC – an interracial effort to secure economic justice. On returning from the nation's capital, Hing sought to organise his fellow Asian Americans. An early member of, and key leader in, the Red Guard Party (a group explicitly modelled on the Black Panthers), Hing would spend the next two decades working with the Asian American movement.⁴⁰

During the 1960s, thousands of American radicals like O'Neil and Hing looked east, to Mao's China, for enlightenment.⁴¹ But, as it turned out, an even greater source of inspiration could be found much closer to home, just ninety miles off the coast of Florida.

* In 1957, Mao helped found the Afro-Asian People's Solidarity Organization, to promote national liberation and Third World solidarity. He also offered support to the African American freedom struggle: 'The evil system of colonialism and imperialism', Mao declared, 'arose and throve with the enslavement of Negroes . . . and it will surely come to its end with the complete emancipation of the black people.' In 1964, meanwhile, he declared: 'People of the world, unite and defeat the US aggressors and all their running dogs! People of the world, be courageous, dare to fight, defy difficulties and advance wave upon wave. Then the whole world will belong to the people. Monsters of all kinds shall be destroyed.'

PART THREE
CUBA

FIDEL

Fidel talking to reporters in New York, during his April 1959 visit
to the United States, just a few months after taking power.

25. GRANMA

We will be free men or martyrs.

– FIDEL CASTRO

In the early hours of Sunday 25 November 1956, a creaking twin-engine leisure yacht set sail from the Mexican port city of Tuxpan, bound for Cuba. At fifty-eight feet long, and with limited deck space, a modest lounge and four small cabins, the *Granma* was designed to accommodate roughly two dozen people. Packed aboard the boat that night, however, were eighty-two men, all members of the 26th of July Movement (M-26-7), a revolutionary organisation committed to ending the rule of President Fulgencio Batista, Cuba's American-backed dictator.

At the head of this band of rebels was Fidel Castro, an enigmatic thirty-year-old lawyer and professional revolutionary who had paid an American expat dentist $15,000 for the vessel, which had been given the affectionate nickname he used for his wife, Hazel. Squeezed in among the compañeros, who included Fidel's younger brother, Raúl, Juan Almeida – one of the few senior revolutionaries of African descent – and the enigmatic Argentine doctor Ernesto 'Che' Guevara, was a substantial arsenal (two anti-tank guns, three Thompson submachine guns, ninety rifles and more than three dozen pistols, plus ammunition), as well as a small quantity of food and medical supplies, and some two thousand gallons of fuel stored in metal cans on deck.[1]

Just days earlier, Mexican police had seized a cache of weapons and arrested several of the movement's activists during a raid on a rebel safe house in an upmarket neighbourhood of the capital. Meanwhile, severe storm warnings had led the local authorities to issue an order prohibiting all sea travel. With the net closing in, and local officials on high alert, the *Granma*'s crew were keen to depart as quietly as possible. As she slipped away from her moorings, all the lights on board were turned out and the yacht was powered by just one engine, running at low speed. The young revolutionaries – 'crouched so closely together' that they were 'almost on top of each other' – held their breath as the boat inched its way down the Tuxpan river and across the harbour, before finally reaching the Gulf of Mexico and the relative sanctuary of open water. After a tense hour, the revolutionaries permitted themselves a moment of emotional release. 'As one', they stood for a stirring rendition of the Cuban national anthem, followed by the rousing 26th July hymn: 'Onward Cubans!' they sang. 'May Cuba reward our heroism; for we are soldiers who are going to free the motherland.'[2]

Cuba, the biggest island in the Antilles, is an enchanting place but also, it is said, one that labours under a curse. Although it had achieved nominal independence in 1898 after the American military 'liberated' the country from Spanish rule, the island was run as a virtual colony of the United States for much of the next fifty years. Under the terms of the so-called Platt Amendment – an American measure that, in 1901, was written into the new Cuban constitution – Washington reserved the formal right to interfere in Cuba's domestic affairs in the event of a breakdown in law and order, or a threat to property rights. The United States also restricted Cuba's ability to pursue an independent foreign policy, including the right to make treaties and to establish commercial relationships with other nations, and insisted on the right to maintain military facilities on the island. These included a major naval base at Guantánamo Bay, which was secured in 1903 with an open-ended lease.[3] Even after relinquishing some formal powers in 1934, Uncle Sam continued to exercise a profound – some would say profoundly distorting – influence over the island's economy and political culture.[4]

On the surface, Cuba in the mid-1950s was doing rather well, thanks in large part to the post-war American economic boom. The price of sugar, Cuba's main export, had remained stable and crop yields had begun to grow, while a substantial growth in tourism from the United States had seen the construction of numerous hotels, casinos and clubs. Meanwhile, Cuba's per capita income, literacy rates and life expectancy ranked among the highest in Latin America. But beneath this healthy veneer lay significant structural problems. Cuba's economy was heavily over-reliant on sugar, which constituted 50 per cent of the island's agricultural production and 80 per cent of its exports (half its sugar was sold to the USA), employed almost a quarter of the workforce and accounted for about 30 per cent of GDP. Moreover, US economic interests, worth some $1 billion ($18 billion in 2018 prices), concentrated in banking, utilities, mining, tourism and agriculture, meant that much of the island's wealth was in the hands of foreign corporations and investors. Partly as a result of this, Cuba's society, with its population of six million, was marred by deep inequality. At the top were some nine hundred thousand who controlled 43 per cent of the nation's income, and who lived a life of luxury in air-conditioned villas, with access to private beach resorts and regular shopping excursions to Miami. For those at the bottom, however, life was starkly different: 1.5 million Cubans were either unemployed, worked as landless labourers or eked out a living as subsistence farmers. Owning just 2 per cent of the nation's wealth, they often survived on a meagre diet of rice, beans and sugar-water.[5]

The island also faced some seemingly intractable political problems. Ever since independence, Cuba's political institutions had been weak, and there was a pervasive culture of gangsterism and corruption.[6] Aside from a brief period of democratic, constitutional rule, which lasted from 1940 to 1952, Cuba's political culture was characterised by instability, intrigue and violence. From 1934, when a self-styled 'revolutionary' government was overthrown by a group of Cuban Army officers, through to the end of the 1950s, one man dominated Cuban politics: Fulgencio Batista.

Born in 1901, of mixed-race peasant stock, Batista joined the army as a private in 1921, following a stint as a labourer. A decade later he was appointed as a military court stenographer, before rising to the very top in 1934 by leading a military takeover of the government.

Batista introduced a new constitution in 1940 and, four years later, stepped down from office following free and fair elections in which the opposition Auténtico Party had triumphed. But the following eight years were extraordinarily corrupt, even by Cuba's own appallingly low standards. The verdict of Louis Pérez, one of Cuba's leading historians, is unsparing: 'Embezzlement, graft, corruption, and malfeasance of public office permeated every branch of national, provincial, and municipal government.'

On 10 March 1952, Batista emerged from retirement to lead a second coup; cancelling the elections that had been scheduled for 1 June, he appointed himself president. During his first period in office, Batista had embarked on progressive reforms and enjoyed a measure of public support. But his second term proved to be quite different. Structural problems were ignored, corruption continued, and in the face of rising popular discontent Batista increasingly relied on repression and brutality to maintain his position: the Cuban Communist Party, the Partido Comunista de Cuba, or PCC, was outlawed, the labour movement and civil organisations were co-opted and dissent was crushed.[7] In September 1955, the *New York Times* lamented how Batista, drunk on the 'heady wine of power', had sold his political soul to the 'devil of dictatorship'.[8] In the months leading up to the *Granma* expedition, Cuba had been rocked by student protests, outbreaks of violence – including an armed assault on an army barracks and the assassination of the chief of military intelligence – and the uncovering of several anti-Batista plots. But this only brought fresh waves of repression and violence from the regime. The island was, it seemed, primed for revolution.[9]

One of the earliest challenges to Batista's second power grab had come from none other than Fidel Castro. Fidel – like both Mao and Lenin before him – had enjoyed a relatively privileged upbringing, thanks to his father, Ángel, an immigrant from Galicia, Spain, who had managed to pull himself up by his bootstraps to become a wealthy landowner. The young Fidel was raised on his father's sugar farm, in Oriente province, which boasted a rambling, plantation-style mansion as well as a bakery, a general store, a blacksmith, a slaughterhouse and a barracks-type building, with dirt floors and palm-leaf roofs, that housed the farm's migrant workers. Near to the house, Fidel recalled, there was a 'big orange grove where my father personally oversaw the pruning, with a big two-handed pair of shears'. Across the thirty or so acres were 'all kinds of fruit trees', including plantains, coconuts, papaya and sugar-apples, as well as forty or so beehives. 'I could', explained Fidel, 'walk through that orange grove with my eyes closed . . . I knew where every single kind of fruit tree was; I'd peel the orange with my fingers, and I'd spend my whole summer and Christmas holidays out there. Nobody ate more oranges than I did.'[10] Fidel's childhood might have been relatively gilded, but the same could not be said for most of his contemporaries. Mayarí – the region where he grew up – was dominated by the all-powerful American-owned sugar companies, such as United Fruit. And with these companies came stark inequalities of wealth and opportunity. Cuban cane-cutters (including the fathers of Fidel's childhood friends) lived in squalid shacks, earning just a dollar a day – sometimes less – during the four months of the sugar harvest, while living hand to mouth during the so-called 'dead time'. The companies' American employees and their families, in contrast, enjoyed a sumptuous lifestyle in gated communities.[11] Fidel later claimed that his passion for social justice had been forged during his childhood: memories of his friends going barefoot because their families could not afford shoes were, he said, seared into his consciousness. This, together with what he described as an 'unquestionably rebellious' temperament, had shaped his political outlook and commitment to revolution.[12]

Fidel's reference to his rebellious streak was telling. As a child, he had earned the nickname El Loco ('The Crazy One') for his habitual refusal to follow the rules or otherwise defer to authority. He clashed repeatedly with his parents – refusing to take regular baths, attempting to organise a strike by his father's farm workers and even, during one outburst, threatening to burn down the family home. Sent to boarding school, first in Santiago and then in Havana, Fidel was also in frequent conflict with his teachers, firing rocks onto the roof of a teacher's house with a makeshift slingshot, fighting with other boys and forging the grades on his end-of-year report card. Although clearly bright, Fidel was a poor student who, by his own admission, 'never paid attention in any lesson', and instead put his energies into mountain climbing and sports – particularly baseball, basketball and football (soccer), at which he excelled.[13]

After high school, Fidel enrolled at the University of Havana, where he eventually specialised in law, diplomatic law and social sciences. The university, whose magnificent buildings dominate Aróstegui Hill in the northern suburb of Vedado, provided an ideal environment for fashioning a revolutionary. From the moment he entered, in the autumn of 1945, he could 'see an atmosphere of force, of fear, of weapons', with the university itself controlled by supporters of the corrupt and unpopular government of Ramón Grau. In no time, Fidel was neglecting his studies in favour of the cut and thrust of student radicalism.[14] At a time when factional disputes – and even elections – were often settled violently, Fidel became adept in the dark arts of street politics, participating in raucous protests and facing down his opponents, a Browning fifteen-shot pistol seldom far from his side. In the spring of 1948, he was even arrested during an investigation into the murder of a local politician (and subsequently released without charge). Fidel, a prize-winning debater, also displayed an early penchant for the long, fiery speeches for which he would later become famous – although, in these days, he sported a pencil-thin moustache rather than a beard, and donned fashionable dark-coloured suits rather than olive-green fatigues.[15]

During this formative period in his life, Fidel's political allegiances lay with the supporters of Eduardo Chibás, the founder and leader of the Orthodox Party (or the Party of the Cuban People) and radio

FIDEL

broadcaster, who used his regular Sunday-evening slot to denounce the theft and corruption that marred the island, and to champion Cuban nationalism. Fidel also began to immerse himself in the politics of anti-imperialism: in 1947, as chairman of the Federation of University Students' Committee for Dominican Democracy, he joined an ill-fated expedition to fight the dictatorship of the Dominican Republic's Rafael Trujillo and was in Bogotá the following spring when a failed uprising took place. These experiences, he later claimed, confirmed his faith in 'irregular' warfare; 'you couldn't fight head-on against an army in Cuba or the Dominican Republic,' he explained, 'because the army had a naval element, an air element, it had everything. It was stupid not to acknowledge that.'[16]

After graduating in 1950, Castro set up a legal practice with two of his classmates, in a somewhat shabby area of Havana, to defend the rights of the poor. Although he had married Mirta Díaz-Balart, the daughter of a prominent supporter of Batista, in October 1948, Fidel's first love remained politics. And, while he had shown some interest in the ideas of Marx and Lenin, he was – at this stage – no communist. Inspired by Cuba's long struggle for independence, Fidel's great hero was José Martí. Born in Havana in January 1853, this poet, political philosopher, journalist and revolutionary had spent most of the 1880s and early 1890s in exile in New York, publishing widely – on culture and the arts, as well as politics. He wrote more than three hundred articles for the *Sun*, then the city's most popular newspaper, and its sister weekly the *Hour*, honing a powerful critique of American imperialism and corporate capitalism, and translating the work of American writers such as Walt Whitman for a Latin American audience. In April 1895, Martí returned to his native Cuba to help lead the nationalist uprising. His death at the hands of the Spanish, on 19 May during the Battle of Dos Ríos, made him a nationalist martyr.[17]

Committed, like Martí, to eliminating the vested interests, the social and economic inequality, and the political corruption that marred his homeland, Fidel railed against US imperialism in Latin

America and demanded 'justice for the workers and Cuban peasantry'. He was preparing to run for a seat in the lower house of Congress, for the Orthodox Party, when Batista launched his coup and abruptly cancelled the elections. A few days later, the mercurial young lawyer distributed a manifesto denouncing this usurpation of power and calling for the restoration of the constitution. 'There is', Fidel stated, 'nothing as bitter in the world as the spectacle of a people that goes to bed free and awakens in slavery.' Invoking the Cuban national anthem, he declared that 'to live in chains' was 'to live in shame!' But with the democratic route now firmly closed off, it did not take long before Fidel began to turn to the politics of revolution.

On Sunday 16 March 1952, Fidel joined other supporters of the Orthodox Party in Havana's Colón Cemetery, for a rally at the grave of Eduardo Chibás (who had committed suicide the previous year). Incensed by the 'tepid' speeches made by the party's leaders, Fidel raised his right arm into the air and shouted out, 'If Batista grabbed power by force, he must be thrown out by force!'[18] Alongside filing lawsuits against the new Cuban regime and penning denunciations of Batista for various newspapers, Fidel also began to build a revolutionary network from his friends' apartment, recruited more than a thousand volunteers, organised clandestine military training and looked for ways to take the fight to Batista. By the end of 1952 he had settled on the idea of seizing a major army base; by the spring of the following year he had selected his target and begun to formulate a detailed plan of operations. Speaking to some 130 followers crammed into a modest farmhouse at Siboney, twenty kilometres east of Santiago de Cuba, on the night of Saturday 25 July 1953, Fidel told his comrades that 'in a few hours you will be victorious or defeated, but regardless of the outcome . . . this Movement will triumph.'[19]

Just after dawn on 26 July, a daring assault began on the Moncada Barracks in Santiago – the country's second-largest military garrison. Fidel's plan was simple enough: use the element of surprise to seize the barracks and its mighty arsenal while most of the soldiers were still in their bunks; simultaneously use smaller groups of fighters to occupy the Palace of Justice next door, as well as the city's hospital and radio station; then demand a return to constitutional government while arousing 'the people' to join the rebellion. The plan was a bold one, but it was also, to say the least, foolhardy. Fidel's band of 150 or so rebels – idealistic young men who had cut their teeth in student politics, alongside labourers, farmworkers and a handful of middle-class professionals – were armed mainly with 0.22-calibre rifles, and never likely to overpower a heavily armed fortress of some one thousand troops. The plan unravelled almost immediately: Castro's forces were spotted by an army patrol shortly after they arrived at the barracks. Within minutes the rebels were pinned down by gunfire. For Castro, 'more than the shooting, I remember the deafening, bitter sounds of the alarm sirens that thwarted our plan.' Although Fidel managed to escape, many of his companions were not so fortunate. More than sixty lost their lives – most of them after having been captured and then tortured. The treatment meted out by the army and security personnel was sickening: many prisoners were beaten with rifle butts, and at least three were dragged to their deaths behind a jeep. Haydée Santamaría, one of two young women involved in the attempted putsch, was said to have been presented with the bloody, gouged-out eyeball of her brother, Abel, during her own interrogation. Haydée's boyfriend, Boris Luis Santa Coloma, was also tortured to death by Batista's henchmen.

In the aftermath of the assault, a number of civilians, wrongly suspected of involvement, were rounded up; some were killed. Fidel himself was finally apprehended on 1 August while sleeping in a small hut on the outskirts of a farm. The dozen or so soldiers who seized him were, he recalled, 'furious. The veins and arteries in their necks, I'll never forget, were all swollen and throbbing.' With the Batista regime claiming, falsely, that Fidel's rebels had slit the throats of the sick soldiers who had been in the Moncada infirmary, it was hardly surprising that 'they wanted to kill us on the spot.' In the event, Fidel's life was spared only because the lieutenant who captured him – Pedro Sarría – was, in contrast to many of his colleagues, a fundamentally decent man. 'Calm down! Take it easy!' Fidel recalled him saying, repeatedly. 'Don't shoot. You can't kill ideas.'[20]

Put on trial in the autumn, charged with organising an armed uprising against the 'Constitutional Powers of the State', Castro mounted his own defence. As he told the court: 'Only one who has been so deeply wounded, who has seen his country so forsaken and justice so vilified, can speak at a moment like this with words that spring from the blood of his heart and the essence of truth.'[21] It was the start of a brilliant courtroom performance, and one of the most famous political speeches in modern political history. Over the course of two hours, Fidel sought to expose the 'horrible, repulsive crimes' that the Batista regime had inflicted on the prisoners and to 'show the nation and the world the infinite misfortune of the Cuban people' who were, he said, 'suffering the cruelest, the most inhuman oppression of their history'. He defended his fellow Moncada rebels as brave, patriotic heroes, dedicated to the cause of freedom and justice, and to securing 'the greatness and happiness of one's country', and condemned the president – a 'tyrant more vicious, more arrogant than ever' – as a 'criminal and a thief'. After outlining his political manifesto – a restoration of constitutional government, comprehensive land reform, granting workers the right to share in the profits of large companies, the elimination of corruption and the recovery of Cuba's stolen wealth – Fidel concluded his lengthy speech with a defiant cry: 'I do not fear prison, as I do not fear the fury of the miserable tyrant who took the lives of 70 of my comrades. Condemn me. It does not matter. History will absolve me.'[22]

Found guilty and sentenced to fifteen years, Fidel was, along with a number of his fellow rebels, incarcerated in a prison on the Isle of Pines, fifty kilometres south of the mainland. Here, he put his time to good use: reading widely, writing numerous letters and working to shore up his nascent opposition movement (which, it was quickly decided, would be named the 26th of July Movement – or M-26-7 – in honour of the attack on Moncada). A number of the M-26-7 leaders tutored their comrades, holding classes in the prison library. Fidel taught seminars in philosophy, world history and public speaking. In his letters, he wrote warmly of his comrades, praising their discipline and spirit, and explaining proudly how, having 'learned to handle weapons', these great young men were now:

> learning to wield books for the important battles of the future. Their discipline is Spartan; their lives, their education is Spartan; everything about them is Spartan, and their faith and commitment are so unshakable that they too will rise to the cry 'With the shield or on a shield!'

Apart from a brief period that saw their privileges suspended and Fidel cast into solitary confinement, the Moncadistas were permitted to receive regular visitors and had plenty of opportunity for exercise, and even to enhance their culinary skills. (Steak with guava jelly, spaghetti, and omelettes were some of Fidel's specialities.) With a regular supply of books, food and, crucially, cigars (the granite floor of his cell was, Fidel confessed, 'strewn with butts'), life could certainly have been a lot worse. In the spring of 1955, it suddenly got a great deal better. That April, in what would prove to be a catastrophic error of judgement, General Batista – basking in the glow of economic growth and American support, and increasingly complacent about his hold on power – granted an amnesty; on 15 May, Fidel, Raúl and eighteen other members of the 26th of July Movement walked free. Within weeks, Fidel – worried that his continued opposition to Batista would land him back in jail – headed into exile. On the afternoon of Thursday 7 July, he headed to Havana Airport and, after kissing his young son Fidelito goodbye, he boarded Mexican Aviation Company flight 566, bound for the port city of Veracruz. In a farewell message that was published in the mass-circulation weekly *Bohemia*, Fidel explained that:

> I am leaving Cuba because all doors of peaceful struggle have been closed to me. Six weeks after being released from prison I am convinced more than ever of the dictatorship's intention to remain in power for twenty years masked in different ways, ruling as now by the use of terror and crime and ignoring the patience of the Cuban people, which has limits . . . I believe the hour has come to take rights and not to beg for them, to fight instead of pleading for them. I will reside somewhere in the Caribbean. From trips such as this, one does not return or else one returns with the tyranny beheaded at one's feet.[23]

26. SHIPWRECK

Government planes strafed and bombed the revolutionary forces
tonight and wiped out 40 members of the 26th of July
Movement's supreme command. Thirty-year-old Fidel Castro,
its leader, was among those killed.
– UPI PRESS RELEASE

According to his biographer, Fidel 'arrived in Mexico with the clear and
specific purpose of organizing and training a rebel force that would land
in Cuba to engage in guerrilla warfare in the Sierra Maestra'. The plan was
for such a force to subsequently defeat the Cuban Army, topple Batista
and establish a new, revolutionary government.[1] The initial months of
exile, though, did not augur well. Perpetually short of money, Fidel too
often preferred to attend baseball games or while away the evenings
in animated and idealistic talk about his grand plans for Cuba, rather
than mastering the organisational detail that was required to launch
a successful revolution. Gradually, the situation began to improve. A
seven-week trip to the United States that autumn, during which he
gave barnstorming speeches to anti-Batista exiles in Philadelphia, New
York and Miami – raising funds, generating publicity and forging
connections with key figures – was a modest success. Weapons were
purchased and new rebels recruited – the most important of whom was
Ernesto 'Che' Guevara, a twenty-seven-year-old medic, Marxist and
committed revolutionary who had spent the previous year travelling
around South America, developing a deep affinity for the continent's
rural peasantry and an equally intense loathing of US imperialism. Che
was enormously impressed by Fidel's 'unshakeable faith' and optimism,
and was 'moved by a feeling of romantic, adventurous sympathy, and
by the conviction that it would be worth dying on an alien beach for
such a pure ideal'. Within hours of their first meeting – and despite
his grave doubts about whether the venture would succeed – Che had

'already become one of his future revolutionaries'.[2]

During these months of exile, Fidel also began to hone his political message. A manifesto, published in early August 1955 and distributed to supporters in Cuba as well as in Mexico, served as 'an open call for revolution, and a frontal attack against the clique of criminals who trample the honor of the nation and rule its destiny counter to its history and the sovereign will of the people'. 'The bridges have been burned,' Fidel declared – 'either we conquer the fatherland at any price so that we can live with dignity and honor, or we shall remain without one.' After a stinging indictment of Batista's mean and oppressive regime, Fidel explained that his movement had been 'formed without hatred for anyone' and that its 'ranks are open to all Cubans who sincerely desire to see political democracy reestablished and social justice introduced in Cuba'. Specific demands included land reform, wage increases, rent cuts, the nationalisation of public utilities, a mass education programme and an end to racial and sexual discrimination. The overall promise was of a new government that would serve the nation 'tirelessly and without self-interest' and produce 'a happier world for the Cuban people'.[3] A statement issued six months later channelled similar sentiments. Fidel characterised the 26th of July Movement as 'the revolutionary organization of the humble, by the humble, and for the humble', and declared that the group constituted:

> The hope of redemption for the Cuban working class, who can hope for nothing from the political cliques; it is the hope of the land for the peasants who live like pariahs in the country whose freedom their grandfathers won; it is the hope of going back home for the émigrés who had to leave their country, where they could not live or work; and it is the hope of daily bread for the hungry and of justice for the forgotten.[4]

In mid-January 1956, the training of Fidel's rebel army began in earnest. The man chosen to oversee this critical endeavour was

Lieutenant Colonel Alberto Bayo, a Cuban who had fought with the Spanish Army in the Rif Mountains of North Africa in the 1920s, studied guerrilla warfare at the Infantry Academy in Toledo and served as an adviser at the war ministry during the Spanish Republic's doomed attempt to face down Franco's nationalists during the civil war. Fleeing, like many of his Republican compatriots, to exile in Mexico City, Bayo had spent his days running a furniture factory, teaching, and mentoring various Latin American revolutionaries. Now, this white-haired sixty-three-year-old, 'intoxicated' by Fidel's enthusiasm and optimism, agreed to sell his business and resign his teaching positions, and 'subjugated' himself to the cause.[5]

Beginning with drill classes, endless marches around the neighbourhood, and basketball, soccer and rowing to improve their agility and physical fitness, the recruits – who now numbered more than sixty – moved on to more serious pursuits: shooting and ballistics, orienteering and then, after relocating to the Santa Rosa ranch twenty-five miles south-east of Mexico City, an intense programme that included more advanced weapons training, simulated combat, night marches and guard duty – all undertaken in makeshift mountain camps.[6] Che, for the first time, now began to entertain the possibility that 'victory was, in fact, possible.'[7]

And then, disaster struck.

On the evening of Wednesday 20 June, Mexican police raided a safe house in the Polanco district of the capital, seizing large quantities of weapons and rounding up several M-26-7 members. Fidel was arrested shortly thereafter and surrounded by armed officers on the street, before being bundled into a police cruiser and taken to the jail of the interior ministry, on Miguel E. Schultz Street. A couple of days later, the Santa Rosa ranch was raided, and more activists – including Che – were apprehended (although by this time much of the arsenal had been moved to a secret location). With clear evidence the group had been plotting an armed rebellion against the Cuban government, Batista pressed for Fidel's extradition. Holed up in jail for the best part of a month, while prominent left-wing lawyers argued for his release and supporters launched a media offensive on his behalf, Fidel became increasingly desperate – pacing 'back and forth like a caged lion' in the compound's central courtyard, concerned that his dreams of revolution had now crumbled into dust.[8]

In the event, the lawyers' arguments, combined with the Mexican government's reluctance to tarnish the country's reputation as a haven for dissidents, won out. The majority of the Cubans were released on 9 July, and two weeks later – following an intervention by former president Lázaro Cárdenas – Fidel was free once more.[9]

This brush with the law, alongside developments back in Cuba – where a 250,000-strong strike by sugar workers, growing urban unrest, and street battles between students and police all signified an intensification of opposition to Batista – added to the exiles' sense of urgency.[10] With the 26th of July Movement bolstered by the arrival of forty new recruits – among them twenty-four-year-old Camilo Cienfugos, the son of a Havana tailor, who had joined the anti-Batista underground in 1954 – Fidel now set about finalising his plans. In August, Frank País, an aspiring twenty-one-year-old teacher and coordinator for the 26th of July Movement in Oriente province, travelled to Mexico to talk strategy. Fidel, who had from the first determined that the rebel army would land in Oriente, in the easternmost part of the country, now discussed with País his plans for coordinated action with the so-called 'llano' – or urban underground. The idea was to distract the Cuban Army with multiple armed uprisings across the province, thereby making it easier for Fidel's rebels to reach the relative sanctuary of the Sierra Maestra, Cuba's largest mountain range.[11] Attempts were also made to establish a unified front among anti-Batista forces. On 30 August, following a meeting in Mexico City, Fidel and José Antonio Echeverría, the twenty-four-year-old student leader and general secretary of the Students' Revolutionary Directorate, issued a joint statement, declaring that they had 'decided to unite solidly their efforts in order to overthrow the tyranny and

The *Granma*, in front of Cuban naval headquarters on 12 June 1959, after being presented to the new revolutionary government.

carry out the Cuban Revolution'. With the country now 'ripe for revolution', M-26-7 and the SRD called for 'students, workers, youth organizations, and all men of dignity' to support the struggle to establish 'social justice, freedom, and democracy', and promised that 'victory will belong to those of us who fight on the side of history.'[12]

In September, the movement's perpetual money worries were solved, courtesy of a $100,000 donation from Cuba's former president Carlos Prío Socarrás – secured after Fidel swam the Río Grande for a clandestine meeting in the Texas border town of McAllen.[13] As well as bringing in fresh supplies of arms, the injection of cash enabled Fidel to finally turn his attention to the question of transport. In late September, after an abortive attempt to purchase a surplus Patrol Torpedo boat from the US Navy, Fidel – who was testing automatic rifles in the hills above Tuxpan with Mexican arms dealer El Cuate ('The Friend') – first laid eyes on the *Granma*. Sitting in a dry dock, and in terrible shape having sunk during a hurricane three years earlier, the vessel did not strike El Cuate as at all suitable (the cabin cruiser was, he pointed out, far too small), but Fidel could not be dissuaded: 'In this boat,' he declared, 'I'm going to Cuba.'[14]

Desperate repairs were still being made to the *Granma* when the call came to depart. With the Mexican police again closing in on the rebels, there was no time to lose. On 19 November, Fidel issued a statement – published in *Alerta*, the official government newspaper in Havana – declaring that, if Cuba's problems were not solved within two weeks, his 26th of July Movement would consider itself 'free to start the revolutionary struggle at any time'. This, he explained, was 'the only possible way out. We strongly reaffirm the promise we made for the year 1956: We will be free men or martyrs.'[15]

On the evening of Saturday 24 November, having dispatched a coded telegram to Frank País in Santiago – 'Book ordered out of print' – that indicated a planned landing at Playa las Coloradas, south of Niquero, on 30 November, Fidel and other M-26-7 members left Mexico City by bus, bound for Tuxpan.[16] The following night, recruits from locations across Mexico assembled at the dockside in torrential rain. Faustino Pérez, a thirty-six-year-old medic, recalled:

> Many 'civilians' crossed the river that night in rented boats; their owners rowed slowly. The 'travellers' gave generous tips hoping to cut down the chances of being turned in. One after the other, the groups came to the prearranged meeting place, using the darkest streets. We were totally convinced of the importance of our mission, and nobody asked questions, or even spoke. A silent embrace among the weeds at the river's edge was the only greeting between men who hadn't seen one another for some time. A short distance away, silent shadows moved toward the river; they were other comrades who were feverishly loading a small boat that could be partly seen in the lights reflected on the water – it was the *Granma*.[17]

On deck, dressed in a billowing black cape, was Fidel, overseeing the final preparations. The moment of truth had arrived.

Any elation that the *Granma*'s crew felt on making it undetected into the Gulf of Mexico proved to be short-lived. Almost immediately, a combination of rough seas, strong winds and the poor state of the boat threatened disaster. Dreadful seasickness struck most of the crew, leaving men lying 'immobile' and 'in strange positions' on the deck, their 'clothes covered in vomit' and their faces etched with anguish.[18] The boat also came perilously close to sinking. One comrade described how, as 'mountainous waves toyed with the small yacht', she began to ship water at an alarming rate. With the bilge pumps failing, the compañeros were forced to bail out the stricken craft by hand. 'We grabbed buckets and started bailing,' recalled Faustino Pérez, 'but the water kept on rising at our feet.' Fidel 'seemed worried' but, just as Pérez was fearing the worst, 'the deck's planks were beginning to reappear. The pumps were working and we all breathed more easily. The *Granma* was invincible. Forces other than purely physical ones had resisted the storm and were driving the ship to her destination.'[19]

In order to avoid detection by the Cuban Navy and Air Force, Fidel had plotted a route that had the *Granma* heading due east, to the tip of the Yucatán Peninsula, before heading south to give Cuba's southern coast a wide berth – and then making a straight dash for the western shore of Oriente province.

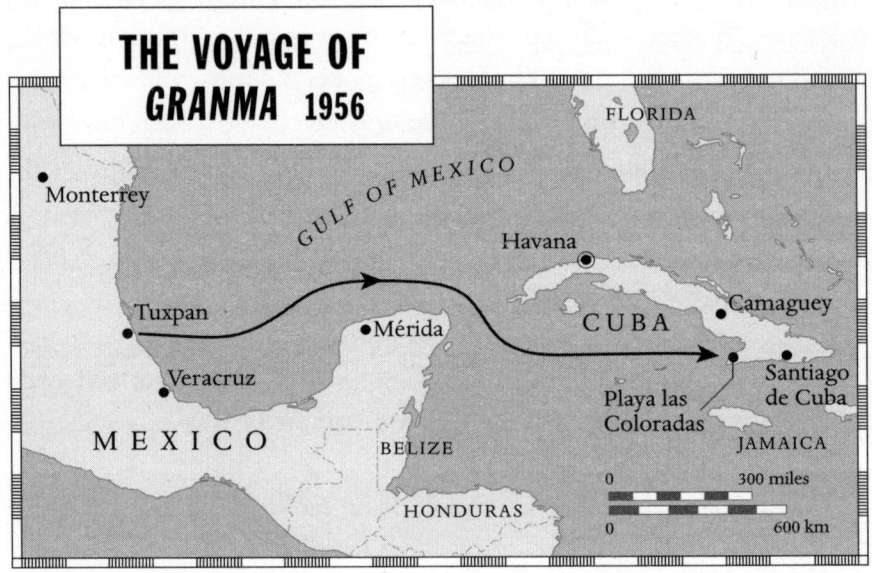

In good weather it should have been possible to make the journey in five days. But a combination of the fierce El Norte winds and the wretched state of the boat's badly worn gears meant that progress was painfully slow.[20] The mood of growing impatience was made worse by hunger. As the weather improved and the rebels' appetites returned, Fidel was forced to impose rationing, as the one hundred Hershey bars, two thousand oranges, half a dozen hams and 4.5 kilos of bread that had been hastily stacked onboard proved woefully inadequate. The original plan had been to land near Niquero on 30 November in coordination with a planned uprising in the nearby city of Santiago de Cuba. But, as dawn broke on the appointed day, the *Granma* had only made it as far as the Cayman Islands. With the ship's radio only able to receive messages, the compañeros were forced to sit and listen helplessly as a bulletin brought news that the revolution had begun without them.

Cuba's second city had, in fact, awoken that morning 'under heavy fire' as up to three hundred activists launched their attack with 'weapons of every caliber . . . spitting fire and lead'. Under the direction of País, the rebels, wearing their trademark drab olive-green fatigues and distinctive red-and-black armbands, chanted 'Down with Batista!' and 'Long live the Revolution!' as they launched a series of attacks. The police station, Customs House and other public buildings came under fire, and for a time the rebels were able to roam the city streets freely. In the end it took several days, and the arrival of 280 elite troops, to restore order. By then, the *Granma* had finally arrived on the island. Although, in the words of one compañero, 'It wasn't a landing, it was a shipwreck.'[21]

In the early hours of Sunday 2 December, the flashing light of the Cabo Cruz lighthouse on the south-western tip of Oriente was finally glimpsed by the *Granma*'s increasingly desperate crew. But as the ship's navigator, Roberto Roque, strained to make out the coast from atop the cabin, he lost his footing and toppled into the murky sea. Fidel ordered the captain to circle back, and the *Granma* spent an hour, using up precious reserves of fuel, in the search for the veteran sailor. Fidel even instructed that the ship's searchlight be turned on, and this at a time when doing so was more dangerous than ever. But, explained Pérez, 'nothing helped. Our comrade was being swallowed by the deep.' Refusing to give up, Fidel 'ordered one more search. We heard the cry, "Here!" again, weaker but inexplicably closer now,' and within minutes the half-drowned navigator was pulled aboard and revived.[22]

As dawn broke, the *Granma* ran aground about a hundred yards from Playa las Coloradas. They could hardly have picked a worse spot. Forced to abandon most of their equipment, the compañeros – proudly wearing their new uniforms and boots, and carrying rifles, knapsacks, cartridge belts and flasks – waded ashore through muddy salt water, only to find themselves faced with seemingly endless mangrove swamps whose 'thick, jumbled net' proved 'hard to penetrate'. It was, confessed Raúl Castro, 'Hell'. They struggled on for several hours before finally reaching dry land, exhausted and hungry, caked in mud, their hands and knees cut to ribbons. Help – and hospitality – soon came in the shape of Angel Pérez, a local charcoal burner, who offered the rebels sanctuary in his shack. While the compañeros scraped the mud from their uniforms and cleaned their weapons, Pérez's family began to roast a pig and some sweet potatoes for their visitors. But then, amid the sounds of shooting and shelling from the vicinity of the mangrove swamp, the men were forced to abandon the feast and seek sanctuary in the local hills. 'Everything', explained Fidel confidant Faustino Pérez, 'had gone awry.'[23]

With Batista's forces now hot on their tails, the rebels' only hope was to reach the Sierra Maestra mountain range to the east, whose high peaks offered relative sanctuary and a chance to regroup. The ragged band of revolutionaries pushed on – often marching at night to avoid the attention of spotter planes, sucking on sugar cane for sustenance and, occasionally, receiving help from local peasant families. But, as Che put it, these were truly 'terrible days'. Malnourished, desperately thirsty, and suffering from fungal infections and painful open blisters, they were 'an army of shadows, ghosts'. By the morning of Wednesday 5 December, the party was on the verge of total collapse – some men were fainting, while others begged for rest. There was no choice but to stop. They had reached a place called Alegría de Pío ('Joy of the Pious'), nothing more than a 'small grove of trees, bordering a sugarcane field on one side and open to some valleys on the other, with dense woods starting farther back'.[24] Most of the men stretched out and slept.

Later that afternoon, Che was leaning against a tree, chatting to a comrade and munching on a couple of crackers and half a sausage, when the first shot rang out. Betrayed by a guide who had left the camp earlier in the day, the compañeros found themselves under attack from Batista's troops. As fighter jets and B-26 Marauder bombers swooped low over the woods, strafing the rebel position, an infantry unit opened fire. Juan Almeida, Fidel's first lieutenant, bellowed out, 'Nobody surrenders! Nobody surrenders!', and the rebels returned fire. One of the men, Universo Sánchez, described how, in the confusion, 'the comrades started falling back toward a plantation that had been set afire by incendiary bombs. I had sores on my feet. I had taken off my boots, knapsack and bandolier.' Pausing to 'sweep up everything', Sánchez lagged behind his retreating comrades, but eventually made it into the neighbouring cane field. If anything the situation was now even worse, as, with Batista's soldiers now just a hundred yards away, the 'hail of bullets went on, digging in the dirt around us'. In the chaos, several revolutionaries were killed, and others scrabbled for cover. Wounded in the neck, Che returned fire with his rifle before dragging himself into the relative safety of an adjoining field.[25]

With many of the *Granma*'s landing party now either killed or captured, and the remainder scattered, the 26th of July Movement's prospects looked pretty bleak. A news release, issued by the United Press and based on information supplied by the Cuban military, reported that the rebels had been 'wiped out' in a 'brief and bloody skirmish, by aircraft and ground troops'. This, together with the claim that the Castro brothers were among those who had been killed, received prominent play – including front-page billing in the *New York Times*. For a time, the reports of Fidel's demise were widely believed.

Although Fidel was still very much alive, the situation for the rebels was far from easy.[26] For several days, Fidel himself commanded the grand total of two men, with just a couple of rifles and 120 rounds of ammunition between them. Much of their time was spent hiding in sugar cane fields, desperately seeking cover as low-flying jets strafed the area with .50-calibre machine guns, causing the very 'earth to shake'. The only sustenance came from sucking on cane stalks and licking the morning dew from the damp leaves. Determined that he would not be taken alive, Fidel took to sleeping with the barrel of his rifle resting against his chin.[27] Finally, with the assistance of sympathetic local peasants, who offered much-needed food and fresh drinking water, and members of a network of farmers that had been recruited by Celia Sánchez – a formidable thirty-six-year-old revolutionary with an unmatched talent for organisational efficiency – Fidel's party reached sanctuary. On the morning of Sunday 16 December, they arrived at Cinco Palmas, the home of an M-26-7 sympathiser, which had been designated as a regrouping point in the event that the rebels became separated. Two days later, Raúl arrived at the ranch. After embracing his brother, Fidel asked how many guns he had managed to save. The answer, it turned out, was five. 'Well!' exclaimed Fidel. 'We have two. That makes seven.' He was overjoyed. 'Now', Fidel declared, 'we've won the war!'[28]

HERBERT MATTHEWS

The veteran *New York Times* correspondent Herbert L. Matthews.
His friend Ernest Hemingway memorably described him as a
'gaunt lighthouse of honesty'.

27. A NEWSPAPERMAN'S NEWSPAPERMAN

A newspaperman who will run a big risk for a mediocre story
is a fool; one who will not run a big risk for a big story should
go into the public relations business.

– HERBERT L. MATTHEWS

When it finally came, the call was short and to the point: 'You will be picked up in an hour. Be sure you are ready.' For the veteran *New York Times* reporter Herbert Lionel Matthews, who had spent much of Friday 15 February 1957 pacing around the *Times* bureau office on Refugio Street, Havana, it was now time for action. He immediately called his wife at the Sevilla-Biltmore Hotel, to ask whether she had already started to do her hair. Nancie, who had just finished mixing up the last of her expensive Italian dye, offered a resigned 'No.' 'Well, don't,' her husband explained. 'We leave at 6.30.' Nancie was packing, somewhat reluctantly, when Herbert arrived back at their suite carrying 'a bundle of hideous dark clothing and a warm jacket bought ostensibly "for a fishing trip"'. Within minutes, the couple were ready to depart. But, as Nancie later wrote, 'I should have remembered that most Cubans, however gloriously brave, are consistently unpunctual.' After waiting around for the best part of two hours, the couple decided to pop around the corner to the Floridita – a favourite haunt of the novelist Ernest Hemingway – for frozen daiquiris and some tasty moro crab. It was 'a combination to stouten a timorous heart', and Nancie's anxieties now gave way to 'excited anticipation'. Eventually, with the hour approaching ten o'clock, a Plymouth sedan pulled up and, after loading their luggage – which included hiking boots, a small box camera and a black newsboy-style cap – they were off, bound for the Sierra Maestra five hundred miles away, and what Herbert would later call the 'biggest scoop of our times'.[1]

*

Matthews – fifty-seven years old, tall, thin, half bald, 'silent as a tomb, precise as a Swiss watch' – was, according to one colleague, 'a newspaperman's newspaperman'. And yet, in his own words, he had 'drifted into the game by accident'.[2] Born in New York City on 10 January 1900, the grandson of Jewish immigrants from Eastern Europe, Herbert grew up in a cultured, bookish household on the Upper West Side. Alongside tennis lessons, horse riding and summer vacations in the Catskill Mountains, the young Herbert loved adventure tales – his favourite book was *Real Soldiers of Fortune*, a collection of biographical stories by Richard Harding Davis, the legendary journalist considered by many to be the world's first modern war correspondent. He was also a keen pianist with the talent, it was said, to pursue it as a career. But Matthews's early life was not without its challenges: he suffered a serious bout of childhood tuberculosis and then, in 1918, his mother, Frances, succumbed to the influenza pandemic.[3] That same year, he signed up with the US Army, but arrived in Bourg, headquarters of the Tank Corps, 'just too late to see any action'.[4] Demobbed in April 1919, he promptly enrolled at Columbia University, where he immersed himself in the study of Romance languages. Matthews might have stayed and carved out an academic career, had it not been for his reluctance to teach. 'I knew', he explained, that 'I should make a very bad teacher, being shy and unsociable' and lacking the 'tolerance, the patience, the humanity . . . and the kindliness which a good teacher needs and is born with'.[5] And so, after graduating in 1922, Matthews answered an advertisement in the *New York Times*, placed by an unnamed publishing company, for a secretary-stenographer, assuming (and hoping) that it would lead to a job at a book publisher's. It turned out, though, that the post was at 'The Gray Lady'* herself. That summer, he started work as secretary to the *New York Times*'s assistant business manager, on a salary of $25 a week.[6]

* The nickname referred both to the paper's conservative, cautious approach to covering the news and to its tradition of printing only in black and white. (It took until 1997 for colour to appear on the front page.)

He hated it.

Thoroughly miserable in the world of business and advertising, Matthews eventually switched to night work so that he could resume graduate studies at Columbia. As he explained, his sole intention was to secure 'a fellowship that would take me abroad for more study'. Matthews succeeded, and he spent the 1925–6 academic year in Europe, mostly in Italy, where he focused his studies on Dante, medieval history and philosophy.[7] On the boat home he met Edith Crosse, a smart and enchanting Englishwoman who went by the name of Nancie; the couple would marry in 1931.[8] Back in New York, Matthews caught up with Arthur Hays Sulzberger, the *Times*'s vice president (later its publisher), who had talked vaguely about a job on his return. He was appointed night assistant to Frederick T. Birchall, the acting managing editor, a post that, as Matthews explained, 'put me into the News Department and began a forceful education in the things that were really happening in the world'.[9]

Matthews now embarked on his apprenticeship: 'reporter, rewrite man, copy-reader, and since I had been abroad and theoretically knew something about Europe, I ended up on the cable desk'.[10] In the spring of 1929, the paper's publisher, Adolph S. Ochs, opted to send Matthews on a five-month tour of the Far East (Japan, Korea, Manchuria and northern China), a trip that was funded by the Carnegie Endowment for International Peace. Matthews was unimpressed by his encounter with the Chinese Nationalist leader, Chiang Kai-shek, whom he thought 'bombastic', but responded well to the 'charm and hospitality of the Japanese'.[11] Returning to the cable desk in New York, Matthews was increasingly convinced that, in order to 'handle stories from foreign countries with some degree of intelligence', it was necessary to acquire 'first-hand knowledge' of what was happening. And so, having enjoyed his fellowship year in Europe, and with the enthusiastic encouragement of Nancie, Matthews quickly agreed to a posting in France, as the number two in the Paris bureau. They set sail in November 1931.[12]

Living in the Parisian suburb of Garches, with his wife and two young children, Matthews's brief was economic and business affairs. He had no great interest in the topic, but wrote with energy about the economic difficulties, social deprivations and political weaknesses caused by the Great Depression – and his stories focused on, among other topics, France's budgetary collapse, financial scandals and the debate over war debts and German reparations.[13]

Matthews was travelling from Paris to Rome on 2 October 1935: the day when, standing on the balcony of the Palazzo Venezia before an adoring crowd, Benito Mussolini announced that Italy – which had long harboured a desire to strengthen its position in the Horn of Africa – was launching a military operation against Emperor Haile Selassie of Ethiopia (then widely known as Abyssinia). On hearing the news, Matthews's only thought was to 'get to Abyssinia as quickly as possible'. 'I was a journalist,' he explained, 'and this was going to be a great story, probably the greatest since World War I, and as I spoke Italian and knew Italy, I felt entitled to cover it from the Italian side.' 'All the old dreams', he noted, 'were surging up, the lure of adventure, the longing to go to strange, far-away places, to face danger, to distinguish myself, to be anything but a "second man" in the Paris bureau living an uninterruptedly humdrum existence.'

Matthews did not know it at the time, but he was 'embarking, not on one adventure' but on 'a whole career of danger, hardships and loneliness'.[14]

It was during a starry night on the edge of the Salt Plain near Dankalia, Matthews later wrote, 'when it first came to me that my dreams were really being fulfilled and that my instincts had not lied to me, and that men really were born to fight and suffer and die, and glory in doing so'. Accompanying an Italian flying column on a hazardous mission, with only one other journalist for company, he described how, that evening, they had:

dined out under the stars in the light of storm-lanterns hung from a nearby tree. The food was excellent, and there was a last precious *fiasco* of Chianti, brought from Assab, to wash it down. 'What more could a man want?' I thought to myself as we stretched out lazily on the ground afterwards, too replete to do anything but puff our cigarettes in silence. Good food, good wine, good fellowship, sentimental music played by a portable gramophone, the half moon spreading a mild glow about the camp, and the spirit of adventure pervading all.

Inevitably, perhaps, Matthews's thoughts turned to 'Paris and the daily grind, with feet stuck under a desk and bowed shoulders poring over newspapers'. 'It amused me', he explained, 'to think that lots of people were feeling sorry for me at the moment – poor, misguided people, who have never learned why men are willing to give up the luxuries of civilization, and leave sweethearts, wives and children for a life of hardship and danger.'[15]

Matthews had, in the role of war reporter, found his métier. Neither the dust, the heat and the terrible flies, nor the interminable ten-week wait at the start of the campaign, dimmed his enthusiasm. In contrast to some of his colleagues, who were content to stay in Addis Ababa and base their stories on official reports from government spokesmen and army headquarters, Matthews championed the importance of getting 'news on the spot'. He understood, instinctively, that 'a situation cannot be understood safely and properly at any distance from the sources of what is happening', and took great pride in having travelled hundreds of miles with the Italian forces, across the strange, inhospitable Ethiopian terrain – a landscape of 'deep bowls and chasms, of fantastically shaped *ambas* and jagged mountain ranges, of flat sands, lava beds and stretches of lovely, rolling green' – in order to witness the fighting up close.[16]

In February 1936, Matthews was with the Italian Northern Army at Enda Jesus as the climactic Battle of Amba Aradam unfolded. His report, which appeared on the front page of the *New York Times* on Monday 17 February 1936, saluted the 'valor', 'ferocity' and 'tactical skill' of the Ethiopians as they resisted the Italian assault. In the end, though, it was a rout. An estimated five thousand Ethiopians were killed, for the loss of just five hundred or so Italians, thanks largely to a tremendous artillery bombardment that had been unleashed by the forces of Il Duce's commander-in-chief, Marshal Pietro Badoglio.[17] Matthews's dispatch was, characteristically, packed with telling detail, based on first-hand observations, and written in the romantic style that had been popularised by an earlier generation of journalists, including Richard Harding Davis and John Reed.[18] Matthews had, he explained, travelled into the little village of Scelicot, where he 'saw the dead of the previous day's battle being buried near where they had fallen, with Amba Aradam and the Priest's Hat* towering in the mist overhead. Some bodies had terrible wounds, made by Ethiopian soft-nosed lead bullets . . . [The] inertness of these burlap-wrapped bodies, some with shoes sticking out, gave a vivid, unforgettable evidence that war is hell.' On the evening of 15 February, with the battle won, he described how, as the sun dipped below the horizon, Marshal Badoglio approached the small group of journalists, his face 'alight with joy and his arms . . . opened in an embracing movement as he approached them'. His voice choking with emotion, Badoglio declared that they had brought him 'good luck. That mountain which has been lying on our stomachs has been won. The enemy is in flight toward the south . . . You have noticed the boldness of our manoeuvres, which show that the Italian soldiers have good legs and marvelous hearts. And now write freely what you have seen. I wish you all good evening and good appetites.'[19]

   Matthews's sympathetic portrait of Badoglio, a Fascist hero, was telling. During the Abyssinian campaign, his own personal fondness for Italians and Italian culture, and his qualified admiration for

---

* The mountain of Amba Aradam was divided into two: a jagged ridge, which the Italians referred to as 'The Herringbone', and a distinctive flat-topped peak that they christened 'The Priest's Hat'.

Mussolini's supposedly modernising, civilising government, inevitably coloured his reporting. As he later put it, 'I chose at that time to deny the validity of the moral issues involved, on the basis that everyone directly concerned – opponents and Italians alike – was doing the same thing. If', he continued, 'you start from the premise that a lot of rascals were having a fight, it is not unnatural to want to see the victory of the rascal you like, and I liked the Italians during that scrimmage more than I did the British or the Abyssinians.'[20] The issues of the day, both in Abyssinia and back in Europe, had, he explained, not affected him personally, and as a journalist still learning his craft he had been 'content to be a mere spectator, to applaud success because it was a success, and to refrain from moral judgment'.[21]

What changed all that was Spain.

When, in the summer of 1936, General Francisco Franco mobilised armies in Morocco and, in alliance with right-wing elements of the military and security forces on the peninsula, sought to overthrow the fledgling Spanish Republic, Matthews, keen to build on his recent experiences in Africa, immediately asked to cover the story. That autumn, he got his wish – arriving in Valencia in November, to follow the Republican side. (William P. Carney was to report on the nationalists.) It was a posting that changed Matthews's life. Writing in 1946, he declared that 'I have already lived six years since the Spanish Civil War ended, and have seen much of greatness and glory and many beautiful things and places since then, and I may, with luck, live another twenty or thirty years.' 'But,' he explained, 'I know, as surely as I know anything in this world, that nothing so wonderful will ever happen to me again as those two and a half years I spent in Spain.' It was in Spain, he continued, that 'one learned that men could be brothers, that nations and frontiers, religions and races were but outer trappings, and that nothing counted, nothing was worth fighting for, but the ideal of liberty.'[22]

Matthews was not alone. Several hundred journalists, eager to cover the story, flocked to the Republican-controlled zone. Among them were Ernest Hemingway, Martha Gellhorn, Jay Allen, Sefton Delmer, Henry Buckley and Louis Delaprée. While some of them were committed leftists, many were simply professional reporters looking for the next scoop. In *We Saw Spain Die*, his impressive and moving account of foreign correspondents in the Spanish Civil War, Paul Preston has shown how, as a result of what they witnessed first-hand – particularly the stoicism of the Republican population – those who arrived without any great political commitments often came to embrace the cause of the beleaguered Spanish Republic.[*][23] Matthews had, in fact, sensed a little of this on arriving in Valencia: 'In my first dispatch,' he wrote, 'I caught dimly some inkling of the heroism and the glory that Spain was to mean.' But for Matthews, as for so many others, it was in Madrid – subjected to a terrible two-and-a-half-year siege – 'where I really was swept off my feet'.[24] Writing in 1938 – the year before the city finally fell to Franco – Matthews declared that 'of all the places to be in this world, Madrid is the most satisfactory. I thought so from the moment I arrived, and whenever I am away from it these days I cannot help longing to return. All of us feel the same way,' he continued, 'so it is more than a personal impression. The drama, the thrills, the electrical optimism, the fighting spirit, the patient courage of these mad and wonderful people – these are things worth living for and seeing with one's own eyes.'[25]

As well as being inspired by the heroic Republican resistance, many of the foreign correspondents – Matthews included – also came to sense that, by supporting a policy of non-intervention even as Nazi Germany and Fascist Italy funnelled men, materiel and military support to the nationalists, the democratic powers were both guilty of a terrible betrayal and committing a catastrophic blunder. 'We knew,

---

* For some, their commitment to the cause pushed them beyond their journalistic duties. As Preston has noted: 'Hemingway drove an ambulance and dispensed advice to military commanders' while 'Jay Allen lobbied tirelessly for the Republic in America, then went into Vichy France to help Spanish refugees and imprisoned international brigaders.'

we just knew,' explained Martha Gellhorn, 'that Spain was the place to stop Fascism. This was it. It was one of those moments in history when there was no doubt.'[26] The combination of intense human suffering and the magnitude of the political ideals at stake meant that, for many correspondents, adopting a position of moral neutrality – what Gellhorn memorably dismissed as 'all that objectivity shit' – was simply untenable.[27] As Matthews put it:

> All of us who lived the Spanish Civil War felt deeply emotional about it . . . I always felt the falseness and hypocrisy of those who claimed to be unbiased, and the foolishness, if not rank stupidity, of editors and readers who demanded 'objectivity' or 'impartiality' of correspondents writing about the war . . . those of us who championed the cause of the Republican government against the Franco Nationalists were right. It was, on balance, the cause of justice, morality, decency.[28]

Matthews's scepticism about journalistic objectivity was also, no doubt, fuelled by his conflicts with the *New York Times*. Under intense criticism from both Catholics and anti-communists,* his editors – notably Neil MacNeil and Clarence Howell, both of whom were staunch Catholics – repeatedly altered or censored his reports, cutting them for length and, notoriously, replacing the numerous references to 'Italian' troops and equipment he had seen on the battlefield with 'insurgent' instead. At the same time they happily printed, without challenge, misleading and at times entirely faked stories by fellow *Times* reporter (and Franco supporter) William P. Carney.[29] Little surprise, then, that Matthews grew increasingly frustrated with his employer's insistence on 'balanced' coverage. 'The publisher', he explained, 'laid

---

* The violence – much of it directed against the Catholic Church – that erupted during the first weeks of the Civil War skewed much foreign opinion in favour of Franco's rebels, while Stalin's support for the Republic made it easier for conservatives to denounce the Republican cause as little more than a Bolshevist plot.

down a mechanical, theoretically impartial, plan of operation – print both sides, equal prominence, equal length, equal treatment.' But, as Matthews noted, 'this often meant equality for the bad with the good – the official handouts hundreds of miles from the front lines with the eye-witness stories, the tricky with the honest, the wrong with the right. I say that not only I, but the truth suffered.'[30]

Although Matthews's sympathy for the Republicans was strong, this did not mean that he was, as one critic has it, 'a rabid red partisan'.[31] In fact, the shy and diffident Matthews retained a fierce commitment to honest reporting. The fundamental job of a journalist, he believed, was to write 'truthfully what he sees and knows on a given day'. Among his colleagues in Spain, Matthews's reputation for integrity was second to none.[32] Constancia de la Mora, director of the Republican government's foreign press office, came to greatly admire this 'lean and lanky' New Yorker's 'passion for fact'. 'He used to come in every evening,' she explained, 'always dressed in his grey flannels, after arduous and dangerous trips to the front, to telephone his story to Paris, whence it was cabled to New York.' De la Mora was struck by the care and effort he put into his reporting. Matthews, she explained, 'used to spend days tracking down some simple fact – how many churches in such and such a small town; what the Government's agricultural programme was achieving in this or that region', and drove to the front 'more often than almost any other reporter'.[33] Ernest Hemingway, meanwhile, described his friend as 'the straightest the ablest and the bravest war correspondent writing today'. At a time when 'faking now is more successful than the truth', Hemingway declared that Matthews stood 'as a gaunt lighthouse of honesty'.[34]

In a letter written just after the nationalist victory, Matthews laid bare his feelings: 'And so it goes. We got beat proper. I guess at the end I was fighting harder than the soldiers – at least on paper. So long as there was hope I played it up strong, all along.'[35] But although the Republican defeat made Matthews 'sick at heart', he 'knew that the fight had not been in vain'. He would also continue to take enormous personal and professional pride in the story that he had told; a story of 'bravery, of tenacity, of discipline and constant decency, of optimism that came from courage and high ideals'.[36]

After a vacation back home, where he licked his wounds, Matthews was, in April 1939, sent to Rome. There, he experienced 'a close-up of Fascism as Mussolini and his country went down the toboggan slide to catastrophe'. Arrested and 'crowded into a small, dark, very dirty and very cold cell' on the orders of the regime, following Italy's declaration of war against the United States on 11 December 1941, Matthews was subsequently interned for five months in Siena.[37] Although, as he put it, 'there is no happiness for a man who is not free and who does not know how long it will be before he can see his wife and children', it could have been worse. 'If I had the choice of any place in Italy for internment,' Matthews conceded, 'I would have picked that lovely, medieval town, which the world has passed by for centuries. I came to know and love every stone of it. I bicycled every morning up and down the Tuscan hills, and as a "natural" experience I have known nothing more thrilling in my life than watching those lovely hills pass from the snows of winter to the fresh green of spring.'[38] After his release, as part of an international prisoner exchange, he spent ten months covering the British defence of India, before returning to Europe to report on the Allied invasion of Italy and Sicily in 1943 – cheating death when a German shell killed three of his British colleagues. At the war's end, he was appointed chief of the London bureau. But in April 1949, after suffering a heart attack while investigating conditions in post-war Germany and frustrated by money problems caused by his increasingly elaborate lifestyle (he had a weakness for bespoke suits, fancy hats, fine wine and art), he decided to return to New York, and a new role on the paper's editorial board. Over the next ten years, Matthews combined his work as an editorial writer with that of a de facto special correspondent. Developing a particular interest in Latin America, he covered major developments in Argentina, Colombia, Ecuador, Brazil, Venezuela – and Cuba.[39]

*

In a special report for the *New York Times*, published on 4 November 1956, Matthews attempted to make sense of the Cuban political situation for his American readers. Acknowledging that the country under Batista had, to all intents and purposes, deteriorated into a military dictatorship, Matthews described an island that, despite a rapidly improving economy, was wracked with 'tension and suppressed anarchy', and pointed to recent sporadic outbreaks of political violence (including the assassination of the head of military intelligence). But although there was a 'genuine revolutionary and often patriotic element' to the violence, he concluded that there were, as yet, 'no signs of a popular or organized revolution'.[40] A month later, in an editorial that Matthews penned in the immediate aftermath of the *Granma* landing, the entire escapade was dismissed as 'pathetic'. 'There was', he declared, 'not the slightest hope that a revolt could succeed in present circumstances.'[41]

Then, in February 1957, Matthews was presented with a glorious opportunity to revisit this question up close.

28. A CHAPTER IN A FANTASTIC NOVEL

A man must go to meet his fate, wherever it may be, whenever it may come. The urge to go out and fight, to pit one's strength and wits against the forces of nature, to seek adventure, risk life and take joy in comradeship and danger – these are deep feelings, so deep that even I who love life and family and luxury and books have yielded to them.

– HERBERT L. MATTHEWS

After regrouping in the foothills of the Sierra Maestra during the early weeks of December 1956, the twenty or so survivors of the *Granma*, together with a handful of new recruits, had headed deeper into the mountains – nearing Pico Caracas, whose summit lay more than four thousand feet above sea level, by year's end.[1] A hundred miles long and thirty miles across at their widest point, the Sierra Maestra, with their towering peaks, steep slopes and dense forests, made an ideal base for Castro's rebel army. In a December 1956 essay published in the leading Cuban magazine *Bohemia*, the young geographer and revolutionary Antonio Núñez Jiménez explained that this was 'the most rugged and least known area in Cuba' and that its 'green mountains, sometimes reaching higher than the clouds', formed 'an intricate labyrinth of valleys and hills, peaks and troughs, which make penetration difficult'. Guerrilla fighters had used the region as a base during Cuba's long struggle for independence from Spain and, with its long association with 'outlaws, squatters, and rebels', it was perhaps not surprising that the writ of the government in Havana ran particularly thin there. Moreover, Castro and his forces stood an excellent chance of winning substantial support from the region's dispossessed, marginalised and impoverished peasantry. By ambushing Batista's forces in a series of hit-and-run attacks, Fidel hoped to negate the huge advantages in manpower and materiel that the Cuban military enjoyed. The ultimate aim: to inspire a mass uprising that would throw off the dictatorship.[2] On 17 January

1957, the rebels attacked a small garrison at La Plata, killing two soldiers and capturing a useful haul of weapons (including eight Springfield rifles and a Thompson submachine gun), food and medical supplies.[3]

What Che described as the 'first victorious battle of the Rebel Army' was, of course, hugely encouraging after all the terrible military setbacks and personal hardships the compañeros had endured.[4] But as Fidel quickly realised, for a man who was widely presumed by many of his countrymen to be dead, winning wider support – let alone inspiring a serious rebellion – was going to be hard. And so, just days after the Battle of La Plata, he sent word to Faustino Pérez, the *Granma* veteran who had been assigned acting chief of M-26-7 operations in Havana. His task: to secure a foreign correspondent who could be smuggled into the mountains and, evading Cuba's strict censorship laws, tell their story to the world.

And so it was that, towards the end of January 1957, Felipe Pazos walked into the Refugio Street office of Ruby Hart Phillips. A 'fast-talking, chain-smoking' reporter, the fifty-eight-year-old Phillips had been working from Cuba since 1937, as correspondent for the *New York Times*, and had an enviable list of contacts that included generals, government officials and President Batista himself. Pazos, who had become friendly with Phillips during his stint as president of the country's national bank, had agreed to serve as a go-between at the urging of his son Javier, an avid M-26-7 supporter. On hearing the news about Fidel's survival, Phillips struggled to contain her excitement, and readily agreed to meet at a more discreet location, away from the prying eyes and ears of the in-house censor. Two days later, she entered the magnificent art deco headquarters of the Bacardi company, near the Cuban defence ministry, for a clandestine meeting with Pazos senior and 'a group of boys' who included Faustino Pérez and René Rodríguez, a fellow veteran of the *Granma*. Phillips, who had from the start been sceptical about the reports of Fidel's death, now asked detailed questions about the landing and subsequent escape into the mountains, in order to assess the veracity of what seemed a truly remarkable tale.

On learning that the rebel leader had specifically requested an interview with a foreign correspondent, Phillips would have felt torn. The opportunity to secure a major international scoop was, of course, enormously tempting. But even before Rodríguez started to make none-too-subtle remarks about the difficulties of smuggling a woman past Batista's troops, Phillips had decided that she could not possibly take on the assignment. All too aware of the prevailing culture of sexism (she published under the byline R. Hart Phillips in order to conceal her gender), she also knew that, if she wrote the story, Batista was certain to have her deported. Leaving a country that she had made her home over the past two decades was too great a wrench, and she left the meeting promising the rebels that she would find them a suitable journalist. Back in the *Times* office, she ran into Ted Scott, the NBC correspondent and editorial writer for the *Havana Post*, and talked it over with him. Scott elected to turn it down for similar reasons, but having just received a letter from Herbert Matthews, thanking him for a recent box of cigars and mentioning plans for a mid-winter trip to Cuba, he suggested the *Times* man as the obvious choice for a 'one-shot' job. Phillips immediately cabled the paper's foreign editor, Emanuel R. Freedman, asking that Matthews come to Havana immediately.

Within days, the legendary war correspondent was in town.[5]

On Sunday 10 February, his first full day in Havana, Matthews had a meeting at the *Times* office with Felipe and Javier Pazos, René Rodríguez and Faustino Pérez to hammer out the arrangements. After being interrogated on the details of Fidel's escape, Javier had a question of his own. Unnerved by the age and apparent frailty of Matthews – who, with his fashionable tailored suit, and pipe clenched between his teeth, resembled a university don rather than a grizzled war reporter – the Cubans then asked whether Matthews would 'send for someone from New York?' 'No,' Matthews explained, 'I'll go myself.' Barely concealing his surprise, Felipe now asked whether Matthews was 'apt at mountain climbing'.[6] Matthews – like Edgar

Snow and John Reed before him – relished the prospect of adventure in the cause of a scoop, despite the dangers (or, perhaps, because of them). As he later explained:

> As if any newspaperman would pass up an opportunity like that! Felipe Pazos could not have known what makes a journalist tick. A newspaperman who will run a big risk for a mediocre story is a fool; one who will not run a big risk for a big story should go into the public relations business.[7]

His final response was dry, but definitive: 'I'll do it.'[8]

The plan to get Matthews into the mountains was straightforward enough: Herbert and Nancie, dressed as wealthy foreign tourists, would be driven across Cuba to Manzanillo, in the south of the island, by Javier Pazos, Liliam Mesa and her husband, Faustino Pérez. Then, while Nancie stayed behind in a safe house, Herbert would be taken by jeep to the edge of the Sierra Maestra before hiking to a remote rendezvous spot, and a meeting with Fidel. While outwardly simple, this would be a journey fraught with danger. In order to suppress the incipient rebellion, the military had set up roadblocks all along the highway in Oriente.[9] To pass through safely, the rebels devised a method that, Herbert explained, was 'as simple as it was effective':

> We took my wife along in the car as 'camouflage'. Cuba [was] at the height of the tourist season and nothing could have looked more innocent than a middle-aged couple of American tourists driving down to Cuba's most beautiful and fertile province with some young friends. The guards would take one look at my wife, hesitate a second, and wave us on with friendly smiles. If we were to be questioned a story was prepared for them. If we were searched the jig would be up.[10]

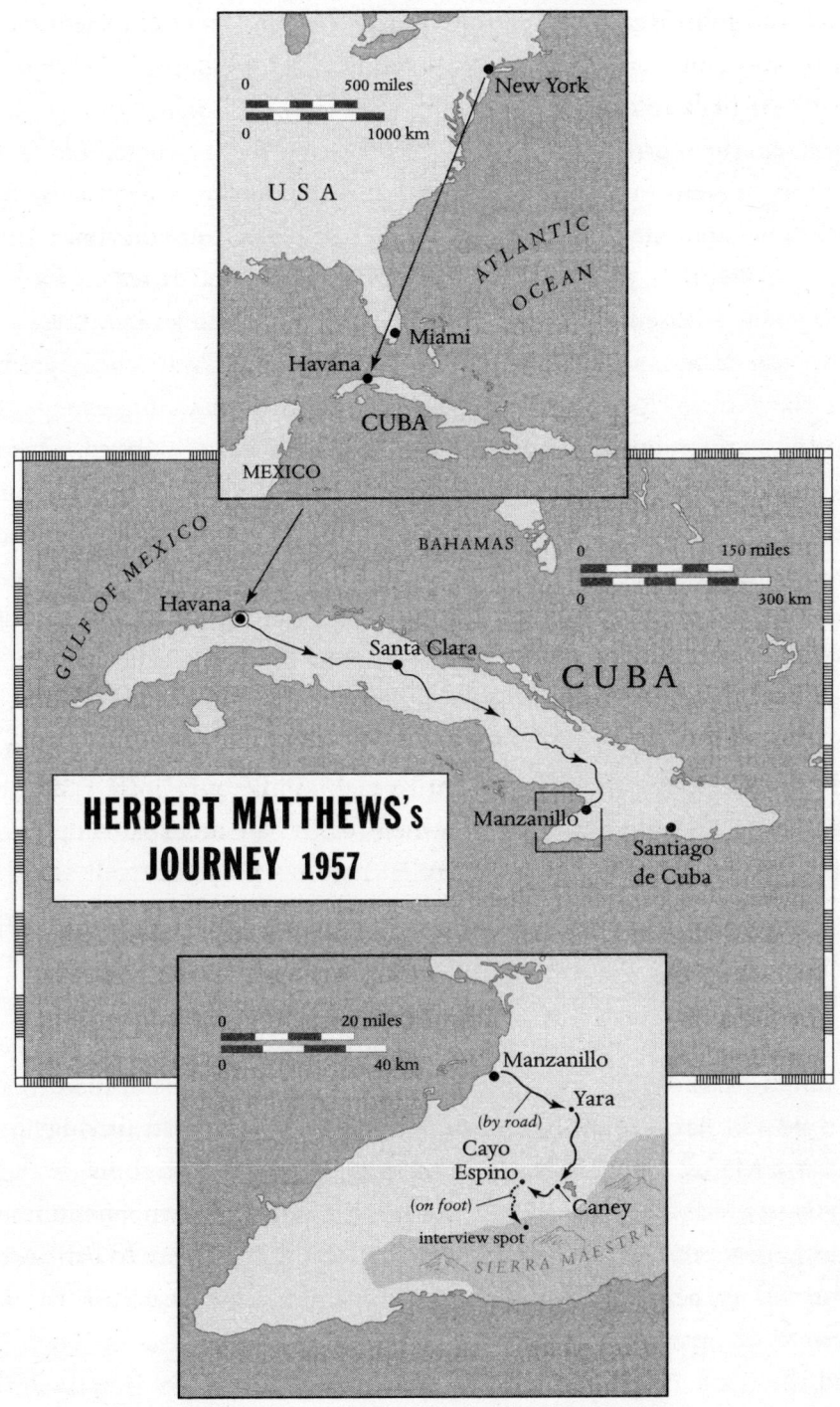

HERBERT MATTHEWS's
JOURNEY 1957

Despite the need for discretion during the long drive, Nancie noted how 'we stopped so many times for thimblefuls of Cuban coffee that a long trail of people had every chance to examine us in detail.' As dawn broke on the morning of Saturday 16 February, the travellers, cold and hungry, arrived in Santa Clara. But Mesa apparently 'had no sense of direction' and, after circling around the same block several times, she stopped to ask a policeman for directions 'to a good hotel'. Luckily, the rebels aroused no suspicions and, after a restorative breakfast of café con leche and fresh rolls, they were on their way once again. As they drew closer to the Sierra Maestra, the main highway was dotted with military roadblocks, and Nancie's heart 'skipped a beat as a soldier stepped into the road and signalled us to stop'. But, she recalled, 'he merely peered at us in friendly fashion. One look at the white chimney-pot hat put on to cover the wreck of my hair and we were waved on.' Finally, just after 2 p.m., and following a series of 'agonizing' wrong turns, they arrived at the home of Pedro and Ena Samuel, schoolteachers who were, according to Herbert, 'typical of the middle-class intellectuals' who would make the Cuban Revolution. The couple were soon surrounded by a group of 'very jolly, friendly people'; 'the kind of men and women' who, Nancie explained, 'you might meet at any Cuban tea party'.[11]

A heavier-than-expected troop presence around Manzanillo led to a frustrating five-hour wait, though it did enable Herbert to grab some much-needed rest. Then, after changing into the old clothes that he had purchased for the trip – 'warm for the cold night air of the mountains and dark for camouflage' – Matthews was bundled into an old US Army jeep, bound for the mountains. The driver, Felipe Guerra Matos, used his expert knowledge of the local back roads and trails to evade Batista's patrols, though the party was stopped at one checkpoint. The guard apparently looked a bit dubious, but Matthews's story about being an 'American sugar planter who could not speak a word of Spanish', off to visit a farm he was interested in buying, did the trick. (Javier Pazos apparently played the role of 'interpreter' to perfection.) Then came 'hours of driving, through sugar-cane and rice fields, across rivers that only jeeps could manage', taking them through the little villages of Yara, Caney and Cayo Espino before, 'after slithering through miles of mud', they 'could go no farther'.[12]

By now it was midnight, and a challenging hike lay in wait. It was, Matthews admitted, 'hard going'.[13] Eventually the party 'turned off the road and slid down a hillside to where a stream, dark brown under the nearly full moon, rushed its muddy way'. 'One of the boys', Matthews recalled, 'slipped and fell full length into the icy cold water. I waded through with the water almost to my knees, and that was hard enough to do without falling. Fifty yards up the slope was the meeting point.' They had reached what they thought was a rendezvous spot, from which rebel soldiers would take them to Fidel. But it was deserted, and, after a frustrating fifteen-minute wait, they decided to push on a bit further up the hill. But, with no sign of any rebels, they eventually stopped 'in a heavy clump of trees and bushes, dripping from the rain, the ground underfoot heavily matted, muddy, and soaked'. 'There,' Matthews explained, 'we sat for a whispered confab. The courier, and another youth who had fought previously with Castro, said they would go up the mountainside and see if they could find any of the rebel troops.' Matthews and his two remaining companions now endured 'a rather agonizing wait of more than two hours, crouched in the mud, not daring to talk or move, trying to snatch a little sleep with our heads on our knees and annoyed maddeningly by the swarms of mosquitoes that were having the feast of their lives'.[14]

Eventually, out of the darkness came the sound of a low, soft double-whistle – the rebels' characteristic call sign. Within minutes a rebel patrol was guiding the party across fields, up steep hills and through the forest, towards Fidel's mountain base. With dawn still two hours away, Matthews finally made it into a heavy grove, where 'the dripping leaves and boughs, the dense vegetation, the mud underfoot, the moonlight – all gave the impression of a tropical forest, more like Brazil than Cuba.' As the weary and relieved journalist stretched out on a blanket, and munched on some soda crackers, talk turned to revolution: speaking in the 'lowest possible whispers' to avoid detection by the Cuban Army, 'one man told me how he had seen his brother's store wrecked and burned by Government troops and his brother dragged out and executed. "I'd rather be here fighting for Fidel, than anywhere in the world now," he said.' Another described how local farmers and sympathetic storekeepers kept the rebels supplied with food, at great personal risk.[15]

As dawn broke, Raúl Castro entered the camp, and 'a few minutes later Fidel himself strode in.' He made a powerful first impression:

> Taking him, as one would at first, by physique and personality,
> this was quite a man – a powerful, six-footer, olive-skinned,
> full-faced, with a straggly beard. He was dressed in an olive gray
> fatigue uniform and carried a rifle with a telescopic sight, of which
> he was very proud.

After some general chit-chat, Matthews and Fidel strolled over to the blanket and sat down. For the next three hours – sustained by tomato juice, ham sandwiches, coffee and some Havana cigars that Fidel broke out especially for the occasion – Matthews listened as the rebel leader held court.[16]

Fidel was, Matthews noted, 'a great talker. His brown eyes flash; his intense face is pushed close to the listener and the whispering voice, as in a stage play, lends a vivid sense of drama.' After recounting how the compañeros had regrouped in the aftermath of the *Granma* landing, Fidel claimed that the morale of his men, who were now taking the fight to Batista, was higher than ever. And although the Cuban Army was equipped with a formidable array of weaponry including bazookas, mortars and fighter jets – much of it supplied by the United States – Fidel was confident: 'We are safe here in the Sierra,' he declared; 'they must come and get us and they cannot.' While 'they never know where we are, we always know where they are'. Moreover,

Herbert Matthews interviewing Fidel in the Sierra Maestra, 17 February 1957.

'a dictatorship', Fidel explained, 'must show that it is omnipotent or it will fall; we are showing that it is impotent.' Talk soon turned to Fidel's plans for the new Cuba. While Matthews found his economic ideas unconvincing ('an economist', he argued, 'would consider them weak'), he was far more receptive to Fidel's talk of liberty and social justice. 'We are fighting', the revolutionary leader explained, 'for a democratic Cuba and an end to the dictatorship.' By the time the meeting drew to a close, Matthews was seriously impressed. Fidel, he noted, 'inspires confidence' and was 'a born leader'. His personality, meanwhile, was 'overpowering'. It was, Matthews wrote:

> easy to see that his men adored him and also to see why he has caught the imagination of the youth of Cuba all over the island. Here was an educated, dedicated fanatic, a man of ideals, of courage and of remarkable qualities of leadership.[17]

Fidel had, in fact, gone to a great deal of trouble to make a favourable impression. Before Matthews's arrival, the rebels had set to work, cleaning up the camp – and their own rather dishevelled state – as best they could. Manuel Fajardo, one of the first peasants to join the rebel army, described how, after being told by Fidel to 'whip things into shape', he 'looked at [himself] and the other guys, our shoes battered, tied with electric wire, full of holes. But we changed as best we could and I went up front, marching like a soldier.' It was, Che recalled, all 'an act'. The rebels also went to elaborate lengths to convey an impression of military strength. At one point during the interview with Matthews, another rebel rushed up to Fidel and announced: 'My *Comandante*, we've succeeded in reaching the Second Column.' In reality, the entire rebel army 'was right there, in front of Matthews'. Fidel, moreover, exuded confidence. Pressed on rumours that he was poised to 'declare a revolutionary government in the Sierra', he suggested that it was a matter of 'when' rather than 'if'. Although the time was not yet ripe, he intended to 'make myself known at the opportune moment'. And, in any case, 'it will have all the more effect for the delay, for now everybody is talking about us. We are sure of ourselves.'[18]

As the interview ended, Matthews made a couple of requests. First, he asked Fidel to sign his name on the folded-over sheets of writing paper on which he had been making notes. Second, he handed his small box camera to one of Fidel's men, and asked him to photograph the two of them together, standing in the clearing and smoking their cigars.[19] As he prepared to depart, Fidel acknowledged the personal risks that his interlocutor had taken: 'You have taken quite a risk in coming here,' he declared, 'but we have the whole area covered, and we will get you out safely.' Fidel was true to his word. As they ploughed their way 'back through the muddy undergrowth', this time in broad daylight, their scout 'went like a homing pigeon through woods and across fields where there were no paths straight to a farmer's house on the edge of the Sierra'. There, Matthews waited in a back room while someone fetched the jeep for the journey back to Manzanillo.[20]

*

Nancie, who had been 'very warmly and comfortably taken care of' by her friendly hosts, was enormously relieved to see her husband safe and well. Although 'utterly tired and unwashed', Herbert – elated, she explained, by the fact that he 'could still show a younger generation of newspapermen how to get a difficult and dangerous story' – could barely conceal his sense of triumph. After a quick snack and a change of clothes, the couple were driven to Santiago, from where they caught a direct flight back to Havana. Despite pressure from Ruby Phillips and Ted Scott to leave immediately for New York, Herbert insisted on tying up a few loose ends. After interviews with student leaders, including José Antonio Echeverría, president of the Federation of University Students, he and Nancie spent the evening of Monday 18 February with Ernest and Mary Hemingway at Finca Vigía, their splendid residence in the hills overlooking Havana. The following morning, before boarding the plane back to New York, Nancie smuggled Herbert's highly sensitive interview notes past customs by hiding them in her girdle. Once the twin-propellor aircraft was safely in the air, she paid a discreet visit to the bathroom in order to retrieve them. By the time she returned to her seat, her husband was already hard at work on a story that, as he well knew, was dynamite.[21]

29. SCOOP!

When the world had given us up for dead, the interview with
Matthews put the lie to our disappearance.
– CHE GUEVARA

'Cuban Rebel Is Visited in Hideout' hit the front page of the *New
York Times* on Sunday 24 February. Alongside a striking photograph
of Fidel, rifle in hand, Matthews explained how the 'rebel leader of
Cuba's youth' was 'fighting hard . . . in the rugged, almost impenetrable
fastness of the Sierra Maestra'. This worldwide scoop was, Matthews
made clear, the 'first sure news that Fidel Castro is still alive and still
in Cuba'. He continued:

> No one connected with the outside world, let alone with the press,
> has seen Señor Castro except this writer. No one in Havana, not
> even at the United States Embassy with all its resources for getting
> information, will know until this report is published that Fidel
> Castro is really in the Sierra Maestra.[1]

At a time when strict censorship laws meant that Cuba's cities had
been crackling with 'the most astonishing rumours', Matthews's
account revealed the shocking truth. All across the southern province
of Oriente, he wrote, thousands of ordinary Cubans 'are heart and
soul with Fidel Castro and the new deal for which they think he
stands'. The fierceness of the government's attempts to suppress
the rebellion, meanwhile, had merely served to further arouse the
population against Havana. The result was that, despite the 'cream'
of the armed forces being deployed to the region, the 'Army men are
fighting a thus-far losing battle to destroy the most dangerous enemy
General Batista has yet faced in a long and adventurous career as a
Cuban leader and dictator'.[2]

After describing the voyage of the *Granma*, and the desperate days that followed, Matthews recounted his own 'elaborate, dangerous' journey from Havana to the rebel base in the Sierra. He had, he explained, been assisted by dozens of Castro supporters who had bravely risked everything to smuggle him past army checkpoints and into the mountains. As for the rebels themselves, they were the 'flaming symbol' of the nationwide opposition to Batista; Fidel and his 26th of July Movement were, Matthews emphasised, deeply committed to 'liberty, democracy, social justice', and planned to restore constitutional

Cuban Rebel Is Visited in Hideout

Castro Is Still Alive and Still Fighting in Mountains

This is the first of three articles by a correspondent of The New York Times who has just returned from a visit to Cuba.

By HERBERT L. MATTHEWS

Fidel Castro, the rebel leader of Cuba's youth, is alive and fighting hard and successfully in the rugged, almost impenetrable fastnesses of the Sierra Maestra, at the southern tip of the island.

President Fulgencio Batista has the cream of his Army around the area, but the Army men are fighting a thus-far losing battle to destroy the most dangerous enemy General Batista has yet faced in a long and adventurous career as a Cuban leader and dictator.

This is the first sure news that Fidel Castro is still alive and still in Cuba. No one connected with the outside world, let alone with the press, has seen Señor Castro except this writer. No one in Havana, not even at the United States Embassy with all its resources for getting information, will know until this report is published that Fidel Castro is really in the Sierra Maestra.

This account, among other things, will break the tightest censorship in the history of the Cuban Republic. The Province of Oriente, with its 2,000,000 inhabitants, its flourishing cities such as Santiago, Holguin and Manzanillo, is shut off from Havana as surely as if it were another country. Havana does

Continued on Page 34, Column 1

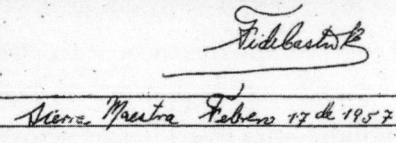

The New York Times

Fidel Castro at a heavily shaded outpost on Feb. 17. He gave the signature to the correspondent who visited him.

Matthews's scoop, which hit the front page of the *New York Times* on 24 February 1957, had an electrifying impact, greatly enhancing the prestige and popular image of Fidel and his rebel army.

government and hold elections. Although their movement was fiercely nationalistic and anti-imperialist, Matthews's American readers had nothing to fear. In fact, Fidel – the 'very picture of idealism and moderation' – had gone out of his way to reassure the 'Yanquis': 'You can be sure', he had told Matthews, that 'we have no animosity toward the United States and the American people.'[3]

When it came to the military situation, Matthews recalled how, on hearing first-hand the story of how the rebels had regrouped in the aftermath of the landing at Playa las Coloradas, 'one got a feeling that [Fidel] is now invincible. Perhaps he isn't, but that is the faith he inspires in his followers.' Fidel certainly did not lack for confidence – 'It is a battle against time,' he explained, 'and time is on our side.' Extraordinarily, Matthews appeared to agree. 'From the looks of things,' he declared, 'General Batista cannot possibly hope to suppress the Castro revolt.'[4]

In the Presidential Palace – a grand neoclassical structure, built in 1920, that boasted interior decoration from Tiffany Studios of New York, and a Salón de los Espejos modelled on the Hall of Mirrors at Versailles – Fulgencio Batista was stunned.[5] His senior military advisers had assured him repeatedly not only that was Fidel dead but that the Sierra Maestra was now protected by a 'ring of steel' that would prevent anyone – rebel or reporter – from passing through undetected. And although his censors had been hard at work that morning, quite literally cutting the story out of every copy of the *Times* prior to them going on sale, it was to no avail. American tourists arriving on the island that Sunday brought with them uncensored copies of the newspaper, and Fidel's supporters in New York had anyway mailed three thousand copies to addresses across Havana. Within hours, the entire capital seemed to be talking about Matthews's extraordinary scoop. Over the coming days, Spanish translations of the story, including Carlos Franqui's piece for the underground newspaper *Revolución*, were passed from hand to hand, pored over at kitchen tables and discussed animatedly all over Cuba.[6]

Batista, though, was desperate to put the genie back into the bottle. Egged on by his public relations adviser, the former CBS executive Edmund Chester – who remained convinced that Fidel was dead – he ordered his minister of defence, Santiago Verdeja, to issue an official rebuttal. 'Before anything else,' it began:

> let me assure you that the opinion of the Government, and I am sure, of the Cuban public also, is that the interview and the adventures described by Correspondent Matthews can be considered as a chapter in a fantastic novel. Mr. Matthews has not interviewed the pro-Communist insurgent, Fidel Castro, and the information came from certain opposition forces.

The government noted that, although the *Times* article featured a photograph of Fidel, it 'seemed strange that, having had an opportunity to penetrate the mountains and having had such an interview, Matthews did not have a photograph taken of himself with the pro-Communist insurgent in order to provide proof of what he wrote'. As for Fidel, the government did not know for sure whether he was 'alive or dead, but if he is alive,' they explained, 'the Government takes the full responsibility for stating that no such supporting forces as Matthews describes actually exist.'[7]

On 28 February, the *Times* published the photograph of Fidel and Matthews together – the Cuban lighting a cigar, the reporter scribbling down some notes – as well as a robust response to the allegations of fabrication. 'The story', Matthews asserted, 'surely speaks for itself' and it was 'hard to believe that anyone reading it can have any doubts'. In addition to the photograph of the two men – which, Matthews explained, had not been deemed of suitable quality to be published originally – he also noted that later editions of the 24 February paper, although not those sent to Cuba, had featured a reproduction of Fidel's signature, alongside the words 'Sierra Maestra Febrero 17 de

1957', which he had secured during the mountain summit. 'The truth will always out,' Matthews declared, 'censorship or no censorship.'[8]

Matthews's invocation of the 'truth' would later stick in the craw of many a conservative critic who accused the correspondent of being at best naïve, and at worst a virtual propagandist.[9] That, though, lay in the future. In the spring of 1957, the response to his electrifying scoop was overwhelmingly positive. His story was picked up by other newspapers, both in the United States and around the world, earning him the admiration of his fellow professionals.[10] Even the press attaché at the US embassy in Havana was moved to write to Matthews – unofficially, of course – to convey his congratulations 'for a piece of journalism reminiscent of the beats of a bygone age'.[11] The dean of Columbia University's School of Journalism, Edward W. Barrett, wrote to congratulate him, as did the university's president, Grayson Kirk. 'I cannot tell you how thrilled I was to read your enormously exciting story . . . about your own visit to Cuba and your successful attempt to make contact with Fidel Castro,' he explained. 'This was', he continued, clearly 'a hazardous exploit and I am happy to know that you have returned safely from it bringing a truly splendid and exciting story'.[12]

In the days that followed the publication of Matthews's extraordinary scoop, messages of support poured into the *New York Times* office at 229 West 43rd Street, and he was also sent enough Cuban cigars to last for the next eighteen months. Writing to Turner Catledge, the managing editor, on 4 March, Matthews recorded his astonishment: 'Never in my thirty-five years on the *Times*,' he explained, have I 'received such a flood of letters and telegrams as I have had this time. Naturally in my old age I appreciate this very much.'[13] Unsurprisingly, perhaps, figures from Cuba's opposition were among those to voice their admiration. Carlos Prío Socarrás, who had been overthrown as Cuba's president in the 1952 coup, wrote to Matthews to 'express to you my appreciation, as a Cuban citizen who was forged in the struggle against tyranny . . . for your enthusiastic defence of freedom in my country, and for the incalculable service that you have done to my homeland, in one of the blackest hours of its history'.[14] Even some within the regime were prepared to break cover, albeit discreetly. Nicolás Rivero, the Cuban representative in the Inter-American Economic and Social Council, wrote to Matthews, confidentially, to explain how his articles on Cuba had touched him deeply. He was, he continued, 'sure that the great majority of the Cuban people share my gratitude to you for your valuable contribution to the cause of Cuban freedom'.[15]

From Cuba, supporters of Fidel's 26th of July Movement, the Federation of University Students and other revolutionary groups were effusive in their praise. From Santiago de Cuba, Fidel's comrades lauded Matthews for having 'rendered a great service to the cause of Liberty and Democracy'.[16] From Havana, two activists with the Students' Revolutionary Directorate (a rival organisation) described Matthews as 'a great soldier for freedom' and 'a hope for the oppressed people who see in your enlightening pen their greatest friend'.[17] Cuban exiles, too, were greatly moved by Matthews's reporting, and urged him – as one put it – to 'continue dedicating your valuable pen to the defense of decency, liberty and justice which we all seek'.[18] 26th of July Movement leaders in the United States also voiced their support. Ernesto F. Betancourt, the official representative of the 26th of July Movement in Washington DC, praised Matthews for having performed 'a great service to the cause of freedom and democracy' while, at the same time, providing 'an example of American journalism at its very best'.[19]

Matthews's larger-than-life story won plenty of admirers among his fellow citizens too. Arthur Steinmetz, a resident of Brooklyn, wrote to Matthews immediately after reading his scoop, saying that the story had 'thrilled me no end'. Steinmetz, whose Flying Fortress had been shot down near Paris in August 1943, had spent three months 'in enemy territory and not so friendly Spain' before managing to escape back to England. Having experienced a 'similar adventure' to the one that Matthews had described in the *Times*, he explained that he had been greatly moved by Matthews's fearlessness in securing the story and inspired by the idealism and courage of the Cuban rebels. 'I hope', he wrote, that 'your heroic followers of Fidel Castro will soon be able to see the daylight.'[20]

In an early sign of the extraordinary hold that Fidel and his revolutionaries would have over the sixties generation, eight students at the University of California, Berkeley declared that they had been so inspired by Matthews's reporting that they intended to head to Cuba themselves. There, disguised as visiting anthropologists, they planned to make for the Sierra Maestra so that they could take up arms alongside the compañeros.[21]

When Matthews returned to Cuba that June, he was greeted by crowds of grateful, enthusiastic supporters, keen to thank him for telling the world the truth about Cuba. But this taste of 'what it was like to be a famous Hollywood actor' was profoundly discomforting. While part of him was, naturally, gratified by all of the praise, he also found the role of 'hero' to be tiring and 'excruciatingly embarrassing'.[22] He had also had concerns, from the very start, about the way in which he was being portrayed 'as a great champion of Fidel Castro' and had, he told Catledge, 'gone to a lot of trouble all along . . . to make everybody understand I was simply fulfilling a journalistic duty'.[23] In fact, back at the start of March, he had written to William M. Porter, attorney for the 26th of July Movement in Miami, declining an invitation to address a rally of Cuban dissidents that was being planned for 10 March – the fifth anniversary of Batista's seizure of power. 'I think our Cuban friends are laboring under a misapprehension,' he explained:

The job I did in Cuba was entirely a work of journalism. Whatever my personal sympathies are, and as you might suppose I am against dictatorships everywhere, and as you saw I was favorably impressed by the opposition in Cuba, I cannot as a journalist allow those feelings to involve the *New York Times* in any way. I went to Cuba to find out what was happening there and to break the strict censorship that President Batista had imposed. I believe we did this effectively. I cannot as a representative of the *New York Times* in any way play a role that affects the internal affairs of Cuba, whatever I feel about the matter.[24]

Matthews's protestations notwithstanding, his interview with Fidel was, quite clearly, a very considerable tonic for the 26th of July Movement. Not only had it provided the first sure news for many of them that Fidel was still alive, but it also conferred legitimacy on their movement.[25] They were the electrifying embodiment of opposition to the dictatorship who supposedly boasted wide and deep support among ordinary Cubans. Their leader, moreover, had been portrayed as a hero – an 'impassioned outlaw dedicated to aiding his suffering people', and a kind of Robin Hood of the Antilles.[26]

Batista would later claim that the publication of the interview with Matthews had given 'considerable propaganda and support' to the rebels and marked the origins of Fidel's emergence as a 'legendary personage'.[27] They might not have agreed on much but on this at least Che Guevara heartily concurred: 'When the world had given us up for dead,' he explained, 'the interview with Matthews put the lie to our disappearance. Thus we can say that the timid stage of the revolution was brought to an end.'[28]

30. FIDEL'S SECRET WEAPONS

Sierra Maestra Press Mission. To our American Friends with Gratitude.
– FIDEL CASTRO

Matthews might have got to the story first, but others soon followed in his wake, encouraged by a rebel leadership for whom, as Che explained, 'the presence of a foreign journalist, American [by] preference, was more important to us at that time than a military victory.'[1] Presenting powerful and evocative images of the rebel fighters as romantic, idealistic, likeable and, above all, dedicated to a just and honourable cause, foreign correspondents became, as one historian has put it, Fidel Castro's 'secret weapon'.[2]

On the evening of Sunday 19 May, the CBS television network broadcast *Rebels of the Sierra Maestra: The Story of Cuba's Jungle Fighters*. Back at the start of April, after weeks of meticulous planning, the reporter Robert Taber and cameraman Wendell Hoffman had travelled six hundred miles from Havana to the Sierra Maestra by way of Santiago. From there, weighed down by heavy recording equipment, they had trekked high up into the mountains to the rebel camp, near to Pico Turquino, the Sierra's highest point. On arrival, they were greeted enthusiastically and quickly informed that, such was the importance of their mission, all encounters with the enemy had been avoided for the previous three weeks so as not to put their lives in danger. After taking photographs of and chatting with the guerrilla soldiers (including three American teenagers who had run away from the Guantánamo Bay naval base to join the revolution), Taber and Hoffman proceeded to hike a little further up the mountain for a meeting with Fidel that would form the centrepiece of the documentary. Seated in front of a memorial bust to José Martí, wearing his cap, military fatigues and thick beard,

Fidel stared directly into Hoffman's camera as he delivered a message for his American audience. 'As Herbert Matthews, the reporter of the *New York Times*, said, the truth will always be known, with or without censorship, because there are always brave reporters, like you two, that will always be risking your lives for seeking things out.' Claiming the support of all the people of the Sierra Maestra, he ridiculed Batista. With Taber next to him, microphone in one hand, cigarette in the other, the Cuban revolutionary declared, in his trademark broken English, 'At this time there's not a one to admit that he's incapable of defeating us. He hopes to obtain *by liar* that which he cannot get by force of arms. Sometimes,' Fidel continued, 'he says that *I am dead*. Another time he says that *there's nobody in the Sierra Maestra*. And when the soldiers are killed in battle, he says they were *died in accident*. Eh. There have been a *great deal of accidents* here in Sierra Maestra last month.'[3]

Throughout the film the rebels were treated sympathetically. As one historian has noted, they were seen 'drawing water ingeniously from hanging vines, peering through dense undergrowth with their rifles poking through the foliage, cooking over open fires' and 'even raiding a beehive in a tree stump for its honey'. The only word of criticism concerned the rather careless way in which they appeared to handle their rifles.[4] Both Taber and Hoffman were clearly impressed by what they saw. Back in New York, Hoffman explained that, during their long chats, Fidel had been absolutely clear that 'this is only the beginning. The last battle will be in the capital.' Taber, who stayed on to broadcast a radio report from the rebel camp, declared that 'within a very short time' Fidel's army had 'grown considerably in strength', and predicted that it would soon be ready to take the fight to Batista in Oriente province. Government claims that Castro's guerrilla army was a figment of the imagination, or had already been defeated, were nothing more than wishful thinking. 'After three weeks with Fidel Castro,' Taber explained, 'this reporter can assert with confidence that, if fiction is being written, it is in the presidential palace in Havana.'[5]

In a series of photo essays published in the men's adventure magazine *Cavalier*, the celebrity journal *Coronet* and *Look*, one of America's premier photography magazines, the freelance photojournalist Andrew St George painted a compelling portrait of the rebels as 'reluctant, altruistic revolutionaries forced to defend a pure people against a barbarous tyrant'.[6] Over the course of some half-dozen trips to the Sierra Maestra, St George produced numerous iconic images of the guerrillas – many of which were widely printed in Cuba's own underground press – and exhilarating, romantic accounts of the rebel army and its leader.[7] They were, he wrote in his October 1957 article for *Cavalier*, gaining 'hundreds of civilian recruits in every township', despite the 'ferocious government persecution'. And, in the figure of Fidel Castro, 'Cuba had found itself a national hero.'[8] Accompanying the rebel army as they were ambushed one May afternoon, St George described how:

> I heard the submachine guns open up ahead with loud, spiteful banging. I squatted down in the grass and listened.
>
> Then all hell broke loose. Captain [Juan] Almeida's scout squad on the right flank had raised an army patrol. The soldiers were perhaps 50 or 60 strong. On any other day it would have gone badly for them. Now the rebel column was strung out thinly for 500 yards.
>
> I found myself carried backward by a running rebel squad . . . and as I watched them, I frog-hopped left and knelt among the thick, leathery underhang of sea-grape tree. There was an explosion of gunfire over us, the bullets thwacking across the tree-trunk with a ripping sound or raising tiny spouts of red mud around our feet.[9]

Batista's troops, though, were soon fleeing in the face of the rebels – who had killed four enemy soldiers for the loss of one of their own. Guillermo Dominguez, a lieutenant whom St George had befriended, had been subjected to repeated bayonetting by Batista's troops prior to his death. In tying his hands behind his back and stabbing him more than a dozen times, Batista's soldiers had appeared to derive a sadistic pleasure.[10]

In contrast to the savagery and barbarism of the regime, Fidel's rebels were portrayed as committed if reluctant revolutionaries – patriots who had been forced to take up arms in order to save their country, and who were now busy setting fire to sugar cane fields, feasting on roasted snake, manning temporary roadblocks and setting up legal tribunals to enforce the rule of law in rebel-controlled territory. In fact, Fidel was keen to present his own fighters as modern-day mambises – the legendary foot soldiers of Cuba's struggle to overthrow Spanish rule – and emphasised both the moral purity and the honour of his men.[11] Questioned on the controversial military tactic of burning the island's sugar crop, Fidel told St George (and the five million American readers of *Look* magazine) that this was a difficult step to take, but justified it on the grounds that it was from the sugar tax that Batista financed the military. Noting how, during Cuba's earlier war for independence, the revolutionaries had burned sugar cane to secure freedom from Spain, he also pointed out that American colonists had thrown tea into Boston Harbor during their own struggle against the British.[12]

As for post-revolutionary Cuba, Fidel was quick to offer reassurance. The aim, he explained, was to create a 'provisional government whose heads are to be elected by civic bodies, like the Lions, Rotarians, groups of lawyers and doctors, religious organizations'. Its aim would be to root out corruption, eradicate illiteracy, encourage industrialisation and create new jobs. Pressed on whether his 26th of July Movement was, in some way, linked to communism, Fidel was emphatic in his denials. The accusation was, he stated, 'absolutely false. Every American newsman who has come here at great personal peril – Herbert Matthews of the *New York Times*, two CBS reporters and yourself – has said this is false.' The movement's support, he declared, came from right across Cuban society, including the middle class.

'We even', Fidel continued, 'have many wealthy sympathizers' and 'merchants, industrial executives, young people, workers' – all of them were 'sick of the gangsterism that rules Cuba'.[13]

Matthews, for his part, would continue to take a positive view of the Cuban revolutionaries. In a report filed while visiting the island in June 1957,* for instance, he described Fidel as 'more than holding his own in his fight against the Government forces that vowed a week ago to liquidate him'. In fact, Matthews explained, Fidel was 'stronger than ever, his prestige has risen throughout Cuba and he is today far and away the greatest figure in the nation-wide opposition to President Fulgencio Batista'. In Oriente province, home to a third of the island's population, Fidel was 'worshipped': 'From poor farmers and workers to the highest levels of conservative, religious elements of society, business and the professions, Señor Castro has', Matthews asserted, 'become the leader and symbol of the struggle against the dictatorship . . . No figure has attained this status in Cuba since the struggle for independence against Spain.'[14] On 2 December, Matthews penned an unsigned editorial in which he described the landing of the *Granma*, a year earlier, as the beginning of 'one of the strangest and most romantic episodes in Cuba's colorful history' and praised Fidel, 'the hero of the youth of Cuba', for having 'made history'.[15] The following March, he again lauded Fidel's 'courage and dynamism', declaring him to be 'the most remarkable and romantic figure to arise in Cuban history since José Martí, the hero of the war of independence'.[16] But by then, concerns that Matthews was too personally involved in the story – that he had crossed the line between editorial opinion and news reporting – had led to his newsroom colleagues blocking further attempts by him to return to Cuba to report on the situation on the ground. Matthews was incensed, arguing that the fact that he had got 'the news, and deeply and expertly and in a true framework of Cuban

* Although no fan of Matthews's reporting, Batista was unwilling to ban the *New York Times* journalist from the island for fear of antagonising the government in Washington.

history and politics', was what should count, 'not the unavoidable fact that I, as inventor of Fidel Castro, am caught up in the chain of events occurring in Cuba'.[17]

Matthews was holidaying in Havana with Nancie when Batista fled in the early hours of New Year's Day 1959. Although he was bitterly disappointed that Jules Dubois of the *Chicago Tribune* won the race to be the first to interview an exultant Fidel, whose forces had almost immediately taken control of Santiago, he 'could not repress a sense of personal triumph'. After all, the bold prediction that he had made back in February 1957 had come to pass.[18] In the weeks and months that followed the overthrow of Batista, Matthews made clear his support for the Cuban Revolution – in print, in public and in private. In an article for the *Times*, published just a week or so after Fidel's triumphant arrival in Havana, he defended the new government amid a backdrop of widespread American revulsion at a wave of retaliatory justice that saw several hundred senior Batista supporters – members of the hated secret police and other security organisations – dispatched by firing squad.[19] Noting the widespread support among ordinary Cubans for what Fidel called 'Operation Truth', Matthews argued that the new Cuban leader was 'not in any sense different in character' from his fellow countrymen and that 'those who want to condemn him must condemn all Cubans, as there are very few Cubans indeed who would disapprove of the executions that have been and are taking place.' In fact, 'in the eyes of nearly all of his compatriots Dr. Fidel Castro is the greatest hero that their history has known.' It was a view that Matthews shared. Fidel, he explained, 'is one of the most extraordinary figures ever to appear on the Latin-American scene' and 'by any standard a man of destiny'.[20] Cuba, Matthews believed, was now 'the happiest country in the world', and the revolutionaries had 'performed a great, a noble, a heroic feat'.[21]

Official mythology notwithstanding, Fidel's triumph was not solely due to the heroism and courage of his guerrilla army. As historians have been quick to point out, a significant role was also played by the urban-based opposition (by no means united in their support for Fidel), who engaged in sabotage, organised strikes and provided the rebel fighters in the Sierra Maestra with a steady and growing supply of arms, medical supplies and hard cash. Tactical alliances with other opposition groups, rooted in the churches, the trades unions, middle-class professional organisations and, eventually, the Cuban Communist Party – which until 1958 had advocated electoral, rather than armed, opposition to Batista – also proved vital. Luck (or what some scholars prefer to call 'contingency') also helped. When José Antonio Echeverría, the charismatic student leader and founder of the Revolutionary Directorate, was gunned down in March 1957 during a doomed attempt to seize the Presidential Palace and assassinate Batista, one of Fidel's most significant potential rivals was removed from the scene. The president might have survived that attack, but the increasing reluctance of his own army to fight, and the ever more savage countermeasures he ordered – censorship, the suspension of constitutional rights, and the abduction, torture and murder of suspected rebels – sealed his fate. The repression not only helped to push Cuban public opinion behind Fidel and his guerrilla fighters; it also proved too much for the Americans, who, in March 1958, finally withdrew their support from the regime.[22]

As Fidel himself was quick to acknowledge, the rebels' success had also relied on the sympathetic reporting of a group of American foreign correspondents who, from February 1957, had risked injury, imprisonment and even death to break Batista's censorship and report directly on the rebels in the Sierra Maestra. Disguising themselves variously as tourists, businessmen, a vacationing teacher and even a Presbyterian minister visiting his flock, these journalists produced a series of highly influential scoops. 'Without a press,' Herbert Matthews later remarked, 'Fidel Castro was a hunted outlaw, leading a small band of youths in a remote jungle area of eastern Cuba, isolated and ineffectual.' But thanks to his 'secret weapons', the rebel leader was able to secure vital publicity, and the money, supplies, new recruits and political support that followed in its wake.

In April 1959, Fidel made a point of saying thank you. In a ceremony at the Cuban embassy in Washington DC, he personally honoured thirteen American journalists – including Matthews, Taber, St George, Hoffman, Jules Dubois and the renowned freelance photojournalist Dickey Chapelle (the only woman in the group, she had written a series of powerful articles for *Reader's Digest*) – for what he viewed as their service to the revolution. In a sign of their importance, Fidel had eighteen-carat gold medals specially commissioned for the occasion. Each was engraved with the journalist's name, and featured Fidel's signature, the words 'Sierra Maestra Press Mission' and the inscription: 'To our American Friends with Gratitude'.[23]

31. 'COMRADE MATTHEWS'

My reputation for never writing anything that is not true – or to
the best of my knowledge true – is sacred to me.
– HERBERT L. MATTHEWS

In July 1959, during a series of lengthy private conversations with
Philip Bonsal, the new American ambassador in Havana, and other
senior embassy officials, Matthews, it was reported, 'appeared wholly
and unswervingly convinced that the [government of Cuba], its aims
and leaders are entirely laudable. He insisted that there are only a few
Communists in the government including armed forces, and that their
influence is not decisive. He felt that concern on this subject displayed
by Embassy and other US governmental agencies was unwarranted,
referring to it as "international McCarthyism".'[1] This was a position
that Matthews also stuck to in public. In a front-page article published
in the *New York Times* on 16 July, he wrote that Cuba was in a period
of 'creation, gestation and transformation', and admitted that there
were some Communists and Communist sympathisers 'in secondary
positions in such fields as motion pictures and culture and a few in
the army'. But, he insisted, 'this is not a Communist revolution in any
sense of the word': 'there are no Communists in positions of control.'[2]

Not everyone was quite so convinced.

He is 'either incredibly naïve about Communism or under Communist
discipline', wrote Vice President Richard M. Nixon in a four-page
memorandum prepared for President Eisenhower, Secretary of State
Christian Herter and CIA Director Allen Dulles, immediately
following a three-hour meeting with Fidel in his office at the US Capitol
building on the afternoon of Sunday 19 April 1959. 'My guess', the vice
president continued, 'is the former and I have already implied his ideas
as to how to run a government or an economy are less developed than

340

those of almost any world figure I have met in fifty countries.' While Nixon struggled to make sense of Cuba's new leader, he was sure of one thing: 'he has those indefinable qualities which make him a leader of men' and 'whatever we think of him he is going to be a great factor in the development of Cuba and very possibly in Latin American affairs generally.' As a result, the American government had 'no choice but at least to try to orient him in the right direction'.[3]

Fidel's meeting with Nixon took place during a tumultuous eleven-day trip to North America, sponsored by the American Society of Newspaper Editors, that saw him visit Boston, Houston, Montreal, New York, Princeton and Washington DC. It was a public relations sensation. A toy company produced some hundred thousand fake beards and caps bearing the slogan 'El Libertador', which sold like hot-cakes, and Fidel was mobbed by huge, adoring crowds wherever he went. Fifteen hundred cheering supporters were on hand on 15 April to greet his arrival at Washington's National Airport; more than eight thousand turned out at Harvard University's Soldiers Field to hear him speak; and ten thousand attended a charity ball held in his honour in Montreal. It was New York, though, that witnessed the most raucous scenes. Such was the size of the crowd welcoming him at Penn Station, it took Fidel a full twenty-four minutes just to cross the street to his hotel. During four jam-packed days in the Big Apple, he visited the floor of the New York Stock Exchange, climbed the Empire State Building, spoke about agrarian reform at Columbia University, met with baseball star Jackie Robinson and the city's mayor, Robert F. Wagner, appeared on *The Ed Sullivan Show*, addressed a rally of thirty-five thousand Cuban Americans in Central Park and took a tour of the Bronx Zoo – where he won over the press, and much of the American public, by eating hot dogs, hugging children and feeding peanuts to the elephants. To the horror of the NYPD, and the delight of many ordinary New Yorkers, Fidel insisted at almost every opportunity on pushing past his bodyguards, abandoning formal protocol, and greeting ordinary New Yorkers. ('I must see the people,' he insisted. 'I want to greet the people.') One evening, in a characteristic move, he abandoned the safety of his hotel and made his way to a nearby Chinese restaurant, where he chatted informally with students and did an impromptu interview for WHOM radio. Fidel's radical politics, beatnik style (he had rejected advice from a PR company to cut his hair and don a suit for the tour) and informal approach gave him major rock 'n' roll appeal. 'I don't know if I'm interested in the Revolution,' remarked one young woman, 'but Fidel Castro is the biggest thing to happen to North American women since Rudolph Valentino.'[4]

Fidel's trip might have been a public relations triumph, but politically it was a disappointment. He was snubbed by President Eisenhower, who, concerned about protecting the dignity of his office, preferred a round of golf at Augusta National to a meeting with Cuba's rabble-rousing new leader. To make matters worse, Fidel reacted poorly to his encounter with the vice president, whom he viewed as patronising and rather high-handed. 'That son-of-a-bitch Nixon,' Fidel allegedly told his aides. 'He treated me badly and he is going to pay for it.'[5]

By the time Fidel next returned to the United States, for the opening of the Fifteenth General Assembly of the United Nations in September 1960, the two nations were on the brink. Washington was particularly alarmed by the Cuban government's radical economic policies that, while popular with many ordinary Cubans, were not welcomed by many of those who had prospered under the old regime. An agrarian reform law enacted in May 1959 had seen many of the larger estates, including those owned by the influential American sugar companies, expropriated. Havana had also launched an aggressive programme of economic intervention and nationalisation – opening formerly private beaches to the public, taking hotels (including the Havana Hilton) and private clubs (such as the Biltmore Yacht and Country Club) into public ownership, and moving against large financial, corporate and industrial interests. With some $1 billion invested on the island in banking, utilities, tourism, mining and agriculture, American business owners had plenty to lose.[6]

If the assault on American economic interests (and the political influence that followed) was not enough, a so-called 'authoritarian turn' caused consternation in Washington. Throughout 1960, for instance, Fidel's government bore down on the free press and media, taking either direct or indirect control of newspapers, radio stations and television companies. That August, the University of Havana was purged – 120 professors were dismissed from their posts – and the independence of the judiciary was eroded. Cuba was, President Eisenhower was warned, 'rapidly being taken to the point of no return'.[7]

As Fidel and his fellow revolutionaries strengthened their hold on Cuba, they turned increasingly to Moscow and the wider communist world for support – signing trade deals, instigating cultural links, welcoming technical experts and advisers to the island, sending high-profile delegations abroad and purchasing sizeable quantities of arms. When, in June 1960, Standard Oil and Texaco, under intense pressure from the Eisenhower government, refused to process the first shipments of Soviet crude, Fidel promptly nationalised the refineries. The Americans then responded by cutting the Cuban sugar quota (under which the US government pledged to purchase a set amount of the crop each year, and for an artificially high price that benefited the American-owned producers). Fidel was outraged, decrying the foreign 'henchmen' who sought to compromise Cuba's independence. The following month, he signed a law nationalising a slew of American firms, including United Fruit, the telephone and electricity companies and all the US-owned sugar mills. He also denounced, in increasingly vocal terms, Washington's 'criminal' history of imperialism in Latin America.[8]

It was a sign of the deteriorating relationship between Cuba and the United States that, in the days before Fidel's arrival for the UN General Assembly, the Cuban delegation struggled to secure hotel accommodation in a city that had welcomed them with such euphoria just eighteen months earlier. In the end, to avoid an embarrassing diplomatic incident, US officials intervened to persuade Edward Spatz, the owner of the plush Shelburne Hotel on Lexington Avenue and 37th Street, to host them. Their stay would be both short and unhappy. Amid wild rumours that the Cubans were plucking and cooking chickens in their rooms, and stubbing out cigars on the carpets, Spatz now demanded an additional $10,000 security deposit, in cash. Furious, Castro stormed out. After meeting with the UN secretary general, Dag Hammarskjöld, and threatening to set up a makeshift camp in Central Park, the Cuban leader accepted an offer of hospitality from the Hotel Theresa, the so-called 'Waldorf of Harlem'. Over the coming days, Castro would receive a rapturous reception from the local African American community, hold court with a succession of political and cultural luminaries – including Malcolm X, Gamal Abdel Nasser, Kwame Nkrumah and Allen Ginsberg – and promote the politics of anti-imperialism, racial equality and leftist revolution with a fervour, and an audacity, that would help to make him an icon of the 1960s.[9]

What really alarmed the Americans was Fidel's evident closeness to the Soviet leader, Nikita Khrushchev. On the afternoon of Tuesday 20 September, Khrushchev's motorcade sped off from the Soviet Mission on Park Avenue, bound for Harlem. Although Khrushchev was horrified by the poor condition of the Theresa, the Cuban leader made an instantly favourable impression. His face, Khrushchev later recalled, was lit up with a kind of goodness 'that sparkled in his eyes'. After a brief but friendly meeting, the two men emerged onto the sidewalk to be greeted by cheering spectators and a scrum of excited journalists. As the photographers snapped away, and the police struggled to maintain control, the leaders embarked on a very public embrace. Pressed by newsmen on whether Fidel was a communist, the Soviet leader parried the question, but declared that, for his part, he was a Fidelista! Three days later, Khrushchev hosted Fidel and other members of the Cuban delegation at a lavish reception at the Soviet Mission, where they feasted on caviar, pigeon, roast lamb and pepper-infused vodka, and exchanged gifts; and both men made an ostentatious show of supporting each other's speeches before the General Assembly.

As *Revolución* editor Carlos Franqui put it: 'the honeymoon between Fidel and the Russians' had begun.[10]

The 'loss' of Cuba, a previously stalwart economic and political ally that lay just ninety miles off the coast of Florida, was a bitter pill for the Americans to swallow. In the rancorous debate that followed about who was to blame, Herbert Matthews quickly found himself in the firing line. *Time* magazine, for instance, attacked him as an apologist for Castro: 'Dazzled from the start by the dashing revolutionary,' they explained, 'Matthews fell into the trap that everywhere awaits the unwary reporter' and 'let emotional bias suspend his judgment.'[11] From the pages of the conservative *National Review* and the *American Legion Magazine*, William F. Buckley Jr attacked Matthews as a cretin and a propagandist who had exerted what he believed was a corrupting and deeply damaging influence on State Department officials.[*] 'It is bad enough', Buckley wrote, 'that Herbert Matthews was hypnotized by Fidel Castro, but it was a calamity that Matthews succeeded in hypnotizing so many other people, in crucial positions of power, on the subject of Castro.' Matthews had, Buckley declared, done 'more than any other single man to bring Fidel Castro to power'. Buckley also took the opportunity to take a dig at Matthews's employer, which at the time was running a high-profile advertising campaign for its 'Help Wanted' section. Above Buckley's tirade was a cartoon, featuring Fidel, rifle in hand, and the paper's famous slogan 'I Got My Job Through the *New York Times*'.[12]

Unsurprisingly, the academic and staunch anti-communist Nathaniel Weyl agreed. In his 1960 polemic, *Red Star Over Cuba*,[†]

---

[*] While Matthews enjoyed access to embassy and mid-ranking State Department officials, and was not shy about making clear to them his own views on the Cuban situation, there is no evidence that he exercised a decisive influence over policy-making.
[†] In private, Matthews quipped that the book 'should have been called "Red Star Over Times Square" since it is mostly about me'. See Jerry W. Knudson, *Roots of Revolution: The Press and Social Change in Latin America* (Lanham, MD: University Press of America, 2010), 80.

he claimed that 'if there was any single American who could be held responsible for the Cuban tragedy it was Herbert L. Matthews of the *New York Times*.' Matthews was, he claimed, 'a man who had always preferred choosing sides to dispassionate reporting', and he identified him as the most important member of a 'fanatical . . . clique of foreign correspondents' who, just a few years earlier, had thrown their support behind Fidel's 26th of July Movement.[13] Meanwhile, the distinguished historian Theodore H. Draper (one of the country's leading authorities on the Cuban Revolution) argued that, 'ever since Herbert Matthews went to the Sierra Maestra in February, 1957, Castro has been toying with sympathetic intellectuals and journalists.' Matthews, he continued, 'was fooled into reporting that Castro commanded a large force which had had many fights with and had inflicted large losses on Batista's troops'. The truth, however, was that in early 1957 Fidel commanded fewer than twenty men. This 'first and most famous of the "eyewitness" reports' had, Draper lamented, 'set a pattern to this day'.[14]

The charge that Matthews had exaggerated the size of Fidel's rebel army, and with it the threat that he posed to Batista in the spring of 1957, was seized on by his critics. Weyl, never one for understatement, accused Matthews of being a 'psychological warfare agent', dedicated to feeding false information to the enemy. 'When an American correspondent takes sides in a foreign civil war,' he proclaimed, 'a proper question is whether his dispatches are designed to inform his own country or to misinform that foreign faction or government which he considers he is fighting.'[15] Although Matthews's more serious critics did not doubt his patriotism,* the charge that he had been either naïve, or a dupe, was given added credence by Fidel himself. Speaking before the Overseas Press Club during his 1959 visit to New

* When it came to Matthews, FBI Director J. Edgar Hoover wrote that 'one can't get much closer to communism without becoming one', and complained that 'sometimes I think I would rather deal with an out-and-out communist than a fellow like this with all his double talk.' See DePalma, *The Man Who Invented Fidel*, 176.

York, the Cuban leader had told the assembled journalists (including a visibly uncomfortable Matthews) that, during that first meeting in the mountains, he had ordered his men to march repeatedly in a circle around the camp, so as to create the impression that he commanded a much larger force. With a mischievous gleam in his eye, Fidel (whom Matthews later complained had a 'childish streak') then attempted to quote Abraham Lincoln's famous dictum: 'You can fool some of the people,' he began, but, after a couple of mangled efforts, he finished by saying, 'Well, you know what I mean.' It is, of course, scarcely believable that a man of Matthews's vast experience would have been taken in by such a ruse. His mistake had been in not making it clear that, although he had received information from independent sources about the rebels' estimated strength, he had not been able to personally verify its accuracy.[16]

Matthews's 16 July 1959 article for the *New York Times*, in which he had dismissed concerns that the Cuban Revolution was Communist, also came back to bite him. One passage in particular had aged badly:

> There seem to be very few in Cuba . . . who believe Fidel Castro is a Communist, is under Communist influence or is a dupe of Communism . . . The point of view among the most experienced and knowledgeable Cubans is as follows: There are no Reds in the Cabinet and none in high positions in the Government or army in the sense of being able to control either governmental or defense policies. The only power worth considering in Cuba is in the hands of Premier Castro, who is not only not Communist but decidedly anti-Communist even though he does not consider it desirable in the present circumstances to attack or destroy the Reds – as he is in a position to do any time he wants.[17]

When Fidel announced, in a long, televised speech on the evening of 1 December 1961, that he was 'a Marxist–Leninist and I shall be to the last days of my life', Matthews's judgement was once again called into question. Worse, early – and, as it turned out, inaccurate – reports of the speech in the United States had Fidel claiming that he had, in fact, been a dedicated Communist since his college days, but had concealed the fact lest it harm his attempts to build a broad base of support.* Matthews's subsequent attempts to correct the original United Press International report, and his continued insistence that Fidel had only turned to communism after taking power (he had officially declared Cuba to be a socialist state back in April), fell on deaf ears.[18] As he complained to his older brother, John, 'It will still never be lived down because the UPI is naturally not going to admit an error . . . and once such stories get around nothing can ever kill them, not even a correction or a retraction.'[19]

Walter Lippmann, one of America's most widely respected and influential journalists, was quick to offer his support. On 18 December, he wrote to Matthews, reassuring him that 'I have never had the slightest doubt about your competence and integrity as a journalist', and expressing his hope that 'you have not been too much annoyed by the little fellows who have been snapping at your heels.'[20] Matthews's colleagues on the *New York Times*, however, were more ambivalent. As the paper's managing editor, Turner Catledge, explained, he and other senior figures at the paper had come to believe that Matthews's critics were, in part, correct. Matthews had, as Catledge put it, 'become emotionally involved with Fidel Castro to such a point that I and other editors questioned his ability to write objectively about him'. In the summer of 1961, convinced that Matthews had 'used poor judgment and had lost his cool in his coverage of Castro', the paper's publisher, Orvil Dryfoos, summoned Matthews to a meeting to inform him that he would no longer be permitted to cover Cuba for the news department. Although Matthews continued to write about

* Matthews later described the forty-eight hours between reading the early reports and receiving a fuller and more accurate copy of Fidel's speech from the CIA documentary service as 'the worst period of my career'. See Herbert Matthews, *A World in Revolution: A Newspaperman's Memoir* (New York: Scribner, 1972), 317.

Cuba for the editorial page, on at least two occasions (in 1963 and 1966) the *Times* rejected long pieces that he had prepared, following trips to the island, on the basis that 'to print his articles would do the *Times* more harm than good.' It was a decision that Catledge came to regret. 'In retrospect,' he wrote in 1971, 'I have the haunting thought that Matthews was more sinned against than sinning.'*[21]

Back in February 1957, Matthews had been inundated with congratulatory telegrams and letters expressing admiration for his brave and truthful reporting from the Sierra Maestra. By the early 1960s the tide had turned. Pamphlets, letters and postcards – addressed to 'Comrade Matthews' or 'The Red Fox' – now poured in, attacking Matthews as a Judas.[22] 'Had I done my country that incalculable injury you have,' wrote Raymond S. Richmond from San Francisco, 'I think I would cut my throat.' Martina Hernandez, who gave no address, did not pull her punches either. 'Why don't you move to Cuba if you like communist Castro and his revolution so much?' 'I want you to know', she continued, 'that we all free Cubans, who are suffering so much, hate you from the bottom of our hearts for all your stupid, communist articles in favour of the monster. Some time, perhaps very soon, you will get what you deserve.'[23] The exiled Cuban journalist José Luis Massó declared that Matthews was 'one of the most repulsive individuals in North American journalism', who had given repeated service to the cause of international communism by defending the criminal tyrant who now governed Cuba.[24] And

* When, in July 1977, the *Times* published an obituary of Matthews that gave prominent play to the criticism of his reporting from both Spain and Cuba, one of his former colleagues from the editorial department, John B. Oakes, mounted a robust defence of one of the paper's most distinguished and loyal reporters from the letters page: 'If Herbert L. Matthews was one of the most "controversial" journalists of his era,' he explained, 'that is only because nothing arouses more bitter controversy among a newspaper's readers than honest reporting that contradicts their emotional preconceptions.' Throughout his career, Oakes continued, 'Matthews never deviated from the truth as he saw it' and 'never permitted either the threat of abuse or the lure of fame to lure him from the highest standards of journalistic integrity'. (John B. Oakes, '"Controversial" Journalist', *New York Times*, 7 August 1977, E16).

when Matthews visited San Juan, Puerto Rico, to publicise his 1961 book *The Cuban Story*, angry Cuban exiles demonstrated outside his hotel. They handed out leaflets which urged him to be 'honest with the people of the United States. You must admit that you were wrong or you must declare yourself against democracy and register yourself as an agent of a foreign power, as the law stipulates.' Lamenting Cuba's turn towards communism and embrace of the Soviet Union, and the erosion of basic freedoms on the island, they pressed Matthews to 'not further deceive the people of the United States. Tell them the truth.'[25] Some of the protesters placed a dozen or so buckets outside the entrance to the Caribe Hilton, and suggested that, if Matthews were to stick his head in one, he might be able to think more clearly.[26] There was a darker side to Matthews's new-found notoriety too: on the afternoon of Monday 14 September 1964, James Kenny – a tall, blue-eyed and handsome young FBI agent who could have come straight out of central casting – walked into the *Times* office to warn that a Cuban exile group based in Miami had determined that Matthews should be killed and were in the process of recruiting a hitman to carry out the job.* Matthews quipped that if the hit was successful it would 'make a good story', but he was clearly unnerved by the news. As the meeting ended, he turned to Kenny and said: 'I hope you can keep me alive.'[27]

If the hate mail, the protesters and the attacks from journalists and academics were not bad enough, Matthews also found himself the repeated target of Mississippi senator and renowned anti-communist James O. Eastland. As chair of the powerful Senate Internal Security Subcommittee, Eastland convened a series of high-profile hearings into the communist threat that was posed by Cuba, in which witnesses lined up to criticise Matthews's judgement, impugn his character and question his motives. In July 1962, Whiting Willauer, Washington's

* Fortunately, the threat came to nought, and Matthews later speculated that $15,000 – the likely cost of killing an editor of the *New York Times*, according to his own investigations – had proved too high a hurdle!

former ambassador to Costa Rica, used the opportunity to place on the record a paper he had prepared, back in 1958, in which he had warned that 'America's most important interests in the Caribbean' were 'facing ultimate extinction at the hands of the International Communist conspiracy'. One reason for this, he explained, was that the American press had consistently failed to reveal 'the true nature of what is going on in Latin America'. Willauer then proceeded to draw a parallel with what, at least in his reading, had happened a couple of decades earlier in China:

> The Edgar Snows of Chinese communism are replaced today by the Herbert Matthews[es] of Caribbean Communists. Neither the Snows nor the Matthews[es] are Communists, and both can be fairly credited with abhorring it – if and when they recognize it. The trouble with this type of journalism is that it is carrying a banner for a cause and, in its hate of the dictators, it is blind to the nature of the forces of communism, which are infiltrating the legitimate revolutionary forces.

'Today, as yesterday,' he continued, 'they fail to see through the agrarian reform; through the rent control measures aimed against the wicked landlords. They do not recognize the familiar Communist plot to liquidate the middle class and other opposition elements.' How, Willauer wondered, was this possible? 'Truly, it seems that even among our highly educated modern press there are many in high places of whom it must be said that "none are so blind as those who will not see".'[28]

It was, however, the explosive testimony of former Cuban ambassador, and onetime Batista confidant, Arthur Gardner, that proved the most damaging. Appearing before the committee on 27 August 1960, he explained that he 'felt that Batista had proved a great friend to this country, and his administration had proved a great ability to develop the country itself . . . And I felt it very strongly that the State Department was influenced, first, by those stories by Herbert Matthews, and then it became a kind of fetish with them.' Matthews, in his judgement, was 'one of those people, the do-gooder type, who the minute you mention the word – anybody as a dictator – is out to try to break him'. In his reports from the Sierra Maestra, Gardner went on, Matthews had 'made Castro appear to be a Robin Hood, a savior for the country'. 'All the newspapers in this country', he complained, 'became sort of hypnotized by the thing.' Gardner even claimed – falsely – that he, with Batista's knowledge, had personally helped Matthews to secure the interview with Fidel, on the condition that 'when he came back he would tell me his reactions . . . To this day,' he explained, 'I have never seen him.'[29]

Matthews was furious. Writing to his old friend Ernest Hemingway, he declared that he was 'not going to let Gardner get away with it'. 'Every word' of the claim about how the interview with Fidel had been secured was, Matthews insisted, 'a lie'. 'In fact,' he continued, 'it is the most extraordinary thing that has ever happened to me in my career. Gardner, of course, was under oath. I am now taking measures to force the Senate Subcommittee to call me so that I may appear and deny every word he said, likewise under oath. This presumably will mean that one of us has perjured himself, and it won't be me. I am gathering quite a bit of testimony to prove my story.'* 'My reasons for putting up a fight in this case', Matthews explained, 'are in the first place that I have spent nearly forty years building up a reputation for professional probity and I am not going to allow anyone to besmirch my reputation at this late date. And in the second place, I think it is important to keep the historic record straight.'[30]

*

* The subcommittee, perhaps wary of diverting attention away from its investigations, never did call Matthews. He had to settle for publishing an article denouncing Gardner as a liar in the *Washington Daily News*, and persuading a friendly New York congressman to read it into the *Congressional Record*. See DePalma, *The Man Who Invented Fidel*, 224–5.

Matthews would defend his reporting on the Cuban Revolution until the end of his life.* In his 1961 book *The Cuban Story*, he was at pains to emphasise his commitment to honest journalism, explaining how 'my reputation for never writing anything that is not true – or to the best of my knowledge true – is sacred to me.'[31] Of his July 1959 claim, for instance, that 'this is not a Communist revolution in any sense of the word', Matthews was unrepentant. The assertion, he stated, had been perfectly true when he made it. Matthews recognised, of course, that Fidel had subsequently changed both his mind and his policies – and, were he to be writing today, he would 'write what is true today'. 'This', he explained, 'is the proper function of journalism.'[32]

Matthews believed that, to truly understand the Cuban Revolution, a good journalist – like a good historian – had to develop empathy for the revolutionaries and their supporters, as well as for the climate in which they were operating.[33] He had long agreed with Benedetto Croce – the distinguished Italian philosopher and historiographer, whom Matthews had befriended during his wartime posting to Italy – who argued that men could not stand outside of events 'and move as in a void. It is necessary to pass through them, to feel the impact and the agony they generate in order to stand above them, rising from suffering to judgment and knowledge.'[34] Being mortal, newspaper correspondents could not possibly hope to eliminate all bias from their reporting. But to dismiss their work on that basis would be to 'reject the only things that really matter – honesty, understanding, compassion and thoroughness'. 'A reader', Matthews declared, 'has a right to the truth and to all the facts, to the best of the writer's ability to find them; he has no right to expect or demand that a correspondent agree with him.'[35]

* He would also continue to defend – albeit with qualifications – the Cuban Revolution. In his 1969 book *Castro: A Political Biography*, he was critical of Fidel for having 'deprived Cubans of basic rights that they should have under any system'. And, while he acknowledged that Fidel had 'brought tragedy to some families', Matthews believed that 'it is demonstrable that he brought a better life to a majority of Cubans – if not always today and for the older generations, then for tomorrow and for the youth' (298–9).

For years, Matthews had been committed to going to where the action was, viewing the situation with his own eyes, and reporting the news as honestly as possible. It would be for history (or, more accurately, for historians) to weigh the evidence and make the final judgement. As for his own legacy, he explained that the 'only monument I want to leave on earth is for some student years from now to consult the files of the *New York Times* for information about the Spanish Civil War, the Cuban Revolution, or other events and places, and find my by-line, and know that he can trust it'.[36]

32. VENCEREMOS!

They saw in [Fidel], I think, the hipster who in the era of the
Organization Man had joyfully defied the system, summoned a dozen
good friends, and overturned a government of wicked old men.
– ARTHUR M. SCHLESINGER JR

The Cuban Revolution was a world historical event, with consequences
that reverberated far beyond the Caribbean – and not just because,
for thirteen fraught days in October 1962, the world teetered on the
brink of nuclear Armageddon over the presence of Soviet missiles
on the island. Under Fidel's leadership, Cuba helped to inspire –
and sometimes sought to actively export – socialism across Latin
America; the island played a leading role in the wider global struggle
against imperialism; and Fidel's revolution, for better or worse,
inspired a generation of sixties radicals in both the United States
and Western Europe.

In the so-called 'Declaration of Havana', which was formally
proclaimed before the National General Assembly of the People
on 2 September 1960, Fidel denounced the 'dominance of Yankee
monopolies over the interests of our people and Yankee manipulation
of governments prostrated before Washington'. Revolutionary Cuba
was, he continued, determined to march 'with all the world and not
with just a part of it'. It was, Fidel declared to the vast, cheering crowds,
'the duty of peasants, workers, intellectuals, Negroes, Indians, young
and old, and women, to fight for their economic, political and social
rights; the duty of oppressed and exploited nations to fight for their
liberation; the duty of each nation to make common cause with all the
oppressed, colonized, exploited peoples, regardless of their location in
the world or the geographical distance that may separate them.' 'All
the peoples of the world', he proclaimed, 'are brothers!'[1]

In the years that followed, as part of Fidel's attempts to assert Cuba's leading role in the global struggle against imperialism, Havana hosted a series of international conferences designed, as one historian has put it, to position Cuba 'as the torch bearer of the post-Bandung* world'. Most famously, in January 1966, some five hundred delegates, representing eighty nations, attended the First Solidarity Conference of the Peoples of Africa, Asia, and Latin America (more commonly known as the Tricontinental Conference). Those present, who included Salvador Allende (Chile), Amílcar Cabral (Guinea-Bissau), Carlos Marighella (Brazil), Nguyen Van Tien (of South Vietnam's National Liberation Front) and the French philosopher-cum-guerrilla fighter Régis Debray, sought to coordinate support for national liberation struggles, advance the cause of Third World solidarity, affirm 'the right of the peoples to meet imperialist violence with revolutionary violence' and denounce US imperialism – which, it was claimed, underpinned a 'worldwide system of exploitation'.[2]

During the 1960s, Havana – motivated by both self-interest and a genuine commitment to revolution – offered support to a host of liberation movements across Latin America and Africa: providing ideological indoctrination and training in guerrilla warfare to at least two thousand Latin Americans between 1961 and 1964; encouraging leftist revolution in Bolivia, Colombia, Guatemala, Venezuela and elsewhere; funnelling weapons to the FLN (Front de Libération Nationale) in Algeria; sending soldiers to support rebels in Zaire (formerly Congo-Léopoldville); providing independence movements in Angola and Guinea-Bissau with military instructors; and even dispatching a column of troops to the Republic of the Congo (also known as Congo-Brazzaville) to support the leftist government of Alphonse Massamba-Débat.[3] There were some successes: Fidel's soldiers thwarted the 1966 attempted coup in Congo-Brazzaville, and

---

* In 1955, representatives from across Africa and Asia met in Bandung, Indonesia, to discuss peace, the role of the Global South in the Cold War, and questions of economic development and decolonisation.

Cuban military instructors and medics remained in Guinea-Bissau until independence from the Portuguese was finally secured in 1974. But in Latin America, Havana's 'revolutionary offensive' failed, its symbolic end coming in the jungles of Bolivia in October 1967 with the capture and subsequent execution of Che Guevara.[4]

As well as providing ideological and practical sustenance to a range of anti-colonial movements across the Global South, the Cuban Revolution also served as something of a lodestar for radicals across Western Europe and the United States, including those involved in the burgeoning struggle for black freedom. Indeed, right from the start, Fidel's uncompromising stance on racial equality had won intense admiration among many African Americans. On coming to power in January 1959, Fidel had immediately committed his government to dismantling the racial segregation that had long marred Cuban society. Within weeks, a host of new laws had been passed that sought to integrate schools, beaches, swimming pools, restaurants and other facilities.[5] Although historians would later question the effectiveness of this attempt to eliminate racism from the island (it was, after all, unrealistic to expect a deeply entrenched system of racial prejudice to be eliminated, overnight, by government decree), at the time the crusade generated a genuine sense of excitement, both inside Cuba and in the United States.[6] The presence of a government, less than one hundred miles off the coast of the segregated South, that was committed – in both word and deed – to ending the colour bar inevitably attracted the attention of black Americans. The New York congressman Adam Clayton Powell Jr – one of only two African Americans in the House of Representatives – flew to Havana just weeks after Fidel had taken power. There, standing alongside El Comandante before a million-strong rally in the capital, he heaped praise on the new government's racial policies.[7] Much of the black press in America was similarly enthusiastic. Writing in the Baltimore *Afro-American* on 7 February 1959, for instance, the legendary reporter Ralph D. Matthews Sr famously declared that:

Every white man who cuffs, deprives, and abuses even the lowest colored person, simply because he is white and the other colored, should have seared upon his conscience the fact that it is possible for the tables to be turned. Castro has proved it in our time.[8]

Fidel's bold action stood in stark contrast to the situation in the United States. There, five years after the US Supreme Court's landmark 1954 ruling that segregated schools were unconstitutional, barely 0.2 per cent of black children in the Deep South were able to attend classes alongside white children. In addition, millions of African Americans across the states of the former Confederacy remained excluded from first-class citizenship, including the right to vote, through a combination of law, economic coercion and outright violence. While the towns and cities of the North might have lacked the 'White Only' signs of the Jim Crow South, a powerful combination of poverty, prejudice and segregation (both formal and informal) kept black Americans firmly 'in their place' – largely segregated, discriminated against in housing and employment, and subjected to police brutality.[9] With the Eisenhower administration continuing to offer a counsel of patience and gradualism in the face of growing demands for meaningful change, it was little wonder that many black Americans glimpsed, in revolutionary Cuba, the possibilities of a new, and much better, world.[10]

One of those black Americans was Robert F. Williams, who, by 1960, had forged a reputation as one of America's foremost black freedom fighters. An uncompromising champion of racial equality (and an advocate of what he called armed self-reliance), the president of the Monroe, North Carolina, branch of the National Association for the Advancement of Colored People (America's largest, and oldest, civil rights organisation) had led by example, facing down the Ku Klux Klan with machine guns and dynamite. Williams would visit Cuba twice in the summer of 1960, and the absence of 'White Only' signs, the integrated schools and his ability to stroll, unhindered, along the streets of Havana, all made a powerful impression on him. Writing in his weekly newsletter, *The Crusader*, Williams told his supporters that 'on the streets of Cuba I learned for the first time in my life what it feels like to be respected as a fellow human being, and to be accepted in the human race.' It was in Cuba, he explained, that 'I realized that I was born and have lived all my life in a land that was never home.'[11] As for the accusations in the American press about Cuba going 'red', Williams had a pithy response: 'If this is communism, I vote for communism.' 'Cuba', he declared, 'is an inspiration for me.'[12]

Williams was far from alone. Richard Gibson, the head of the New York chapter of the Fair Play for Cuba Committee* – and the first African American journalist to be employed by CBS – dashed off a postcard to a friend from the Havana Riviera Hotel, sending 'greetings from a really free country, where our kind of people are given a tremendous welcome'. 'The progress here', Gibson declared, was 'incredible'.[13] For the pioneering African American historian John Henrik Clarke, the Cuban Revolution had 'challenged all oppressive regimes throughout the world and given hope to people still longing to be free'.[14] The black playwright Julian Mayfield was similarly star-struck, describing Fidel as 'a beautiful man. He is a hero, we know – one of the few of our times, almost anachronistic – but his manner is that of a young fellow who has done what had to be done and he cannot understand what all the excitement is about . . . and when we think of what they have done to change the world and make the Washington golf-player tremble in his boots – well, it's something to think about.'[15]

In their enthusiasm for the Cuban Revolution, African Americans were joined by a generation of white sixties radicals who were attracted by the Cuban leader's charisma, machismo and audacity, identified strongly with the 'hip' and 'beatnik' style of the Fidelistas and cheered on Havana's uncompromising support for anti-colonialism and anti-racism. These young white students were, as one leading historian of the New Left has put it, inspired by what they saw as Fidel's attempt to

* The FPCC was founded by left-liberal supporters of the Cuban Revolution, including the journalist Robert Taber, in April 1960.

'direct human history, to take hold of one's environment and shape it, to institutionalize better human values'.[16] Todd Gitlin, who in 1963–4 served as president of Students for a Democratic Society, America's largest and most influential New Left organisation, recalled seeing:

> the black-and-white footage of bearded Cubans wearing fatigues, smoking big cigars, grinning big grins to the cheers of throngs deliriously happy at the news that Batista had fled; and we cheered too. The overthrow of a brutal dictator, yes. But more, on the face of the striding barbudos [bearded revolutionaries] surrounded by adoring crowds we read redemption – a revolt of young people, underdogs, who might just cleanse one scrap of earth of the bloodletting and misery we had heard about all our lives. From a living room in the Bronx we saluted our unruly champions.[17]

Castro's extraordinary ability to attract the support of young, liberal, middle-class Americans had been observed by the historian and public intellectual Arthur M. Schlesinger Jr in the spring of 1959, when Cuba's new leader had drawn a huge crowd on a visit to his own Harvard University. Schlesinger, who as a special assistant to President John F. Kennedy would have a ringside seat as Washington sought to deal with the 'Castro problem', explained how 'the undergraduates saw in him, I think, the hipster who in the era of the Organization Man had joyfully defied the system, summoned a dozen good friends and overturned a government of wicked old men.'[18] Certainly, in the Cuba of Fidel Castro, young leftists like Gitlin saw an alternative to capitalism, imperialism and racism that was neither constrained by the rigid doctrinal disputes of the 'Old Left' – which, among other things, pitted Communists, Trotskyists and social democrats against each other – nor tainted by the mass murders and human rights violations that had scarred the Soviet experiment.[19]

Fidel's appeal was by no means restricted to the United States. Haunted by Khrushchev's revelations in February 1956 about the crimes that had been committed by Stalin, and appalled by the Soviet Union's brutal response to the Hungarian uprising later that same year, a generation of European progressives, as well as left-wing artists and intellectuals, gravitated towards the Cuban Revolution for inspiration. As the renowned Marxist historian and lifelong communist Eric Hobsbawm observed, the revolution could hardly have been better designed to appeal to Western leftists. After all, it 'had everything: romance, heroism in the mountains, ex-student leaders with the selfless generosity of youth . . . a jubilant people, in a tropical tourist paradise pulsing with rumba rhythms'. And lacking, during its early years at least, a fixed ideological position,* it could be welcomed enthusiastically across the political Left.[20]

In February 1960, the French intellectuals Jean-Paul Sartre and Simone de Beauvoir had travelled to Cuba in order to see the revolution for themselves.[21] Landing in Havana during the middle of the carnival celebrations, they were immediately smitten: 'The gaiety of the place', declared de Beauvoir, 'exploded like a miracle under the blue sky.'[22] Based in the luxurious Hotel Nacional on the Malecón, the city's historic esplanade, the couple were shown the sights of the old town, introduced to leading revolutionaries and feted by some of the island's most prominent novelists, artists, poets and playwrights.[23] On one famous occasion, immortalised by the legendary photographer Alberto Korda, they paid a midnight visit to Cuba's National Bank, where they were ushered through the lobby, past rebel soldiers, into the director's office. There, over strong coffee and fine cigars, they chatted for more than two hours with Che Guevara, who had recently been appointed as the bank's director: 'I am first of all a doctor,' Che said, 'then somewhat of a soldier, and finally, as you see, a banker.'[24] Sartre and de Beauvoir were also given a personal tour of the island by Fidel, who drove them around in his jeep, visiting sugar cane fields,

* Fidel declared Revolutionary Cuba to be a socialist nation on 1 May 1961; on 2 December that same year he came out as a Marxist–Leninist, proclaiming that 'Marxism or scientific socialism has become the revolutionary movement of the working class.'

new agricultural cooperatives and tourist developments on the newly public beaches, as well as a former rebel hideout. They also had time to see the sights of Santiago, and to enjoy a memorable fishing trip in the waterways of the Península de Zapata.[25]

The visit of the French existentialists was headline news. Carlos Franqui, the editor of *Revolución*, recalled how the couple were 'everywhere: at meetings, on the street, in the carnival, out in the country, on television'.[26] Greeted with chants and jostled by cheering, boisterous crowds, their names were even incorporated into a popular carnival refrain.[27] The enthusiasm was mutual: Sartre and de Beauvoir were clearly impressed by what they found in Cuba, with de Beauvoir later describing how the revolution was characterised not by 'machinery' or 'bureaucracy', 'but a direct contact between leaders and people, and a mass of seething and slightly confused hopes. It wouldn't last forever, but it was a comforting sight. For the first time in our lives, we were witnessing happiness that had been attained by violence,' and it 'restored a pleasure in just being alive that I thought I had lost forever'.[28] Sartre was, if anything, even more effusive. In a series of articles that were published in the leading French daily *France-Soir* later that summer, he lauded Cuba's organic, bottom-up revolution: a political project that, as he saw it, was free from ideological hang-ups and, above all else, an exercise in 'direct democracy'.[29] As for the Cuban revolutionaries, they had formed a 'cult of energy'. Liberated from the 'latifundias of sleep', they 'live energy, they exercise it, they invent it, perhaps'. Che – at least in Sartre's telling – was the archetypal existentialist hero: a man defiant in the face of injustice, and absolutely committed to action.[30] As for Fidel – a man 'who fought, who is fighting, for a whole people' with 'no other interest than theirs' – he was a kind of everyday superman.[31] The desire of the Cubans to defend their hard-won freedom and to maintain the revolution had Sartre's full-throated support: 'The Cubans must win,' Sartre declared, 'or we will lose all, even hope.'[32]

*

The reality on the ground in Cuba, of course, did not always match up to the high ideals. In fact, there had been voices of caution right from the start. The black poet and playwright LeRoi Jones (later known as Amiri Baraka) might have been won over while visiting Cuba in July 1960 but, on the eve of his departure to Havana, his good friend and fellow Greenwich Village poet Gilbert Sorrentino had told him, bluntly, 'I don't trust guys in uniforms.'³³ And while Allen Ginsberg may have viewed Fidel as an 'honest rat', his fellow beat poet Gregory Corso reminded him that, for all their apparent good humour and playfulness, the barbudos also carried Sten guns. It was a prescient observation: during a 1965 trip to Havana, Ginsberg would witness first-hand the Cuban government's repression of homosexuals. After speaking out once too often ('The worst thing I said was that I'd heard by rumour that Raúl Castro was gay. And the second worst thing I said was that Che Guevara was cute.'), Fidel had him bundled onto the next plane out of Havana.³⁴ Fidel's support for Leonid Brezhnev's brutal crushing of the Prague Spring (and, with it, the dream of communism with a human face) in August 1968 also disappointed many of his foreign admirers. Three years later, Sartre and de Beauvoir, appalled by growing censorship in Cuba, felt compelled to denounce Havana's 'use of repressive measures against intellectuals and writers'. Fidel's response was swift: 'Cuba's door', he declared, 'is definitely, definitively and eternally closed to you.'³⁵

Robert F. Williams had learned about the limits of the Cuban Revolution some years earlier. Williams and his family had fled to Cuba in the autumn of 1961 to escape trumped-up kidnapping charges that had been laid after they had taken a white couple into their home to protect them from an angry crowd of black protesters during civil rights disturbances in Monroe, North Carolina. From exile in Havana, Williams continued to support the black freedom struggle in the United States: publishing his *Crusader* newsletter and broadcasting 'Radio Free Dixie', a mix of music, news about the civil rights struggle and his own powerful political commentary, to the South. But, despite his personal friendship with Fidel, he soon ran into difficulties – money failed to arrive, promised support never materialised and he was pressured to alter the content of his broadcasts. Williams's forceful personality probably did not help. On touring the foreign ministry and noticing its all-white staff, Williams's wife, Mabel, recalled that 'Rob told them it looks like Mississippi in here.' ('I thought', she said, 'they would shoot him for sure.') But there were serious political disagreements too: the Cubans, deferring to the official communist line, insisted that class trumped race. Black nationalism, it was said, would alienate the white working class – who were the 'primary revolutionary force'. Unwilling to become what he termed a 'socialist Uncle Tom', Williams left Cuba for Beijing in 1965. Writing to Fidel the following year, Williams declared that he would 'always be a friend of the Cuban Revolution', but he deplored the fact that 'while in Cuba all of my work for the Afro-American struggle was sabotaged.'[36]

Such disillusionment would not, though, significantly diminish Cuba's hold over American and Western European radicals. A new generation of French leftists, for instance, developed a deep sympathy for the Cuban Revolution over their shared support for Algeria's Front de Libération Nationale, to whom Fidel sent arms, troops and, later, medical support.[37] The Cuban government's steadfast support for the Vietnamese struggle for national liberation (Fidel declared 1967 to be the 'Year of Heroic Vietnam'), meanwhile, earned the approval of much of the global anti-war movement.[38] In February 1968, at the height of sixties activism, it was the German student leader Rudi Dutschke who ensured that Che Guevara's famous slogan 'The Duty of a Revolutionary is to Make the Revolution' ('Die Pflicht des Revolutionärs ist es, Revolution zu machen') appeared on a giant banner that stretched around the lecture hall at West Berlin's Free University during the International Vietnam Congress.[39]

For American radicals, Cuba continued to serve as both an inspiration and a haven. Stokely Carmichael, the former leader of the Student Nonviolent Coordinating Committee (one of the key civil rights groups of the early 1960s), and later populariser of the 'Black Power' slogan, visited Havana in August 1967 to attend the First Conference of the Latin American Solidarity Organisation.[40] He described the experience as 'mind blowing. I mean, here were brothers and sisters from around the whole world, Jack, especially the "third world", who were struggling to liberate humanity from colonialism [and] economic exploitation.'[41] It was in Cuba that, for Carmichael:

> the international struggle became tangible, a human reality, names, faces, stories, no longer an abstraction, and our struggle in Mississippi or Harlem was part and parcel of this great international and historical motion.[42]

Cuba was, he proclaimed, 'a shining example of hope in our hemisphere'.[43] Two years later, Angela Davis, the controversial UCLA philosophy professor and Black Power militant, visited the island as part of a delegation from the American Communist Party. Viewing, up close, what she believed was a socialist society made thrillingly real, the trip marked 'a great climax' in her life. 'Politically,' she explained, 'I felt infinitely more mature . . . it seemed like the Cubans' limitless revolutionary enthusiasm had left a permanent mark on my existence.'[44]

Carmichael and Davis were not alone. The Black Panthers, opponents of the Vietnam War, revolutionary firebrands like Mark Rudd (who led the 1968 occupation of Columbia University) and Bernardine Dohrn (founder of the terrorist group the Weather Underground), as well as activists in an array of social justice movements were among those who, inspired by the Cuban Revolution's social achievements in education, healthcare and housing; its championing of liberation struggles (including its support for the North Vietnamese); and its willingness to face down the superpower to the north, continued to look to Havana during the 1960s and beyond.[45] During 1969, in what has been described as 'one of the most imaginative enterprises ever undertaken by the American Left', SDS, which had long championed the Cuban Revolution, founded the Venceremos Brigade.*[46] Initially formed to supply volunteers to help with the Cuban sugar harvest, in the coming years it would send many thousands of Americans – white college students, New Leftists and activists with the African American, Chicano, Asian American, Native American and women's movements – to the island, in defiance of the American travel ban, to live and work alongside ordinary Cubans, demonstrate solidarity with the revolution and learn lessons about radical political organising that they could then apply to the effort to build a more just and equal society back home.[47] For the brigadistas, the experience was transformative. As one of them recalled, 'I came back from Cuba feeling much less isolated. We are not a few hundred thousand valiant but impotent souls struggling alone within the wasteland of Amerika – we are part of an international movement.'[48] Mark Rudd returned from Cuba 'fired up with the flame of socialist revolution' and determined to adapt the strategies of guerrilla warfare for the struggle in 'the imperialist homeland'. 'Like a Christian seeking to emulate the life of Christ,' he recalled, 'I passionately wanted to be a revolutionary like Che, no matter what the price.'[49]

Little wonder, then, that the American authorities were worried. As a top-secret FBI report noted, under the leadership of Fidel Castro, Cuba had come to serve 'as the inspiration for the American radical movement in its avowed aim to bring down the American system that it so fiercely despises'. Cuba was, it continued, 'their Mecca, their Yennan [sic], their shrine, the "first liberat[ed] territory in the Western Hemisphere", where they can see the model of the new society to which they aspire'.[50]

Herbert Matthews was, of course, not responsible for the extraordinary appeal of the Cuban Revolution among sixties radicals. Matthews might have been lauded as the 'Best Friend of the Cuban People', might have

* The name, which means 'We Shall Win', was taken from a Cuban revolutionary slogan.

HERBERT MATTHEWS

personally felt that the revolutionaries' success in overthrowing Batista 'had been my triumph, along with others', might have been buttered up by Fidel Castro, who told him that 'without your help . . . the revolution in Cuba would never have been.'[51] But, in the final analysis, it was Fidel's charisma, his radical ideas and the enigmatic qualities of the barbudos that drew those who were seeking a more humane and authentic alternative to the mid-century Cold War status quo. Matthews did not initiate the Cuban Revolution; he was not, or at least not quite, 'the man who invented Fidel' (as his biographer, Anthony DePalma, has it); and to attribute Fidel's triumph to his reporting is, as the *Hispanic American Historical Review* noted, 'as absurd as blaming a meteorologist for a thunderstorm'.[52] That said, by presenting the rebel leader to the world in such heroic terms in February 1957, Herbert Lionel Matthews had certainly helped to give history a mighty shove.

EPILOGUE

The world that went to pieces at the end of the 1990s was the world shaped by the impact of the Russian Revolution of 1917.
– ERIC HOBSBAWM

In a piece written to commemorate the thirty-first anniversary of the Bolshevik seizure of power in Russia, penned just a year before the founding of his own People's Republic of China, Mao declared that the October Revolution had 'opened up wide possibilities for the emancipation of the peoples of the world' and 'created a new front of revolutions against world imperialism, extending from the proletarians of the West . . . to the oppressed peoples of the East'. 'The long-suffering people of China', Mao continued, 'must win their liberation' and, buoyed as they were by the continued success of the Soviet Communist Party, 'they firmly believe they can.' 'The radiance of the October Revolution', he proclaimed, 'shines upon us.'[1]

A dozen years later, during a meeting in Havana with Sergei Pavlov, the leader of the Komsomol (or youth division of the Communist Party of the Soviet Union), Fidel Castro – keen to butter up his Russian guest and fired up by having recently read John Reed's *Ten Days That Shook the World** – similarly sought to extol the importance and enduring influence of the October Revolution. 'You know,' he explained, 'the Cuban Revolution didn't begin two years back: it began in 1917.' 'If it hadn't been for your revolution,' he noted, 'our revolution wouldn't have happened.'[2]

Although both Mao and Fidel, keen to secure Moscow's support, were exaggerating for effect, their central point remained true. The

---

* Fidel described *Ten Days* as 'a most interesting and useful book'. Noting the fight with external enemies that the Bolsheviks had faced in the immediate aftermath of their revolution, he added that the slanders that Cuba was facing were just repeats of those aimed at the Bolsheviks years ago.

Russian Revolution not only created the world's first communist state, but it birthed a worldwide revolutionary movement that saw Leninist parties, dedicated to establishing workers' states and committed to central economic planning, take power across swathes of Central and Eastern Europe (notably Hungary, Czechoslovakia, Poland and East Germany), Asia (including Vietnam, Laos and North Korea – as well as China) and Africa (Angola, Mozambique). With Cuba's embrace of socialism in the spring of 1961, communism even gained a foothold in Latin America. For much of what Eric Hobsbawm has termed the 'Short Twentieth Century',* the leaders of the Soviet Union, and their supporters, claimed to have pioneered an alternative and superior system to capitalism, one that was destined by history to triumph. Moreover, aside from a brief period during the 1930s and early 1940s when capitalist democracies (and social democrats) united with their communist opponents to take the fight to fascism, the international politics of the Short Twentieth Century were, in the seven decades that followed the October Revolution, dominated by what Hobsbawm has characterised as 'a secular struggle by the forces of the old order against social revolution'. As he points out, this was a revolution that was believed by its opponents to be 'embodied in, allied with, or dependent on the fortunes of the Soviet Union and international communism'. It is, then, no exaggeration to say that 'the world that went to pieces at the end of the 1980s', with the fall of the Berlin Wall and the subsequent collapse of the USSR, 'was the world shaped by the impact of the Russian Revolution of 1917.'[3]

The Russian Revolution, of course, would almost certainly not have happened – at least not in the way that it did – had Lenin not made it back to Petrograd from exile in Switzerland in the spring of 1917. It was Lenin who, unlike many of his colleagues, saw the opportunity for his party to seize sole power and establish what he believed would

* Hobsbawm's twentieth century runs from the outbreak of the Great War in 1914 to the collapse of the USSR in 1991.

be a genuinely soviet system of government. As a result, he attacked the Provisional Government, opposed all attempts to forge an alliance with other socialist parties and denounced the continuation of Russia's involvement in the Great War with a relentlessness, and a ferocity, that made him stand out even among his fellow revolutionaries. In the autumn of 1917, helped by the deteriorating situation on the Eastern Front and the mistakes of his enemies, Lenin's prediction that Russia was passing from the first stage of revolution (in which power was temporarily in the hands of the bourgeoisie) to the second stage (which would see it placed in the hands of the proletariat) was proved spectacularly right. But the Old Man's journey back to Russia aboard the so-called sealed train, though fraught with personal risk, was far from heroic. Not only had Lenin made a deal with the devil in order to pass through German territory unmolested but – according to the well-founded rumours that immediately began to circulate – he had also taken vast quantities of German gold to fund what Kerensky decried as the destruction of Russia. If the journey home itself was something of an embarrassment, the arrival at the Finland Station – with its sea of cheering faces, and Lenin's iconic speech from atop an armoured car – was altogether different. This was an event that marked out Lenin as the hero, arriving home to popular acclamation, poised to wage a heroic struggle on behalf of the impoverished, disenfranchised and long-suffering masses. Tellingly, one of the few statues of Lenin that remains on public view in post-Soviet Russia is the giant bronze monument that stands in front of the Finland Station in modern-day St Petersburg. Designed by the sculptor Sergei A. Evseev and the architects Vladimir Shchuko and V. G. Helfreich, the statue, which was unveiled in 1926, depicts Lenin – left hand clutching his lapel, right arm raised shoulder-high, palm forwards and thumb pointing up[*] – addressing the crowds from the top of an armoured car (rendered, here, in stone).[4]

---

[*] The so-called 'taxi-hailing' pose proved enormously influential and was a common feature of many of the statues of Lenin that would later adorn the Soviet Union.

EPILOGUE

In China, the Long March certainly helped to secure Mao's leadership over the Chinese Communist movement, but the year-long retreat from the Nationalist armies, although a military disaster, also became a founding myth of the People's Republic. Not only did the march demonstrate the extraordinary commitment, courage and endurance of the Red Army, but their ultimate deliverance from the hands of their enemies served as proof that the Communists had been uniquely ordained to build a new China, one that would deliver power to the peasants and workers. In Cuba, meanwhile, the fiasco of the *Granma* landing was quickly woven into a wider story in which a ragtag army of young, idealistic guerrilla fighters overthrew a hated, corrupt and oppressive dictatorship. In February 1966, having merged two newspapers – *Revolución* and *Hoy* – the first issue of the official newspaper of the Central Committee of the Communist Party of Cuba (and de facto mouthpiece of Fidel's revolutionary government) hit the newsstands. Its title: *Granma*. And in a pavilion erected on the grounds of Havana's Museum of the Revolution (the former Presidential Palace) sits the yacht herself – symbolising, in physical form, the spirit of the Cuban Revolution.*

Popular understanding of the Russian, Chinese and Cuban revolutions was shaped, in decisive and consequential ways, by three extraordinary journalists: John Reed, Edgar Snow and Herbert Matthews. They were, as we have seen, very different characters: Reed, the poet and bohemian; Snow, the goofy, sometimes diffident boy from the Midwest; and Matthews, the scholar with a taste for fine wines, tailored suits and works of art. They differed, too, in their politics. Reed was an avowed socialist who took up arms for the fledgling Bolshevik state and went on to help found what became the Communist Party of the United States of America. Snow, a former advertising executive, was a social democrat and

---

* On special state occasions, a replica of the vessel is taken out on parade.

admirer of Franklin D. Roosevelt.* Committed to the right to equal opportunity, free speech, a free press and freedom of assembly, Snow believed that modern capitalist economies should be run for the benefit of the many, not the few.†5 And Herbert Matthews was a classic mid-century liberal (he had supported Adlai Stevenson over Dwight D. Eisenhower in the 1952 and 1956 presidential elections), at ease among the intellectual and cultural elite, and whose close friends included Ernest Hemingway and Grayson Kirk, president of Columbia University.[6]

Reed, Snow and Matthews were 'super-empowered individuals' – defined by the journalist Thomas L. Friedman as those who prove to be far more influential than their status, or circumstances, would ordinarily warrant.[7] Reed was, in the words of Leon Trotsky, an 'extraordinarily keen observer', 'able to transcribe upon the pages of his book the feelings and passions of the deciding days' of the Russian Revolution.[8] His gripping *Ten Days That Shook the World* not only helped to create a model for what a proper, modern revolution should look and feel like, but it was also tremendously effective in winning sympathy for the Soviet cause.[9] Meanwhile, Snow's sympathetic portrayal of the Chinese Communists as agrarian reformers and

* According to his first wife, Helen Foster, 'the only photograph that Ed ever put up that I know of was his own famous portrait of Mao . . . The only other person he ever subsequently so honored was President Franklin D. Roosevelt; in his last election campaign, Ed put a big poster of F.D.R. on our front door in a solidly Republican town.' See Helen Foster Snow, *My China Years*, 202.

† During the Second World War, Snow, along with Helen and good friend the New Zealander Rewi Alley, attempted to put these ideals into action, founding the short-lived Chinese Industrial Cooperatives (or Indusco). A combination of local, mobile industrial units, more established enterprises (mining, mass production lines) in places safe from Japanese attack, and social institutions including clinics, schools, vocational centres and lunchrooms would all be run based on the principle of cooperation between workers, consumers and government. The aim: to deliver 'human rehabilitation, economic progress and democratic education'. See Jerry Israel, '"Mao's Mr America": Edgar Snow's Images of China', *Pacific Historical Review*, vol. 47, no. 1 (February 1978), 118–20. In the 1948 election, Snow supported FDR's former vice president, Henry Wallace, who, running as a Progressive, challenged Harry Truman from the left.

idealists was politically transformative: his 'image-making' and 'image-breaking' book reverberated widely. Smashing for good the notion that the Communists were nothing more than 'Red bandits', *Red Star Over China* helped to create a positive, romantic image of Mao and the revolutionary movement that he led, both within China and without (American policy-makers, public officials and military leaders were among those affected).[10] Such was the book's influence that, according to the scholar Julia Lovell, without Snow 'both a domestic and international cult of Mao would be hard to imagine'. Even today, some nine decades after its publication, *Red Star Over China* remains the key source for contemporary historians writing about Mao's early life and the Long March. As for Matthews, there was, and remains, a widespread consensus that – for better or worse – his February 1957 scoop for the *New York Times* was decisive in establishing the popular image of Fidel as a romantic revolutionary: an idealistic rebel, committed to overthrowing a brutal dictatorship and bringing social justice to the Cuban people.

The adventures and accomplishments of Reed, Snow and Matthews also tell us something about the role of the journalist in American political culture. As the twentieth century unfolded, American journalists – increasingly aware of their own subjectivities – retreated from 'the austere posture of objectivist factuality' that had formerly defined the profession. In recalling his time at the *New York Evening Post*, where he worked from 1902 to 1906, Reed's great mentor Lincoln Steffens described how he and his fellow journalists were expected to 'report the news as it happened, like machines, without prejudice, color, and without style; all alike'. 'Humor or any sign of personality in our reports was', he explained, 'caught, rebuked, and, in time, suppressed.' In contrast to this dry emphasis on 'facts', a new generation of reporters embraced 'interpretative reporting', or journalism with a 'point of view'.[11] Reed, Snow and Matthews, in their various ways, were 'activist journalists' who mobilised their skills and position to support a foreign political cause; in particular, they made revolutionary leaders and revolutionary causes more palatable for a US – and, more broadly, a Western – audience. Given that the three did little to disguise their sympathies, it is not surprising that they became lightning rods for conservatives: Reed, hounded by the authorities, fled into exile, and an early death, in Russia; Snow was denounced as an 'apologist' for Chinese Communism during the Cold War, and found his journalistic career stymied; Matthews was persistently attacked as being either a fool or a traitor. But while they were criticised for their partisanship, the journalists themselves were strikingly reluctant to abandon entirely the journalistic search for the 'truth'. Reed, for instance, wrote as an admitted partisan with an emotional stake in events, while simultaneously insisting that he had 'tried to see events with the eye of a conscientious reporter, interested in setting down the truth'.[12] And, as he emphasised repeatedly, his famous book was based not only on his own first-hand experiences, but also on a formidable trove of documents, newspapers and other printed material. Snow was, as he saw it, the eyes and ears of the average American, an observer on the hunt for the facts. Indeed, the whole purpose of his trip into Red China had been, as he put it, to cut through the propaganda (on both sides) and uncover 'credible evidence' that would assist 'dispassionate observers seeking the truth'.[13] Similarly, Matthews, who privately viewed the Cuban Revolution as a 'great, noble and heroic feat', asserted that the fundamental task of the journalist was to write 'truthfully what he sees and knows on a given day', and he claimed never to have written anything that he 'did not believe to be true'.[14]

It is, of course, easy to sneer at all this. Given what we now know – about the Gulag and the show trials in Russia; the mass famines and the assorted horrors of the Great Leap Forward and the Cultural Revolution in China; and the economic hardships, crushing of free speech and assault on basic democratic rights in Cuba – the accounts produced by Reed, Snow and Matthews appear, at best, hopelessly naïve. But this would be a profound mistake, reading back into the past a future that was, at that point in time, not known (and, in a fundamental sense, unknowable). Reed, Snow and Matthews were, it should be stressed, operating at a moment when the revolutions, and revolutionary movements, that they were writing about were characterised by genuine optimism and a palpable sense of possibility that had not yet been tainted, or tested, by the messy realities of wielding – and holding on to – state power. Reed, clearly, was swept along by the excitement on the streets of Petrograd in the autumn of 1917; Snow, given a carefully curated tour of Red China by Mao and his comrades, was impressed by what he saw, which contrasted favourably with the chaos, corruption and violence that marred much of Nationalist-controlled China; Matthews, like so many others, was taken in by Fidel's charm and charisma, and impressed by the idealism of his guerrilla fighters. After the bitter disappointment of the Spanish Civil War, he seems to have hoped that this time the angels would triumph.

From the streets of Petrograd during the heady autumn of 1917 to Mao's stunning victory in October 1949 and Fidel's triumphant arrival in Havana in January 1959, the social, economic, political and cultural history of the twentieth century was transformed in dramatic and profound ways by the Russian, Chinese and Cuban revolutions.

These momentous events were, of course, shaped decisively by the personal charisma, strategic acumen, ruthless determination and political ideology of Lenin, Mao and Fidel, as well as by the loyalty and ardour of their followers. But the enduring influence of their revolutions – particularly their global resonance and wider popular appeal, not least in the United States – also owed much to the extraordinary courage, thirst for adventure and literary brilliance of John Reed, Edgar Snow and Herbert Matthews: three journalists who shook the world.

ACKNOWLEDGEMENTS

I have incurred many debts while researching and writing this book, and it is a particular pleasure to be able to place on record my thanks to those individuals and institutions that have helped me along the way.

The School of History at the University of Leeds has been my professional and academic redoubt for more than two decades now, and I could not have wished for a more supportive or congenial home. With her characteristic wisdom, Andrea Major, my then Head of School, granted me a year's sabbatical for the 2022–3 academic year, which I was able to dedicate, full-time, to writing. Her successor, Sanjoy Bhattacharya, has been similarly supportive. Financial assistance from the staff research fund helped to defray some of the costs of publication, and colleagues including Nir Arielli, Simon Ball, Alex Bamji, Kate Dossett, Shane Doyle, Claire Eldridge, Sean Fear, William Gould, Will Jackson, Elisabeth Leake (now, sadly for us, at Tufts) and Eline van Ommen offered staunch support and friendship. Meanwhile, a Franklin Research Grant, awarded by the American Philosophical Society, facilitated much of the archival research that underpinned the project. Among other things, it enabled me to employ a brilliant research assistant, Nikita Shepard, who undertook several deep dives into the Herbert Lionel Matthews Papers at Columbia University's Butler Library. Nikita furnished me with hundreds of documents, responded to my persistent queries and undertook invaluable follow-up research with admirable efficiency.

I would also like to thank the staff of the Houghton Library at Harvard for copying materials from the John Reed Papers, and to John Ulrich, who undertook some additional research in the collections there for me. Stuart Hinds and Becky Briggs Becker at LaBudde Special Collections,

ACKNOWLEDGEMENTS

University of Missouri-Kansas City, could not have been more helpful in reproducing numerous documents from the Edgar Snow Papers, as well as securing some of the images that appear in this book. I would also like to record my sincere thanks to Sian Snow, who provided me with materials from her personal collection and commented on the draft chapters that deal with her father's life. Although she does not agree with everything I have written, her careful and thoughtful responses were incredibly helpful. Thanks, too, to Jannick Harmsen for undertaking research on my behalf at the Roosevelt Institute for American Studies, Middelburg, and to Scott Hamm for obtaining materials from the National Archives at College Park. At Leeds, the wonderful staff of the Brotherton Library (especially Tim Wright), were incredibly helpful in tracking down obscure newspaper articles, securing inter-library loans (including microfilms) and organising subscriptions to some major online databases. Meanwhile, librarians and archivists at Syracuse, the Wisconsin Historical Society, the University of Pennsylvania, the Hoover Institution and Yale University helped me to track down important materials, while Morgan Svedlund at the Swedish National Archives very kindly provided me with a copy of a report by the secret police.

Katharine Aylett, Stephan Petzold, Joshua Newmark, and Ian Hall and Eva Janicki-Hall translated materials for me from, respectively, Russian, German, Spanish and Swedish. For responding to my questions, furnishing insights and advice, and sharing their thoughts, I would like to thank Say Burgin, Anthony DePalma, Andrew Hartman, Catherine Merridale, China Miéville, Robert A. Rosenstone and Ronald Suny. I am also grateful to Ben Ambridge, who shared an early draft of his fascinating book on classic story tropes with me. At Leeds, my brilliant colleagues Peter Anderson, Adam Cathcart, James Harris and Rob Hornsby not only answered innumerable questions and provided advice about what to read, but they also gave generously of their time to read draft chapters – and, in the case of James and Rob, entire sections – offering insightful comments and suggestions that greatly improved the manuscript. Any remaining errors of fact or interpretation are, of course, entirely down to me.

My fantastic agent, Sally Holloway, was an early champion of this project, and I remain grateful for her energy, insight and expertise. At Faber, Laura Hassan and Fred Baty supported this book enthusiastically, and offered thoughtful and careful advice about how to make it fly. Silvia Crompton copy-edited the manuscript with great care and skill, Bill Donohoe produced a wonderful set of journey maps and Melanie Gee compiled the thoughtful and helpful index. Meanwhile, Kate Ward shepherded the book, and its author, expertly through the production process.

For raising my spirits and cheering me on these past years, I am particularly grateful to my friends (Stephan Petzold deserves a special shout-out). Most of all, though, I want to acknowledge the incredible love and support of my family. My father, Brian, showed a keen interest in the book, and its progress, during what turned out to be the final months of his life, while my mother, Marilyn, and Emma, Ian, Barney and Matilda have been brilliant. János has (depending on how you view these things) either continued to keep my feet on the ground or kept me on my toes. During the writing of this book, we embarked on a new and extraordinary chapter in our journey together, by becoming parents to the most amazing little boy. And it is to Brody that this book is dedicated, with all the love in the world.

IMAGE CREDITS

p. 7 Keystone-France/Gamma-Keystone via Getty Images; p. 46 Hulton Archive/Getty Images; p. 55 Fine Art Images/Heritage Images/Getty Images; p. 103 Sovfoto/Universal Images Group via Getty Images; p. 138 Slava Katamidze Collection/Getty Images; p. 157 Bettmann/Getty Images; p. 199 Mondadori via Getty Images; p. 207 Helen Foster Snow Papers, L. Tom Perry Special Colletions, BYU Library, Brigham Young University; p. 241 Edgar Snow Papers, LaBudde Special Collections, University of Missouri. Reproduced with the kind permission of Sian Snow; p. 273 I. C. Rapoport/Getty Images; p. 291 Bettmann/Getty Images; p. 299 Herbert Matthews Papers, Columbia University Rare Book & Manuscript Library; p. 321 Associated Press/Alamy Stock Photo; p. 325 From the New York Times. © 1957 The New York Times Company. All rights reserved. Used under license.

SELECT BIBLIOGRAPHY

Below is a list of the major archival and published primary sources I have used. Full details of all secondary works cited can be found in the endnotes.

ARCHIVAL SOURCES

Netherlands

Roosevelt Institute for American Studies, Middelburg
Military Intelligence Reports: Surveillance of Radicals in the United States, 1917–1941

United Kingdom

Brotherton Library, University of Leeds
Arthur Ransome Papers

United States of America

Rare Book & Manuscript Library, Columbia University
Lincoln Steffens Papers, 1863–1936
Herbert Lionel Matthews Papers, 1909–2002
Oral History Archives: Bennett Cerf; Helen Foster Snow

Houghton Library, Harvard University
John Reed Papers

National Archives, College Park, Maryland
Records of the Foreign Service Posts of the Department of State, United States Embassy, Russia 1918: File 800 (Reed, John – Appointment by People's Commissariat as Consul to New York)
Reed: Transcript of the examination [of Reed by officials when returning to New York] forwarded by Assistant Secretary of the Treasury Department to Secretary of State, 9 May 1918, and other documents in Department of State (Record Group 59), File 360d. 1121 R25

Hoover Institution Library & Archives
Anthony DePalma Papers
Helen Foster Snow, 'Notes on the Sian Incident, 1936', 51, in Nym Wales Papers, Box 17, Folder 1

Manuscripts & Archives, Yale University
Louise Bryant Papers

LaBudde Special Collections, University of Missouri-Kansas City
Edgar Snow Papers
Henry Mitchell Papers

Kislak Center for Special Collections, Rare Books and Manuscripts, University of Pennsylvania
Boni & Liveright and Horace Liveright Correspondence

Wisconsin Historical Society
SDS Papers

Special Collections Research Center, Syracuse University
Granville Hicks Papers

NEWSPAPERS AND MAGAZINES

The Liberator
The Masses
New Republic

PUBLISHED PRIMARY SOURCES

The Collected Works of Vladimir Lenin at www.marxists.org/archive/lenin/works/cw/index.htm
American Politics and Society: Students for a Democratic Society, Vietnam Veterans Against the War, and the anti-Vietnam War Movement (1958–1981) (ProQuest History Vault)
Russia in Transition: The Diplomatic Papers of David R. Francis (Frederick, Maryland: University Publications of America, 1985)
Testimony of Mr John Reed, 'Bolshevik Propaganda: Hearings Before a Subcommittee of the Committee on the Judiciary, United States Senate', 20 February 1919, 566, at https://ia600201.us.archive.org/32/items/cu31924030480051/cu31924030480051.pdf
Foreign Relations of the United States, 1918, Volume I: Russia (Washington: Department of State)
Foreign Relations of the United States, 1955–1957, Volume IV: American Republics: Multilateral; Mexico; Caribbean (Washington: Department of State)
Communist Threat to the United States Through the Caribbean: Hearing Before the

SELECT BIBLIOGRAPHY

Subcommittee to Investigate The Administration of Internal Security Act and Other Security Laws

Independent Voices (underground press archive) at www.jstor.org/site/reveal-digital/independent-voices/

They Knew Lenin: Reminiscences of Foreign Contemporaries (Honolulu: University Press of the Pacific, 2005)

World War 1 and Revolution in Russia (Gale Research)

Angelica Balabanoff (Angelika Balabanova), *My Life as a Rebel* (New York: Harper & Brothers, 1938)

Otto Braun, *A Comintern Agent in China, 1932–1939* (Stanford: Stanford University Press, 1982)

Louise Bryant, *Six Red Months in Russia* (Portland, Oregon: Powell's Press, 2002)

George Buchanan, *My Mission to Russia and Other Diplomatic Memories, vol. II* (London: Cassell and Company Ltd., 1923)

Fidel Castro and Ignacio Ramonet, tr. Andrew Hurley, *My Life* (New York: Scribner, 2009)

Chen Chang-Feng, *On the Long March with Chairman Mao* (Peking: Foreign Languages Press, 1972)

David Deutschmann and Deborah Shnookal, *Fidel Castro Reader* (Melbourne: Ocean Press, 2007)

Charles Egleston, ed., *The House of Boni & Liveright, 1917–1933: A Documentary Volume* (Detroit: Gale, 2004)

Comrade Elmsted, 'In the Same Train as Ilyich: Memories of the Driver of the Train (in Finland)', *Leningradskaya Pravda*, 16 April 1924, no. 87, 3

David R. Francis, *Russia from the American Embassy: April 1916–November 1918* (New York: Scribner, 1921)

Carlos Franqui, *The Twelve* (New York: Lyle Stuart Inc., 1968)

Carlos Franqui, *Diary of the Cuban Revolution* (New York: The Viking Press, 1976)

Ernesto 'Che' Guevara, *Reminiscences of the Cuban Revolutionary War* (London: Harper Perennial, 2009)

Eric Homberger, ed., *John Reed and the Russian Revolution: Uncollected Articles, Letters and Speeches on Russia, 1917–1920* (Basingstoke: Macmillan, 1992)

Nadezhda Krupskaya, 'Reminiscences of Lenin: Last Months in Emigration' at www.marxists.org/archive/krupskaya/works/rol/rol21.htm

Zina Lilina (Zina Zinovieva), 'Comrade Lenin Departs for Russia', *Leningradskaya Pravda*, 15 April 1924, no. 87 David E. Lowes, ed., *Bessie Beatty on Revolutionary Russia* (Red Revenant, 2017)

Herbert L. Matthews, 'Cuban Rebel Is Visited in Hideout', *New York Times*, 24 February 1957

Herbert L. Matthews, *The Cuban Story* (New York: George Braziller, 1961)

Herbert L. Matthews, *The Education of a Correspondent* (New York: Harcourt, Brace and Company, 1946)

Herbert L. Matthews, *Revolution in Cuba: An Essay in Understanding* (New York: Scribner, 1975)

SELECT BIBLIOGRAPHY

Herbert L. Matthews, *A World in Revolution: A Newspaperman's Memoir* (New York: Scribner, 1972)

John Newsinger, ed., *Shaking the World: John Reed's Revolutionary Journalism* (London: Bookmarks, 1998)

Colonel B. V. Nikitin, *The Fatal Years: Fresh Revelations on a Chapter of Underground History* (London: William Hodge and Company Ltd., 1938)

Fritz Platten, *Die Reise Lenins durch Deutschland im plombierten Wagen* (Berlin: Neuer Deutscher Verlag, 1924)

Karl Radek, 'Through Germany in the Sealed Coach' (1924) at www.marxists.org/archive/radek/1924/xx/train.htm

F. F. Raskolnikov, 'Comrade Lenin's Arrival in Russia' at www.marxists.org/archive/raskolnikov/1925/kronstadt-petrograd-1917/cho4.htm

John Reed, *Ten Days That Shook the World* (London: Penguin, 2007)

George Safarov, 'Comrade Lenin', *Leningradskaya Pravda*, 16 April 1924, no. 87

Tony Saich, ed., *The Rise to Power of the Chinese Communist Party: Documents and Analysis* (London: Routledge, 2015)

Stuart Schram, ed., *Mao's Road to Power: Revolutionary Writings 1912–1949, Volume I: The Pre-Marxist Period, 1912–1920* (Armonk, NY: M. E. Sharpe, 1993)

Stuart Schram, ed., *Mao's Road to Power: Revolutionary Writings 1912–1949, Volume II: National Revolution and Social Revolution, December 1920–June 1927* (Armonk, NY: M. E. Sharpe, 1994)

Stuart Schram, ed., *Mao's Road to Power: Revolutionary Writings 1912–1949, Volume III: From the Jinggangshan to the Establishment of the Jiangxi Soviets, July 1927–December 1930* (Armonk, NY: M. E. Sharpe, 1995)

Stuart Schram, ed., *Mao's Road to Power: Revolutionary Writings 1912–1949, Volume IV: The Rise and Fall of the Chinese Soviet Republic, 1931–1934* (Armonk, NY: M. E. Sharpe, 1997)

Stuart Schram, ed., *Mao's Road to Power: Revolutionary Writings 1912–1949, Volume V: Toward the Second United Front, January 1935–July 1937* (Armonk, NY: M. E. Sharpe, 1998)

Alexander Shlyapnikov, tr. Richard Chappell, *On the Eve of 1917* (London: Allison & Busby, 1982)

Agnes Smedley, *The Great Road: The Life and Times of Chu Teh* (New York: Modern Reader, 1956)

Edgar Snow, *Journey to the Beginning* (London: Victor Gollancz Ltd., 1960)

Edgar Snow, *Random Notes on Red China* (Cambridge, MA: Harvard University Press, 1957)

Edgar Snow, *Red China Today: The Other Side of the River* (Harmondsworth: Penguin, 1970)

Edgar Snow, *Red Star Over China*, first revised and enlarged edition (London: Grove Press UK, 1988)

Helen Foster Snow, *My China Years* (London: Harrap, 1985)

Lois Wheeler Snow, *Edgar Snow's China: A Personal Account of the Chinese Revolution Compiled from the Writings of Edgar Snow* (New York: Random House, 1981)

SELECT BIBLIOGRAPHY

G. Sokolnikov, 'The Return of V. I. Lenin from Exile', *Leningradskaya Pravda*, 18 April 1928, no. 90

N. N. Sukhanov (edited, abridged and translated by Joel Carmichael), *The Russian Revolution 1917: A Personal Record* (Princeton: Princeton University Press, 1984)

Wang Xing, ed., *China Remembers Edgar Snow* (Beijing: Beijing Review, 1982)

Albert Rhys Williams, *Journey into Revolution: Petrograd, 1917–1918* (Chicago: Quadrangle Books, 1969)

Z. A. B. Zeman, ed., *Germany and the Revolution in Russia, 1915–1918: Documents from the Archives of the German Foreign Ministry* (London: Oxford University Press, 1958)

Grigory Zinoviev, 'The Arrival of V. I. Lenin in Russia', in Platten, *Die Reise Lenins durch Deutschland im plombierten Wagen*

ENDNOTES

Prologue

1 Micheline Aharonian Marcom, '8 Epic Journeys in Literature', *Electric Lit*, 21 October 2020, at https://electricliterature.com/8-epics-journeys-in-literature/. See also Joseph Campbell, *The Hero with a Thousand Faces* (New York: Pantheon Books, 1949), and Christopher Booker, *The Seven Basic Plots: Why We Tell Stories* (London: Continuum, 2004), 69–106

PART ONE: RUSSIA
LENIN

1: Zurich

1 Nadezhda Krupskaya, 'Reminiscences of Lenin: Last Months in Emigration' at www.marxists.org/archive/krupskaya/works/rol/rol21.htm (accessed 11 November 2022); Victor Sebestyen, *Lenin the Dictator* (London: Weidenfeld & Nicolson, 2017), 262–3; Catherine Merridale, *Lenin on the Train* (London: Allen Lane, 2016), 132–3

2 China Miéville, *October: The Story of the Russian Revolution* (London: Verso, 2018), 28; https://en.wikipedia.org/wiki/Russian_Empire_Census (accessed 17 November 2022)

3 Miéville, *October*, 15

4 Miéville, *October*, 32

5 Miéville, *October*, 35–8

6 George Buchanan, *My Mission to Russia and Other Diplomatic Memories, vol. II* (London: Cassell and Company Ltd., 1923), 49

7 Buchanan, *My Mission to Russia*, 50

8 Buchanan, *My Mission to Russia*, 56–7

9 Merridale, *Lenin on the Train*, 97–107

10 Merridale, *Lenin on the Train*, 107–8

11 Merridale, *Lenin on the Train*, 108

12 Merridale, *Lenin on the Train*, 108–13

13 Merridale, *Lenin on the Train*, 113; Miéville, *October*, 59, 64–5, 82

14 Quoted in Helen Rappaport, *Caught in the Revolution: Petrograd 1917* (London: Windmill Books, 2017), 132–3 (see also xxii, 55)

15 R. H. Bruce Lockhart, *Memoirs of a British Agent* (London: Pan Books, 2002), 169–70

16 Orlando Figes, *A People's Tragedy: The Russian Revolution 1891–1924* (London: Pimlico, 1997), 142–5; for Lenin's country estate, see www.ephotozine.com/photo/lenin-house-museum-at-lenino-kokushkino-45898290 (accessed 20 November 2024)

17 Figes, *A People's Tragedy*, 145

18 Figes, *A People's Tragedy*, 145–6

19 Figes, *A People's Tragedy*, 147–8; Sebestyen, *Lenin the Dictator*, 100

20 Figes, *A People's Tragedy*, 148–50

21 Figes, *A People's Tragedy*, 151–4

22 Sebestyen, *Lenin the Dictator*, 151

23 See, for example, Helen Rappaport, *Conspirator: Lenin in Exile* (London: Windmill Books, 2010)

24 Sebestyen, *Lenin the Dictator*, 165–8

25 Figes, *A People's Tragedy*, 191–2

26 Sebestyen, *Lenin the Dictator*, 171, 173

27 Sebestyen, *Lenin the Dictator*, 179–80

28 Rappaport, *Conspirator*, 216–18; Merridale, *Lenin on the Train*, 78–80

29 Merridale, *Lenin on the Train*, 72–3

30 Merridale, *Lenin on the Train*, 80–1

31 'The Conference of the RSDLP Groups Abroad', 19 February/4 March 1915, at www.marxists.org/archive/lenin/works/1915/feb/19.htm (accessed 15 November 2022); see also Merridale, *Lenin on the Train*, 83–4

32 Merridale, *Lenin on the Train*, 85–6; Vasil Kolarov, 'At the Zimmerwald Conference', in *They Knew Lenin* (Honolulu: University Press of the Pacific, 2005), 70–1

33 Manifesto, International Socialist Conference at Zimmerwald, September 1915, at www.marxists.org/history/international/social-democracy/zimmerwald/manifesto-1915.htm (accessed 15 November 2022)

34 V. I. Lenin, 'The Draft Resolution of the Left Wing at Zimmerwald', c. 20 August/2 September 1915, at www.marxists.org/archive/lenin/works/1915/aug/20.htm (accessed 15 November 2022)

35 Merridale, *Lenin on the Train*, 87–8

36 Merridale, *Lenin on the Train*, 88–92

37 Merridale, *Lenin on the Train*, 93–4

38 Krupskaya, 'Reminiscences of Lenin'

39 Lenin, 'Telegram to the Bolsheviks Leaving for Russia' at www.marxists.org/archive/lenin/works/1917/mar/06.htm (accessed 11 November 2022)

40 Lenin, 'Letters from Afar: First Letter – The First Stage of the First Revolution', written 7/20 March, and published in *Pravda*, nos. 14 & 15 (21/22 March), at www.marxists.org/archive/lenin/works/1917/lfafar/first.htm (accessed 11 November 2022)

41 Lenin, 'Letters from Afar: Third Letter – Concerning a Proletarian Militia', written 11/24 March, at www.marxists.org/archive/lenin/works/1917/lfafar/third.htm (accessed 20 November 2024)

42 Sebestyen, *Lenin the Dictator*, 263

43 Krupskaya, 'Reminiscences of Lenin'

2: Caged Lion

1 Zinoviev, 'The Arrival of V. I. Lenin in Russia', in Platten, *Die Reise Lenins durch Deutschland im plombierten Wagen* (Berlin: Neuer Deutscher Verlag, 1924), 67

ENDNOTES

2 Sebestyen, *Lenin the Dictator*, 199–200; Grigory Yevseyevich Zinovyev at www.
   britannica.com/biography/Grigory-Yevseyevich-Zinovyev (accessed 21 November
   2022)

3 Zinoviev, 'The Arrival of V. I. Lenin in Russia', 67–8

4 Merridale, *Lenin on the Train*, 6

5 Zinoviev, 'The Arrival of V. I. Lenin in Russia', 68; Krupskaya, 'Reminiscences of
   Lenin'; Sebestyen, *Lenin the Dictator*, 263–4

6 Sebestyen, *Lenin the Dictator*, 264; Merridale, *Lenin on the Train*, 135

7 Lenin, 'Principles Involved in the War Issue', December 1916, at www.marxists.
   org/archive/lenin/works/1916/dec/00b.htm (accessed 21 November 2022)

8 Karl Radek, 'Through Germany in the Sealed Coach' (1924) at www.marxists.org/
   archive/radek/1924/xx/train.htm (accessed 21 November 2022)

9 Stefan Zweig, 'The Sealed Train', in Zweig, *Decisive Moments in History: Twelve
   Historical Miniatures* (Riverside, CA: Ariadne Press, 1999), 242–3

10 Radek, 'Through Germany in the Sealed Coach'

11 Merridale, *Lenin on the Train*, 135–6

12 Alfred Erich Senn, *The Russian Revolution in Switzerland, 1914–1917* (Madison:
    University of Wisconsin Press, 1971), 222; Rappaport, *Conspirator*, 265

13 Sebestyen, *Lenin the Dictator*, 272

14 Sebestyen, *Lenin the Dictator*, 272

15 Merridale, *Lenin on the Train*, 58–66; Michael Pearson, *The Sealed Train: Journey to
    Revolution, Lenin – 1917* (London: Fontana, 1989), 30–1, 67–9

16 Merridale, *Lenin on the Train*, 136–8; Sebestyen, *Lenin the Dictator*, 272–3

17 Merridale, *Lenin on the Train*, 139; Sebestyen, *Lenin the Dictator*, 273

18 'The Minister in Copenhagen to the Foreign Ministry', Telegram no. 528, 2 April
    1917, in Z. A. B. Zeman, ed., *Germany and the Revolution in Russia, 1915–1918:
    Documents from the Archives of the German Foreign Ministry* (London: Oxford
    University Press, 1958), 31

19 'The State Secretary to the Foreign Ministry Liaison Officer at General
    Headquarters', Telegram no. 461, 23 March 1917, in Zeman, ed., *Germany and the
    Revolution in Russia*, 26; and 'The Liaison Officer at General Headquarters to the
    Foreign Ministry', Telegram no. 371, 25 March 1917, in Zeman, ed., *Germany and
    the Revolution in Russia*, 26

20 Merridale, *Lenin on the Train*, 140

21 Willi Münzenberg, 'Lenin and We', in *They Knew Lenin*, 85–6

22 'The Minister in Bern to the Foreign Ministry', Telegram no. 603, 4 April 1917, in
    Zeman, ed., *Germany and the Revolution in Russia*, 35–6

23 'The Minister in Bern to the Chancellor', Report no. 970, 5 April 1917, in Zeman,
    ed., *Germany and the Revolution in Russia*, 38–9

24 'The Under State Secretary to the Minister in Bern', Telegram no. 394, 5 April
    1917, in Zeman, ed., *Germany and the Revolution in Russia*, 37–8

25 J. Ley, 'A Memorable Day in April', *New Statesman*, 19 April 1958, 496–8

26 Julio Álvarez del Vayo, *The Last Optimist* (New York: Viking Press, 1950), 123–4

27 Pearson, *The Sealed Train*, 90–2

28 Rappaport, *Conspirator*, 269; Merridale, *Lenin on the Train*, 145; Pearson, *The Sealed Train*, 92–3

29 Lenin, 'Farewell Letter to the Swiss Workers', 26 March/8 April 1917, at www.marxists.org/archive/lenin/works/1917/mar/26b.htm (accessed 24 November 2022)

30 Fritz Platten, 'Lenin's Return', in *They Knew Lenin*, 91

31 Pearson, *The Sealed Train*, 93; Platten, *Die Reise Lenins durch Deutschland*, 35

32 Merridale, *Lenin on the Train*, 145

33 Pearson, *The Sealed Train*, 93–5; Rappaport, *Conspirator*, 269–71

34 Zinoviev, 'The Arrival of V. I. Lenin in Russia', 69

35 Merridale, *Lenin on the Train*, 146

36 Merridale, *Lenin on the Train*, 147–8; Pearson, *The Sealed Train*, 95–7; Platten, *Die Reise Lenins durch Deutschland*, 35

37 Merridale, *Lenin on the Train*, 148; Pearson, *The Sealed Train*, 97–8

3. The Sealed Train

1 Pearson, *The Sealed Train*, 97–9; Merridale, *Lenin on the Train*, 148–9, 143; https://peoplepill.com/people/arwed-von-der-planitz (accessed 28 November 2022); www.fernsehserien.de/der-zug/episodenguide/0/9603 (accessed 28 November 2022)

2 Pearson, *The Sealed Train*, 99; Merridale, *Lenin on the Train*, 149; Rappaport, *Conspirator*, 271

3 Merridale, *Lenin on the Train*, 149–50; Pearson, *The Sealed Train*, 102; '125 Years of Maggi in Germany' at www.interpack.com/en/Discover/Tightly_Packed_Magazine/FOOD_INDUSTRY_PACKAGING/News/125_years_of_Maggi_in_Germany (accessed 28 November 2022)

4 Merridale, *Lenin on the Train*, 150

5 Merridale, *Lenin on the Train*, 150–1; Pearson, *The Sealed Train*, 102–4, 108; Rappaport, *Conspirator*, 272; Radek, 'Through Germany in the Sealed Coach'

6 Merridale, *Lenin on the Train*, 152

7 Zinoviev, 'The Arrival of V. I. Lenin in Russia', 114

8 Krupskaya, 'Reminiscences of Lenin'

9 Merridale, *Lenin on the Train*, 153

10 Pearson, *The Sealed Train*, 116–17

11 Radek, 'Through Germany in the Sealed Coach'

12 G. Sokolnikov, 'The Return of V. I. Lenin from Emigration [Exile]', *Leningradskaya Pravda*, 18 April 1928, no. 90; Radek, 'Through Germany in the Sealed Coach'; Platten, 'Lenin's Return', 91–2

13 Pearson, *The Sealed Train*, 122–3

14 Radek, 'Through Germany in the Sealed Coach'

15 Merridale, *Lenin on the Train*, 159; Pearson, *The Sealed Train*, 125, 127; Zinoviev, 'The Arrival of V. I. Lenin in Russia', 69

16 Merridale, *Lenin on the Train*, 159–60; Pearson, *The Sealed Train*, 126–31; 'Memorandum by Ow-Wachendorf, Berlin', 11 April 1917, in Zeman, ed., *Germany and the Revolution in Russia*, 44–5. On Swedish permission see 'The Minister in Stockholm to the Foreign Ministry', Telegram no. 600, 10 April

1917, in Zeman, ed., *Germany and the Revolution in Russia*, 44

17 Merridale, *Lenin on the Train*, 160–1

18 Merridale, *Lenin on the Train*, 164–5; Radek, 'Through Germany in the Sealed Coach'; Platten, *Die Reise Lenins durch Deutschland*, 38; Radek, 'Lenin's "Sealed Train"', *New York Times*, 19 February 1922, 92

19 Merridale, *Lenin on the Train*, 165; Pearson, *The Sealed Train*, 134

20 Radek, 'Through Germany in the Sealed Coach'; Radek, 'Lenin's "Sealed Train"', 92; Merridale, *Lenin on the Train*, 165–8; Otto Grimlund, 'On the Way to the Homeland', in *They Knew Lenin*, 95–6

21 'Memo concerning the revolutionaries belonging to the so-called "Lenin Group" travelling from Switzerland to Russia via Germany', 1, secret police report dated 16 April 1917, in: National Archives, Stockholm, State Police Bureau for the Supervision of Foreigners in the Realm, vol. E3:2, VPM 1916–1917; Radek, 'Through Germany in the Sealed Coach'; Merridale, *Lenin on the Train*, 192–4

22 Merridale, *Lenin on the Train*, 193–7; 'Memo concerning the revolutionaries belonging to the so-called "Lenin Group" travelling from Switzerland to Russia via Germany', 2, secret police report dated 16 April 1917, in: National Archives, Stockholm, State Police Bureau for the Supervision of Foreigners in the Realm, vol. E3:2, VPM 1916–1917

23 Merridale, *Lenin on the Train*, 196; Radek, 'Through Germany in the Sealed Coach'

24 Merridale, *Lenin on the Train*, 197–8; Hugo Sillén, 'Meetings with Lenin', in *They Knew Lenin*, 97

25 Merridale, *Lenin on the Train*, 198–9

26 Merridale, *Lenin on the Train*, 199–200; Pearson, *The Sealed Train*, 143

27 Merridale, *Lenin on the Train*, 200–1

28 Merridale, *Lenin on the Train*, 202

29 Zinoviev, 'The Arrival of V. I. Lenin in Russia', 69–70

30 'Memorandum by Ow-Wachendorf, Berlin', 31 March 1917, in Zeman, ed., *Germany and the Revolution in Russia*, 29–30

31 'Memorandum recording interviews with Mr Keskula, Stockholm, 19 May 1917', 2, in FO 371/3012 – US and Russia; Russian and Esiland, *World War I and Revolution in Russia* (Gale Research); Esmé Howard, *Theatre of Life: Life Seen from the Stalls, 1905–1936* (London: Hodder and Stoughton Ltd., 1936), 264

32 Pearson, *The Sealed Train*, 101

33 Platten, *Die Reise Lenins durch Deutschland*, 38

34 Merridale, *Lenin on the Train*, 206–7

35 Pearson, *The Sealed Train*, 144–5; Merridale, *Lenin on the Train*, 207–8

36 Colonel B. V. Nikitin, *The Fatal Years: Fresh Revelations on a Chapter of Underground History* (London: William Hodge and Company Ltd., 1938), 54–5; Merridale, *Lenin on the Train*, 208

37 'Calls Soviet Foe of Trade Unionism', *New York Times*, 4 December 1919, 7

38 Pearson, *The Sealed Train*, 145

39 Merridale, *Lenin on the Train*, 209–10; Rappaport, *Conspirator*, 277; Krupskaya, 'Reminiscences of Lenin'

40 Krupskaya, 'Reminiscences of Lenin'

41 Merridale, *Lenin on the Train*, 210–11

42 Merridale, *Lenin on the Train*, 213; Pearson, *The Sealed Train*, 151

43 F. F. Raskolnikov, 'Kronstadt and Petrograd in 1917, IV: The April Days' at www.marxists.org/archive/raskolnikov/1925/kronstadt-petrograd-1917/ch04.htm (accessed 12 December 2022)

44 Comrade Elmsted, 'In the Same Train as Ilyich: Memories of the Driver of the Train (in Finland)', *Leningradskaya Pravda*, 16 April 1924, no. 87, 3

4. From the Finland Station

1 Edmund Wilson, *To the Finland Station: A Study in the Writing and Acting of History* (London: Penguin Books, 1972), 547

2 Merridale, *Lenin on the Train*, 96–7, 112

3 N. N. Sukhanov (edited, abridged and translated by Joel Carmichael), *The Russian Revolution 1917: A Personal Record* (Princeton: Princeton University Press, 1984), 269–70; see also Sokolnikov, 'The Return of V. I. Lenin from Emigration [Exile]'

4 Sukhanov, *The Russian Revolution 1917*, 270

5 Sukhanov, *The Russian Revolution 1917*, 272–3

6 Sukhanov, *The Russian Revolution 1917*, 274–5; Rappaport, *Caught in the Revolution*, 163; Merridale, *Lenin on the Train*, 220–1

7 Sukhanov, *The Russian Revolution 1917*, 276, 277–8; Merridale, *Lenin on the Train*, 221; Rappaport, *Caught in the Revolution*, 166. On the mansion, see www.saint-petersburg.com/mansions/kschessinska-mansion/ (accessed 3 January 2023)

8 Sukhanov, *The Russian Revolution 1917*, 276, 278, 279; Merridale, *Lenin on the Train*, 222

9 Sukhanov, *The Russian Revolution 1917*, 280; Merridale, *Lenin on the Train*, 223

10 Sebestyen, *Lenin the Dictator*, 289; Sukhanov, *The Russian Revolution 1917*, 285

11 Sukhanov, *The Russian Revolution 1917*, 281–2, 284; Merridale, *Lenin on the Train*, 223; Raskolnikov, 'Kronstadt and Petrograd in 1917, IV: The April Days'

12 Miéville, *October*, 110

13 Sukhanov, *The Russian Revolution 1917*, 282

14 Raskolnikov, 'Kronstadt and Petrograd in 1917, IV: The April Days'

15 Sukhanov, *The Russian Revolution 1917*, 285

16 Raskolnikov, 'Kronstadt and Petrograd in 1917, IV: The April Days'

17 Marcel Liebman, *Leninism Under Lenin* (Chicago: Haymarket Books, 2016), 129

18 Merridale, *Lenin on the Train*, 226, 229; Radek, 'Through Germany in the Sealed Coach'

19 Robert Service, *Lenin: A Political Life, Volume 2: Worlds in Collision* (Basingstoke: Macmillan, 1995), 156

20 Christopher Read, *Lenin: A Revolutionary Life* (New York: Routledge, 2005), 146–7

21 Lenin, 'The Tasks of the Proletariat in the Present Revolution [aka The April Theses]', originally published in *Pravda*, 7 April 1917, at www.marxists.org/archive/lenin/works/1917/apr/04.htm (accessed 6 January 2023)

22 Liebman, *Leninism Under Lenin*, 121

ENDNOTES

23 Liebman, *Leninism Under Lenin*, 124, 127

24 Liebman, *Leninism Under Lenin*, 127; David Lane, 'Revisiting Lenin's theory of socialist revolution on the 150th anniversary of his birth', https://blogs.lse.ac.uk/europpblog/2020/04/22/revisiting-lenins-theory-of-socialist-revolution-on-the-150th-anniversary-of-his-birth/ (accessed 6 January 2023)

25 See, for example, Jonathan Frankel, 'Lenin's Doctrinal Revolution of April 1917', *Journal of Contemporary History*, vol. 4, no. 2 (April 1969), 117–42; Lars T. Lih, 'A Fully Armed Historiography', *Canadian-American Slavic Studies*, vol. 53 (2019), 72–89; John Marot, 'Leninism, Bolshevism, and Social-Democratic Political Theory', *Historical Materialism*, vol. 22, nos. 3–4 (2014), 129–71. See also Miéville, *October*, 112. The leading revisionist in this debate is Lars T. Lih.

26 Liebman, *Leninism Under Lenin*, 127; Robert Service, 'Lenin as Historical Personality', in Silvio Pons and Stephen A. Smith, eds., *The Cambridge History of Communism: Volume 1, World Revolution and Socialism in One Country, 1917–1941* (Cambridge: Cambridge University Press, 2017), 127

27 Sebestyen, *Lenin the Dictator*, 292

28 Merridale, *Lenin on the Train*, 229

29 Sebestyen, *Lenin the Dictator*, 292

30 Liebman, *Leninism Under Lenin*, 131

31 See, for example, James Ryan, '"War Against War": The Significance of the Great War in the Thought of V. I. Lenin on Violence, 1914–1921', in Christopher Read et al., eds, *Russia's Home Front in War and Revolution, 1914–1922, Book 4: Reintegration – The Struggle for the State* (Bloomington: Slavica, 2018), 257–78

32 Service, *Lenin: A Political Life, Volume 2*, 156–7

33 Merridale, *Lenin on the Train*, 230–2; Miéville, *October*, 114

34 Buchanan to Balfour, 22 April 1917, 371/3012 – All-Russian Meeting of Councils of Labour and Soldiers Deputies, *World War I and Revolution in Russia*. Buchanan did, though, concede that Lenin was 'an honest fanatic, possessed of considerable oratorical powers' and, given the 'present unsettled state of affairs', one could not completely rule out the possibility that he would 'make his influence felt'.

35 Donald C. Thompson, *Donald Thompson in Russia* (New York: The Century Co., 1918), 160 (letter of 18 April/1 May)

36 Rappaport, *Caught in the Revolution*, 166

JOHN REED

5. Across the War World

1 John Reed, 'The Fall of the Russian Bastille', *New York Tribune Magazine*, 25 March 1917, in Eric Homberger, ed., *John Reed and the Russian Revolution: Uncollected Articles, Letters and Speeches on Russia, 1917–1920* (Basingstoke: Macmillan, 1992), 7. See also John Reed, 'Russia', *The Masses*, May 1917, in Homberger, ed., *John Reed and the Russian Revolution*, 15

2 Robert A. Rosenstone, *Romantic Revolutionary* (Harmondsworth: Penguin, 1982), 281

3 John Reed and Louise Bryant, 'The Russian Peace', *The Masses*, July 1917, in

ENDNOTES

Homberger, ed., *John Reed and the Russian Revolution*, 17

4 Virginia Gardner, '*Friend and Lover': The Life of Louise Bryant* (New York: Horizon Press, 1982), 81

5 Rosenstone, *Romantic Revolutionary*, 10–12, 15

6 Rosenstone, *Romantic Revolutionary*, 12–13, 17, 24–5, 37–8. See also Bertram D. Wolfe, 'The Harvard Man in the Kremlin Wall', *American Heritage*, vol. 11, no. 2 (February 1960), and Edwin R. Bingham, 'Oregon's Romantic Rebels: John Reed and Charles Erskine Scott Wood', *The Pacific Northwest Quarterly*, vol. 50, no. 3 (July 1959), 77–90

7 Reed, 'Almost Thirty', *New Republic*, 15 April 1936, 268–9; Rosenstone, *Romantic Revolutionary*, 38

8 Reed, 'Almost Thirty', 268. A full version of this essay, which was not published until after Reed's death, can be found in *John Reed: Adventures of a Young Man* (San Francisco: City Lights, 1975), 125–44

9 Rosenstone, *Romantic Revolutionary*, 39–42

10 See, for example, Rosenstone, *Romantic Revolutionary*, 57, 45

11 'Who were the tycoons of the Gilded Age? Meet the ruthless "robber barons" who made millions', *History Extra* (November 2016) at www.historyextra.com/period/victorian/rise-of-the-robber-barons/ (accessed 1 November 2024); William V. Shannon, 'The Political Machine I: Rise and Fall the Age of the Bosses', *American Heritage*, vol. 20, no. 4 (June 1969) at www.americanheritage.com/political-machine-i-rise-and-fall-age-bosses; Michael McGerr, *A Fierce Discontent: The Rise and Fall of the Progressive Movement in America, 1870–1920* (New York: Oxford University Press, 2005)

12 On the Wobblies, see Patrick Renshaw, *The Wobblies: The Story of the IWW and Syndicalism in the United States* (Chicago: Ivan R. Dee, 1999), and Eric Thomas Chester, *The Wobblies in Their Heyday: The Rise and Destruction of the IWW During the World War I Era* (Amherst, MA: Levellers Press, 2016)

13 Rosenstone, *Romantic Revolutionary*, 44–6

14 Reed, 'Almost Thirty'

15 Rosenstone, *Romantic Revolutionary*, 60–75, 81, 83

16 Rosenstone, *Romantic Revolutionary*, 78, 83; Bertram D. Wolfe, 'The Harvard Man in the Kremlin Wall'; 'John Reed', *Spartacus Educational*: https://spartacus-educational.com/Jreed.htm

17 Rosenstone, *Romantic Revolutionary*, 83; John Reed, 'Almost Thirty'

18 David C. Duke, *John Reed* (Boston: Twayne Publishers, 1987), 11

19 Rosenstone, *Romantic Revolutionary*, 109–110

20 Rosenstone, *Romantic Revolutionary*, 119–21; Homberger, ed., *John Reed and the Russian Revolution*, 47–9

21 Reed, 'War in Paterson', *The Masses*, June 1913, 14–17

22 Duke, *John Reed*, 15–16; Rosenstone, *Romantic Revolutionary*, 164–6

23 Reed, 'What About Mexico?', *The Masses*, June 1914

24 Reed, *Insurgent Mexico*, chapter V: The Funeral of Abram Gonzales: www.gutenberg.org/files/48108/48108-h/48108-h.html#the-funeral-of-abram-gonzales

25 Rosenstone, *Romantic Revolutionary*, 166–7

26 Reed, 'The Colorado War', *Metropolitan*, July 1914, quoted in www.wsws.org/en/articles/2020/12/03/reed-d03.html

27 www.wsws.org/en/articles/2020/12/03/reed-d03.html

28 Duke, *John Reed*, 20; Rosenstone, *Romantic Revolutionary*, 215–23

29 Rosenstone, *Romantic Revolutionary*, 233–5

30 Michael Munk, 'The Romance of John Reed and Louise Bryant: New Documents Clarify How They Met', *Oregon Historical Quarterly*, vol. 109, no. 3 (Fall 2008)

31 Rosenstone, *Romantic Revolutionary*, 232, 238–9

32 Munk, 'The Romance of John Reed and Louise Bryant'

33 Barbara Gelb, *So Short a Time: A Biography of John Reed and Louise Bryant* (New York: W. W. Norton, 1973), 79; Rosenstone, *Romantic Revolutionary*, 241

34 Rosenstone, *Romantic Revolutionary*, 255, 261–2

35 Reed, 'The Traders' War', *The Masses*, September 1914, 16–17

36 Rosenstone, *Romantic Revolutionary*, 180–3, 189–90

37 Reed, 'Whose War?', *The Masses*, April 1917, 11

38 Reed, 'Almost Thirty'

39 Rosenstone, *Romantic Revolutionary*, 282; Granville Hicks, *John Reed: The Making of a Revolutionary*, 249–50

40 Bryant and Reed, 'News from France', *The Masses*, October 1917, 5 (Marxists Internet Archive)

41 Reed, 'Across the War World', 1, in John Reed Papers (hereafter JRP), Box: 11 Identifier: MS Am 1091 (1179), Houghton Library, Harvard University

42 SS *United States*, Scandinavian America Line, at www.norwayheritage.com/p_ship.asp?sh=unist

43 Reed, 'Across the War World', 1

44 Reed, 'Across the War World', 2–3

45 Reed, 'Across the War World', 4–5

46 Reed, 'Across the War World', 5

47 Reed, 'Across the War World', 6–7

48 'A Letter from John Reed', *The Masses*, November–December 1917, in Homberger, ed., *John Reed and the Russian Revolution*, 19

49 Rosenstone, *Romantic Revolutionary*, 282; Hicks, *John Reed*, 250

50 Bryant, *Six Red Months in Russia* (Portland, OR: Powell's Press, 2002), 2

51 Reed, 'Across the War World', 8

52 Reed, 'Across the War World', 8–9

53 Reed, 'Across the War World', 9

6. Scandinavia in Wartime

1 See, for example, Pasi Ihalainen and Tiina Kinnunen, 'Reform and Revolution in Scandinavia, 1917–1919', *Scandinavian Journal of History*, vol. 44, no. 2 (2019), 143–9; Karen Gram-Skjoldager, 'Denmark during the First World War: Neutral policy, economy and culture', *Journal of Modern European History*, vol. 17, no. 2 (2019), 234–50; Karl Erik Haug, 'Norway', in *International Encyclopedia of the First World War*: https://encyclopedia.1914-1918-online.net/article/norway;

www.britannica.com/place/Norway/World-War-I-and-the-interwar-years. See also Claes Ahlund, ed., *Scandinavia in the First World War: Studies in the War Experience of the Northern Neutrals* (Lund: Nordic Academic Press, 2012)

2 Reed, 'Scandinavia in Wartime', 1–2, in JRP, Box: 1 Identifier: MS Am 1091 (136), Houghton Library, Harvard University

3 Reed, 'Scandinavia in Wartime', 2–3

4 Reed, 'Scandinavia in Wartime', 3

5 Reed, 'Scandinavia in Wartime', 4

6 Reed, 'Scandinavia in Wartime', 5

7 Reed, 'Scandinavia in Wartime', 6–7

8 Reed, 'Scandinavia in Wartime', 6

9 Reed, 'Scandinavia in Wartime', 5; Rosenstone, *Romantic Revolutionary*, 283

10 Reed, 'Scandinavia in Wartime', 7–8

11 Reed, 'Scandinavia in Wartime', 8

12 Reed, 'Scandinavia in Wartime', 9–10

13 Reed, 'Scandinavia in Wartime', 10

14 Reed, 'Scandinavia in Wartime', 10

7. Red Russia – Entrance

1 Reed, 'Red Russia – 1. Entrance', 2–3, in JRP, Box: 11 Identifier: MS Am 1091 (1182), Houghton Library, Harvard University

2 Reed, 'Red Russia – 1. Entrance', 3

3 Reed, 'Red Russia – 1. Entrance', 3–4

4 Merridale, *Lenin on the Train*, 3

5 Bryant, *Six Red Months in Russia*, 3

6 Reed, 'Red Russia – 1. Entrance', 4

7 Bryant, *Six Red Months in Russia*, 3

8 Reed, 'Red Russia – 1. Entrance', 5

9 Reed, 'Red Russia – 1. Entrance', 5–6

10 Bryant, *Six Red Months in Russia*, 5–6

11 Reed, 'Red Russia – 1. Entrance', 13

12 Reed, 'Red Russia – 1. Entrance', 13

13 Bryant, *Six Red Months in Russia*, 7

14 Reed, 'Red Russia – 1. Entrance', 13–14

15 Reed, 'Red Russia – 1. Entrance', 14

16 Reed, 'Red Russia – 1. Entrance', 14

17 Reed, 'Red Russia – 1. Entrance', 15

18 Reed, 'Red Russia – 1. Entrance', 15

19 Reed, 'Red Russia – 1. Entrance', 15–16; Bryant, *Six Red Months in Russia*, 9–10

20 Bryant, *Six Red Months in Russia*, 10–11

21 Bryant, *Six Red Months in Russia*, 12

22 Alec Luhn, 'Story of cities #8: St Petersburg – is the "city built on bones" starting to crumble?', *Guardian*, 23 March 2016, www.theguardian.com/cities/2016/mar/23/story-of-cities-8-st-petersburg-city-built-on-bones-starting-to-crumble

23 Bryant, *Six Red Months in Russia*, 18

8. Red Petrograd

1 www.historichotelsthenandnow.com/angleterrestpetersburg.html; https://
guideforyou-russia.com/what-to-see/hotels/angleterre-hotel/; https://
mahlerfoundation.org/mahler/locations/russia/st-petersburg/1907-hotel-d-
angleterre/; Homberger, ed., *John Reed and the Russian Revolution*, 133
2 Bryant, *Six Red Months in Russia*, 14–15
3 Bryant, *Six Red Months in Russia*, 20; Reed, *Ten Days That Shook the World*, 37–8
4 Reed, *Ten Days*, 38–9; Bryant, *Six Red Months in Russia*, 21–2
5 Bryant, *Six Red Months in Russia*, 22–3
6 Reed, *Ten Days*, 39–40
7 Reed to Boardman Robinson, 17 September 1917, in Homberger, ed., *John Reed and the Russian Revolution*, 26
8 Rosenstone, *Romantic Revolutionary*, 287–8; Reed to Sally Robinson, 16 September 1917, in Homberger, ed., *John Reed and the Russian Revolution*, 23–4
9 Reed, *Ten Days*, 43; John Reed, 'Red Russia: The Triumph of the Bolsheviki', *The Liberator*, vol. 1, no. 1 (March 1918), 14–21, at www.marxists.org/archive/reed/1918/red-russia1.htm#f1 (accessed 23 August 2022)
10 Miéville, *October*, 85, 92–4; Merridale, *Lenin on the Train*, 118
11 Miéville, *October*, 58, 90
12 Quoted in Merridale, *Lenin on the Train*, 127
13 Rosenstone, *Romantic Revolutionary*, 286; Miéville, *October*, 117–20, 123, 143, 162–4, 193. Milyukov note at www.dhr.history.vt.edu/modules/eu/mod03_1917/evidence_detail_30.html (accessed 6 September 2022)
14 Merridale, *Lenin on the Train*, 112
15 Sheila Fitzpatrick, *The Russian Revolution* (Oxford: Oxford University Press, 2017), 60–1
16 Miéville, *October*, 225–31
17 Reed, 'Red Russia: The Triumph of the Bolsheviki'
18 Reed, 'Red Russia: The Triumph of the Bolsheviki'
19 Reed, 'Red Russia: The Triumph of the Bolsheviki'

9. October

1 Reed, *Ten Days*, 104–5; Albert Rhys Williams, *Journey into Revolution: Petrograd, 1917–1918* (Chicago: Quadrangle Books, 1969), 117
2 Reed, *Ten Days*, 105
3 Miéville, *October*, 260–2
4 Leon Trotsky, *The History of the Russian Revolution* (London: Pluto Press, 1997), 999
5 'Meeting of the Central Committee of the RSDLP (B), October 10 (23), 1917', at www.marxists.org/archive/lenin/works/1917/oct/10a.htm (accessed 8 September 2022)

6 Miéville, *October*, 262–3

7 Reed, *Ten Days*, 59

8 Miéville, *October*, 264

9 Miéville, *October*, 260

10 Miéville, *October*, 259–60, 271; Reed, *Ten Days*, 71; Alexander Rabinowitch, *The Bolsheviks Come to Power: The Revolution of 1917 in Petrograd* (New York: W. W. Norton, 1976), 232

11 Miéville, *October*, 273–4

12 Reed, *Ten Days*, 73

13 Reed, *Ten Days*, 75–6

14 Miéville, *October*, 275–6

15 Reed, *Ten Days*, 78–81

16 Miéville, *October*, 277–8, 279, 283, 284

17 Reed, *Ten Days*, 88–9

18 Reed, *Ten Days*, 89–90

19 Reed, *Ten Days*, 90

20 Reed, *Ten Days*, 91–2

21 Miéville, *October*, 287

22 Reed, *Ten Days*, 92–3

23 Reed, *Ten Days*, 94–5

24 Reed, *Ten Days*, 95

25 Reed, *Ten Days*, 54–5

26 Williams, *Journey into Revolution*, 105

27 Reed, *Ten Days*, 96

28 Williams, *Journey into Revolution*, 108; Miéville, *October*, 289–90

29 Reed, *Ten Days*, 97–8; Miéville, *October*, 289–90

30 Reed, *Ten Days*, 98

31 Miéville, *October*, 294; Reed, *Ten Days*, 99–100

32 Reed, *Ten Days*, 100–4; Miéville, *October*, 295–7

33 Reed, *Ten Days*, 104

34 Reed, *Ten Days*, 104

35 Reed, *Ten Days*, 106; Miéville, *October*, 297

36 Bryant, *Six Red Months in Russia*, 56

37 Reed, *Ten Days*, 106–7

38 Reed, *Ten Days*, 107; Miéville, *October*, 297–8

39 Bryant, *Six Red Months in Russia*, 58; Williams, *Journey into Revolution*, 118–19

40 Miéville, *October*, 290–3, 300–1

41 Reed, *Ten Days*, 108–9

42 Reed, *Ten Days*, 110

43 Reed, *Ten Days*, 110–11

44 Reed, *Ten Days*, 111–12

45 Reed, *Ten Days*, 112–16; Miéville, *October*, 303–4

46 Reed, *Ten Days*, 116

ENDNOTES

10. The Commissariat

1 Fitzpatrick, *The Russian Revolution*, 65–73; Miéville, *October*, 306–12. On Western involvement in the civil war, see Anna Reid, *A Nasty Little War: The West's Fight to Reverse the Russian Revolution* (London: John Murray, 2023)

2 Reed, 'Red Russia: The Triumph of the Bolsheviki'

3 Reed, 'Foreign Affairs', *The Liberator*, June 1918, in Homberger, ed., *John Reed and the Russian Revolution*, 144–51

4 Reed, 'Foreign Affairs', 146–7

5 Reed, 'How Soviet Russia Conquered Imperial Germany', *The Liberator*, January 1919, in Homberger, ed., *John Reed and the Russian Revolution*, 237; Williams, *Journey into Revolution*, 169

6 Reed, 'How Soviet Russia Conquered Imperial Germany', 237–8

7 Testimony of Mr John Reed, 'Bolshevik Propaganda: Hearings Before a Subcommittee of the Committee on the Judiciary, United States Senate', 20 February 1919, 566, at https://ia600201.us.archive.org/32/items/cu31924030480051/cu31924030480051.pdf (accessed 20 September 2022)

8 Reed, 'How Soviet Russia Conquered Imperial Germany', 238–9, 241–4; Homberger, ed., *John Reed and the Russian Revolution*, 158–9; Rosenstone, *Romantic Revolutionary*, 307–8

9 Rosenstone, *Romantic Revolutionary*, 309

10 Homberger, *John Reed and the Russian Revolution*, 159–60; Williams, *Journey into Revolution*, 219–20, 223–4

11 See, for instance, Richard B. Spence, 'John Reed, American Spy?', *American Communist History*, 13:1 (2014), 39–63

12 Williams, *Journey into Revolution*, 201; Telegram, Francis to Secretary of State, 30 January 1918, in Department of State (Record Group 59), File 360d. 1121 R25, College Park

13 'John Reed Cables the *Call* News of the Bolshevik Revolt', *New York Call*, 22 November 1917, in Homberger, ed., *John Reed and the Russian Revolution*, 69

14 Excerpts of speeches by Rheinstein, Williams and Reed, 10/23 January, in Records of the Foreign Service Posts of the Department of State, United States Embassy, Russia 1918: File 800 (Reed, John – Appointment by People's Commissariat as Consul to New York), NARA, College Park; Williams, *Journey into Revolution*, 207–8

15 Rosenstone, *Romantic Revolutionary*, 311–12, 323

16 Telegram, Schmedeman (Christiania) to Secretary of State, 19 February 1918, in Department of State (Record Group 59), File 360d. 1121 R25; Williams, *Journey into Revolution*, 208

17 Rosenstone, *Romantic Revolutionary*, 313

18 Telegram, Francis to Lansing, 29 January 1918, in Records of the Foreign Service Posts of the Department of State, United States Embassy, Russia 1918: File 800 (Reed, John – Appointment by People's Commissariat as Consul to New York)

19 Williams. *Journey into Revolution*, 207–8

20 Rosenstone, *Romantic Revolutionary*, 313–14

ENDNOTES

21 Rappaport, *Caught in the Revolution*, 11

22 David R. Francis, *Russia from the American Embassy: April 1916–November 1918* (New York: Scribner, 1921), 168; The Ambassador in Russia (Francis) to the Secretary of State, 31 January 1918, File No. 861.00/1053, *Foreign Relations of the United States, 1918, Volume I: Russia* at https://history.state.gov/historicaldocuments/frus1918Russiav01 (accessed 22 September 2022); Rappaport, *Caught in the Revolution*, 9–11

23 Rosenstone, *Romantic Revolutionary*, 314; Homberger, ed., *John Reed and the Russian Revolution*, 162; Williams, *Journey into Revolution*, 220–1

24 Telegram, Francis to Secretary of State, 6 February 1918, Records of the Foreign Service Posts of the Department of State, United States Embassy, Russia 1918: File 800 (Reed, John – Appointment by People's Commissariat as Consul to New York). See also 'Drop Reed as Consul?', *New York Times*, 18 February 1918, 2

25 Telegram, Francis to Secretary of State, 6 February 1918, Records of the Foreign Service Posts of the Department of State, United States Embassy, Russia 1918: File 800 (Reed, John – Appointment by People's Commissariat as Consul to New York)

26 Telegram, for Harrison from Bell, 12 February 1918, Department of State (Record Group 59), File 360d. 1121 R25; Telegram, Bell from Harrison, 16 February 1918, Department of State (Record Group 59), File 360d. 1121 R25; Homberger, ed., *John Reed and the Russian Revolution*, 164

27 Homberger, ed., *John Reed and the Russian Revolution*, 165; Rosenstone, *Romantic Revolutionary*, 315; Hicks, *John Reed*, 297

28 'Editor John Reed', *Social-Demokraten*, 21 February 1918 – Translation, dispatch no. 695, encl. no. 2, Department of State (Record Group 59), File 360d. 1121 R25; George Nicholas Ifft to Secretary of State, 26 February 1918, re: Intercepted Mail of Mr John Reed, Department of State (Record Group 59), File 360d. 1121 R25; Homberger, ed., *John Reed and the Russian Revolution*, 166

29 Telegram, Ifft to Secretary of State, re: Intercepted Mail of Mr John Reed, 28 February 1918

30 See telegrams from Christiania to Secretary of State, 7 and 14 March, Department of State (Record Group 59), File 360d. 1121 R25

31 Department of State to American Consul, Christiania, 25 March 1918, Department of State (Record Group 59), File 360d. 1121 R25

32 Sisson to Creel, 24 April 1918, Department of State (Record Group 59), File 360d. 1121 R25; Rosenstone, *Romantic Revolutionary*, 317

33 Report of the examination of John Silas Reed, arriving on the SS *Bergensfjord*, 28 April, Department of State (Record Group 59), File 360d. 1121 R25

34 Gardner, '*Friend and Lover*', 135–6; Gelb, *So Short a Time*, 200; Rosenstone, *Romantic Revolutionary*, 317–18

35 Mike Gold, 'John Reed: He Loved the People', *The New Masses*, vol. 37, no. 5, 22 October 1940, 9–10, at www.marxists.org/history/usa/pubs/new-masses/1940/v37no5-oct-22-1940-NM.pdf (accessed 23 September 2022). On the history of the Brevoort Hotel, see http://daytoninmanhattan.blogspot.com/2020/12/the-lost-brevoort-house-15-fifth-avenue.html (accessed 23 September 2022)

ENDNOTES

11. Blocked

1 Rosenstone, *Romantic Revolutionary*, 324; Homberger, ed., *John Reed and the Russian Revolution*, 166–7

2 Rosenstone, *Romantic Revolutionary*, 325, 427; Homberger, ed., *John Reed and the Russian Revolution*, 168

3 Rosenstone, *Romantic Revolutionary*, 325–6

4 Rosenstone, *Romantic Revolutionary*, 325–6; Hicks, *John Reed*, 306

5 Art Young, *On My Way* (New York: Horace Liveright, 1928), 111–12: www.marxists.org/subject/art/cartoons-drawings/young/On-My-Way-Art%20Young.pdf (accessed 4 October 2022)

6 Homberger, ed., *John Reed and the Russian Revolution*, 174

7 On Carnegie Hall, see https://npgallery.nps.gov/GetAsset/5b82f3e2-d183-472f-88f1-e4c82ffca307/ (accessed 4 October 2022)

8 Perkins report, 'IN RE: John Reed et al., Bolshevik Meeting at Carnegie Hall – Seditious Talk', 20 May 1918, 1–3, *US Military Intelligence Reports: Surveillance of Radicals in the United States, 1917–1941*, reel 4, RIAS

9 Reed to Steffens, 9 June 1918, in Lincoln Steffens Papers, Box 11, Reed, John, Croton-on-Hudson, NY, 9 June [1918?], Rare Book & Manuscript Library, Columbia University

10 Steffens to Reed, 17 June 1918, in Granville Hicks Papers, Box 80, 'Lincoln Steffens Letters to John Reed', Special Collections Research Center, Syracuse University

11 Reed to William Franklin Sands, 4 June 1918, Department of State (Record Group 59), File 360d. 1121 R25

12 William Franklin Sands to Frank Lyon Polk, 5 June 1918, Department of State (Record Group 59), File 360d. 1121 R25; Spence, 'John Reed, American Spy?', 44–5

13 Rosenstone, *Romantic Revolutionary*, 315; Homberger, ed., *John Reed and the Russian Revolution*, 161–2; Spence, 'John Reed, American Spy?', 45–6; Williams, *Journey into Revolution*, 221–2

14 Sisson to Creel, 24 April 1918, Department of State (Record Group 59), File 360d. 1121 R25

15 'The Masses Trial Begins', *New York Times*, 1 October 1918, 18; Rosenstone, *Romantic Revolutionary*, 327–30; Homberger, ed., *John Reed and the Russian Revolution*, 175; www.mtsu.edu/first-amendment/article/289/debs-v-united-states (accessed 7 October 2022)

16 Rosenstone, *Romantic Revolutionary*, 331

17 Rosenstone, *Romantic Revolutionary*, 330

18 Rosenstone, *Romantic Revolutionary*, 330; 'Knit a Strait-Jacket for Your Soldier Boy', *The Masses*, vol. 9, no. 10 (August 1917), 42

19 United States of America vs. The Masses Publishing Company, Max Eastman, Floyd Dell, C. Merrill Rogers Jr, Arthur Young and John Reed, Testimony of John Reed, 3 October 1918, 655–56, Hicks Papers, Syracuse

20 Reed Testimony, 660

21 Reed Testimony, 661–2

22 Reed Testimony, 666–7

23 Reed Testimony, 667

24 Reed Testimony, 668

25 Reed Testimony, 665–6, 676–7

26 'Masses Case Nears End', *New York Times*, 5 October 1918, 11

27 'Masses Jury Disagrees', *New York Times*, 6 October 1918, 9; Hicks, *John Reed*, 320

12. *Ten Days That Shook the World*

1 Max Eastman, *Heroes I Have Known* (New York: Simon & Schuster, 1942), 223–4

2 Gardner, *'Friend and Lover'*, 146; Hicks, *John Reed*, 325; Rosenstone, *Romantic Revolutionary*, 335; Daniel W. Lehman, *John Reed and the Writing of Revolution*, 184; Preface to Reed, *Ten Days That Shook the World*, 13

3 Homberger, ed., *John Reed and the Russian Revolution*, 175–6; John Reed, Preface to *Ten Days*, 13

4 Reed, *Ted Days*, 77

5 Lehman, *John Reed and the Writing of Revolution*, 184. Much of this paragraph – summarising the book's structure – is based on Lehman, *John Reed*, 176–84

6 Lehman, *John Reed and the Writing of Revolution*, 180–1

7 Reed, *Ten Days*, 218

8 Reed, *Ten Days*, 230

9 Reed, *Ten Days*, 10

10 Reed, *Ten Days*, 27–8

11 Reed, *Ten Days*, 13

12 Charles Egleston, ed., *The House of Boni & Liveright, 1917–1933: A Documentary Volume*, 5, 19, 20–1; Walker Gilmer, *Horace Liveright: Publisher of the Twenties* (New York: David Lews, 1970), 1–3, 4–5. See also Tom Dardis, *Firebrand: The Life of Horace Liveright* (New York: Random House, 1995), 3–24

13 Gilmer, *Horace Liveright*, 11; Dardis, *Firebrand*, 52–5; Egleston, ed., *The House of Boni & Liveright*, 24–5

14 Egleston, ed., *The House of Boni & Liveright*, 25–6; Gilmer, *Horace Liveright*, 16; Dardis, *Firebrand*, 57

15 Gilmer, *Horace Liveright*, 81–3

16 Egleston, ed., *The House of Boni & Liveright*, 21

17 Dardis, *Firebrand*, 45–6

18 Egleston, ed., *The House of Boni & Liveright*, 32–3; Boni & Liveright, Inc. to John Reed (Miss Louise Bryant), 11 June 1920: Royalty Statement to the period ended 31 March 1920. Inflation calculator at www.officialdata.org/us/inflation/ (calculated at 2022 prices). $500 is cited by Rosenstone, *Romantic Revolutionary*, 346

19 Egleston, ed., *The House of Boni & Liveright*, 32

20 Eadmonn MacAlpine, *Revolutionary Age*, 12 April 1919, 5

21 Floyd Dell, 'Lenine and His Time', *The Liberator*, 1 May 1919, 44–5. See also *The Nation*, 3 May 1919, 699, and *New Republic*, 31 May 1919, 161

22 Charles E. Russell, 'Bolshevism, In Theory and Practice, As Friend and Opponent See It', *New York Times*, 27 April 1919, 86, 238. On Russell, see Robert Miraldi, *The Pen Is Mightier: The Muckraking Life of Charles Edward Russell* (New York:

ENDNOTES

Palgrave Macmillan, 2003)

23 John Philip Morris, 'Books: Reed on Comrade Lenine', *Chicago Daily Tribune*, 24
May 1919, 12

24 Harold Edmund Stearns at https://prabook.com/web/harold.stearns/3762879
(accessed 19 October 2022); for *The Dial*, see https://en.wikipedia.org/wiki/The_
Dial (accessed 19 October 2022)

25 Stearns, 'The Unending Revolution', *The Dial*, vol. XLVI, 22 March 1919, 301–3

26 Reed to Bryant, 25 March 1919; Boni & Liveright, Inc. to John Reed (Miss Louise
Bryant), 11 June 1920: Royalty Statement to the period ended 31 March 1920

27 Emma Goldman, *Living My Life, Volume II* (New York: Knopf, 1934), 684

28 *Bill Haywood's Book: The Autobiography of William D. Haywood* (New York:
International Publishers, 1929), 308

29 Hicks, *John Reed*, 341. See also, for example, the advertisement in *The New Justice*
(Los Angeles), 1 May 1919, 17

30 Reed, 'Dear Comrade' letter, 16 May 1919. See also Liveright to Reed, 22 April
1919, and Samuel Lavit (business agent with International Association of Machinists,
District #55) to Boni & Liveright, 1 April 1919

31 Hicks, *John Reed*, 341

32 Reed, 'On Bolshevism, Russian and American' (Letter to the *New York Times*,
refused publication), *Revolutionary Age*, 12 April 1919, 6

13. American Bolshevik

1 Reed quoted in Homberger, ed., *John Reed and the Russian Revolution*, 191–2. See
also Reed, 'Why Political Democracy Must Go', *New York Communist*, 21 June
1919, 7. The series began in the 15 May edition, and ran over six issues.

2 Friend cited in Lincoln Steffens, *John Reed: Under the Kremlin* (Chicago: Printed by
Will Ransom for the Walden Book Shop, 1922), 13

3 Max Eastman, *Love and Revolution: My Journey through an Epoch* (New York:
Random House, 1964), 106

4 Steffens, *John Reed: Under the Kremlin*, 12–13

5 For a discussion of this, see Homberger, ed., *John Reed and the Russian
Revolution*, 180–9, 193–200; Rosenstone, *Romantic Revolutionary*, 339–42, 347,
350–6; 'Manifesto of the Left Wing Section of the Socialist Party of New York',
Revolutionary Age, 22 March 1919, 4–5

6 Rosenstone, *Romantic Revolutionary*, 358–61; Homberger, ed., *John Reed and the
Russian Revolution*, 200–1; Hicks, *John Reed*, 366–8

7 Quoted in Rosenstone, *Romantic Revolutionary*, 357

8 Rosenstone, *Romantic Revolutionary*, 358

9 Rosenstone, *Romantic Revolutionary*, 361; Homberger, ed., *John Reed and the
Russian Revolution*, 201; Hicks, *John Reed*, 369–71

10 Rosenstone, *Romantic Revolutionary*, 361–2; Hicks, *John Reed*, 372

11 Reed, 'The Bolsheviks in 1919: Notebook Entries', in Homberger, ed., *John Reed
and the Russian Revolution*, 267

12 Letter to Bryant, 13 May 1920, in Hicks, *John Reed*, 381–2

13 Rosenstone, *Romantic Revolutionary*, 362; Hicks, *John Reed*, 372. On the West's support for the White counter-revolution, see Reid, *A Nasty Little War*.

14 Reed, 'Soviet Russia Now', *The Liberator*, December 1920–January 1921 (written July 1920), in Homberger, ed., *John Reed and the Russian Revolution*, 270–1

15 Reed, 'Soviet Russia Now', 272

16 Reed, 'Soviet Russia Now', 273

17 Reed, 'Soviet Russia Now', 268

18 Reed, 'Soviet Russia Now', 269

19 Reed, 'Soviet Russia Now', 273

20 Reed, 'Soviet Russia Now', 278–9

21 Reed, 'Soviet Russia Now', 274–5

22 Rosenstone, *Romantic Revolutionary*, 366–7

23 Goldman, *Living My Life*, chapter 52, at https://theanarchistlibrary.org/library/emma-goldman-living-my-life (accessed 25 October 2022)

24 Rosenstone, *Romantic Revolutionary*, 366–70; Homberger, ed., *John Reed and the Russian Revolution*, 203–7; Hicks, *John Reed*, 378–86

25 Rosenstone, *Romantic Revolutionary*, 372–3, 374; Hicks, *John Reed*, 390–1

26 Rosenstone, *Romantic Revolutionary*, 373

27 Homberger, ed., *John Reed and the Russian Revolution*, 209–10; Rosenstone, *Romantic Revolutionary*, 374–5

28 Rosenstone, *Romantic Revolutionary*, 375–6

29 Reed, 'The World Congress of the Communist International', *The Communist* (UCP: New York), no. 10 (c. 5 November 1920), 4–5, at www.marxists.org/history/usa/parties/cpusa/1920/09/0901-reed-worldcong.pdf (accessed 25 October 2022)

14. The Harvard Man in the Kremlin Wall

1 Bryant, 'The Last Days with John Reed', *The Liberator*, February 1921, at www.marxists.org/archive/bryant/works/1920/john-reed.htm (accessed 25 October 2022); Rosenstone, *Romantic Revolutionary*, 379–81

2 Rosenstone, *Romantic Revolutionary*, 381; 'John Reed's Death Caused by Eating Unwashed Fruit', *New York Call*, 3 November 1920, 5

3 'John Reed's Death Caused by Eating Unwashed Fruit', *New York Call* – Hicks Papers, Syracuse University, 5; Bryant, 'The Last Days with John Reed'; Rosenstone, *Romantic Revolutionary*, 381–2

4 Bryant, 'The Last Days with John Reed'

5 Barbara Evans Clements, *Bolshevik Feminist: The Life of Aleksandra Kollontai* (Bloomington: Indiana University Press, 1979), chapter 8: The Workers' Opposition, at https://publish.iupress.indiana.edu/read/bolshevik-feminist-the-life-of-aleksandra-kollontai/section/a9bb4d03-aed5-472c-89b2-3b9c74d9a9d9 (accessed 26 October 2022)

6 Bryant, 'The Last Days with John Reed'; Gardner, *'Friend and Lover'*, 208

7 Baku Congress of the Peoples of the East: Appendix to the Report of the Fourth Session – John Reed's Speech, at www.marxists.org/history/international/comintern/baku/ch04a.htm (accessed 26 October 2022)

ENDNOTES

8 Benjamin Gitlow, *The Whole of Their Lives: Communism in America, a Personal History and Intimate Portrayal of Its Leaders* (Boston: The Americanist Library, 1965 – originally published 1948 by Scribner), 32–4

9 Theodore Draper, *The Roots of American Communism* (New Brunswick: Transaction Publishers, 2003), 285; Homberger, ed., *John Reed and the Russian Revolution*, 213–15

10 Goldman, *Living My Life*, chapter 51, at https://theanarchistlibrary.org/library/emma-goldman-living-my-life (accessed 26 October 2022)

11 Angelica Balabanoff, *My Life as a Rebel* (New York: Harper & Brothers, 1938), 243–4

12 Balabanoff, *My Life as a Rebel*, 275

13 Balabanoff, *My Life as a Rebel*, 291

14 Colonel Mathew C. Smith to J. Edgar Hoover, 10 June 1921 (10058-94), *Military Intelligence Reports: Surveillance of Radicals in the United States, 1917–1941*, reel 33

15 Draper, *The Roots of American Communism*, 291. See also David C. Duke, *Distant Obligations: Modern American Writers and Foreign Causes* (New York: Oxford University Press, 1983), 130–6

16 'Thousands Mourn Death of Reed, Rebel-Poet-Artist', *New York Call*, 20 October 1929, 2–3 – Hicks Papers, Syracuse University

17 'Workers Cheer Cause for Which Reed Died', *New York Call*, 26 October 1920, 1 – Hicks Papers, Syracuse University

18 'John Reed', *The Liberator*, vol. 3, no. 12, December 1920, 6

19 'John Reed', *New York Call*, 26 October 1920, Hicks Papers, Syracuse University

15. Afterlives

1 Michael Quin, 'Definition of a Name', *Partisan* (Hollywood-Carmel JRC), vol. 1, no. 3 (1934), 7 – cited in Laurie Ann Alexandre, *The John Reed Clubs: A Historical Reclamation of the Role of Revolutionary Writers in the Depression*, MA thesis, California State University, Northridge, June 1977, 3. On Quin, see Harry Carlisle, 'Mike Quin (1906–1947): A Biographical Sketch', in Carlisle, ed., *On The Drumhead: A Selection from the Writing of Mike Quin* (San Francisco: The Pacific Publishers Foundation, Inc., 1948), xix–xxxviii

2 Alan Wald, *Exiles from a Future Time: The Forging of the Mid-Twentieth-Century Literary Left* (Chapel Hill: University of North Carolina Press, 2002), 105

3 Draper, *The Roots of American Communism*, 115, 120–1

4 Michael Gold, 'John Reed and the Real Thing', *The New Masses*, vol. 3, no. 7, November 1927, 7

5 Homberger, 'Proletarian Literature and the John Reed Clubs, 1929–1935', *Journal of American Studies*, vol. 13, no. 2 (August 1979), 233–4

6 Homberger, 'Proletarian Literature and the John Reed Clubs, 1929–1935', 234–5

7 Michael Denning, *The Cultural Front: The Laboring of American Culture in the Twentieth Century* (London: Verso, 1998), 205–11; Malcolm Cowley, 'From a Coffee Pot', in *The Dream of the Golden Mountains: Remembering the 1930s* (New York: Viking Press, 1980), 140–1

8 For a good history of the New Left, see Van Gosse, *Rethinking the New Left: An Interpretative History* (New York: Palgrave Macmillan, 2005)

9 Todd Gitlin, 'The Underground Press and its Cave-In', in Geoffrey Rips, Anne Janow-itz and Nancy J. Peters, eds, *The Campaign Against the Underground Press* (San Francis-co: City Lights Bookstore, 1981), 21. For Reed's influence on the anti-war movement, see Carl Davidson and Greg Calvert, 'The International Days of Resistance or 10 Days to Shake the Empire', *New Left Notes*, vol. 2, no. 43 (4 December 1967), 1, 3

10 Dick Roberts, '10 Days that Shook the World', *The Militant*, 11 December 1967, 3, at www.marxists.org/history/etol/newspape/themilitant/1967/v31n45-dec-11-1967-mil.pdf (accessed 1 November 2022)

11 'Moscow – The Day of the People', *The Rag* (Austin, Texas), 15 April 1974, 8–9

12 'Statement by the Minister of Defense and Political Prisoner, Pun Plamondon, to the People in the Youth Colony (Woodstock Nation) Concerning Self-Purge and Self-Discipline, August 12, 1970', *Sun/Dance*, issue 2 (October 1970), 2. For a brief description of the White Panther Party, see Grace Elizabeth Hale, *A Nation of Outsiders: How the White Middle Class Fell in Love with Rebellion in Postwar America* (Oxford: Oxford University Press, 2011), 222–3

13 John Frazier, 'John Reed's Unblinking Stare', *The American Scholar*, vol. 71, no. 3 (Summer 2002), 38

14 Jim Poe, 'Forty Years Later, *Reds* Is Still One of the Best Films Ever Made About Revolutionary Politics', *Jacobin*, 2 December 2021, at https://jacobin.com/2021/12/reds-history-film-warren-beatty-john-reed-louise-bryant-russian-revolution (accessed 7 November 2022). See also Richard Grenier, 'Bolshevism for the 80s', *Commentary*, March 1982, at www.commentary.org/articles/richard-grenier/bolshevism-for-the-80s/ (accessed 7 November 2022)

15 Robert D. Warth, 'On the Historiography of the Russian Revolution', *Slavic Review*, vol. 26, no. 2 (June 1967), 250

16 Rosenstone, '*October* as History', *Rethinking History*, vol. 5, no. 2 (2001), 255–6, 259, 262

17 Peter Martin, *China's Civilian Army: The Making of Wolf Warrior Diplomacy* (Oxford: Oxford University Press, 2021), 25; Qiang Zhai, *The Dragon, the Lion, and the Eagle: Chinese/British/American Relations, 1949–1958* (Kent, OH: The Kent State University Press, 1994), 7; Barbara Barnouin and Yu Changgen, *Zhou Enlai: A Political Life* (Hong Kong: The Chinese University Press, 2006), 20

PART TWO: CHINA
MAO

16. Annihilation

1 Harrison E. Salisbury, *The Long March: The Untold Story* (London: Pan Books, 1986), 16–17; Philip Short, *Mao: A Life* (New York: Henry Holt and Company, 1999), 313–14; Jung Chang and Jon Halliday, *Mao: The Unknown Story* (London: Jonathan Cape, 2005), 125

2 Chang and Halliday, *Mao*, 125; Dick Wilson, *The Long March 1935: The Epic of Chinese Communism's Survival* (London: Hamish Hamilton, 1971), 53

3 Short, *Mao: A Life*, 314

ENDNOTES

4 Wilson, *The Long March*, 57; Short, *Mao: A Life*, 314

5 Short, *Mao: A Life*, 314–15; Jonathan D. Spence, *The Search for Modern China*, 397

6 Short, *Mao: A Life*, 19–23; Alexander V. Pantsov with Steven I. Levine, *Mao: The Real Story* (New York: Simon & Schuster Paperbacks, 2012), 12–14

7 Edgar Snow, *Red Star Over China* (hereafter *RSOC*), 132

8 Snow, *RSOC*, 132–3

9 Short, *Mao: A Life*, 28–9; Snow, *RSOC*, 133. See also Pantsov, *Mao: The Real Story*, 15–17

10 Short, *Mao: A Life*, 27

11 Snow, *RSOC*, 138; Short, *Mao: A Life*, 30, 36–7

12 Snow, *RSOC*, 133–4, 136; Short, *Mao: A Life*, 33

13 Snow, *RSOC*, 135; Short, *Mao: A Life*, 34–5

14 Short, *Mao: A Life*, 39–41; Pantsov, *Mao: The Real Story*, 31–5

15 Snow, *RSOC*, 140–1

16 Snow, *RSOC*, 142; Short, *Mao: A Life*, 49–50, 56

17 Snow, *RSOC*, 143

18 Short, *Mao: A Life*, 52–3

19 Snow, *RSOC*, 144

20 Snow, *RSOC*, 145–6

21 Lee Feigon, *Mao: A Reinterpretation* (Chicago: Ivan R. Dee, 2002), 18; Snow, *RSOC*, 145–6; Short, *Mao: A Life*, 56–7; Pantsov, *Mao: The Real Story*, 39–40

22 Short, *Mao: A Life*, 57

23 Short, *Mao: A Life*, 58–9

24 Snow, *RSOC*, 147

25 Snow, *RSOC*, 147

26 Short, *Mao: A Life*, 71–2; Feigon, *Mao: A Reinterpretation*, 19; 'Public Announcement Inviting Students to the Workers' Evening School', 30 October 1917, in Stuart R. Schram, ed., *Mao's Road to Power, Volume I* (Armonk, NY: M. E. Sharpe, 1993), 143

27 Short, *Mao: A Life*, 73

28 Short, *Mao: A Life*, 80–1, 84

29 Snow, *RSOC*, 152

30 Snow, *RSOC*, 151

31 Feigon, *Mao: A Reinterpretation*, 20; Short, *Mao: A Life*, 86–7

32 Feigon, *Mao: A Reinterpretation*, 20

33 Short, *Mao: A Life*, 86, 87; Snow, *RSOC*, 152

34 Michael Lynch, *Mao* (New York: Henry Holt, 2000), 46

35 Lynch, *Mao*, 47; Short, *Mao: A Life*, 102

36 Short, *Mao: A Life*, 93–4; Pantsov, *Mao: The Real Story*, 63–4

37 'Letter to Xiao Xudong, Cai Linbin, and the Other Members in France', 1 December 1920, in Schram, ed., *Mao's Road to Power, Volume II* (Armonk, NY: M. E. Sharpe, 1994), 9

38 'Report on the Affairs of the New People's Study Society (no. 2)', Summer 1921, in Schram, ed., *Mao's Road to Power, Volume II*, 62

ENDNOTES

39 Short, *Mao: A Life*, 119–20
40 Short, *Mao: A Life*, 123, 124–33
41 Short, *Mao: A Life*, 135, 138–9; Spence, *The Search for Modern China*, 314–16
42 'An Analysis of the Various Classes among the Chinese Peasantry and Their Attitudes toward the Revolution', January 1926, in Schram, ed., *Mao's Road to Power, Volume II*, 307–8
43 'Report on the Peasant Movement in Hunan', February 1927, in Schram, ed., *Mao's Road to Power, Volume II*, 430. See also Pantsov, *Mao: The Real Story*, 172–3
44 'Report on the Peasant Movement in Hunan', 434–5
45 Short, *Mao: A Life*, 164–7; Spence, *The Search for Modern China*, 323–31; Lynch, *Mao*, 60
46 Lynch, *Mao*, 60–1; Feigon, *Mao: A Reinterpretation*, 39
47 Short, *Mao: A Life*, 152
48 Short, *Mao: A Life*, 179–80, 187–8; Feigon, *Mao: A Reinterpretation*, 42
49 'Latest Directive of the All-China Peasant Association', 13 June 1927, in Schram, ed., *Mao's Road to Power, Volume II*, 516
50 Short, *Mao: A Life*, 196–7, 209–10
51 Short, *Mao: A Life*, 196, 200–7
52 Snow, *RSOC*, 165–6
53 Short, *Mao: A Life*, 209, 211–13
54 Short, *Mao: A Life*, 213
55 Short, *Mao: A Life*, 222–3
56 Short, *Mao: A Life*, 219–20, 228
57 Short, *Mao: A Life*, 219
58 Short, *Mao: A Life*, 231–2; Pantsov, *Mao: The Real Story*, 214–15
59 Short, *Mao: A Life*, 232–3, 236
60 Brantly Womack, 'From Urban Radical to Rural Revolutionary: Mao from the 1920s to 1937', in Timothy Cheek, ed., *A Critical Introduction to Mao* (Cambridge: Cambridge University Press, 2010), 79
61 Lynch, *Mao*, 70
62 Womack, 'From Urban Radical to Rural Revolutionary', 79–80; Feigon, *Mao: A Reinterpretation*, 49; 'Xunwu Investigation', May 1930, in Schram, ed., *Mao's Road to Power, Volume III* (Armonk, NY: M. E. Sharpe, 1995), 296–418
63 Lynch, *Mao*, 72–5. See also Feigon, *Mao: A Reinterpretation*, 51–3
64 Womack, 'From Urban Radical to Rural Revolutionary', 79–80; Feigon, *Mao: A Reinterpretation*, 49
65 Feigon, *Mao: A Reinterpretation*, 55; Womack, 'From Urban Radical to Rural Revolutionary', 81–2. See also Benjamin Yang, *From Revolution to Politics: Chinese Communists on the Long March* (Boulder: Westview Press, 1990), 96–7
66 'Conclusions Regarding the Report of the Central Executive Committee', 27 January 1934, in Schram, ed., *Mao's Road to Power, Volume IV* (Armonk, NY: M. E. Sharpe, 1997), 716; Womack, 'From Urban Radical to Rural Revolutionary', 82
67 Womack, 'From Urban Radical to Rural Revolutionary', 82

17. Exodus

1 Wilson, *The Long March*, 74

2 Lily Xiao Hong Lee and Sue Wiles, *Women of the Long March* (St Leonards, Australia: Allen & Unwin, 1999), 22–3; Salisbury, *The Long March*, 50–1

3 Zhang Wentian, 'All for the Defense of the Soviet' (29 September 1934), in Tony Saich, ed., *The Rise to Power of the Chinese Communist Party: Documents and Analysis* (London: Routledge, 2015), 635–40. See also 'Commentary D: The Rise and Fall of the Soviet Movement in Central China, 1931–January 1935', 523

4 Sun Shuyun, *The Long March: The True History of Communist China's Founding Myth* (New York: Anchor Books, 2006), 64

5 Salisbury, *The Long March*, 60–1; Sun, *The Long March*, 65–6

6 See Lee and Wiles, *Women of the Long March*, and Helen Praeger Young, *Choosing Revolution: Chinese Women Soldiers on the Long March* (Urbana: University of Illinois Press, 2001) – especially chapter 7

7 Short, *Mao: A Life*, 316–17. See also Lee and Wiles, *Women of the Long March*, 9–23

8 Lee and Wiles, *Women of the Long March*, 25

9 Salisbury, *The Long March*, 60–7

10 Young, *Choosing Revolution*, 190

11 Salisbury, *The Long March*, 60–7

12 Young, *Choosing Revolution*, 193, 202

13 Wilson, *The Long March*, 77

14 Salisbury, *The Long March*, 95–6

15 Sun, *The Long March*, 74

16 Salisbury, *The Long March*, 92–5

17 Sun, *The Long March*, 74

18 Sun, *The Long March*, 74

19 Sun, *The Long March*, 74–5

20 Sun, *The Long March*, 77–8

21 The debate on casualties continues to rage; 'official' histories of the Long March place the death toll at fifty thousand. For more, see Karen Gernant, 'Attrition Sustained by the First Front Army of the Chinese Red Army on the Long March, 1934–35', *Journal of Asian History*, vol. 19, no. 2 (1985), 171

18. Zunyi

1 Salisbury, *The Long March*, 105; Agnes Smedley, *The Great Road: The Life and Times of Chu Teh* (New York: Modern Reader, 1956), 313–14; https://en.wikipedia.org/wiki/Mount_Langshan

2 Smedley, *The Great Road*, 314

3 Short, *Mao: A Life*, 2, 3–4; Wilson, *The Long March*, 80

4 Short, *Mao: A Life*, 5

5 Short, *Mao: A Life*, 5, 8; Salisbury, *The Long March*, 106–7

6 Salisbury, *The Long March*, 107

7 Smedley, *The Great Road*, 315–16

8 Short, *Mao: A Life*, 8–9; Salisbury, *The Long March*, 111–12

9 Short, *Mao: A Life*, 9–10; Salisbury, *The Long March*, 114–15

10 Salisbury, *The Long March*, 114, 116

11 Gernant, 'Attrition Sustained by the First Front Army', 173

12 Wilson, *The Long March*, 86

13 Wilson, *The Long March*, 86–8

14 Wilson, *The Long March*, 88–90

15 Salisbury, *The Long March*, 118–19; Short, *Mao: A Life*, 10–11; Yang, 'The Zunyi Conference as One Step in Mao's Rise to Power: A Survey of Historical Studies of the Chinese Communist Party', *The China Quarterly*, vol. 106 (June 1986), 237; Young, *Choosing Revolution*, 197

16 Yang, 'The Zunyi Conference as One Step in Mao's Rise to Power', 241

17 Short, *Mao: A Life*, 10

18 Otto Braun, *A Comintern Agent in China, 1932–1939* (Stanford: Stanford University Press, 1982), 96

19 Braun, *A Comintern Agent in China*, 98; Short, *Mao: A Life*, 11; Salisbury, *The Long March*, 121–2

20 Salisbury, *The Long March*, 122; Stuart R. Schram, 'The Writings of Mao Zedong, 1935–1937', in Schram, ed., *Mao's Road to Power, Volume V* (Armonk, NY: M. E. Sharpe, 1998), xxxviii–xxxix

21 Yang, 'The Zunyi Conference as One Step in Mao's Rise to Power', 245, 247; Braun, *A Comintern Agent in China*, 98–9; 'The Outline Resolution of the Enlarged Politburo Meeting on Summing Up Experiences and Lessons in Smashing the Fifth "Encirclement Campaign" (28 February 1935)', in Saich, ed., *The Rise to Power of the Chinese Communist Party*, 642; Short, *Mao: A Life*, 12–13; Salisbury, *The Long March*, 123–4

22 Yang, 'The Zunyi Conference as One Step in Mao's Rise to Power', 245–6; Salisbury, *The Long March*, 120–1, 123–6; Short, *Mao: A Life*, 12–14. For further analysis of the resolutions passed at the Zunyi Conference, see Yang, *From Revolution to Politics*, 112–23

19. The Bridge of Chains

1 Salisbury, *The Long March*, 119

2 Short, *Mao: A Life*, 321–2; Salisbury, *The Long March*, 127–8

3 Lee and Wiles, *Women of the Long March*, 33–4, 262–3; Short, *Mao: A Life*, 322; Young, *Choosing Revolution*, 202–3

4 Short, *Mao: A Life*, 321–2; Salisbury, *The Long March*, 127–8

5 'Loushan Pass', 28 February 1935, in Schram, ed., *Mao's Road to Power, Volume V*, 8

6 Schram, 'The Writings of Mao Zedong', xl–xli; Short, *Mao: A Life*, 322–4

7 Braun, *A Comintern Agent in China*, 114

8 Schram, 'The Writings of Mao Zedong', xl–xli; Short, *Mao: A Life*, 322–4. On the discontent with Mao's tactics, see also Yang, *From Revolution to Politics*, 127

9 Short, *Mao: A Life*, 324

10 Short, *Mao: A Life*, 324

11 Short, *Mao: A Life*, 324; Salisbury, *The Long March*, 197–8

12 Wilson, *The Long March*, 140; Smedley, *The Great Road*, 319

13 Salisbury, *The Long March*, 199

14 Salisbury, *The Long March*, 222–8; Short, *Mao: A Life*, 325

15 Salisbury, *The Long March*, 222

16 Snow, *RSOC*, 198–9

17 Short, *Mao: A Life*, 326–7

18 Chen Chang-Feng, *On the Long March with Chairman Mao* (Peking: Foreign Languages Press, 1972), 66

19 Wilson, *The Long March*, 178. See also Braun, *A Comintern Agent in China*, 122; Young, *Choosing Revolution*, 207; Lily Xiao Hong Lee, *Biographical Dictionary of Chinese Women, Volume 2: Twentieth Century*, 270

20 Short, *Mao: A Life*, 317–18; Schram, 'The Writings of Mao Zedong', xli–xlvi; Lynch, *Mao*, 93–5; Pantsov, *Mao: The Real Story*, 283–7. On the power clash between Mao and Zhang, and for a summary of Zhang's activities in northern Sichuan, see Yang, *From Revolution to Politics*, 129–61

21 Short, *Mao: A Life*, 331–2

22 Smedley, *The Great Road*, 337

23 Chen, *On the Long March with Chairman Mao*, 81

24 Braun, *A Comintern Agent in China*, 136–7. See also Smedley, *The Great Road*, 338; Young, *Choosing Revolution*, 213

25 Short, *Mao: A Life*, 332, 334–5

26 Short, *Mao: A Life*, 335

27 Chen, *On the Long March with Chairman Mao*, 91–3

28 Lynch, *Mao*, 86; Gernant, 'Attrition Sustained by the First Front Army', 186

29 Mao, 'On Tactics Against Japanese Imperialism', 27 December 1935, in Schram, ed., *Mao's Road to Power, Volume V*, 92

30 On alternative, revisionist histories of the Long March see, for instance, Anthony Garavente, 'Commentary: Solving the Mystery of the Long March, 1934–1936', *Bulletin of Concerned Asian Scholars*, vol. 27, no. 3 (1995), 57–69, and Frederick S. Litten, 'The Myth of the "Turning Point" – Towards a New Understanding of the Long March', *Bochumer Jahrbuch zur Ostasienforschung*, Band 25 (2001), at https://litten.de/fulltext/loma.pdf

31 Mao, 'On Tactics Against Japanese Imperialism', 92

EDGAR SNOW

20. Red China Beckons

1 Snow to L. M. McBride, 1 June 1936, Edgar Snow Papers (hereafter ESP), Folder 10

2 Helen Foster Snow, *My China Years* (London: Harrap, 1985), 181–2; Snow, *RSOC*, first revised and enlarged edition (London: Grove Press, 1988), 41

3 John Maxwell Hamilton, *Edgar Snow: A Biography* (Bloomington: Indiana

University Press, 1988), 1–8; Snow, *Journey to the Beginning* (London: Victor Gollancz Ltd., 1960), 13–14

4 Hamilton, *Edgar Snow*, 9–10
5 Snow, *Journey to the Beginning*, 28–9
6 Hamilton, *Edgar Snow*, 12–14; Robert M. Farnsworth, *From Vagabond to Journalist: Edgar Snow in Asia, 1928–1941* (Columbia: University of Missouri Press, 1996), 10–13; S. Bernard Thomas, *Season of High Adventure: Edgar Snow in China* (Berkeley: University of California Press, 1996), 31. On 1927 dollars, see www.in2013dollars.com/us/inflation/1927?amount=800
7 Hamilton, *Edgar Snow*, 14–15
8 Snow, *Journey to the Beginning*, 3
9 Thomas, *Season of High Adventure*, 34–5; Hamilton, *Edgar Snow*, 17; Farnsworth, *From Vagabond to Journalist*, 16–18. On the *Radnor*'s arrival, see 'Annual Report of the Board of Harbor Commissioners of the Territory of Hawaii', 1 July 1927 to 30 June 1928, 92, at https://core.ac.uk/download/pdf/77122865.pdf (accessed 16 January 2023)
10 Hamilton, *Edgar Snow*, 17–18; Thomas, *Season of High Adventure*, 36; Edgar Snow, 'A First Class Stowaway', *New York Herald Tribune Sunday Magazine*, 21 October 1928, 10
11 Hamilton, *Edgar Snow*, 18–19; Farnsworth, *From Vagabond to Journalist*, 19
12 Hamilton, *Edgar Snow*, 19
13 Thomas, *Season of High Adventure*, 43–4
14 Snow, *Journey to the Beginning*, 3–4
15 Snow, *Journey to the Beginning*, 16, 17
16 Snow, *Journey to the Beginning*, 18; Farnsworth, *From Vagabond to Journalist*, 21
17 Thomas, *Season of High Adventure*, 49–50; Hamilton, *Edgar Snow*, 23–4
18 Thomas, *Season of High Adventure*, 50–3; Hamilton, *Edgar Snow*, 25–6
19 Snow, 'Saving 250,000 Lives', *China Weekly Review*, 3 August 1929
20 Snow, *Journey to the Beginning*, 32–3
21 Snow, *Journey to the Beginning*, 33; Hamilton, *Edgar Snow*, 31–3, 37
22 Hamilton, *Edgar Snow*, 33
23 Snow, *Journey to the Beginning*, 67
24 Snow, *Journey to the Beginning*, 75–7
25 Thomas, *Season of High Adventure*, 66, 69
26 Hamilton, *Edgar Snow*, 38; http://disasterhistory.org/central-china-flood-1931 (accessed 18 January 2023)
27 Snow, 'In the Wake of China's Flood', *The China Weekly Review*, 23 January 1932
28 Hamilton, *Edgar Snow*, 38–9; Thomas, *Season of High Adventure*, 80–1
29 Hamilton, *Edgar Snow*, 39
30 Hamilton, *Edgar Snow*, 39–41; Thomas, *Season of High Adventure*, 83–4; Snow, *Journey to the Beginning*, 100–1
31 Thomas, *Season of High Adventure*, 84, 87
32 Snow, *Journey to the Beginning*, 101
33 Thomas, *Season of High Adventure*, 101–5; Foster Snow, *My China Years*, 24–34, 54

34 Foster Snow, *My China Years*, 148–9; Thomas, *Season of High Adventure*, 107, 109

35 Snow, *Journey to the Beginning*, 119

36 Hamilton, *Edgar Snow*, 49, 51–2, 55–6; Thomas, *Season of High Adventure*, 108–9. On the 1938 Nobel Prize, see www.nobelprize.org/prizes/literature/1938/summary/ (accessed 25 January 2023)

37 Snow, *Journey to the Beginning*, 143–4

38 Hamilton, *Edgar Snow*, 57–9; Thomas, *Season of High Adventure*, 122–3

39 Snow, *Journey to the Beginning*, 145

40 Snow, *Journey to the Beginning*, 146

41 Thomas, *Season of High Adventure*, 90

42 Thomas, *Season of High Adventure*, 90–6

43 Hamilton, *Edgar Snow*, 54

44 Hamilton, *Edgar Snow*, 63

45 Thomas, *Season of High Adventure*, 96

46 Snow, *RSOC*, 35–7

47 Hamilton, *Edgar Snow*, 60–3; Snow, *RSOC*, 38

48 Hamilton, *Edgar Snow*, 63–4; Bennett A. Cerf, 'A Matter of Timing', *Publishers Weekly*, 12 February 1938, 838

49 Cerf, 'A Matter of Timing', 838–9

50 Thomas, *Season of High Adventure*, 126; Hamilton, *Edgar Snow*, 65–6

51 Edgar Snow to Nelson T. Johnson, 6 February 1937, 2, ESP, Folder 11

52 Hamilton, *Edgar Snow*, 67–8; Thomas, *Season of High Adventure*, 131–3; Snow, *Journey to the Beginning*, 152

53 Hamilton, *Edgar Snow*, 69; Thomas, *Season of High Adventure*, 131

54 Snow, *RSOC*, 39; Snow, *Journey to the Beginning*, 152

21. The Road to Red China

1 Edgar Snow diary, Book 11, June 1936, 2, Folder 120; Snow, *RSOC*, 46

2 Snow, *RSOC*, 43–4

3 Edgar Snow diary, Book 11, June 1936, 8, Folder 120

4 Snow, *Journey to the Beginning*, 153; Snow, *RSOC*, 43–5, 46–7; Snow diary, Book 11, June 1936, 7, Folder 120

5 Snow, *RSOC*, 47, 50–1

6 Snow, *RSOC*, 52–3

7 Thomas, *Season of High Adventure*, 134–5; Hamilton, *Edgar Snow*, 70

8 Hamilton, *Edgar Snow*, 70; Snow, *RSOC*, 51

9 Snow, *RSOC*, 54; Snow, *Journey to the Beginning*, 154–5

10 Snow, *RSOC*, 54–5

11 Snow, *RSOC*, 55–6

12 Snow, *Journey to the Beginning*, 155

13 Snow, *RSOC*, 56–7

14 Snow, *Journey to the Beginning*, 155; Thomas, *Season of High Adventure*, 135

15 Snow, *RSOC*, 57–9

16 Snow, *RSOC*, 63–4

17 Snow, *RSOC*, 65–6; Snow diary, book 12, 8–18 July 1936, 1, Folder 121
18 Snow, *RSOC*, 66; Snow diary, book 12, 8–18 July 1936, 1, Folder 121
19 Snow, *Journey to the Beginning*, 156
20 Snow, *RSOC*, 67
21 Snow, *RSOC*, 67–9; Snow diary, book 12, 8–18 July 1936, 1–2, Folder 121
22 Snow, *RSOC*, 70–1
23 Snow diary, book 13, 3–4, Folder 122
24 Snow, *Journey to the Beginning*, 159; Thomas, *Season of High Adventure*, 136
25 Snow diary, book 12, 8–18 July 1936, 3, Folder 121
26 Snow diary, book 12, 8–18 July 1936, 4, Folder 121
27 Snow diary, book 12, 8–18 July 1936, 3, Folder 121

22. The Red Capital

1 Snow, *RSOC*, 77, 81; Snow diary, book 12, 8–18 July 1936, 4–5, Folder 121
2 Snow, *RSOC*, 82
3 Snow diary, book 12, 8–18 July 1936, 5, Folder 121
4 Snow diary, book 12, 8–18 July 1936, 4, Folder 121
5 Snow diary, book 12, 8–18 July 1936, 5, Folder 121
6 Snow, *RSOC*, 84–5
7 Snow diary, book 12, 8–18 July 1936, 6, Folder 121; Snow, *RSOC*, 89
8 Snow diary, book 12, 8–18 July 1936, 6, Folder 121
9 Snow, *Journey to the Beginning*, 159–60
10 Snow diary, book 12, 8–18 July 1936, 6, Folder 121
11 Snow, *Journey to the Beginning*, 159–60
12 Snow diary, book 12, 8–18 July 1936, 6, Folder 121
13 Snow, *RSOC*, 90
14 Snow, *Red China Today: The Other Side of the River* (Harmondsworth: Penguin, 1970), 141
15 Snow, *RSOC*, 93
16 Hamilton, *Edgar Snow*, 71
17 Snow diary, book 12, 8–18 July 1936, 7, 9, Folder 121
18 Snow diary, book 12, 8–18 July 1936, 9–10, Folder 121
19 Snow, *Journey to the Beginning*, 176
20 Snow, *Random Notes on Red China* (Cambridge, MA: Harvard University Press, 1957), 117–18
21 Snow, *Journey to the Beginning*, 176–7
22 Snow, *Journey to the Beginning*, 175–6
23 Snow, *RSOC*, 258
24 Snow, *RSOC*, 284–9
25 Snow, *RSOC*, 348–9
26 Snow, *Random Notes on Red China*, 119; Snow, *RSOC*, 368; Snow, *Journey to the Beginning*, 179–80
27 Snow, *Journey to the Beginning*, 178
28 Snow, *RSOC*, 368

29 Snow, *Random Notes on Red China*, 119–20
30 Snow, *Random Notes on Red China*, 120–1
31 Snow, *Random Notes on Red China*, 121–2
32 Snow, *Random Notes on Red China*, 122–3
33 Snow, *Random Notes on Red China*, 123–4
34 'Fear for Edgar Snow', *Kansas City Times*, 27 October 1936, 1; 'Deny Edgar Snow Death', 'Articles, circa 1920–1939', ESP, Folder 553
35 Snow, *RSOC*, 368–9; Snow, *Journey to the Beginning*, 182
36 Foster Snow, *My China Years*, 198; Foster Snow, 'Notes on the Sian Incident, 1936', 51, in Nym Wales Papers, Box 17, Folder 1, Hoover Institution Library and Archives

23. *Red Star Over China*

1 Snow to McBride, 29 December 1936, 1, 2, Folder 10
2 Ishikawa Yoshihiro, *How the 'Red Star' Rose: Edgar Snow and Early Images of Mao Zedong* (Hong Kong: The Chinese University of Hong Kong Press, 2022), 214–15; Hamilton, *Edgar Snow*, 80
3 Snow, undated letter to Mr Ti Ti Li, c. December 1936, 'Correspondence, 1936', ESP, Folder 10; Thomas, *Season of High Adventure*, 171
4 Yoshihiro, *How the 'Red Star' Rose*, 211–12
5 Foster Snow, *My China Years*, 219, 202–3; Foster Snow, 'Notes on the Sian Incident', 53–4
6 Foster Snow, 'Notes on the Sian Incident, 54
7 Hamilton, *Edgar Snow*, 84
8 Thomas, *Season of High Adventure*, 172
9 Snow, *RSOC*, 90, 89–96
10 Thomas, *Season of High Adventure*, 169
11 Hamilton, *Edgar Snow*, 85
12 'China's Red Army', *Times Literary Supplement*, 23 October 1937, 771
13 W. N. Ewer, 'Lost Country where only One White Man Has Trod', *Daily Herald*, 11 October 1937, 10. See also 'Communists in China', *New Statesman and Nation*, 6 November 1937, 766
14 Bennett Cerf, 'A Matter of Timing', 3
15 Thomas, *Season of High Adventure*, 170
16 'Red Star Over China', *The Atlantic*, May 1938. See also Pearl S. Buck, 'Asia Book-Shelf', *Asia*, vol. 38 (March 1938), 202–3
17 'China's United Front', *Saturday Review*, vol. 17, no. 10, 1 January 1938, 6
18 'Red China', *New Republic*, 12 January 1938, 287; 'Books: Chinese Reds', *Time*, 10 January 1938
19 'Books: A Marco Polo Out of Red China', *New Yorker*, 8 January 1938, 79
20 Hamilton, *Edgar Snow*, 80–3; Thomas, *Season of High Adventure*, 152–3
21 Hamilton, *Edgar Snow*, 83
22 Hamilton, *Edgar Snow*, 83–4; Thomas, *Season of High Adventure*, 170–1
23 Thomas, *Season of High Adventure*, 171

ENDNOTES

24. Maoism

1 Snow, *RSOC*, 409

2 www.ohiocountylibrary.org/wheeling-history/5655#speach (accessed 16 February 2023)

3 On the FBI investigation, see, for instance, Stephen J. Farnsworth, 'Seeing Red: The FBI and Edgar Snow', *Journalism History*, vol. 28, no. 3 (2002), 137–45

4 Hamilton, *Edgar Snow*, 199–201

5 'Red Star Over Independence Square: The Strange Case of Edgar Snow and the *Saturday Evening Post*', *Plain Talk*, September 1947

6 Hamilton, *Edgar Snow*, 205

7 Memorandum, G. H. Scatterday to A. H. Belmont, 28 June 1960, re: 'Edgar Snow', 1–4, in FBI Edgar Snow File (100-267865), Henry Mitchell Papers, Folder 3, University of Missouri-Kansas City

8 Hamilton, *Edgar Snow*, 55

9 Farnsworth, 'Seeing Red: The FBI and Edgar Snow', 138

10 Willard Edwards, 'Tell Plot for 3 Reds to Run US Intelligence', *Chicago Daily Tribune*, 16 February 1952, A5; 'Snow Denies Charge He Ever Was a Red', *New York Times*, 17 February 1952, 15

11 Farnsworth, 'Seeing Red: The FBI and Edgar Snow', 142; Hamilton, *Edgar Snow*, 206–7

12 Anthony Kubek, *How the Far East Was Lost: American Policy and the Creation of Communist China, 1941–1949* (New York: Twin Circle Publishing Co., Inc., 1972), 371

13 Julia Lovell, *Maoism: A Global History* (London: Vintage, 2019), 62

14 Lovell, *Maoism*, 7

15 Lovell, *Maoism*, 8–9, 26, 59

16 This section is based on Lovell, *Maoism*, 26–59. See also Timothy Cheek, 'Mao, Revolution, and Memory', 13–15, in Cheek, ed., *A Critical Introduction to Mao* (Cambridge: Cambridge University Press, 2010)

17 Lovell, *Maoism*, 26, 62

18 Yoshihiro, *How the 'Red Star' Rose*, 229–40; Hamilton, *Edgar Snow*, 93–4; Lovell, *Maoism*, 84

19 Lovell, *Maoism*, 84

20 Dong Leshan, 'Edgar Snow and "Red Star Over China"', in Wang Xing, ed., *China Remembers Edgar Snow* (Beijing: Beijing Review, 1982), 59–60

21 Zhao Rongsheng, 'Snow Led Us to Yanan', in Wang, ed., *China Remembers Edgar Snow*, 67–9

22 See, for example, Anne-Marie Brady, *Making the Foreign Serve China: Managing Foreigners in the People's Republic* (Lanham: Rowman & Littlefield Publishers, Inc., 2003), especially 45–50. On Mao's 'pawn', see S. C. M. Paine, 'Edgar Snow and Shaping US Perceptions of the Chinese Civil War', in Andrea J. Drew et al., eds, *From Quills to Tweets: How America Communicates About War and Revolution* (Washington DC: Georgetown University Press, 2019), 136

23 Lovell, *Maoism*, 61

24 Yoshihiro, *How the 'Red Star' Rose*, 199–204; Lovell, *Maoism*, 76–7

25 Hamilton, *Edgar Snow*, 95

26 Snow to Johnson, 6 February 1937, 2

27 Hamilton, *Edgar Snow*, 89

28 Kenneth E. Shewmaker, *Americans and Chinese Communists, 1927–1945: A Persuading Encounter* (Ithaca: Cornell University Press, 1971), 60

29 Wang, ed., *China Remembers Edgar Snow*, 57

30 Snow, letter to *Kansas City Star*, 23 June 1939, 2, Folder 11

31 Lovell, *Maoism*, 77

32 Lovell, *Maoism*, 83

33 Lovell, *Maoism*, 83

34 Nelson Mandela, *Long Walk to Freedom* (London: Abacus, 1995), 325–6

35 Loren Glass, *Rebel Publisher: Grove Press and the Revolution of the Word* (New York: Seven Stories Press, 2013), 145

36 Ann Loehr, 'For Edgar Snow, Revolutionary Journalist', *Space City!*, 24 February 1972, 5; University of Wisconsin Committee to End the War in Vietnam, 'Organizing a Vietnam Protest Committee' (c. 1966), 11, Vietnam Summer project, Folder: 201739-010-0015, Date: 1 January 1966–31 December 1967, Fred Halstead Papers, 1956–1978; Students for a Democratic Society printed pamphlets: Carl Wittman, 'Seminar on Marxism', 7, New York, SDS, Folder: 201772-039-0678, Date: 1 January 1960–31 December 1970, Students for a Democratic Society Papers, 1958–1970; San Diego State SDS, 'SDS Newsletter', 1 March 1968, 1, Students for a Democratic Society locality file: Nebraska and New Hampshire, Folder: 201772-024-0004, Date: 1 January 1965–31 December 1969, Students for a Democratic Society Papers, 1958–1970; John Sinclair, *Guitar Army: Rock & Revolution with MC5 and the White Panther Party* (New York: Douglas, 1972), 300; Georgetown Radical Union, 'Books for Freaks and Revolutionaries', c. August 1970; 'Red Star Over China: A Speech by Vicki Garvin', *Control, Conflict and Change*, 11 January 1972, available at https://archives.wayne.edu/repositories/2/archival_objects/665104. On the CCC, see https://archives.wayne.edu/repositories/2/archival_objects/664805 and Say Burgin, *Organizing Your Own: The White Fight for Black Power in Detroit* (New York: New York University Press, 2024). Charles A. Haynie, *A Memoir of the New Left: The Political Autobiography of Charles A. Haynie* (Knoxville: University of Tennessee Press, 2009), 16

37 Lovell, *Maoism*, 277

38 Lovell, *Maoism*, 278

39 Lovell, *Maoism*, 82–3; 'Alex Hing, Former Minister of Information for the Red Guard Party and Founding Member of I Wor Kuen', interviewed by Fred Ho and Steve Yip, in Fred Ho, ed., *Legacy to Liberation: Politics and Culture of Revolutionary Asian Pacific America* (San Francisco: Beg Red Media/AK Press, 2000), 279–83

40 Karen L. Ishizuka, *Serve the People: Making Asian America in the Long Sixties* (London: Verso, 2018), 81–2. On the Asian American movement in general, see, for instance, Daryl Joji Maeda, *Rethinking the Asian American Movement* (New York: Routledge, 2012). The first issue of *Yellow Seeds* (April 1972) – newspaper

of a radical, inter-ethnic organisation founded in Philadelphia in 1971, to 'serve the needs' of the residents of Chinatown – carried an obituary for Edgar Snow, who had died from pancreatic cancer two months earlier. Snow was, they said, an 'authority on China', a 'close friend' of many of the country's leaders, and a man whose efforts had 'played a large role in promoting friendship and understanding between the Chinese and American peoples'. See Maeda, 77–9, and 'A Friend of China Dies', *Yellow Seeds*, vol. 1, no. 1 (April 1972), 6, available at www.marxists. org/history/erol/ncm-1a/yellow-seeds/v1n1.pdf (accessed 8 March 2023)

41 On Maoism and American radicals during the long 1960s, see, for example, Max Elbaum, *Revolution in the Air: Sixties Radicals Turn to Lenin, Mao and Che* (London: Verso, 2018); Robeson Taj Frazier, *The East Is Black: Cold War China in the Black Radical Imagination* (Durham, NC: Duke University Press, 2014); and Robin D. G. Kelley and Betsy Esch, 'Black Like Mao: Red China and Black Revolution', *Souls: Critical Journal of Black Politics & Culture*, vol. 1, no. 4 (1999). On the Black Panther Party, specifically, see Sean L. Malloy, *Out of Oakland: Black Panther Party Internationalism During the Cold War* (Ithaca: Cornell University Press, 2017)

PART THREE: CUBA
FIDEL

25. *Granma*

1 Herbert L. Matthews, *Revolution in Cuba: An Essay in Understanding* (New York: Scribner, 1975), 71–2; Hugh Thomas, *Cuba: or The Pursuit of Freedom* (New York: Da Capo Press, 1998), 891, 894. The name of the yacht is usually ascribed to Robert Erickson's grandmother. For more on this, see Peter Swanson, 'The Amazing True Story of Fidel Castro's Motoryacht', *Passagemaker: The World's Cruising Authority*, 23 February 2018, at www.passagemaker.com/trawler-news/granma-yacht-changed-history

2 Thomas, *Cuba*, 888, 891; Carlos Franqui, *Diary of the Cuban Revolution* (New York: The Viking Press, 1976), 121–2; Ernesto 'Che' Guevara, *Reminiscences of the Cuban Revolutionary War* (London: Harper Perennial, 2009), 139; Julia E. Sweig, *Inside the Cuban Revolution: Fidel Castro and the Urban Underground* (Cambridge, MA: Harvard University Press, 2002)

3 Jorge Castañeda, *Compañero: The Life and Death of Che Guevara* (London: Bloomsbury, 1997), 78, 80; Aviva Chomsky, *A History of the Cuban Revolution* (Chichester: Wiley-Blackwell, 2011), 24–5; http://history.state.gov/ milestones/1899-1913/Platt (accessed 13 September 2013); Thomas, *Cuba*, chapters xxxv–l

4 Chomsky, *A History of the Cuban Revolution*, 24

5 Chomsky, *A History of the Cuban Revolution*, 24, 33–4; Castañeda, *Compañero*, 78–9; Thomas, *Cuba*, 893; Matthews, *Revolution in Cuba*, 34–9; James O'Connor, *The Origins of Socialism in Cuba* (Ithaca: Cornell University Press, 1970), especially 1, 20; 'Memorandum from the Director of the Office of Middle American

ENDNOTES

Affairs (Wieland) to the Assistant Secretary of State for Inter-American Affairs (Rubottom), 19 December 1957, re: Policy Recommendation for Restoration of Normalcy in Cuba', in *Foreign Relations of the United States, 1955–1957, Volume IV: American Republics: Multilateral; Mexico; Caribbean*, 870

6 Castañeda, *Compañero*, 80, 81, 82; Chomsky, *A History of the Cuban Revolution*, 28

7 Chomsky, *A History of the Cuban Revolution*, 28–33; Matthews, *Revolution in Cuba*, 29–34; Max Boot, 'M-26-7: Castro's Improbable Comeback, 1952–1959', in Boot, *Invisible Armies*, 430–1; Sweig, *Inside the Cuban Revolution*, 4

8 'Another Dictatorship', *New York Times*, 22 September 1955, 30

9 Thomas, *Cuba*, 883–5, 889–90; Leycester Coltman, *The Real Fidel Castro* (New Haven: Yale University Press, 2003), 109; Chomsky, *A History of the Cuban Revolution*, 34; 'Cuba: Hit-Run Revolt', *Time*, 10 December 1956; 'Student Disorders Have Cuba Worried', *New York Times*, 7 December 1955, 10; 'Cuba Suppresses Plot for Revolt', *New York Times*, 4 April 1956, 9; '17 Cubans Arrested; Revolt Data Seized', *New York Times*, 4 May 1956, 9; Matthews, 'Cuba a Live Volcano of Political Unrest', *New York Times*, 6 May 1956, 186; '17 Arrested in Cuba in Anti-Batista Plot', *New York Times*, 27 June 1956, 2; 'Cuban Army Aide Slain by Gunmen', *New York Times*, 29 October 1956, 6; Matthews, 'Cuba's Violence Is Found Normal', *New York Times*, 4 November 1956, 4

10 Fidel Castro and Ignacio Ramonet, tr. Andrew Hurley, *My Life* (New York: Scribner, 2009), 28–30

11 Tony Perrottet, *Cuba Libre! Che, Fidel, and the Improbable Revolution* (New York: Blue Rider Press, 2019), 34; Tad Szulc, *Fidel: A Critical Portrait* (London: Coronet Books, 1989), 94–5

12 Castro, *My Life*, 42, 81

13 Castro, *My Life*, 57, 68–9, 70–4, 79

14 Castro, *My Life*, 91

15 Thomas, *Cuba*, 810–23; Boot, 'M-26-7', 429–31; Matthews, *Revolution in Cuba*, 41–7; Castañeda, *Compañero*, 82; Coltman, *The Real Fidel Castro*, 18; www.cubatechtravel.com/destination/extrahotel/9613/havana-university (accessed 17 September 2023). On the Browning, see Castro, *My Life*, 95. See also Simon Hall, *Ten Days in Harlem*, 12–13

16 Castro, *My Life*, 84–5, 89, 92–3, 97–9

17 Simon Hall, *Ten Days in Harlem: Fidel Castro and the Making of the 1960s* (London: Faber & Faber, 2020), 13

18 Thomas, *Cuba*, 817–21; Boot, 'M-26-7', 430–1; Sweig, *Inside the Cuban Revolution*, 5; Szulc, *Fidel*, 234

19 Szulc, *Fidel*, 234–72; Franqui, 'The Attack on the Moncada Barracks: Recollections', in *Diary of the Cuban Revolution*, 56–7. See also Lillian Guerra, *Heroes, Martyrs, and Political Messiahs in Revolutionary Cuba, 1946–1958* (New Haven: Yale University Press, 2018), 122–3, 125–7

20 Thomas, *Cuba*, 835–41; Boot, 'M-26-7', 431–2; Matthews, *Revolution in Cuba*, 49, 55–63; Coltman, *The Real Fidel Castro*, 75–6, 82; www.pbs.org/wgbh/amex/castro/peopleevents/e_moncada.html (accessed 17 September 2023); Chomsky, *A*

History of the Cuban Revolution, 36–7; Castro, *My Life*, 129. See also Matthews, 'Batista Is Facing Fateful Decisions', *New York Times*, 22 October 1953, 15. On the interrogation of Haydée Santamaría, see Franqui, 'The Attack on the Moncada Barracks: Recollections', 61. On Fidel's brush with death, see Castro, *My Life*, 161–5. See also Guerra, *Heroes, Martyrs, and Political Messiahs*, 128–9

21 Castro, 'History Will Absolve Me', in David Deutschmann and Deborah Shnookal, *Fidel Castro Reader* (Melbourne: Ocean Press, 2007), 46

22 Boot, 'M-26-7', 432; Matthews, *Revolution in Cuba*, 64–5; Thomas, *Cuba*, 843; Coltman, *The Real Fidel Castro*, 87–8, 90; 'Cuba Begins Trial of 100 for Revolt', *New York Times*, 22 September 1953, 19; Castro, 'History Will Absolve Me', in Deutschmann and Shnookal, *Fidel Castro Reader*, 55, 59, 66–7

23 Coltman, *The Real Fidel Castro*, 93–101; Matthews, *Revolution in Cuba*, 67–8; Thomas, *Cuba*, 862–3. See Castro's letters from prison (especially those of 18 December 1953, 22 December 1953, 24 March 1955) in Franqui, *Diary of the Cuban Revolution*, 66, 68, 71, 73; Fidel Castro, letter, 7 July 1955, in Franqui, *Diary of the Cuban Revolution*, 90; Szulc, *Fidel*, 349–50

26. Shipwreck

1 Szulc, *Fidel*, 351

2 Szulc, *Fidel*, 353, 360–3; Robert E. Quirk, *Fidel Castro* (New York: W. W. Norton, 1995), 87–102

3 'Manifesto No. 1 to the People of Cuba – August 8, 1955', in Luis Plazas, 'Revolutionary Manifestos and Fidel Castro's Road to Power' (2014 MA thesis, University of Central Florida), 73–84, available at https://stars.library.ucf.edu/cgi/viewcontent.cgi?article=5785&context=etd (accessed 8 January 2021)

4 Castro, 'Statement', 19 March 1956, in Franqui, *Diary of the Cuban Revolution*, 100–1

5 Szulc, *Fidel*, 376, 352–3

6 Szulc, *Fidel*, 378–9, 387–8

7 Guevara, *Reminiscences*, 137

8 Szulc, *Fidel*, 391–2; Coltman, 107; Franqui, *Diary of the Cuban Revolution*, 104–5

9 Szulc, *Fidel*, 394–5; Coltman, 107

10 Szulc, *Fidel*, 374–5

11 Szulc, *Fidel*, 353, 396; Sweig, *Inside the Cuban Revolution*, 2, 12–13

12 Szulc, *Fidel*, 396; 'Mexico Pact – September 1956', in Plazas, 'Revolutionary Manifestos and Fidel Castro's Road to Power', 92–3

13 Quirk, *Fidel Castro*, 114

14 Perrottet, *Cuba Libre!*, 756; Szulc, 398–400

15 Coltman, 111–12; Franqui, *Diary of the Cuban Revolution*, 111

16 Szulc, *Fidel*, 403–4; Quirk, *Fidel Castro*, 119–20

17 Franqui, *Diary of the Cuban Revolution*, 121–2

18 Guevara, *Reminiscences*, 139

19 Franqui, *Diary of the Cuban Revolution*, 122

20 Franqui, *Diary of the Cuban Revolution*, 122; Matthews, *Revolution in Cuba*, 71–2

21 Matthews, *Revolution in Cuba*, 71–2; Thomas, *Cuba*, 891, 894–7; Franqui, *Diary of the Cuban Revolution*, 120, 124; 'Cuba: Hit-Run Revolt', *Time*; Enzo Infante, 'Santiago Uprising: A Harbinger of Victory', *The Militant*, vol. 60, no. 9 (4 March 1996). The phrase 'shipwreck', often attributed to Che Guevara, was most likely used first by Juan Manuel Márquez – see Peter Hulme, *Cuba's Wild East: A Literary Geography of Oriente* (Liverpool: Liverpool University Press, 2011), 321, n. 13

22 Perrottet, *Cuba Libre!*, 90; Szulc, *Fidel*, 408–9; Franqui, *Diary of the Cuban Revolution*, 123

23 Franqui, *Diary of the Cuban Revolution*, 123–4, 129; Guevara, *Reminiscences*, 9, 140–1; Thomas, *Cuba*, 897; Matthews, *Revolution in Cuba*, 72; Boot, 'M-26-7', 427–8; Castañeda, *Compañero*, 99

24 Guevara, *Reminiscences*, 9–10, 141; Thomas, *Cuba*, 897–8; Franqui, *Diary of the Cuban Revolution*, 124

25 Guevara, *Reminiscences*, 10–12; Franqui, *Diary of the Cuban Revolution*, 125, 129; Franqui, *The Twelve* (New York: Lyle Stuart Inc., 1968), 55–7; Castro and Ramonet, *My Life*, 182–3; Boot, 'M-26-7', 428; Thomas, *Cuba*, 898–9; 'July 26 Movement appealed to soldiers and youth in Cuba to join revolutionary struggle', *The Militant*, vol. 68, no. 3 (26 January 2004)

26 UPI News Release, in Franqui, *Diary of the Cuban Revolution*, 126; Quirk, *Fidel Castro*, 123

27 Castro, *My Life*, 183–4; Franqui, *The Twelve*, 59

28 Perrottet, *Cuba Libre!*, 95–8; Tony Perrottet, 'How Cuba Remembers Its Revolutionary Past and Present', *Smithsonian Magazine*, October 2016, available at www.smithsonianmag.com/history/cuba-remembers-revolutionary-past-present-180960447/ (accessed 11 January 2021). For Celia Sánchez, see Nancy Stout, *One Day in December: Celia Sánchez and the Cuban Revolution* (New York: Monthly Review Press, 2013) – especially chapter 4, 120

HERBERT MATTHEWS

27. A Newspaperman's Newspaperman

1 Matthews, *The Cuban Story* (New York: George Braziller, 1961), 23–4; Nancie Matthews, 'Matthews' Journey to Sierra Maestra: Wife's Version', *Times Talk*, vol. 10, no. 7 (March 1957), 8; Anthony DePalma, *The Man Who Invented Fidel: Cuba, Castro, and Herbert L. Matthews of the New York Times* (New York: Public Affairs, 2006), 71–2; Perrottet, *Cuba Libre!*, 120–1

2 Matthews, *The Education of a Correspondent* (New York: Harcourt, Brace and Company, 1946), 3

3 DePalma, *The Man Who Invented Fidel*, 42–6

4 Matthews, *The Education of a Correspondent*, 6

5 Matthews, *The Education of a Correspondent*, 4

6 Matthews, *The Education of a Correspondent*, 3–5

7 Matthews, *The Education of a Correspondent*, 5, 13

8 DePalma, *The Man Who Invented Fidel*, 49

ENDNOTES

9 Matthews, *The Education of a Correspondent*, 14
10 Matthews, *The Education of a Correspondent*, 14–15
11 Matthews, *The Education of a Correspondent*, 15–16
12 Matthews, *The Education of a Correspondent*, 17; DePalma, *The Man Who Invented Fidel*, 49–50
13 Matthews, *The Education of a Correspondent*, 18–19
14 Matthews, *The Education of a Correspondent*, 21–2, 31
15 Matthews, *The Education of a Correspondent*, 7–8
16 Matthews, *The Education of a Correspondent*, 37–9, 42; DePalma, *The Man Who Invented Fidel*, 51–2
17 Matthews, '80,000 Ethiopians Routed By Foe in 6-Day Battle; Italians Gain in North', *New York Times*, 17 February 1936, 1, 6
18 DePalma, *The Man Who Invented Fidel*, 52
19 Matthews, '80,000 Ethiopians Routed By Foe in 6-Day Battle', 6
20 Paul Preston, *We Saw Spain Die: Foreign Correspondents in the Spanish Civil War* (London: Constable, 2009), 51–2; Matthews, *The Education of a Correspondent*, 28
21 Matthews, *The Education of a Correspondent*, 21
22 Matthews, *The Education of a Correspondent*, 67
23 Preston, *We Saw Spain Die*, 18; Matthews, *The Education of a Correspondent*, 95. See also David Deacon, 'Elective and Experiential Affinities: British and American Foreign Correspondents and the Spanish Civil War', *Journalism Studies*, vol. 9, no. 3 (2008), 392–408
24 Matthews, *The Education of a Correspondent*, 91
25 Preston, *We Saw Spain Die*, 52
26 Phillip Knightley, *The First Casualty: From the Crimea to the Falklands: The War Correspondent as Hero, Propagandist, and Myth Maker* (London: Pan Books, 1989), 210
27 Preston, *We Saw Spain Die*, 23
28 Preston, *We Saw Spain Die*, 23; Matthews, *A World in Revolution: A Newspaperman's Memoir* (New York: Scribner, 1972), 11–12, 17–18
29 Preston, *We Saw Spain Die*, 22–3; DePalma, *The Man Who Invented Fidel*, 57–9; Matthews, *A World in Revolution*, 20
30 Deacon, 'Elective and Experiential Affinities', 404
31 Preston, *We Saw Spain Die*, 23
32 Matthews, *A World in Revolution*, 19; Preston, *We Saw Spain Die*, 117
33 Constancia de la Mora, *In Place of Splendour: The Autobiography of a Spanish Woman* (London: Michael Joseph, 1940), 288–9. On de la Mora, see Preston, *We Saw Spain Die*, 109–13
34 Preston, *We Saw Spain Die*, 149
35 DePalma, *The Man Who Invented Fidel*, 60
36 Matthews, *The Education of a Correspondent*, 192
37 Matthews, *The Education of a Correspondent*, 195, 202, 209–11
38 Matthews, *The Education of a Correspondent*, 210
39 Wolfgang Saxon, 'Newspaperman's Newspaperman', *New York Times*, 31 July 1977,

36; DePalma, *The Man Who Invented Fidel*, 42–65; Perrottet, *Cuba Libre!*, 120; 'Biographical Note', Herbert L. Matthews Papers (hereafter HLMP), Columbia University

40 Matthews, 'Cuba's Violence Is Found Normal', *New York Times*, 4

41 Matthews, 'The Violent Cubans' (editorial), *New York Times*, 4 December 1956, 38

28. A Chapter in a Fantastic Novel

1 Thomas, *Cuba*, 899–904; Matthews, *Revolution in Cuba*, 77–8; Manuel Fajardo, 'Recollections', in Franqui, *Diary of the Cuban Revolution*, 134; http://peakery.com/pico-caracas/ (accessed 20 September 2023)

2 Thomas, *Cuba*, 904–8; Chomsky, *A History of the Cuban Revolution*, 38–9; Boot, 'M-26-7', 436; Coltman, *The Real Fidel Castro*, 118; Hulme, *Cuba's Wild East*, 314–15

3 Guevara, *Reminiscences*, 19; Quirk, *Fidel Castro*, 130; Núñez Jiménez quoted in Hulme, *Cuba's Wild East*, 313

4 Guevara, *Reminiscences*, 20

5 DePalma, *The Man Who Invented Fidel*, 14–15, 35–8; Perrottet, *Cuba Libre!*, 122–3; Ruby Hart Phillips, *Cuba: Island of Paradox* (New York: McDowell, Obolensky, 1959), 298–9; Matthews, *The Cuban Story*, 18–21

6 Perrottet, *Cuba Libre!*, 123; DePalma, *The Man Who Invented Fidel*, 40–1; Matthews, *The Cuban Story*, 21–2

7 Matthews, *The Cuban Story*, 22

8 DePalma, *The Man Who Invented Fidel*, 41

9 Matthews, *The Cuban Story*, 24; DePalma, *The Man Who Invented Fidel*, 72

10 Matthews, *The Cuban Story*, 32

11 Nancie Matthews, 'Matthews' Journey to Sierra Maestra: Wife's Version', 8

12 Matthews, *The Cuban Story*, 33; DePalma, *The Man Who Invented Fidel*, 74–5

13 Matthews, *The Cuban Story*, 34

14 Matthews, *The Cuban Story*, 34

15 Matthews, *The Cuban Story*, 34–5

16 Matthews, *The Cuban Story*, 36

17 Matthews, *The Cuban Story*, 36–8. See also Matthews's original notes of the interview with Fidel, available at https://dlc.library.columbia.edu/catalog/ldpd:113193

18 Franqui, *The Twelve*, 76, 102; Franqui, *Diary of the Cuban Revolution*, 139; DePalma, *The Man Who Invented Fidel*, 81–4; Matthews, *The Cuban Story*, 37

19 DePalma, *The Man Who Invented Fidel*, 88–9

20 Matthews, *The Cuban Story*, 39

21 Nancie Matthews, 'Matthews' Journey to Sierra Maestra: Wife's Version', 8; Matthews, *The Cuban Story*, 40, 43–4; DePalma, *The Man Who Invented Fidel*, 89, 91–2; Perrottet, *Cuba Libre!*, 125–6

29. Scoop!

1 Matthews, 'Cuban Rebel Is Visited in Hideout', *New York Times*, 24 February 1957, 1

2 Matthews, 'Cuban Rebel Is Visited in Hideout', 34

3 Matthews, 'Cuban Rebel Is Visited in Hideout', 34

4 Matthews, 'Cuban Rebel Is Visited in Hideout', 34

5 www.lonelyplanet.com/cuba/havana/attractions/museo-de-la-revolucion/a/poi-sig/369753/358014; Perrottet, *Cuba Libre!*, 136

6 Perrottet, *Cuba Libre!*, 131; DePalma, *The Man Who Invented Fidel*, 102, 104–5; Franqui, *Diary of the Cuban Revolution*, 144–5

7 Matthews, *The Cuban Story*, 45–7

8 Matthews, *The Cuban Story*, 47–8

9 DePalma, *The Man Who Invented Fidel*, 190–7

10 DePalma, *The Man Who Invented Fidel*, 105–6

11 Richard G. Cushing to Matthews, 26 February 1957, in HLMP, Box 1, Folder 26

12 Edward W. Barrett to Matthews, 6 March 1957, and Grayson Kirk to Matthews, 1 March 1957, in HLMP, Box 1, Folder 26

13 Matthews to Turner Catledge, 4 March 1957, in HLMP, Box 1, Folder 26

14 Carlos Prío Socarrás to Matthews, 18 March 1957, in HLMP, Box 1, Folder 26. See also José R. Andreu to Matthews, 19 March 1957, in HLMP, Box 1, Folder 26

15 Nicolás Rivero to Matthews, 17 March 1957, in HLMP, Box 1, Folder 26

16 26th July Movement, Santiago de Cuba, to Matthews, 13 March 1957, in HLMP, Box 1, Folder 26

17 Faure Chomón Mediavilla and Victor Bravo (Revolutionary Directory) to Matthews, 17 April 1957, in HLMP, Box 1, Folder 26

18 J. A. Valladares to Matthews, 1 March 1957, in HLMP, Box 1, Folder 26. See also Rene L. Diaz to Matthews, 25 February 1957, and Mario D. Masip to Matthews, 22 April 1957, in HLMP, Box 1, Folder 26

19 Betancourt to Matthews, 27 March 1957, in HLMP, Box 1, Folder 26. See also Arnaldo G. Barrón to Matthews, c. 5 March 1957, in HLMP, Box 1, Folder 26

20 Arthur Steinmetz to Matthews, 24 February 1957, in HLMP, Box 1, Folder 26

21 DePalma, *The Man Who Invented Fidel*, 107

22 Matthews, *The Cuban Story*, 50–1; DePalma, *The Man Who Invented Fidel*, 118

23 Matthews to Turner Catledge, 4 March 1957, in HLMP, Box 1, Folder 26

24 Matthews to William M. Porter, 1 March 1957, in HLMP, Box 1, Folder 26. For the invitation, see Porter to Matthews, 1 March 1957

25 Teresa Casuso, *Cuba and Castro* (New York: Random House, 1961), 126–7

26 DePalma, *The Man Who Invented Fidel*, 115

27 Matthews, *The Cuban Story*, 49

28 Guevara, 'One Year of Combat', *El Cubano Libre*, no. 3 (January 1958), available at www.hartford-hwp.com/archives/43b/066.html (accessed 16 January 2021)

30. Fidel's Secret Weapons

1 Guerra, *Heroes, Martyrs, and Political Messiahs*, 245

2 Guerra, *Heroes, Martyrs, and Political Messiahs*, 245

3 Leonard Ray Teel, *Reporting the Cuban Revolution: How Castro Manipulated American Journalists* (Baton Rouge: Louisiana State University Press, 2015), 61–4; DePalma, *The Man Who Invented Fidel*, 116–17; Hulme, *Cuba's Wild East*, 348–52

4 DePalma, *The Man Who Invented Fidel*, 117

5 Teel, *Reporting the Cuban Revolution*, 64

6 Guerra, *Heroes, Martyrs, and Political Messiahs*, 245

7 Guerra, *Heroes, Martyrs, and Political Messiahs*, 246; Teel, *Reporting the Cuban Revolution*, 69, 103–4

8 Teel, *Reporting the Cuban Revolution*, 84

9 Andrew St George, 'How I Found Castro, the Cuban Guerrilla', *Cavalier*, October 1957, 58, quoted in Teel, *Reporting the Cuban Revolution*, 85–6

10 Teel, *Reporting the Cuban Revolution*, 85–6

11 Guerra, *Heroes, Martyrs, and Political Messiahs*, 251–2

12 Teel, *Reporting the Cuban Revolution*, 114–17

13 Teel, *Reporting the Cuban Revolution*, 117

14 Matthews, 'Castro Rebels Gain In Face of Offensive By the Cuban Army', *New York Times*, 9 June 1957, 1

15 Matthews, 'Castro's Anniversary', *New York Times*, 2 December 1957, 26

16 Matthews, 'Cuba Seen on Eve of Grave Events', *New York Times*, 23 March 1958, E10

17 Teel, *Reporting the Cuban Revolution*, 105; DePalma, *The Man Who Invented Fidel*, 126–9

18 DePalma, *The Man Who Invented Fidel*, 139–40, 143; Matthews, *The Cuban Story*, 88

19 Perrottet, *Cuba Libre!*, 327–9; DePalma, *The Man Who Invented Fidel*, 150–1

20 Matthews, 'Castro Aims Reflect Character of Cubans', *New York Times*, 18 January 1959, E6

21 DePalma, *The Man Who Invented Fidel*, 153

22 Simon Hall, *1956: The World in Revolt* (London: Faber & Faber, 2016), 369. On the position of the Popular Socialist Party (official name of the Cuban Communist Party), see Samuel Farber, 'The Cuban Communists in the Early Stages of the Cuban Revolution: Revolutionaries of Reformists', *Latin American Research Review*, vol. 18, no. 1 (1983), 59–83

23 Teel, *Reporting the Cuban Revolution*, 1–4, 9. On Chapelle, see 171–2

31. 'Comrade Matthews'

1 'Telegram from the Embassy in Cuba to the Department of State, 14 July 1959', in *Foreign Relations of the United States, 1958–1960, Volume VI: Cuba*, at https://history.state.gov/historicaldocuments/frus1958-60v06/d333 (accessed 30 June 2023)

2 Matthews, 'Cuba Has a One-Man Rule And It Is Called Non-Red', *New York Times*, 16 July 1959, 1, 2

3 Rough draft of summary of conversation between the vice president and Fidel Castro, 10 April 1959, in *Diplomatic History*, vol. 4, no. 4 (Fall 1980), 431. For a discussion of Nixon's meeting with Fidel, see Jeffrey J. Safford, 'The Nixon-Castro Meeting of 19 April 1959', *Diplomatic History*, vol. 4, no. 4 (Fall 1980), 425–31

4 Alan McPherson, 'The Limits of Populist Diplomacy: Fidel Castro's April 1959 Trip to North America', *Diplomacy and Statecraft*, vol. 18, no. 1 (2007), 237–8; Perrottet, *Cuba Libre!*, 330–2; DePalma, *The Man Who Invented Fidel*, 154–62

5 Alan McPherson, 'The Limits of Populist Diplomacy', 244, 247

6 Hall, *Ten Days in Harlem*, 21–3

7 Hall, *Ten Days in Harlem*, 23–4

8 Hall, *Ten Days in Harlem*, 24–5

9 For a comprehensive account of this trip, see Hall, *Ten Days in Harlem*. See also Brenda Gayle Plummer, 'Castro in Harlem: A Cold War Watershed', in Allen Hunter, ed., *Rethinking the Cold War* (Philadelphia: Temple University Press, 1997), chapter 6

10 Hall, *Ten Days in Harlem*, 65–70, 121–31

11 Anthony DePalma, 'Myths of the Enemy: Castro, Cuba and Herbert L. Matthews of the *New York Times*', Working Paper #313 – July 2004, Helen Kellogg Institute for International Studies, 11, available at https://kellogg.nd.edu/sites/default/files/old_files/documents/313_0.pdf (accessed 12 October 2023)

12 DePalma, *The Man Who Invented Fidel*, 196–7; William F. Buckley Jr, 'I Got My Job Through the *New York Times*', *American Legion Magazine*, vol. 70, no. 3 (March 1961), 18, 19, 46–8, available at https://archive.legion.org/node/1942

13 Nathaniel Weyl, *Red Star Over Cuba: The Russian Assault on the Western Hemisphere* (New York: The Devlin-Adair Company, 1960), 133, 169

14 Theodore Draper, *Castro's Revolution: Myths and Realities* (London: Thames and Hudson, 1962), 171

15 Weyl, *Red Star Over Cuba*, 170

16 DePalma, *The Man Who Invented Fidel*, 158–9; Matthews letter to Theodore Draper in Draper, *Castro's Revolution*, 196

17 Richard E. Welch Jr, 'Herbert L. Matthews and the Cuban Revolution', *The Historian*, vol. 47, no. 1 (November 1984), 5

18 DePalma, *The Man Who Invented Fidel*, 190–1

19 DePalma, *The Man Who Invented Fidel*, 192

20 Walter Lippmann to Matthews, 18 December 1961, in HLMP, Box 1, Folder 16

21 Turner Catledge, *My Life and The Times* (New York: Harper & Row, 1971), 265–8; Thomas G. Paterson, *Contesting Castro: The United States and the Triumph of the Cuban Revolution* (New York: Oxford University Press, 1994), 80; Hulme, *Cuba's Wild East*, 334–5; DePalma, *The Man Who Invented Fidel*, 199–200; Jerry W. Knudson, *Roots of Revolution: The Press and Social Change in Latin America* (Lanham, MD: University Press of America, 2010), 80, 82

22 Welch Jr, 'Herbert L. Matthews and the Cuban Revolution', 13

23 DePalma, *The Man Who Invented Fidel*, 195

24 José Luis Massó, 'Matthews Again', n.d., in HLMP, Box 6, Folder 2

25 'Herbert Matthews en Puerto Rico', 10, in HLMP, Box 6, Folder 2

26 'Grupo Cubanos Mota Piquete a Matthews', 11, in HLMP, Box 6, Folder 2

27 Matthews, *A World in Revolution*, 324–5, and Matthews's contemporaneous notes of the incident in HLMP, Box 9, Folder 10 (quote from p. 1)

ENDNOTES

28 Testimony of Whiting Willauer, 27 July 1962, in *Communist Threat to the United States Through the Caribbean: Hearing Before the Subcommittee to Investigate the Administration of Internal Security Act and Other Security Laws*, 883

29 Testimony of Arthur Gardner, 27 August 1960, in *Communist Threat to the United States Through the Caribbean: Hearing Before the Subcommittee to Investigate the Administration of Internal Security Act and Other Security Laws*, Part 9, 663–80, available at www.cia.gov/readingroom/docs/CIA-RDP91-00965R000200030001-5.pdf (accessed 7 July 2023)

30 Matthews to Ernest Hemingway, 2 January 1961, in HLMP, Box 2, Folder 6

31 Matthews, *The Cuban Story*, 50

32 Matthews, *The Cuban Story*, 290

33 Matthews, *The Cuban Story*, 288

34 Matthews, *Education of a Correspondent*, 11–12

35 Matthews, *The Cuban Story*, 303

36 Matthews, *The Cuban Story*, 311

32. Venceremos!

1 'The Declaration of Havana', 2 September 1960, at www.walterlippmann.com/fc-09-02-1960.html (accessed 5 July 2023)

2 John A. Gronbeck-Tedesco, 'The Left in Transition: The Cuban Revolution in US Third World Politics', *Journal of Latin American Studies*, vol. 40, no. 4 (November 2008), 659–60; Manuel Barcia, 'Locking Horns with the Northern Empire: Anti-American Imperialism at the Conference of 1966 in Havana', *The Journal of Transatlantic Studies*, vol. 7, no. 3 (2009), 208–17; Jonathan C. Brown, *Cuba's Revolutionary World* (Cambridge, MA: Harvard University Press, 2017), 97–8; Robert Buzzanco, 'Fidel Castro (1926–2016) and Global Solidarity', *The Sixties: A Journal of History, Politics and Culture*, vol. 10, no. 2, 275; 'Resolutions Adopted by the Conference' at www.latinamericanstudies.org/tricon/tricon5.htm (accessed 2 July 2019). See also Ali Raza, 'Dispatches from Havana: The Cold War, Afro-Asian Solidarities, and Culture Wars in Pakistan', *Journal of World History*, vol. 30, no. 1–2 (June 2019), 223–46

3 Piero Gleijeses, 'Cuba and the Cold War, 1959–1980', in Melvyn P. Leffler and Odd Arne Westad, eds, *The Cambridge History of the Cold War, Volume II, Crises and Détente* (Cambridge: Cambridge University Press, 2010), 330–3, 340–1; Gleijeses, *Conflicting Missions: Havana, Washington, and Africa, 1959–1976* (Chapel Hill: University of North Carolina Press, 2002), 21; Jorge I. Domínguez, *To Make a World Safe for Revolution: Cuba's Foreign Policy* (Cambridge, MA: Harvard University Press, 1989), 119–26; Chomsky, *A History of the Cuban Revolution*, 100–5. For a detailed history of Cuba's promotion and support of liberation movements and socialist revolution overseas, see Gleijeses, *Conflicting Missions*, and Jonathan C. Brown, *Cuba's Revolutionary World*. On Havana's attempts to fashion a global anti-imperialist movement, see, for example, Manuel Barcia, 'Locking Horns with the Northern Empire', 208–17

4 Gleijeses, 'Cuba and the Cold War, 1959–1980', 335

ENDNOTES

5 Chomsky, *A History of the Cuban Revolution*, 134–6; Devyn Spence Benson, *Antiracism in Cuba: The Unfinished Revolution* (Chapel Hill: University of North Carolina Press, 2016), 1–3; Guerra, *Visions of Power in Cuba: Revolution, Redemption, and Resistance, 1959–1971* (Chapel Hill: University of North Carolina Press, 2012), 54–6

6 The most famous revisionist critique of Castro's Cuba and race is Carlos Moore, *Castro, the Blacks, and Africa* (Los Angeles: Center for Afro-American Studies, University of California, Los Angeles, 1988). See also Guerra, *Visions of Power in Cuba*, 265–78. For a concise summary of the historiographical debate, see Benson, *Antiracism in Cuba*, 18–21

7 Timothy B. Tyson, *Radio Free Dixie: Robert F. Williams & the Roots of Black Power* (Chapel Hill: University of North Carolina Press, 1999), 221; Van Gosse, *Where the Boys Are: Cuba, Cold War America and the Making of a New Left* (New York: Verso, 1993), 120–1; Adam Clayton Powell Jr, *Adam by Adam: The Autobiography of Adam Clayton Powell Jr* (New York: Kensington Publishing, 1994), 189–94

8 Gosse, *Where the Boys Are*, 122. On the wider history of Cuba and Afro-America, see, for instance, Manning Marable, 'Race and Revolution in Cuba: African American Perspectives', *Souls*, vol. 1, no. 2 (1999), 6–17; Lisa Brock and Digna Castañeda Fuertes, eds, *Between Race and Empire: African-Americans and Cubans Before the Cuban Revolution* (Philadelphia: Temple University Press, 1998) – which contains 'The African-American Press Greets the Cuban Revolution' by Van Gosse, 266–80; Gronbeck-Tedesco, *Cuba, the United States, and Cultures of the Transnational Left, 1930–1975* (Cambridge: Cambridge University Press, 2015), 198–234; Besenia Rodriguez, '"De la Esclavitud Yanqui a la Libertad Cubana": US Black Radicals, the Cuban Revolution, and the Formation of a Tricontinental Ideology', *Radical History Review*, 92 (Spring 2005), 62–87; Cynthia A. Young, *Soul Power: Culture, Radicalism, and the Making of a US Third World Left* (Durham: Duke University Press, 2006), especially 18–53; Young, 'Havana Up in Harlem: LeRoi Jones, Harold Cruse and the Making of a Cultural Revolution', *Science & Society*, vol. 65, no. 1 (Spring 2001), 12–38; and H. Timothy Lovelace Jr, 'William Worthy's Passport: Travel Restrictions and the Cold War Struggle for Civil and Human Rights', *Journal of American History* (June 2016), 107–31

9 Thomas J. Sugrue, *Sweet Land of Liberty: The Forgotten Struggle for Civil Rights in the North* (New York: Random House, 2009), xv; Matthew D. Lassiter, 'De Jure/ De Facto Segregation: The Long Shadow of a National Myth', in Matthew D. Lassiter and Joseph Crespino, eds, *The Myth of Southern Exceptionalism* (New York: Oxford University Press, 209), 25–48; Chin Jou, 'Neither Welcomed, Nor Refused: Race and Restaurants in Postwar New York City', *Journal of Urban History*, vol. 40, no. 2 (2014), 232–51; Brian Purnell, 'Desegregating the Jim Crow North: Racial Discrimination in the Postwar Bronx and the Fight to Integrate the Castle Hill Beach Club (1953–1973)', *Afro-Americans in New York Life and History*, vol. 33, no. 2 (July 2009), 47–78. See also Brian Purnell and Jeanne Theoharis, 'Histories of Racism and Resistance, Seen and Unseen: How and Why to Think about the Jim Crow North', in Brian Purnell and Jeanne Theoharis, eds, *The Strange Careers of the*

426

Jim Crow North: Segregation and Struggle outside of the South (New York: New York University Press, 2019), 1–42

10 Hall, *1956: The World in Revolt* (London: Faber & Faber, 2016), 248–51, 386. There was, in fact, a long history of African Americans identifying with Cuba's struggles against racism. See, for instance, Lovelace Jr, 'William Worthy's Passport', 112; Brock and Castañeda Fuertes, eds, *Between Race and Empire*; and Frank Andre Guridy, *Forging Diaspora: Afro-Cubans and African Americans in a World of Empire and Jim Crow* (Chapel Hill: University of North Carolina Press, 2010)

11 Tyson, *Radio Free Dixie*, especially 149, 150–65; Robert F. Williams, 'The Streets of Cuba', *The Crusader*, 3 September 1960; Besenia Rodriguez, 'De la Esclavitud Yanqui a la Libertad Cubana', 73–8

12 Translation of interview with Robert F. Williams while in Cuba, published in *Revolución*, 14 July 1960; translation by Paul Joseph Lalli, 1 August 1960, in Fair Play for Cuba Committee, FBI file, 99-4196-91, 3

13 Postcard to Irene Rose, sent 6 July 1960, Richard T. Gibson Papers, Box 12, Folder 11, Gelman Library, George Washington University

14 Statement by John Henrik Clarke, July 1960, John Henrik Clarke Papers, Box 35, Folder 24, Schomburg; Lovelace Jr, 'William Worthy's Passport', 113. Worthy travelled to Cuba several times and was eventually convicted for violating the State Department's travel ban, a verdict that he overturned in the US Supreme Court.

15 Julian Mayfield to 'Maga', 25 September 1960, in Julian Mayfield Papers, Box 7, Folder 2, Schomburg

16 Gosse, *Where the Boys Are*, 162–3

17 Quoted in Teishan A. Latner, *Cuban Revolution in America: Havana and the Making of a United States Left, 1968–1992* (Chapel Hill: University of North Carolina Press, 2018), 17

18 Arthur M. Schlesinger Jr, *A Thousand Days: John F. Kennedy in the White House* (Boston: Houghton Mifflin, 1965), 220

19 Latner, *Cuban Revolution in America*, 12

20 Eric Hobsbawm, 'The Cuban Revolution and Its Aftermath', in Leslie Bethell, ed., *Viva La Revolución: Eric Hobsbawm on Latin America* (London: Little, Brown, 2016), 262

21 William Rowlandson, *Sartre in Cuba – Cuba in Sartre* (Cham, Switzerland: Palgrave Macmillan, 2018), 2

22 Rowlandson, *Sartre in Cuba – Cuba in Sartre*, 4

23 Rowlandson, *Sartre in Cuba – Cuba in Sartre*, 4–5, 59

24 Rowlandson, *Sartre in Cuba – Cuba in Sartre*, 50–2; Jean-Paul Sartre, *Sartre on Cuba* (Westport, CT: Greenwood Press, 1974), 94, 98–9

25 Rowlandson, *Sartre in Cuba – Cuba in Sartre*, 5; Sartre, *Sartre on Cuba*, 138–9

26 Carlos Franqui, *Family Portrait with Fidel* (New York: Random House, 1984), 68

27 Rowlandson, *Sartre in Cuba – Cuba in Sartre*, 4–5

28 Eugene Wolters, 'Incredible Candid Photos of Jean-Paul Sartre and Simone de Beauvoir in Cuba', 20 June 2014, at www.critical-theory.com/incredible-candid-photos-of-jean-paul-sartre-and-simone-de-beauvoir-in-cuba/ (accessed 4 March

2019); Rowlandson, *Sartre in Cuba – Cuba in Sartre*, 97; Simone de Beauvoir, *Force of Circumstance* (London: Penguin, 1983), 503

29 Rowlandson, *Sartre in Cuba – Cuba in Sartre*, 30

30 Rowlandson, *Sartre in Cuba – Cuba in Sartre*, 53, 54, 55

31 Rowlandson, *Sartre in Cuba – Cuba in Sartre*, 33; Sartre, *Sartre on Cuba*, 44

32 Sartre, *Sartre on Cuba*, 146

33 LeRoi Jones, 'Cuba Libre', in Rosemari Mealy, *Fidel & Malcolm X: Memories of a Meeting* (Baltimore: Black Classic Press, 2013), 62–78 (originally published in *Evergreen Review*, November/December 1960); Gosse, *Where the Boys Are*, 183–7

34 Bill Morgan, ed., *An Accidental Autobiography: The Selected Letters of Gregory Corso* (New York: New Directions Publishing, 2003), 263–4; Barry Miles, *Ginsberg: Beat Poet* (London: Virgin Books, 2010), 272, 337–48, 349–51; Michael Schumacher, *Dharma Lion: A Critical Biography of Allen Ginsberg* (New York: St. Martin's Press, 1992), 419–28; Morgan, *I Celebrate Myself: The Somewhat Private Life of Allen Ginsberg* (London: Penguin, 2006), 402–3; José Quiroga, *Cuban Palimpsests* (Minneapolis: University of Minnesota Press, 2005), 235 n. 28. On the Cuban government's sustained campaign against homosexuals, see, for instance, Guerra, *Visions of Power in Cuba*, 227–9, 245–55

35 Rowlandson, *Sartre in Cuba – Cuba in Sartre*, 88–9. The protest was triggered by the arrest and humiliation of the poet Heberto Padilla. See Guerra, *Visions of Power in Cuba*, 353–60

36 Tyson, *Radio Free Dixie*, 285, 292–4; letter, Robert F. Williams to Castro, 28 August 1966, Richard T. Gibson Papers, Box 13, Folder 5, George Washington University

37 Kepa Artaraz and Karen Luyckx, 'The French New Left and the Cuban Revolution 1959–1971: Parallel Histories?', *Modern and Contemporary France*, vol. 17, no. 1 (2009), 71

38 Deutschmann and Shnookal, eds, *Fidel Castro Reader*, 12, 285

39 Mark Kurlansky, *1968: The Year that Rocked the World* (London: Jonathan Cape, 2004), 149; Timothy Scott Brown, *West Germany and the Global Sixties: The Anti-Authoritarian Revolt, 1962–1978* (Cambridge: Cambridge University Press, 2013), 234

40 See Sarah Seidman, 'Tricontinental Routes of Solidarity: Stokely Carmichael in Cuba', *Journal of Transnational American Studies*, vol. 4, no. 2 (2012)

41 Gronbeck-Tedesco, 'The Left in Transition', 665

42 Latner, *Cuban Revolution in America*, 47–8

43 'Solidarity with Latin America', in Stokely Carmichael, *Stokely Speaks* (Chicago: Chicago Review Press, 2007), 101, 104–5

44 Angela Davis, *Angela Davis: An Autobiography* (London: Arrow Books, 1976), 202–10, 216

45 Latner, *Cuban Revolution in America*, 4–9. See also Gronbeck-Tedesco, 'The Left in Transition', 651–73; Anne Garland Mahler, 'The Global South in the Belly of the Beast: Viewing African American Civil Rights through a Tricontinental Lens', *Latin American Research Review*, vol. 50, no. 1 (2015), 95–116; and Young, *Soul Power*, 8–9, 20–1, 23–53

46 Tom Hayden, *Listen, Yankee! Why Cuba Matters* (New York: Seven Stories Press, 2015), 111. See also 103, 7–8

47 See 'The Venceremos Brigades, Cuba, and the US Left', in Latner, *Cuban Revolution in America*, 27–74

48 Latner, *Cuban Revolution in America*, 35

49 Hayden, *Listen, Yankee!*, 110; Mark Rudd, '1968: Organizing vs. Activism' at www.markrudd.com/index5cf2 (accessed 6 July 2023)

50 FBI Files: Weatherman (Part 1B), 2, at www.sds-1960s.org/sds_wuo/weather/weath1b.pdf (accessed 6 July 2023)

51 Matthews, *The Cuban Story*, 88; DePalma, *The Man Who Invented Fidel*, 158

52 Paterson, *Contesting Castro*, 80

Epilogue

1 Mao, 'Revolutionary Forces of the World Unite, Fight Against Imperialist Aggression!', *For a Lasting Peace, For a People's Democracy*, 21 (1948), available at www.marxists.org/reference/archive/mao/selected-works/volume-4/mswv4_44.htm (accessed 1 August 2023)

2 Service, *Comrades! A History of World Communism*, 345; Report to the TsK KPSS from S. Pavlov, Secretary of the TsK VLKSM (All-Union Young Communists League), regarding a visit of the VLKSM delegation to Cuba, February 1961, in *Fond 89: The Soviet Communist Party on Trial*, reel 1.999, Opisi 28, File 5. I am grateful to Robert Hornsby for translating the relevant portions of this document for me.

3 Eric Hobsbawm, *The Age of Extremes: 1914–1991*, 4, 56

4 https://en.wikipedia.org/wiki/Statue_of_Lenin_at_Finland_Station; Brandon Taylor, 'Later Soviet Sculpture', *Third Text*, vol. 51 (Summer 2000), 48–9; Victoria E. Bonnell, 'The Leader's Two Bodies: A Study in the Iconography of the "Vozhd"', *Russian History*, vol. 23, no. 1/4 (1996), 124

5 For a good summary of Snow's politics, see Snow, 'Why I Am for Wallace' (24 February 1948), ESP, Folder 266

6 On Stevenson, see Ross D. Mackenzie, 'Matthews on Campus: Cuba, Castro, and Communists', *Yale Daily News*, 6 December 1960, 1. The paper was reporting on Matthews having taken up a prestigious Chubb Fellowship at Yale's Timothy Dwight College. See HLMP, Box 9, Folder 11

7 Friedman cited in Paine, 'Edgar Snow and Shaping US Perceptions of the Chinese Civil War', 131

8 Trotsky, *The History of the Russian Revolution*, 1199

9 James Rodgers, *Assignment Moscow: Reporting on Russia from Lenin to Putin* (London: I. B. Tauris, 2020), 19; Draper, *The Roots of American Communism*, 115

10 Shewmaker, *Americans and Chinese Communists*, 58; Paine, 'Edgar Snow and Shaping US Perceptions of the Chinese Civil War', 133–4; Nicholas R. Clifford, 'White China, Red China: Lighting Out for the Territory with Edgar Snow', *New England Review*, vol. 18, no. 2 (Spring 1997), 103. According to Clifford, *Red Star Over China* 'has done more than any other single work to fix the image of Chinese Communism in the American mind'

ENDNOTES

11 Peter Novick, *That Noble Dream: The 'Objectivity Question' and the American Historical Profession* (Cambridge: Cambridge University Press, 1988), 42–3, 161–3

12 Reed, *Ten Days*, 13

13 Snow, *RSOC*, 35; Hamilton, *Edgar Snow*, 147

14 DePalma, *The Man Who Invented Fidel*, 153; Matthews, *World in Revolution*, 19

INDEX

Page numbers followed by 'n' refer to a footnote on the same page.

26th of July Movement (Cuba): ambushing and treatment by Batista's troops, 334–5; arrest and imprisonment in Mexico, 289–90; Batista's troops attack landing party, 296–7; Battle of La Plata, 314; donations to, 292, 338; expansion, 287–8, 290, 334; foreign correspondents as 'secret weapon', 332, 338–9; formation, 282; in Havana, 314; Matthews's *Times* report on *see under* Matthews, Herbert; Moncada Barracks attack, 282–4; other documentaries and reports on, 332–5, 339; overthrow Batista, 337; praise Matthews's *Times* report, 329; regroup at Cinco Palmas, 298; run aground at Playa las Coloradas, 295–6; Santiago de Cuba uprising, 294–5; Sierra Maestra base, 313, 319–22, 332–5, 346–7; sugar crop burning, 335; tactical alliances, 290–2, 338; training in Mexico, 288–9; trial and prison sentence for Moncada Barracks attack, 284–5; US students join, 330, 332; voyage on *Granma* to Cuba, 275–6, *291*, 293–5, *294*, 312, 371

Afro-American (newspaper), 357–8
Alegría de Pío, 296–7
Alerta (newspaper), 292
Alexander II, Tsar of Russia, 14
Alexander III, Tsar of Russia, 14
Alexandra, Tsarina of Russia, 10
All-Russian Congress of Soviets of Workers' and Soldiers' Deputies: Second All-Russian Congress opening, 94–6, 97, 100–1; Third All-Russian Congress opening, 108, 118
Allen, Jay, 308, 308n
Almeida, Juan, 297, 334
Amba Aradam, Battle of, 305
American Federation of Labor (AFL), 139–40
American Legion Magazine, 345
The American Magazine, 60–1

American Red Cross Mission, 107
American Socialist Party, 59, 132
An-chia-pan, 247–8
Ansai, 233
'The April Theses' (Lenin), 49–51
Armand, Inessa, 9, 27
Atlantic (magazine), 255
Auténtico Party (Cuba), 278
'Autumn Harvest Uprising' (Hunan), 170–1
Axelrod, Pavel, 75

Badoglio, Pietro, 306
Baku, 140, 143–4, 145
Balabanova, Angelika, 21, 145, 145n
Bao'an, 239–41, 243, 244–5
Baraka, Amiri, 363
Barrett, Edward W., 328
Batista, Fulgencio: attempts to extradite Castro, 289–90; Castro on, 282, 284; failed assassination attempt, 338; first presidency of Cuba, 277; grants amnesty to 26th of July Movement prisoners, 285; overthrown by revolutionaries, 337; response to Matthews's scoop on Castro, 326–7, 331; second presidency of Cuba, 278, 282, 334–5, 338; unwillingness to ban Matthews from Cuba, 336n
Battle of Amba Aradam, 305
Battle of La Plata, 314
Battle of Lazikou Pass, 203
Battle of Loushan Pass, 194
Battle of Xiang River, 180–2
Bayo, Alberto, 289
Beatty, Bessie, 96
Beatty, Warren: *Reds* (film), 152
Beauvoir, Simone de, 361–2, 363
Beijing: Japanese invasion, 251, 256; Mao in, 165–6; Peking University, 166; Snow in, 219–21, 265; student demonstration, 221; student protests at, 166n
Beijing – Bao'an journey (Snow), *228*; Ansai to Pai Chia P'ing, 233; arrival at Bao'an, 239;

co-travellers and escorts, 229, 230–1, 237; departure, 209–10, 224; first encounter with Red warrior, 232–3; interviews en route, 233–5; packing and supplies, 209–10, 231; in Pai Chia P'ing, 233–5; Pai Chia P'ing to Bao'an, 237–9; planning and permissions, 209, 223–4, 227–8; village hospitality en route, 231–2, 237–8; in Xi'an, 225–8; Xi'an to Yan'an, 229–30; Yan'an to Ansai, 231–3

Beloostrov, 43, 81

Berlin, 35–6, 364

Bern: Grigory Zinoviev in, 21; Lenin addresses meeting before departure, 27; Zimmerwald Conference, 18–19

Betancourt, Ernesto F., 329

Birchall, Frederick T., 303

Blum, Oscar, 29

Bo Gu, 160, 186, 190–1, 192, 241, 244, 244n

Bohemia (magazine), 286, 313

Bolsheviks: accompany Lenin on Zurich – Petrograd journey, 28; arrests by Provisional Government in July Days, 86, 86n; under attack from Tsarist secret police, 19; Bolshevik Central Committee, 21, 49; Cheka (secret police), 134, 137; commandeer Matilda Kshesinskaya's mansion, 47; greet Lenin at Beloostrov, 42–3; greet Lenin at Petrograd, 44–8; growing support for, 86–7; hiring gangs of robbers, 16; Lenin agitates for revolution amongst, 16; Lenin's long speech to at Kshesinskaya's mansion, 48–9; and Mensheviks, split of RSDLP, 15, 21; moderate line taken by, 42, 48, 51, 52; October Revolution events, 88–101; *Pravda* (newspaper), 19, 20, 42, 49, 51, 52, 142; threatened by Provisional Government, 89–90, 91; two-stage theory of revolution, 51; withdraw from Provisional Council of the Russian Republic, 84

Boni, Albert, 124–5

Boni & Liveright publishers, 124–6, *126*

Bonsal, Philip, 340

Braun, Otto, 160, 186, 190, 191–2, 195, 202

Britain: ambassador to Russia (George Buchanan), 10–11, 41, 53; ambassador to Sweden (Esmé Howard), 40–1; military/naval activities, 25, 68, 69, 71; officials in Finland, 40–2; officials in Nova Scotia, 29, 69

Brockdorff-Rantzau, Ulrich von, 25

Broński, Mieczysław, 9

Bryant, Louise:
CHARACTERISTICS: Reed on, 64

JOURNALISM: *The Masses*, 57–8, 64; *New York American*, 58; reporting Great War, 58; *Spectator*, 63

LIFE: childhood and education, 63; in Croton, New York, 64–5; death, 144n; first days in Petrograd, 82–4; interview with Mathew C. Smith, 145–6; journey to Russia *see* New York City – Petrograd journey; in Moscow, 141; portrayal in *Reds* (film), 152; Reed's death and funeral, 142–3; relationship with John Reed, 64–5, 113, 152; returns to New York City, 109; witnesses October Revolution, 88, 90, 91–101

QUOTED: on brewing revolution(s), 66–7; on the February Revolution, 57–8; on Hotel Angleterre, Petrograd, 82; on 'Red Petrograd', 81; on Reed, 141, 144–5; on Reed's funeral, 143; on revolutionary soldiers in Finland, 78

Buchanan, Sir George, 10–11, 41, 53

Buck, Pearl S., 220

Buckley, Henry, 308

Buckley, William F. Jr, 345

Bühring, Ulrich von, 29–31, 33

Bukharin, Nikolai, 142

Bulletin de la Presse (newspaper summary), 124

Bureau of International Revolutionary Propaganda, Russia, 105–7, 142

Burma: Snow in, 216

Cárdenas, Lázaro, 290

Carmichael, Stokely, 364–5

Carmon, Walt, 148

Carney, William P., 307, 309

Castro, Fidel, *273*
CHARACTERISTICS: broken English, 333; charisma, 359, 367; cigar smoking, *273*, 285, *321*; dress, 280, 342; energy, 280, 336; hair and facial hair, 280, 320, 342; intensity, 320; leadership qualities, 321, 341; oratory style, 280, 284, 287; physique, 320; rebellious streak, 279–80

GOVERNMENT OF: anti-racism policies (and limits of), 357–9, 363–4; authoritarianism, 343, 363; Declaration of Havana, 355; economic intervention and nationalism, 342–3; links with communism, 343, 344–5, 347–8; repression of homosexuals, 363; supports global liberation and revolutionary movements, 356–7, 364–5; takes power, 337

INFLUENCES: José Martí, 281; witnessing inequalities as a child, 279

LIFE: arrest and imprisonment in Mexico, 289–90; arrest during murder investigation,

280; attends Fifteenth General Assembly of the United Nations, 342; biography, 287; childhood and family, 278–80; education, 280; in Havana, 281–2; holds ceremony of thanks to foreign journalists, 339; interview with Herbert Matthews, 320–2, *321*, 346–7, 352; interview with Jules Dubois, 337; interview with Nixon, 340–1, 342; interviews with Taber and Hoffman, 332–3; leaves Cuba for Mexico, 285–6; legal work, 281, 282; meetings with Khrushchev, 344; meets Sartre and de Beauvoir, 361–2; in Mexico, 287; relationship with Mirta Díaz-Balart, 281; requests interview with foreign correspondent, 314; rumours of death at Alegría de Pío, 297, 314, 326, 327; trial and prison sentence for Moncada Barracks attack, 284–5; trip to North America (1959), *273*, 340–2, 346–7, 360; trip to US (1955), 287–8; trip to US (1960), 342–4

QUOTED: on aims for revolutionary Cuba, 335, 355; on barring Sartre and de Beauvoir, 363; on Batista regime and own political manifesto, 284; on Batista's coup, 282; on bravery of foreign correspondents, 322, 333; on childhood farm, 279; on distancing from communism, 335–6; on ending the dictatorship, 321; on failed Moncado Barracks attack, 283; on futility of fighting national army head-on, 281; on identification with communism, 347, 361; on intention to start the revolution, 292; on Nixon's attitude, 342; on October Revolution, 368, 368n; on prison comrades, 285; on reasons for leaving Cuba, 286; on reunion with Raúl at Cinco Palmas, 298; on revolutionary purpose of 26th of July Movement, 288; on strength of Sierra Maestra base, 320, 322, 333; on taking the fight to Havana, 333; on *Ten Days That Shook the World*, 368n; on tricking Matthews at Sierra Maestra base, 347; on wish to meet New Yorkers, 341–2

REVOLUTIONARY ACTIVITY: agrees to unite with Student's Revolutionary Directorate, 290–2; creates 26th of July Movement, 282; distributes manifesto, 288; fights dictatorship in Dominican Republic, 281; Moncado Barracks attack, 282–4; prepares to stand for Orthodox Party, 282; rally at grave of Eduardo Chibás, 282; recruits Alberto Bayo, 289; recruits Che Guevara, 287–8; student radicalism, 280–1; takes power, 337; *see also* 26th of July Movement (Cuba)

Castro, Raúl, 275, 285, 296, 298, 320, 363
Catledge, Turner, 328, 330, 348, 349
Cavalier (magazine), 334
cave dwellings, Shaanxi province, 230, 232, 237
CCP *see* Chinese Communist Party (CCP)
Central Daily (newspaper), 178
Cerf, Bennett, 254
Changsha, 162–3, 167, 169
Chapelle, Dickey, 339
Cheka (Bolshevik secret police), 134, 137
Chen Chang-Feng, 198, 203
Chernyshevsky, Nikolay, 14
Chester, Edmund, 327
Chiang Kai-shek: appointed commander-in-chief of National Revolutionary Army, 170; attempts to crush communists, 159–60, 169–70, 172–4; avoids conflict with Japan, 218, 220; flees to Taiwan, 262n; Herbert Matthews on, 303; kidnapping and release, 256; Snow on, 222; trip to rally support for Guomindang, 178; *see also* National Revolutionary Army (China)
Chibás, Eduardo, 280–1, 282
Chicago Daily News, 218
Chicago Tribune (newspaper), 127–8, 337
China: Ansai, 233; Bao'an, 239–41, 243, 244–5; Beijing *see* Beijing; Changsha, 162–3, 167, 169; An-chia-pan, 247–8; Dadu River, 196–8; flood, 217; food shortages, 162, 185, 215, 238; Fu-ts'un, 247; Gansu province, 203; Great Snow Mountains, 198–200; 'Green Gang', 170; Guangchang, 160; Guiyang, 193, 194; Guizhou province, 184–94; Hunan province, 160–1, 163–4, 168, 169, 170–1, 183–4; Jiangxi *see* Jiangxi; Jinggangshan, 171–3, 179n; Langshan (Mount Lang), 183–4; Lianghekou, 200–1; Liping, 186; Loess Plateau, 229–30; losses under Treaty of Versailles, 166n; Luding bridge, 196–8, 198n; Manchuria province, 217; medicines, 225–6; normalising relations with United States, 261n; poverty, 162, 185, 216, 238; Ruijin Library, 178, 181; Saratsi, 215; Shaanxi province *see* Shaanxi province; Shanghai *see* Shanghai; Sichuan province, 193, 195–203; Suiyuan province, 215, 215n; West's exploitation of, 213–14; Wu River, 187; Wuhan, 169; Xi'an, 225–8, 248–9; Xiang River, 180–2; Xiasiwan, 203; Yan'an, 230–1, 265; Yangtze River, 193, 217; Yunnan province, 216; Zunyi, 186–92
HOSTILITIES WITH JAPAN: Beijing, 251, 256; Japan's 'Strong China' policy, 215n; Jinan

occupation, 215; Manchuria, 217; propaganda and Red Army morale, 252n; Shanghai, 218, 256

MILITARY: National Revolutionary Army *see* National Revolutionary Army (China); Northern Expedition (of CCP – Guomindang United Front), 169–71; Red Army *see* Red Army (China)

POLITICS AND POWER: Chinese Communist Party (CCP) *see* Chinese Communist Party (CCP); creation of Chinese Soviet Republic, 173, 174; Guomindang *see* Guomindang; organisation of village soviets, 242; People's Republic of China establishment, 258; Qing government, 162, 163; Republic of China establishment, 163

REVOLUTIONARY MOVEMENTS AND ACTIVITIES: 'Autumn Harvest Uprising', 170–1; Changsha rice riots, 162–3; May Fourth Movement, 166–7; Northern Expedition of CCP – Guomindang United Front, 169–71; Poor People's League, 231, 247; student movement, 220–1; Wuchang uprising, 163

China Weekly Review (magazine), 214, 215–16

Chinese Communist Party (CCP): alliance with Guomindang, 167–8, 256, 258n; base at Bao'an, 239–41, 243, 244–5; Central Committee, 168, 169, 171, 192; establishes Red Army, 170; establishment and growth of, 167; ideological schism over peasantry, 169; Military Commission, 184–5, 201; military leadership overhaul, 192; Politburo, 171, 186–7, 192, 195; *see also* Red Army (China)

Chkheidze, Nikolai, 45–6

Christiana (now Oslo), 71, 111

Churchill, Winston, 31

Cienfugos, Camilo, 290

Clarke, John Henrik, 359

Cleveland, Ohio, 115

Colorado Fuel and Iron Company, 63

Comintern (Communist International), 132, 139–40, 145; Executive Committee (ECCI), 133, 137, 139

Communist Labor Party (CLP) (US), 132, 148n

Communist Party of the United States of America (CPUSA), 132, 148, 148n, 365

Congo-Brazzaville, 356–7

Coronet (journal), 334

Corso, Gregory, 363

Council of People's Commissars (Russia), 102

Cowley, Michael, 255

Crabb, Dan, 212–13

Croce, Benedetto, 353

Crosse, Edith 'Nancie', 301, 303, 316–18, 323, 337

Croton, New York, 64–5

Crusader (newsletter), 363

Cuba: Alegría de Pío, 296–7; Guantánamo Bay naval base, 276; Havana *see* Havana; inequalities, 276–7, 279; La Plata, 314; Manzanillo, 316, 318, 322–3; Moncado Barracks, 282–4; Playa las Coloradas, 295–6; Santiago de Cuba, 282–4, 294–5, 337; Sierra Maestra mountains, 313, 319–22, 332–5, 346–7; sugar production, 276, 277, 279, 290

POLITICS AND POWER: Auténtico Party, 278; Batista's first presidency, 277; Batista's second presidency, 278, 282, 334–5, 338; Castro's government *see under* Castro, Fidel; corruption, 277, 278; Cuban Communist Party (PCC), 278, 338; nationalist uprising, 281; Orthodox Party, 280–1, 282

RELATIONSHIP WITH UNITED STATES, 343; business relations sour, 342, 343; Cuba as virtual colony, 276; deteriorating political relationship with Castro, 342, 343–4; Senate Internal Security Subcommittee hearings on Cuba's communist threat, 350–2, 352n; US ambassador (Philip Bonsal), 340; US withdraws support for Batista regime, 338; work of Venceremos Brigade, 366

REVOLUTION: Batista is overthrown, 337; Battle of La Plata, 314; as inspiration for radicals worldwide, 357–62, 364–6; Matthews's *Times* report on *see under* Matthews, Herbert; Moncado Barracks attack, 282–4; other documentaries and reports on, 332–5, 339; role of foreign correspondents, 338–9; Santiago de Cuba uprising, 294–5; as world historical event, 355; *see also* 26th of July Movement (Cuba)

REVOLUTIONARY MOVEMENTS (OTHER): Cuban Communist Party (PCC), 278, 338; farmer network of Castro sympathisers, 298; growing opposition to Batista, 290, 334; Revolutionary Directorate, 338; student protests and radicalism, 278, 280, 281, 290; Students Revolutionary Directorate (SRD), 290–2, 329; urban-based opposition, 290, 338; violence towards army, 278

Cuban Communist Party (PCC), 278, 338

Dadu River, 196–8

Daily Herald (newspaper), 209, 250, 254

INDEX

Davis, Angela, 365
de la Mora, Constancia, 310
Debs, Eugene V., 59, 118
Delaprée, Louis, 308
Dell, Floyd, 127
DePalma, Anthony, 367
The Dial (magazine), 128
Díaz-Balart, Mirta, 281
Dohrn, Bernardine, 365
Dominguez, Guillermo, 334–5
Dominican Republic, 281
Dong Biwu, 199–200
Dong Leshan, 265
Draper, Theodore H., 346
Dryfoos, Orvil, 348
Dubois, Jules, 337, 339
Dutschke, Rudi, 364
Dzerzhinsky, 'Iron Felix', 134

Eastland, James O., 350
Eastman, Max, 61, 118–19, 120, 122n, 131–2,
    147; *Heroes I Have Known*, 121
Echeverría, José Antonio, 290–2, 323, 338
economic blockade (Great War), 25, 34, 71, 134
Eisenstein, Sergei: *October* (film), 152–3
Ethiopia: Second Italo-Ethiopian War, 304–7
Ewer, William Norman, 254
Executive Committee of the Comintern (ECCI),
    133, 137, 139

Die Fackel (newspaper), 105–6
Fair Play for Cuba Committee (US), 359, 359n
Fajardo, Manuel, 322
Faroe Islands, 69
February Revolution (Russia): events of, 11–12;
    Gregory Zinoviev learns of, 21; jubilation
    following, 13; Lenin learns of, 9, 19–20; Reed
    and Bryant's response to, 57–8, 75
Feigon, Lee: *Mao: A Reinterpretation*, 252n
Figes, Orlando, 14
Finland: independence, 39n, 84; Lenin flees to,
    86n; Lenin in, 16; Lenin's passage through, 42;
    political status, 16; Reed's first passage through,
    77–80; Reed's imprisonment in, 138; Reed's
    second passage through, 132–3; revolutionary
    soldiers in, 78; Tornio, 40, 41–2, 77–8
Finland Station, Petrograd, 44–6, 81, 370n
First World War *see* Great War
Flakserman, Galina, 89
Fleming, Peter, 254
food shortages: China, 162; Russia, 11, 12, 82,
    134, 135; Sweden, 72, 73

Foster Snow, Helen 'Peg':
    LIFE: in Beijing, 219; relationship with Edgar
        Snow, 219, 262
    QUOTED: on *Red Star Over China*, 251; on Snow,
        219, 249, 372n; on Snow's journey, 209–10
    WORK AND WRITING: founds Chinese
        Industrial Cooperatives, 372n; input to *Red
        Star Over China*, 251; *My China Years*, 372n; as
        'Nym Wales', 219n; trip to Red territory, 251
France: Paris, 303–4
France-Soir (newspaper), 362
Francis, David R., 109–10
Franco, Francisco, 307; *see also* Spain: Civil War
Frankfurt, 35
Franqui, Carlos, 326, 345, 362
French Information Bureau, Petrograd, 124
Friedman, Thomas L., 372
Fu-ts'un, 247

Ganetsky, Yakov, 22, 36, 37
Gansu province, 203
Gardner, Arthur, 350–1
Gellert, Hugo, 147
Germany: Berlin, 35–6, 364; Frankfurt, 35;
    Gottmadingen, 29–30; Great War losses and
    hardships, 23, 25, 34; International Vietnam
    Congress, 364; Lenin's passage through, 29–36;
    negotiations over Lenin's passage through, 23–
    6; Russian revolutionary propaganda directed
    towards, 105–6; Singen, 33; Social Democratic
    Party (SPD), 17, 23; Stuttgart, 34–5
Gibson, Richard, 359
Ginsberg, Allen, 363
Giovannitti, Arturo, 147
Gitlin, Todd, 150–1, 360
Gold, Mike, 113, 149
Goldman, Emma, 129, 137; *Living My Life*,
    144–5
Gompers, Samuel, 139
Gottmadingen, 29–30
Granma (cabin cruiser), 275–6, 291, 293–5, 294,
    312, 371
Granma (newspaper), 371
Great War: Bryant reports on, 58; conscription
    (US), 66; economic blockade, 25, 34, 71,
    134; German losses and hardships, 23, 25, 34;
    Haparanda (Sweden)'s strategic importance,
    39; Kerensky Offensive, 85; Lenin on, 17–18,
    23, 47, 48, 50; Norwegian hardships, 71–2;
    outbreak, 17; Reed (reports) on, 63, 65–6,
    71–2, 119–20; Russian losses and hardships,

435

10–11, 12, 23, 82, 85; socialist anti-war sentiment, 17–18; submarine warfare, 25, 65, 69; Swedish hardships, 72, 73; Treaty of Versailles, 166n

'Green Gang' (China), 170

Green, Henry, 58

Grimm, Robert, 18, 24, 26

Gruner, Harold, 41, 42n

Guangchang, 160

Guantánamo Bay naval base, 276

Guchkov, Alexander, 85

Guevara, Ernesto 'Che': on banking, 361; on Castro, 287; Ginsberg on, 363; injured at Alegría de Pío, 296–7; on La Plata victory, 314; on Matthews's interview, 322, 331, 332; recruited by Castro, 287–8; Sartre on, 362; slogan, 364

Guiyang, 193, 194

Guizhou province, 184–94

Gumberg, Alex, 96, 109

Guomindang (China): accepts aid from Soviet Union, 168; alliance with CCP, 167–8, 256, 258n; *Central Daily* (newspaper), 178; as de facto government of Republic of China, 169; military *see* National Revolutionary Army; *see also* Chiang Kai-shek

Halifax, Nova Scotia, 69

Haparanda, 39–40, 77

Harper's (magazine), 212

Harvard Monthly (magazine), 59

Harvard University, 58–9, 60, 360

Hatem, George, 227–8, 228n; accompanies Snow on journey to Bao'an, 229–32, 237–40

Havana: 26th of July Movement in, 314; Castro in, 281, 282; First Conference of the Latin American Solidarity Organisation, 365; Ginsberg in, 363; Matthews in, 323, 337; Sartre and de Beauvoir in, 361–2, 363; Tricontinental Conference, 356; University of, 280, 281, 343; Williams in, 363–4

Havana – Sierra Maestra journey (Matthews), 301, 315–19, 317, 325

Havana Post (newspaper),-315

Hawaii, 212

Hays, Arthur Garfield, 122n

Haywood, William Dudley 'Big Bill', 61, 62, 129

He Long, 251

He Zhuguo, 248

He Zizhen, 179, 193–4, 240

Hemingway, Ernest, 301, 308, 308n, 310, 323, 352, 372

Hing, Alex, 270

Hispanic American Historical Review (journal), 367

Hobsbawm, Eric, 361, 369, 369n

Hoffman, Wendell, 332–3, 339

Hoover, J. Edgar, 145, 259–60, 346n

Hotel Angleterre, Petrograd, 82

Hour (magazine), 281

Howard, Sir Esmé, 40–1

Howell, Clarence, 309

Hoy (newspaper), 371

Hsu Ping, 224

Hsu Teh-li, 241

Hu Yuzhi, 264

Huili, 195

Hunan province, 160–1, 163–4, 168, 169, 170–1, 183–4

Hunan Self-Study University, 167

Huysmans, Camille, 74–5

Ifft, George N., 111

Independent (newspaper), 114

India, 311

Industrial Workers of the World (IWW) (US), 59–60, 61–2, 64, 118, 129, 140

International Socialist Bureau, 74–5

'Internationale' (anthem), 29, 38, 135

Iskra (newspaper), 15, 24

Israel, Jerry, 372n

Italy, 304–7, 311

Jacobin (magazine), 152

Janson, Wilhelm, 34–5

Japan: hostilities with China *see under* China; Snow in, 213

Jerome, Charles, 58

Jiang Kanghu, 163

Jiangxi: base of First Front Red Army, 159, 160, 173–4; fate of those left behind, 179; Long March from *see* Long March (Jiangxi – Shaanxi);

Jiménez, Antonio Núñez, 313

Jinggangshan, 171–3, 179n

Jocelyn, Ed: *The Long March: The True Story [...]*, 198n

John Reed Clubs, 148–50

Johnson, Nelson T., 223–4

Jones, LeRoi, 363

Josephson, Matthew, 150

journeys: Castro *see* Tuxpan – Playa las Coloradas journey; Lenin *see* Zurich – Petrograd journey; Mao *see* Long March (Jiangxi – Shaanxi);

INDEX

Matthews *see* Havana – Sierra Maestra journey;
Reed *see* New York City – Petrograd journey;
Snow *see* Beijing – Bao'an journey
Joyce, James, 27
July Days (Russia, 1917), 86, 86n
Jung Chang: *Mao: The Unknown Story*, 198n

Kamenev, Lev, 19, 42–3, 48, 49, 51, 52, 89,
  133–4
Karsavina, Tamara, 82
Kenny, James, 350
Kerensky, Alexander: allows Lenin to enter
  Russia, 41; declining popularity, 86; defiant
  speech to Provisional Council, 91, 122; flees
  Winter Palace, 93; on imperative to suppress
  Kornilov, 78; on Lenin, 52; Lenin on, 19, 20;
  made head of Provisional Government, 78,
  85; 'Speedy' persona, 85–6; on welcoming
  the fight, 90; *see also* Provisional Government
  (Russia)
Kerensky Offensive, 85
Kesküla, Alexander, 40–1
Khrushchev, Nikita, 344, 360–1
Kirk, Grayson, 328
Knox, General Alfred, 11–12
Knudson, Jerry W.: *Roots of Revolution: The Press
  and Social Change in Latin America*, 345n
Kollontai, Aleksandra, 142
Kornilov, Lavr, 78, 79, 86
Krasin, Leonid, 16
Kresty Prison occupation, 11
Krupskaya, Nadezhda: accompanies Lenin on
  journey to Russia, 27, 31; learns of February
  Revolution, 9; on Lenin, 19, 20, 22, 49; in
  Siberia with Lenin, 15
Kshesinskaya, Matilda, 47
Kubek, Anthony: *How the Far East Was Lost*,
  262–3

La Plata, Battle of, 314
Lampoon (magazine), 59
Langshan (Mount Lang), Hunan, 183–4
Lazikou Pass, Battle of, 203
Lebedev-Polianskii, Pavel, 52
Left Front (magazine), 149
Lenin, Vladimir Ilyich (born Vladimir Ilyich
  Ulyanov), 7
  CHARACTERISTICS: dress, 7, 38, 43; eyes and
  gaze, 38, 40, 133; mannerisms, 133; religion/
  atheism, 13, 14; 'taxi-hailing' pose, 370, 370n
  IDEOLOGY: condones violence and theft, 16;
  influence of Nikolay Chernyshevsky, 14;

radicalism, 52; revolutionary defeatism, 18, 19,
  47, 48–51; revolutionary Marxism, 14, 15
  LIFE: adopts alias, 13n; biography, 49, 52;
  brief return to Russia after 1905 revolution,
  16; childhood and family, 13–14; education,
  13–14; evades arrest, 86n, 89; exile in
  Europe, 15–16, 17; exile to Siberia, 14–15;
  imprisonment on suspicion of spying, 17;
  journey back to Russia *see* Zurich – Petrograd
  journey; learns of February Revolution, 9,
  19–20; relationship with Inessa Armand, 9,
  27; relationship with Nadezhda Krupskaya
  see Krupskaya, Nadezhda; statues of, 370; in
  Zurich, 9, 17
  POLITICAL ACTIVITY: addresses meeting in
  Bern, 27; agitates for revolution, 15–16;
  attends Zimmerwald Conference, 18–19;
  drafts resolution ratifying October Revolution,
  101; gains broader workers' support, 52; heads
  Council of People's Commissars, 102; leads
  Bolsheviks in RSDLP, 15; loses Bolshevik
  support, 48–9, 51–2; loses influence in Russia,
  19; meetings in Stockholm en route to Russia,
  37–8; organises St Petersburg workers, 14;
  revokes Reed's consulship, 109–10; speech at
  farewell banquet, Zurich, 28; speech at Second
  All-Russian Congress of Soviets opening, 95;
  speeches on return to Petrograd, 46–7, 46,
  48–9; speeches to soldiers, 53; starts *Iskra*
  newspaper, 15; student demonstrations,
  14; wins debate for adopting resolution for
  revolution, 89
  QUOTED: on Alexander Kerensky, 20; on
  beginning a series of revolutions, 28; on
  being back on native soil, 42; on 'bourgeois'
  socialism, 15, 48; on clothing purchases, 38;
  on fallacy of 'democratic peace', 17–18; on
  February Revolution, 9; on Germany's SDP,
  17, 23; on Great War, 17–18, 23, 47, 48, 50;
  on need for armed uprising, 16, 19–20; on
  October Revolution, 95; on refusing to meet
  Wilhelm Janson on train, 35; on resolution for
  revolution, 89; on revolutionary government,
  50–1; on Robert Grimm, 24; on Roman
  Malinovsky, 42; on theft to fund the party, 16;
  on the upcoming struggle, 27
  WRITINGS: 'The April Theses', 49–51;
  Imperialism: The Highest Stage of Capitalism, 17
Ley, J., 27
Li Chiang-lin, 237
Lianghekou, 200–1
The Liberator (magazine), 114, 127

Liebman, Marcel, 51
Life (magazine), 250
Lin Biao, 195, 240, 241
Liping, 186
Lippmann, Walter, 348
Liu Bocheng, 184, 196
Liu Lung-hue, 231
Liu Shaoqi, 224
Liveright, Horace, 124–5, 129
Lockhart, R. H. Bruce, 13
Loess Plateau, 229–30
Long March (Jiangxi – Shaanxi) (Mao and Red
   Army), *177, 199*; arrival at Shaanxi, 203; Battle
   of Lazikou Pass, 203; Battle of Loushan Pass,
   194; civilian and military marchers, 178–9;
   climbing Langshan, 183; clothing, 199, 202;
   conflicting narratives, 198n; crossing Sichuan
   grasslands, 201–3; Dadu River battle and
   crossing, 196–8, 198n; departure and initial
   successes, 178–80; disease, 202; equipment
   and supplies taken and abandoned, 176–7,
   178, 181; exhaustion, 195, 200, 202; fate of
   those left behind, 179; food shortages, 199,
   202; freezing, 183, 199–200, 202; joining
   and separation from Zhang's Fourth Front
   Army, 200–1; leaving and retaking Zunyi,
   193–4; legendary status of, 204–5, 371; at
   Lianghekou, 200–1; lice, 180; at Liping,
   186; losses, 181–2, 184, 187, 193, 200,
   201n, 202, 204; Military Commission and
   Politburo meetings en route, 184–5, 186–7,
   190–2, 195, 201; navigating land of the Yi,
   195–6; overview of, 204; preparations, 176–8;
   propaganda about fighting Japanese, 252n;
   silent marching, 179–80; singing, 180; Snow
   on, 197–8; surprise capture of Zunyi, 186–90;
   through Gansu, 203; through Great Snow
   Mountains, 198–200; through Guizhou to
   Zunyi, 184–6; Wu River battle and crossing,
   187; Xiang River battle and crossing, 180–2;
   Yangtze River crossing attempt, 193; Zunyi
   Conference, 190–2; Zunyi to Huili, 194–5
Look (magazine), 334, 335
Los Angeles, 150
Loushan Pass, Battle of, 194
Lovell, Julia, 373; *Maoism: A Global History*, 263,
   264–5, 268
Ludendorff, Erich, 27, 29–31
Luding bridge, 196–8, 198n
Ludlow Massacre, 63
Lvov, Prince, 12, 78, 84, 85

M-26-7 *see* 26th of July Movement (Cuba)
Ma Haide *see* Hatem, George
MacAlpine, Eadmonn, 126
MacNeil, Neil, 309
Madame Sun Yat-Sen, 221–2, 224
Maggi plant, Singen, 33
Malinovsky, Roman, 42
Malmö, 36–7
Manchuria province, 217
Mandela, Nelson, 268
Manzanillo, 316, 318, 322–3
Mao Zedong, *157, 199, 241*
   CHARACTERISTICS: dress, 176, 203; man of the
      people, 252
   IDEOLOGY: importance of anti-elitist education,
      165; importance of physical fitness, 164–5;
      justification for revolutionary violence, 168–9;
      Maoism, 263–4; need for land reform to secure
      revolutionary success, 173, 174; need for
      Russian-style revolution, 167; need for strong,
      centralised state, 164; revolutionary potential
      of peasantry, 168–9
   INFLUENCES: anarchism at Peking University,
      166; father, 161; first encounter with socialism,
      163; October Revolution, 166–7; Qing
      brutality towards Changsha rioters, 162–3; Sun
      Tzu, 172; teachers, 164; Zheng Guanying, 162
   LIFE: in Beijing, 165–6; brief career in
      revolutionary army, 163; childhood and family,
      160–1; education, 161–5; in Hunan, 163–5;
      malaria, 176; meetings with Snow, 240–1, *241*,
      265–7; in Shanghai, 167; Snow's photograph
      of, *157*, 268n; wives and children, 179, 179n,
      193–4, 240; works as assistant librarian, 165–6
   MILITARY AND POLITICAL CAREER: in CCP,
      167–8; as Chairman of Chinese Soviet
      Republic, 173–4; challenge from Lin Biao,
      195; challenge from Wang Ming, 268;
      co-founds Afro-Asian People's Solidarity
      Organization, 270n; in Communist Party's
      Central Committee, 168, 169; expelled from
      Politburo, 171; with First Front Red Army
      at Jiangxi base, 173–4; guerrilla tactics, 174,
      191; in Guomindang, 168; joins forces with
      Zhu De, 172; leads troops at Jinggangshan,
      171–3, 179n; Long March *see* Long March
      (Jiangxi – Shaanxi); in Northern Expedition
      and 'Autumn Harvest Uprising', 169–71;
      proclaims formation of People's Republic
      of China, 258; regains political power, 192;
      removal as Chairman, 174; rivalry with Zhang
      Guotao, 200–1

QUOTED: on African American freedom struggle, 270n; on Bo Gu, 191; on childhood, 160, 161; on defeating US aggressors, 270n; on early enthusiasm with socialism, 163; on Edgar Snow, 258, 266; on end of Long March, 203; on escape from Nationalist militia, 171; on influential teacher, 164; on key messages for CCP, 241; on land reform to secure revolutionary success, 173; in *Little Red Book*, 263; on living conditions in Beijing, 165; on Long March route, 195; on Long March success and symbolism, 204–5; on mobilising the masses, 175; on need for Russian-style revolution, 167; on need for violent revolution, 168–9, 263; on October Revolution, 368; on Otto Braun, 191; on 'paper tiger' imperialists and reactionaries, 264; on physical fitness, 164, 165; on Qing brutality towards Changsha rice riots, 162–3; on relationship with father, 161; on revolutionary potential of peasantry, 168–9
WRITINGS: *New Youth* article, 164; poetry, 194
Maoism, 263–4
Mariinsky Palace, Petrograd, 91
'Marseillaise' (anthem), 33, 45, 46, 97, 102
Martí, José, 281
Martov, Yuli, 14, 15, 16, 24, 96
The Masses (magazine): Bryant writes for, 57–8, 64; Reed writes for, 57–8, 61–2, 65; Reed's election to board of, 61; suppression and trials under 1917 Espionage Act, 108, 114, 115, 118–20, 129
Massó, José Luis, 349
Matthews, Herbert, *299*
  BOOKS: *Castro: A Political Biography*, 353n; *The Cuban Story*, 350, 353; *A World in Revolution: A Newspaperman's Memoir*, 348n
  CHARACTERISTICS: attention to detail, 310; enjoyment of luxuries, 311; honesty, 299, 310; physique, 299, 302, 310; shyness, 302, 310, 330; taste for adventure, 304, 305, 315–16
  JOURNALISM: backlash against reporting on Castro and Cuban Revolution, 345–52, 349n; blocked by colleagues from further news reporting on Cuba, 348–9; blocked by colleagues from further reporting from Cuba, 336–7; Castro scoop *see* REPORT ON CASTRO AND FOLLOWERS (below); defended by John B. Oakes, 349n; defends own reporting, 352–4, 352n; experiences censorship, 308, 326; in Germany, 311; in India, 311; interview with Castro, 320–2, *321*, 346–7, 352; later articles on Castro and the Cuban Revolution, 336–7,
340, 347; *New York Times*, 303–4, 306, 308–9, 311–12, 336, 337, 340, 347; receives medal from Castro, 339; war reporting in Ethiopia, 304–7; war reporting in Italy and Sicily, 311; war reporting in Spain, 307–10
  LIFE: arrest and imprisonment in Rome, 311; biography, 367; childhood and family, 302; education, 302, 303; in Ethiopia, 304–7; Far East tour, 303; fellowship year in Europe, 303; in Havana, 337; heart attack, 311; internment in Siena, 311; journey to Sierra Maestra, 301, 315–19, *317*, 325; in London, 311; in New York City, 302, 303, 311; in Paris, 303–4; receives hate mail and death threats, 349, 350; relationship with Edith 'Nancie' Crosse, 303; return journey from Sierra Maestra, 322–3; returns to Cuba, 330; in Rome, 311; in Spain, 307–11; works as assistant business manager at *New York Times*, 302
  QUOTED: on apprenticeship at *New York Times*, 303; on authenticity of *Times* article, 327, 328; on Castro, 320, 321, 326, 336, 337, 347, 353n; on Castro's government, 337, 340, 347, 353n; on Cuban political situation, 312; on discomfort at 'hero' treatment, 330; on empathy, 353; on Ethiopian landscape, 305; on Fascism, 308–9, 311; on *Granma* landing, 312; on the ideal of liberty, 307; on interview with Castro, 301; on journalistic objectivity and truth, 307, 309, 330–1, 353, 354, 374; on journey to Sierra Maestra, 316, 318–19, 325; on Madrid, 308; on *New York Times* policy of balance over truth, 309–10; on prison cell, 311; on response to *Times* article, 328; on revolutionary Cubans, 324, 325–6; on role of foreign correspondents in Cuban Revolution, 338–9; on Second Italo-Ethiopian War, 304, 306, 307; on Siena, 311; on Spanish Civil War, 307, 308–9, 310–11; on taking risks for big stories, 301, 316; on travel and adventure, 303, 304, 305, 313; on Wiel's *Red Star Over Cuba*, 345n; on wish to defend himself before Senate Internal Security Subcommittee, 352
  REPORT ON CASTRO AND FOLLOWERS, *325*; Batista's attempts to suppress, 326–7; content, 324–6; immediate positive responses to, 326–7, 328–30, 373; interview with Castro, 320–2, *321*, 346–7, 352
Matthews, Ralph D. Sr, 357–8
May Fourth Movement (China), 166–7
Mayfield, Julian, 359
McBride, L. M., 209, 250

McCarthy, Joseph R., 259

Mensheviks: and Bolsheviks, split of RSDLP, 15, 21; *Pravda's* sympathies with, 42; response to Bolsheviks' criminal activity, 16; welcome Lenin back to Russia, 45–6; *see also* Martov, Yuli

Merridale, Catherine, 19, 33; *Lenin on the Train*, 86n

Mesa, Liliam, 316, 318

Metropolitan Magazine, 61, 62, 63

Mexico: Castro and 26th of July Movement in, 285–93; revolution (Reed on), 62

Miéville, China, 9

The Militant (magazine), 151

Military Revolutionary Committee (MRC) (Russia), 89, 90, 91, 96, 100

Milyukov, Pavel, 24, 85

Missouri (the 'Show-Me state'), 267, 267n

Moncado Barracks, Santiago de Cuba, 282–4

Morris, John Philip, 127–8

Moscow: Bolshevik government relocated to, 133–4; falls to Bolsheviks at end of October Revolution, 102, 123; jubilation following February Revolution, 13; Kremlin, 139, 142; mass funeral of revolutionaries, 123–4; Reed in, 133–4, 139–40, 141; Reed's funeral, 142–3

Mukden (now Shenyang), 217

Münzenberg, Willi, 26

Mussolini, Benito, 304, 307, 311

National Review (magazine), 345

National Revolutionary Army (China): Battle of Dadu Bridge, 196–8; encirclement campaigns, 159–60, 172–4, 180–1; Guiyang occupation, 193; last outpost at Yan'an, 230–1; losses to Red Army, 187, 194, 203; Northeastern Army, 223, 226, 247; Northwestern Army, 225; overwhelm Communist forces, 160, 170; truce with Red Army, 223, 226, 256; wave of terror with 'Green Gang', 170; *see also* Chiang Kai-shek; Guomindang (China)

Néry, Amélie de, 13

New Culture Movement (China), 166

The New Masses (magazine), 149, 149n

New Republic (magazine), 255

New York American (newspaper), 58

New York Call (newspaper), 66, 108, 114, 141, 146, 147

New York City: Boni & Liveright publishers, 124–6, *126*; Castro in, 341–2, 346–7; Fifteenth General Assembly of United Nations, 342; José Martí in, 281; Matthews in, 302, 303, 311;

Reed in, *55*, 60–1, 64, 121; Reed's memorial service, 147; Reed's speech at Carnegie Hall, 115–16; Snow in, 211; writers' school, 149

New York City – Moscow journey (Reed), 132–3

New York City – Petrograd journey (Reed), *67*; arrival at Petrograd, 81–2; Christiana to Stockholm, 71–2; clearance to travel, 66; co-travellers, 68–9, 72, 76–7, 79–80, 81; departure, 68; at Halifax, Nova Scotia, 69; return to New York City, 108–13; sea crossings to Norway, 68–70; at Stockholm, 72–5; Stockholm to Tornio, 76–7; Tornio to Petrograd, 77–81

New York Evening Post, 373

New York Herald Tribune Sunday Magazine, 217

New York Sun (newspaper), 218, 281

New York Times, 120, 127, 130, 261–2, 297, 302, 302n, 303, 306, 308–9, 312, 314, 315, 327, 337, 340, 345, 347, 348–9, 349n; Herbert Matthews's report on Castro and followers *see under* Matthews, Herbert

New York Tribune (newspaper), 112, 119, 120

New York World (newspaper), 62

New Yorker (magazine), 255

New Youth (magazine), 164

Nicholas II, Tsar of Russia, 10–11, 12, 16, 47, 84

Nikitin, Boris, 41

Nixon, Richard M., 340–1, 342

Nobs, Ernst, 26–7

Northern Expedition of CCP – Guomindang United Front, 169–71

Norway: Christiana (now Oslo), 71, 111; Great War hardships, 71–2

Nova Scotia: Reed and co-travellers detained at, 69; Trotsky interned at, 29

Oakes, John B., 349n

Ochs, Adolph S., 303

October (film), 152–3

October Revolution (Russia): build-up to, 82–7; events of, 88–101; immediate aftermath, 102–7, 122–4; influence on worldwide revolutionary movement, 166–7, 368–9

Okhrana (secret police, Russia), 19, 42, 84

O'Neil, Dennis, 269–70

Orthodox Party (Cuba), 280–1, 282

Oslo *see* Christiana (now Oslo)

Pai Chia P'ing, 233–5

País, Frank, 290, 292, 295

Palace Square, Petrograd, 104–5; Winter Palace, 90, 92–3, 96–101, 139

Panin, Anton (M. S. Makadzyub), 75
Paris, 303–4
Partido Comunista de Cuba (PCC), 278, 338
Partisan Review (magazine), 149
Parvus (Alexander Helphand), 24–5, 38
Paterson, New Jersey, 61–2
Pavlov, Sergei, 368
Pavlovsky Regiment, mutiny, 11
Pazos, Felipe, 314, 315
Pazos, Javier, 314, 315, 316, 318–19
Pearson, Michael: *The Sealed Train*, 34n
Peking University, 166; *see also* Beijing
Peng Dehuai, 172
Pérez, Angel, 296
Pérez, Faustino, 293, 295, 296, 314, 316
Pérez, Louis, 278
Perkins, L. S., 115–16
Petrograd (formerly and now St Petersburg):
    continuance of cultural activities, 82–3;
    February Revolution events, 11–12; Finland
    Station, 44–6, 81, 370n; French Information
    Bureau, 124; Hotel Angleterre, 82; jubilation
    following February Revolution, 13, 20;
    Kerensky places under martial law, 78; Lenin
    agitates for Bolshevik revolution, 16; Lenin
    arrives after journey from Zurich, 44–6, 370;
    Lenin organises workers, 14; Mariinsky Palace,
    91; Matilda Kshesinskaya's mansion, 47–9;
    October revolution build-up, 82–7; October
    revolution events, 88–101; Palace Square,
    104–5; power vacuum, 10; Reed and Bryant's
    first days in, 82–4; Reed arrives after journey
    from New York City, 81–2; second congress of
    Comintern opening ceremony, 139; Smolny
    Institute, 88, 94–6, 100–1, 105; statue of
    Lenin, 370; Winter Palace, 90, 92–3, 96–101,
    139
Petrograd Soviet of Workers' and Soldiers'
    Deputies: authorises Military Revolutionary
    Committee, 90; dual power arrangement with
    Provisional Government, 50, 85; formation,
    12; growing support for, 90; Lenin on, 20,
    48–9, 50; Mensheviks in, 44, 45–6; resolution
    for revolution, 89; resolution ratifying October
    Revolution, 101; threatened by Provisional
    Government, 91; *see also* All-Russian Congress
    of Soviets of Workers' and Soldiers' Deputies
Philadelphia, 115
Phillips, Ruby Hart, 314–15
Pien Chang-wu, 248
Plain Talk (magazine), 260
Plamondon, Lawrence 'Pun', 152

Planitz, Arwed Edler von der, 31, 33
Platten, Fritz, 18, 26, 28, 35
Playa las Coloradas, 295–6
Poe, Jim, 152
Polk, Frank, 117
Poor People's League (China), 231, 247
Popper, David H., 255
Poronin, Galicia (now Poland), 17
Porter, William M., 330
Portland, Oregon, 58, 63–4
Potemkin (battleship), 69
Powell, Adam Clayton Jr, 357
Pravda (newspaper), 19, 20, 42, 49, 51, 52, 142
Preston, Paul: *We Saw Spain Die*, 308, 308n
Prokopovich, Sergei, 97–8
Provisional Committee of the State Duma
    (Russia), 12
Provisional Council of the Russian Republic, 84
Provisional Government (Russia): Bolshevik
    arrests in July Days, 86, 86n; Bolshevik
    'vigilant control' policy over, 48; Bolsheviks
    overthrow in October Revolution, 88–93,
    96–101; declining power and popularity, 52,
    85–6; dual power arrangement with Petrograd
    Soviet, 50, 85; fails to negotiate Lenin's passage
    home, 24, 39; formation, 12, 84; Kornilov's
    attempted coup d'état, 78, 79–81; Lenin's
    views on, 20, 39, 42, 46, 48, 50; liberal
    reforms, 84; places Petrograd under martial
    law, 78; threatens Bolsheviks, 89–90, 91;
    Winter Palace headquarters, 90, 92–3, 96–101,
    139; *see also* Kerensky, Alexander

Qian Xijun, 193–4
Queen Victoria (steamer), 36
Quin, Mike, 148

Radek, Karl: accepts financial aid on Lenin's
    behalf, 38; accompanies Lenin on journey, 27,
    34–5, 34n, 36, 37; alleged behaviour on trip
    to Baku, 143–4; attends Reed's funeral, 142;
    heads Bureau of the Press, 105; on journey
    with Lenin, 23–4, 35; on Lenin's boots,
    38; pre-war activities, 18; Reed's animosity
    towards, 146; secretary of executive committee
    of Comintern, 139, 140; on Swedish
    breakfasts, 37
Radnor (merchant ship), 212
The Rag (newspaper), 151–2
Raskolnikov, Fedor, 42–3, 49
Rasputin, 10
Ravich, Olga, 27, 28

Reader's Digest (magazine), 339

Red Army (China): battles with Nationalist troops, 159–60, 172–3, 181–2, 187, 194, 196–8, 203; education opportunities, 233, 235, 240, 243–4, 245; establishment, 170; Jiangxi base of First Front Red Army, 159, 160, 173–4; Long March *see* Long March (Jiangxi – Shaanxi); Mao and Zhu join forces, 172; Peng's troops join others at Jinggangshan, 172; planning to evacuate Jiangxi base, 160, 176–8; reception by peasants, 238–9, 244; singing, 180, 189–90, 235, 238; Snow impressed by, 238, 242–4, 245–6; treatment of civilians and their property, 172, 238, 239, 242–3; treatment of enemies, 174; treatment of political prisoners, 243; truce with Nationalist Army, 223, 226, 256; victory over Nationalist troops, 258; Young Vanguards, 234; Zhang Guotao's Fourth Front Army, 193, 200–1

Red Army (Russia), 134, 136

Red Army University (China), 178, 178n

red flag, symbolism, 12, 40, 44, 83

Red Guard Party (US), 270

Red Guards (Russia), 87, 98–9, 102, 108, 117, 123

Red Star Over China see under Snow, Edgar

Reds (film), 152

Reed, Horatio 'Ray', 58–9

Reed, John ('Jack'), *55, 103, 138*

  AFTERLIVES: doubts about commitment to communism, 143–6; inspiration to 'New Left' in US, 150–1; John Reed Clubs, 148–50; *Reds* (film), 152

  ARCHIVE: contents and importance of, 108–9, 112, 121; held by US officials, 112, 116–18; returned to Reed, 120

  CHARACTERISTICS: appearance during writing *Ten Days*, 121; effect of Finland imprisonment and Baku trip, 141; loss of smile, 131–2; oratory style, 115, 149

  JOURNALISM: *The American Magazine*, 60–1; *Die Fackel*, 105–6; fine reputation, 62–3; *Harvard Monthly*, 59; *Independent*, 114; *Lampoon*, 59; *The Liberator*, 114; *The Masses*, 57–8, 61–2, 65; *Metropolitan Magazine*, 61, 62, 63; *New York Call*, 108, 114; *New York Tribune*, 119, 120; *New York World*, 62; reporting Great War, 63, 65, 119–20; reporting labour unrest and strikes, 61–2, 63; reporting Ludlow Massacre, 63; reporting Mexico revolution, 62; reporting October Revolution, 105–6, 108; *Die Russische Revolution in Bildern*, 106; *Saturday Evening Post*, 61

  LIFE: arrest in Paterson, 61; arrest in Philadelphia, 115; avoids conscription, 66; brief Russian consulship, 109–10, 112, 118; childhood and family, 58–9; in Croton, New York, 64–5; education, 58, 59, 60; in Europe and Russia, 63, 65; failed attempts to return to US, 137–8; first days in Petrograd, 82–4; first journey to Russia *see* New York City – Petrograd journey; funeral, 142–3; illness and death, 141–2, 144–5; imprisonment in Finland, 138; indictment and trial under the 1917 Espionage Act, 108, 110–11, 114, 119–20; in Moscow, 141; in New York City, 55, 60–1, 64, 121; in Petrograd after October Revolution, 102–8; relationship with Louise Bryant, 64–5, 113, 152; return to New York City, 108–13; second journey to Russia, 132–3; spy theory about, 107, 117n; surgery to remove kidney, 65, 66; tributes and memorial in New York, 146–7; trip to Baku, 140–1, 143–4, 145; witnesses October Revolution, 88, 90, 91–101; works for American Red Cross Mission, 107; works for Bureau of International Revolutionary Propaganda, Russia, 105–7

  POLITICAL INTERESTS AND ACTIVITY: in Baku, 143; in Christiana, 111; in Russia, 88, 90, 91–101, 105–8, 117–18, 133–4, 135, 145; in Stockholm, 74–5; in US, 59, 60, 61, 114–16, 130, 131–2, 149

  QUOTED: on American socialism, 60; on Boris Reinstein, 105; on bourgeois life in St Petersburg, 83; on brewing revolution(s), 63, 66–7; on the Cheka, 137; on consulship, 109, 112; on Edgar Sisson, 118; on February Revolution, 57–8, 75; on Great War, 65–6, 71–2, 119–20; on importance of archive, 112, 116, 117; on importance of recognising new Soviet regime, 116; on industrial unionism, 140; on involvement with American Red Cross Mission, 107; on journey to Russia, 68, 69, 70, 72, 76, 77, 78, 79; on Kamenev, 133–4; on Lenin, 133; on Louise Bryant, 64; on Ludlow Massacre, 63; on Mexican revolution, 62; on need for temporary dictatorship of the proletariat, 131; on October Revolution and aftermath, 90, 92, 93–4, 95, 98–100, 101, 102–4, 108, 113, 123, 124; on optimism for Russia's future, 136; on Pancho Villa, 62; on Petrograd before the October revolution, 83, 84, 86, 87; on political intentions now back in US, 112; on revolutionists in Serpukhov,

135; on rumours of Kornilov's attempted coup d'état, 79; on Russian civil service after October Revolution, 104–6; on Russian severe winter, 134, 135; on second congress of Comintern spectacle, 139; on second journey to Russia, 133; on silk workers' strike, Paterson, 61–2; on Smolny Institute, 94; on Social Revolutionaries, 137; on solidarity with Russian workers, 143; on Stockholm life and socialism, 73, 74; on *Ten Days*, 116, 117, 121, 128, 129–30; on Trotsky, 133; on working for Bureau of International Revolutionary Propaganda, 105, 106

TEN DAYS THAT SHOOK THE WORLD, *126*; banning in Stalinist Russia, 152; content and style, 122–3, 127, 128, 372; contract with Boni & Liveright, 125; discounted distribution, 129–30; Fidel reads, 368, 368n; film adaptation, 152–3; initial contract with Macmillan, 116, 117; International Publishers reprint, 151; Lenin's views on, 134, 134n; posthumous importance and success, 149, 151–3; publication and reception, 125–30; Reed on, 116, 117, 121, 128, 129–30; sources, 124; Trotsky's views on, 372; writing of, 121, 122; Zhou reads, 153

Reinstein, Boris, 105, 142
Revolución (newspaper), 326, 345, 362, 371
Revolutionary Age (magazine), 126
revolutionary defeatism, 18, 19, 47, 48–51
revolutionary defencism, 42, 48
Revolutionary Directorate (Cuba), 338
Riotte, Torsten, 33n
Rivero, Nicolás, 329
'robber barons' (US), 59
Roberts, Dick, 151
Robins, Raymond, 107
Robinson, Boardman 'Mike', 84
Rodríguez, René, 314–15
Romberg, Gisbert von, 23, 24, 26
Rome, 311
Roosevelt, Franklin D., 257, 372, 372n
Roque, Roberto, 295
Rosmer, Alfred, 144
Rosset, Barney, 269
Rudd, Mark, 365, 366
Ruijin Library, 178, 181
Russell, Charles E., 127
Russia: Beloostrov, 43, 81; food shortages, 11, 12, 82, 134, 135; fuel shortages, 134–5; Great War losses, 10–11, 23, 85; liberal reforms, 84; Moscow *see* Moscow; Petrograd *see* Petrograd; population characteristics, 9–10; rebuilding

and renewal, 136; Serpukhov, 135–6; severe winter, 134–5

MILITARY/NAVY: at Beloostrov, 81; education for, 136; Kerensky Offensive, 85; Kornilov's attempted coup d'état, 78, 79–81, 86; Military Revolutionary Committee (MRC), 89, 90, 91, 96, 100; outside Winter Palace, 97–8; Red Army, 134, 136; Red Guards, 87, 98–9, 102, 108, 117, 123; revolutionaries, 11–12, 44, 45, 52, 78, 86n, 87, 90, 91–2, 97–100, 102–4; at Tornio, 41, 42, 78; at Vyborg, 80; White Guards, 102, 123

POLITICS AND POWER: All-Russian Congress of Soviets of Workers' and Soldiers' Deputies, 94–6, 97, 100–1, 108, 118; Bureau of International Revolutionary Propaganda, 105–7, 142; Cheka (Bolshevik secret police), 134, 137; civil service departments after October Revolution, 104–5, 136; Council of People's Commissars, 102; influence of Rasputin, 10; Kornilov's attempted coup d'état, 78, 79–81, 86; Okhrana (Tsarist secret police), 19, 42, 84; Petrograd Soviet *see* Petrograd Soviet of Workers' and Soldiers' Deputies; power vacuum during Great War, 10; Provisional Committee of the State Duma, 12; Provisional Council of the Russian Republic, 84; Provisional Government *see* Provisional Government; Russian Social Democratic Labour Party (RSDLP), 15, 21; State Duma, 12, 16; Tsar Nicholas II abdicates, 12, 84; Tsar Nicholas II as supreme autocrat, 10

REVOLUTIONS: 1905, 16, 21; February 1917 *see* February Revolution; October 1917 *see* October Revolution

Russian exiles: returning to Russia, 68, 72, 77; in Shanghai, 213
Russian Social Democratic Labour Party (RSDLP): Bolshevik/Menshevik split, 15, 21
Die Russische Revolution in Bildern (news-sheet), 106
Ryazanov, David, 29

Samuel, Pedro and Ena, 318
Sánchez, Celia, 298
Sánchez, Universo, 297
Sands, William Franklin, 117
Santa Coloma, Boris Luis, 283
Santamaría, Abel, 283
Santamaría, Haydée, 283
Santiago de Cuba, 294–5, 337; Moncado Barracks, 282–4

Saratsi, 215

Sartre, Jean-Paul, 361–2, 363

Saturday Evening Post, 61, 260, 262

Saturday Review of Literature (magazine), 255

Schaffhausen, 29

Schlesinger, Arthur M. Jr, 360

Scott, Ted, 315

Scottsboro Boys, 150

Serpukhov, 135–6

Service, Robert, 49, 52

Shaanxi province: Ansai, 233; Bao'an, 239–41, 243, 244–5; cave dwellings, 230, 232, 237; An-chia-pan, 247–8; Fu-ts'un, 247; Loess Plateau, 229–30; Pai Chia P'ing, 233–5; Xi'an, 225–8, 248–9; Xiasiwan, 203; Yan'an, 230–1, 265

Shanghai: Japanese hostilities, 218, 256; Mao in, 167; population characteristics, 213–14; Snow in, 213–14, 218, 219, 221–2

Shao Li-tzu, 226

Shinyo Maru (steamship), 212–13

Shlyapnikov, Alexander, 45–6

Shreider, Grigory, 97–8

Siberia: Lenin's exile in, 14–15

Sichuan province, 193, 195–203

Siena, 311

Sierra Maestra (mountain range), 313, 319–22, 332–5, 346–7

Sillén, Hugo, 38

Singen, 33

Sisson, Edgar, 117–18

Sklarz, Georg, 25–6

Smedley, Agnes, 224, 224n, 251; *The Great Road*, 201–2

Smith, Mathew C., 145–6

Smolny Institute, Petrograd, 88, 94–6, 100–1, 105

Snow, Edgar, *207*, *241*

  BOOKS: *Battle for Asia*, 260n; *Far Eastern Front*, 218; *Journey to the Beginning*, 240n; *Living China* (editor), 220; *Red Star Over China see* RED STAR OVER CHINA (below); Yunnan travel book, 220

  CHARACTERISTICS: diffidence, 371; taste for adventure, 210, 219

  FORMATIVE EXPERIENCES AND LEARNING: armed 'harvest bandits', 211; learning from Madame Sun Yat-sen, 221–2; travels around Asia, 216, 221

  JOURNALISM: *Chicago Daily News*, 218; *China Weekly Review*, 214, 215–16; as Consolidated Press Association 'roving correspondent', 216; *Daily Herald*, 209; at educational institutions,

210, 211; *Harper's*, 212; *Life*, 250; meetings with Mao Zedong, 240–1, *241*, 265–7; meetings with Zhou Enlai, 233–5; *New York Herald Tribune Sunday Magazine*, 217; *New York Sun*, 218; notes from journey to Red territory, 240, 248–9, 267; other interviews in Red territory, 241–2, 244; photographs Mao Zedong, *157*, 268n; photography, 250; *Saturday Evening Post*, 260, 262; work drying up, 262

  LIFE: aboard the *Shinyo Maru*, 212–13; in Bao'an and northern Shaanxi, 239–45; in Beijing, 219–21, 265; in Burma, 216; childhood and family, 210; education, 210, 211; friendships, 220, 221–2; in Geneva, 262; in Hawaii, 212; in Japan, 213; journey to Bao'an *see* Beijing – Bao'an journey; journey to India, 216; journey up Yangtze, 217; in Manchuria, 217; in New York, 211; railway journey across China, 215; relationship with Helen Foster, 219, 262; relationship with Lois Wheeler, 262; reputational damage after *Red Star Over China*, 259–62; return to Beijing, 245–9; return to US, 262; road trip to Los Angeles, 210–11; rumours of death in Xi'an, 248; in Shanghai, 213–14, 218, 219, 221–2; world travel, 211–12

  OTHER WORK: founds Chinese Industrial Cooperatives, 372n; teaching, 220, 262; translations, 220

  QUOTED: on appeal of Chinese Communism, 246; on Beijing, 219–20; on Chiang Kai-shek, 222; on departure from Bao'an, 245; on desire to travel the world, 211; on famine in Saratsi, 215; on historical significance of Shaanxi province, 225, 229; on Japanese invasion of Manchuria, 217; on liberal take on Chinese communism, 260n; on Long March events, 197–8; on Mao Zedong, 240, 252–3, 266; on need to tell China's story, 223–4, 250, 374; on October Revolution and aftermath, 222; on optimism in Bao'an, 245, 246; on organisation at Bao'an, 238–9; on organisation of village soviets, 242; on own political beliefs, 261–2; on Pastor Wang, 226; on peasant uprising in Burma, 216; on political morality of Chinese Communists, 267; on Red Army's characteristics, 235, 238, 239, 242–4, 245–6, 252; on *Red Star Over China*, 223, 250, 253, 254, 267; on return journey to Beijing, 246, 247–8, 249; on revolution as necessary last resort, 222; on road trip experiences, 211;

on Shaanxi landscape, 229, 230, 246, 247; on Shanghai, 214; on Shanghai war, 218; on Shao Li-tzu, 226; on significance of trip to Bao'an, 209, 223–4; on student demonstration in Beijing, 221; on Teng Fa, 227; on terrain and people in Northern Shaanxi, 237–9; on vulnerability during trip to Bao-an, 231; on welcome at Bao'an, 239; on Xi'an, 225–6; on Zhou Enlai, 234–5

RED STAR OVER CHINA, 253; characterisation of Communism and Mao in, 252–3, 257, 266–7, 268, 372–3; content and style, 251–2; enduring global influence, 268–70; Helen Foster's input, 251; Mao's influence over content, 265–6; notes for, 240, 248–9, 267; publication and reception in US, 254–7, 262–3; publisher's advance, 223; reputational damage from, 259–62; role in popularising Maoism, 264, 373; translation and reception in China, 263, 264–5

Socarrás, Carlos Prío, 292, 328–9
Social Democratic Party (SPD) (Germany), 17, 23
Social Democrats (Sweden), 74
Social-Demokraten (newspaper), 111
Socialist International, 18
Socialist Revolutionaries (Russia), 83, 96, 137
Socialist Workers Party (US), 151
Sokolnikov, Grigory, 27
Sorrentino, Gilbert, 363
Soviet of Workers' and Soldiers' Deputies ('soviets'), 50, 57; Petrograd *see* Petrograd Soviet of Workers' and Soldiers' Deputies
Spain: Civil War, 307–11
Spectator (Portland newspaper), 63
Spence, Richard B., 117n
St George, Andrew, 334–5, 339
St Petersburg *see* Petrograd
Stalin, Joseph, 16, 42, 51, 89, 256, 270, 361
Stearns, Harold, 128
Steffens, Lincoln, 60, 116–17, 120, 131, 373
Steinmetz, Arthur, 329–30
Stockholm, 37–8, 72–5
Students for a Democratic Society (SDS) (US), 150–1, 269, 360; Venceremos Brigade, 366
Students' Revolutionary Directorate (SRD) (Cuba), 290–2, 329
Stuttgart, 34–5
Su Shuyun: *The Long March: The True History [...]*, 198n
submarine warfare, 25, 65, 69
Suiyuan province, 215, 215n

Sukhanov, Nikolai, 44, 47, 49
Sulzberger, Arthur Hays, 303
Sun Tzu: *The Art of War*, 172
Sun Yat-sen, 167, 169
Sweden: Great War hardships, 73; Haparanda, 39–40, 77; Lenin's passage through, 36–40; Malmö, 36–7; Reed's passage through, 72–7; socialism in, 74–5; Stockholm, 37–8, 72–5
Switzerland: Bern, 18–19, 21, 27; Schaffhausen, 29; Thayngen, 29; Zimmerwald Conference, 18–19; Zurich *see* Zurich

Taber, Robert, 332–3, 339, 359n
Ten Days That Shook the World see under Reed, John
Teng Fa, 227
Thayngen, 29
Thompson, Donald C., 53
'The Three Main Rules of Discipline [...]' (marching song), 189–90
Time (magazine), 345
Times Literary Review (newspaper), 254
Tornio, 40, 41–2, 77–8
Treaty of Versailles, 166n
Tricontinental Conference, Havana, 356
Trotsky, Leon: appoints Reed as consul, 109; *The Bolsheviki and World Peace*, 125; expelled from Soviet Union, 152; internment in Nova Scotia, 29; on October Revolution and new order, 89, 95, 96; organizes and arms Red Guards, 102, 133; Reed on, 109, 133, 152; on *Ten Days That Shook the World*, 372; Winter Palace memo, 104
Trujillo, Rafael, 281
Tuxpan – Playa las Coloradas journey (Castro and 26th of July Movement), 275–6, *291*, 293–5, *294*, 312, 371

Ulyanov, Alexander, 14
United Nations: Fifteenth General Assembly, 342
United States: ambassador to China (Nelson T. Johnson), 223–4; ambassador to Russia (David R. Francis), 109–10; American Red Cross Mission, 107; China Lobby, 262, 262n; Cleveland, Ohio, 115; conscription, 66; consul to Christiania (George N. Ifft), 111; corporate and political corruption, 59, 60n; enters the Great War, 65; Harvard University, 58–9, 60, 360; influence of *Red Star Over China* on countercultural and radical groups, 269–70; labour unions, unrests and strikes, 61–2, 63, 139–40; Los Angeles, 150; Missouri (the

'Show-Me state'), 267, 267n; New York City
see New York City; normalising relations with
People's Republic of China, 261n; Paterson,
New Jersey, 61–2; Philadelphia, 115; Portland,
Oregon, 58, 63–4; racism and civil rights
movement, 357–9, 363–5; Second Red Scare,
258–62; underground newspapers, 151, 151n
RELATIONSHIP WITH CUBA: ambassador to
Cuba (Philip Bonsal), 340; business relations
sour, 342, 343; Castro's trip to, 340–2, 346–7,
360; Cuba as virtual colony, 276; deteriorating
political relationship with Castro, 342, 343–4;
Senate Internal Security Subcommittee hearings
on Cuba's communist threat, 350–2, 352n; US
withdraws support from Batista regime, 338
SOCIALISM IN: American Socialist Party, 59,
132; Communist Labor Party, 132, 148n;
Communist Party of the United States of
America (CPUSA), 132, 148, 148n, 365; Fair
Play for Cuba Committee, 359, 359n; 'golden
age', 59; at Harvard, 60; Industrial Workers of
the World (IWW), 59–60, 61–2, 64, 118, 129,
140; John Reed Clubs, 148–50; 'New Left',
150–1, 359–60; Red Guard Party, 270; Socialist
Workers Party, 151; Students for a Democratic
Society (SDS), 150–1, 269, 360, 366
United States (steamer), 68–70
Utley, Freda, 260

Vandiver, Willard Duncan, 267n
Vayo, Julio Álvarez del, 27
Venceremos Brigade (US), 366
Verdeja, Santiago, 327
Vietnam: Cuban interests in war, 364, 365;
International Vietnam Congress, Berlin, 364;
US anti-war movement, 151, 269, 365
Villa, Pancho, 62
Volksrecht (newspaper), 26–7

Wang Jiaxiang, 191–2
Wang Jicheng, 187, 188–9
Wang Ming, 268
Wang, Pastor, 226–7, 231
Wang Quanyuan, 179–80
Washington Daily News, 352n
Welch, Robert, 260
Wenzhai (magazine), 264
Weyl, Nathaniel: *Red Star Over Cuba*, 345–6
Wheeler, Lois, 262
White Guards (Russia), 102, 123
Willauer, Whiting, 350–1
Williams, Rhys, 94–5, 98n, 105, 106, 109

Williams, Robert F., 358–9, 363–4
Wilson, Edmund, 44
Winter Palace, Petrograd, 90, 92–3, 96–101, 139;
see also Palace Square, Petrograd
'Wobblies' *see* Industrial Workers of the World
(IWW) (US)
Wu Lianping, 266
Wu River, 187
Wuchang, 163
Wuhan, 169
Wuolijoki, Hella, 133

Xi'an, 225–8, 248–9
Xiang River, Battle of, 180–2
Xiangjiang Ribao (newspaper), 163
Xiao Yedan, 196
Xiasiwan, 203

Yan'an, 230–1, 265
Yanda zhoukan (magazine), 264
Yang Changji, 164, 165
Yang Dengwu, 196–7
Yang Hucheng, 225, 247
Yangtze River: flood, 217; Red Army's failed
crossing attempt, 193
Yi people, China, 195–6
Young, Art, 115, 119
Yuan Jiliu, 164
Yunnan province, 216

Zalkind, Ivan, 109
Zhang Guotao, 193, 200–1
Zhang Wentian, 177, 192
Zhang Xueliang, 223, 226, 248, 256
Zhao Rongsheng, 265
Zhen Guanying: *Words of Warning to an Affluent
Age*, 162
Zheng Guanying, 162
Zhou Enlai, 160, 191, 192, 192n, 195, *199*, 226,
256; meetings with Snow, 233–5; reads *Ten
Days*, 153
Zhu De, 160, 172, 185, 195, *199*, 251;
biography, 201
Zimmermann, Arthur, 25
Zimmerwald Conference, Bern, 18–19
Zimmerwald Left, 19
Zinoviev, Grigory: accompanies Lenin on journey
to Russia, 27, 29, 36, 40; alleged behaviour on
trip to Baku, 143–4; appearance and character,
21; as Lenin's right-hand man, 21; on October
Revolution (newspaper leader), 92; orders Reed
to go to Baku, 140; plans return with Lenin to

Russia, 22–3; Reed's animosity towards, 146; supports Lenin's doctrine of 'revolutionary socialism', 18

Zunyi, 186–92

Zurich: Lenin departs, 28–9; Lenin in, 9, 17; Lenin's farewell banquet, 28; reaction to Lenin's journey, 26–7; *Volksrecht* (newspaper), 26–7

Zurich – Petrograd journey (Lenin), *32*; arrival at Petrograd, 44–6, 370; arrival in Russia (Beloostrov), 42–3; Baltic Sea crossing, 36; British attempts to thwart, 41; Churchill on, 31; co-travellers, 27; customs delays at Schaffhausen and Thayngen, 29; departure, 28–9; extraterritorial rights granted to train carriage, 26, 33, 35; Finnish border post at Tornio, 40, 41–2; Finnish leg, 42; German soldiers excitedly meet travellers at Frankfurt, 35; hostile reactions to, 26–7, 28–9; 'Internationale' accompanies, 29, 38; layover in Berlin, 35–6; Lenin declines meeting with Wilhelm Janson at Stuttgart, 34–5; Lenin prepares comrades for possible arrest, 39; Lenin writes 'The April Theses' during, 49; 'Marseillaise' accompanies, 33, 45; planning and negotiations with Germany, 23–6; rejected stratagems, 22, 25–6; rowdy behaviour on train, 33–4; 'sealed train' across Germany, 29–36; Swedish leg, 36–40; toilet arrangements on train, 31, 34; well-wishers, 29, 38, 43

Zweig, Stefan, 23